TOWARD EFFECTIVE SOCIAL WORK PRACTICE

107820

Edited by
Morley D. Glicken
Arizona State University

MSS Information Corporation
655 Madison Avenue, New York, N.Y. 10021

This is a custom-made book of readings prepared for the courses taught by the editor, as well as for related courses and for college and university libraries. For information about our program, please write to:

MSS INFORMATION CORPORATION
655 Madison Avenue
New York, New York 10021

MSS wishes to express its appreciation to the authors of the articles in the collection for their cooperation in making their work available in this format.

Library of Congress Cataloging in Publication Data

Glicken, Morley D   comp.
    Toward effective social work practice.

    1. Social service—Addresses, essays, lectures.
I. Title.
HV40.G58   361'.008   74-6248
ISBN 0-8422-5171-5
ISBN 0-8422-0401-6 (pbk.)

CONTENTS

PREFACE

Any author who believes that his work might help improve the quality and effectiveness of practice must certainly be ready to defend his point of view in the real world of social work practice. A just criticism of academics is that they fail to consider that real world in their work. Perhaps the reader will be inclined to agree when faced with this compilation of articles. Perhaps these works are so many pieces of a not very precise whole. Perhaps, however, and this is the author's hope, the articles presented in this collection will help the reader begin to see the gestalt of social work practice. If this is the case, the author would like to believe that this collection might strengthen a view of the generalist as sophisticated specialist operating in a world which reduces all data to instantaneous obsolescence, and who requires a grasp of how complex are the solutions to problems of modern society.

This collection, including articles by the author and by other social work writers, is not meant to reflect a necessary author bias in terms of articles selected. Consistent with the author's belief, social work is a broad, complex field. What represents truth for one may be an absurdity for another. And so the student looking for a concrete, easily understood answer to treating social problems may be disappointed. He may wonder why contradictory information is included, or why the author seems to disagree strongly with certain points of view presented by others he has included in this collection. Or, if he is particularly literary, he may be appalled by the writing, bored by the content, and incensed at the simplicity of the thinking. Such is the risk one takes in selecting articles for such a collection.

For the author, the articles selected represent nothing more than ideas which need to be considered, issues which are not easily reduced to yes or no answers, and most important, guides for the student to expand and redirect his continued search for information.

Organizationally, the book moves from articles dealing with individuals to works concerning the larger, more complex systems of institutions such as community and government. Consistent with the author's notion of the worker as sophisticated generalist is the belief that workers must be able to operate effectively in a variety of complex social situations. Consequently, material included covers areas of concern which broadly relate to a worker involved in highly generic but increasingly sophisticated practice, as demands on the worker become more and more complex.

For help in preparing this collection, the author would like to thank in particular his wife, Ginnie Glicken, and Elise Morris of the Graduate School of Social Service Administration, Arizona State University, Tempe. Both offered generously of their time and assistance, and were most helpful in organizing the material in a relatively minimal length of time to meet a self-imposed deadline. Additionally, Dean Horace Lundberg of the Graduate School of Social Service Administration provided necessary school resources which significantly eased the author's burden in preparing this collection of articles.

Effective Social Work Intervention in Direct Practice: Implications for Education

By Scott Briar

Dr. Briar is Dean of the School of Social Work at the University of Washington.

It is encouraging that educating for practice effectiveness was selected as the theme for the 1973 Annual Program Meeting of the Council on Social Work Education. For the first time in several years, I am moved to allow myself to use the word "relevant" since it seems to me quite likely that effectiveness will be one of the most important issues confronting our profession over the next decade.

The Issue of Social Work Effectiveness

Social work and social work education currently are under broad attack from various sources.[1] A central theme of these attacks is that social workers and social work programs are not effective and therefore deserve less financial support. This charge is embarrassing because the profession cannot readily refute it. While it probably is true that some of the critics are using the question of effectiveness to mask other motives for attacking social programs, we lack the credibility to make a countercharge if we cannot satisfactorily answer the ineffectiveness criticism. If all we can say is, "Well, we can't prove we are effective, but that's not the real reason you are attacking us," then *social workers'* motives also may be questioned. Moreover, we owe it to our supporters and to our clients to know how effective we are and to demonstrate what we are doing to increase our effectiveness.

The Challenge

The charge of ineffectiveness poses a most fundamental challenge to the profession and to social work education. Over the past fifteen years or so, the profession has responded to a succession of challenges. We

The author expresses his appreciation to Anthony Ishisaka, Trova Hutchins, Ronda Connaway, and Naomi Streshinsky for their valuable suggestions in the preparation of this paper.

FACING THE CHALLENGE: Plenary Session Papers from the 19th Annual Program Meeting of the Council on Social Work Education, 1973, pp. 17-30.

have faced the need to incorporate social perspectives in social work education and practice, to increase our capacity for social and political action, to grapple with the problems of poverty, and to deal with racism in our own house. No one would argue that we have solved *any* of these problems—they remain central issues for us—but our efforts to respond to these and other challenges have altered the face of social work education and have led to profound changes in the profession.

The challenge of effectiveness is at once more fundamental and, in some ways, more difficult than those we have confronted before. More fundamental because if the profession is weakened or crippled by attacks that are justified on the grounds of our ineffectiveness, then clearly social work will be less able to contribute to the solution of problems such as racism and poverty. And the charge of ineffectiveness is especially difficult because while it is clear *what* needs to be done—namely to develop more effective ways of achieving our objectives—it seems less than obvious *how* it can be done.

Let me make clear my realization that decisions about support for social work and social programs are ultimately political decisions. Even if today we could show beyond doubt that social workers are extremely effective at what they do, we still would be in trouble. This is not, however, the same as saying that effectiveness is irrelevant to such decisions. In these days of cost-benefit analysis, one of the first questions to be asked about a program is whether it has demonstrated effectiveness. If we cannot show this, or at least demonstrate that we are making substantial efforts to increase our effectiveness, we lose on the first round and our standing in the political arena is thereby seriously weakened. Our efforts to improve our situation politically may fall short if we do not make a vigorous effort to deal with the effectiveness issue.

While my charge is to discuss effectiveness in relation to education for direct practice roles, I want to emphasize that, in my opinion, the burden falls with equal force on practitioners working with macro-systems. Direct practice in social work has carried the brunt of the ineffectiveness charge only because more is known about the effectiveness of direct service practitioners. I doubt that other social workers would fare much better if the evidence were in.

Research Literature

We should begin by reviewing briefly what is known about the effectiveness of social workers engaged in direct practice. I will not attempt to repeat the litany of outcome studies in great detail. The results of those studies have been reviewed and summarized in numerous places and most social work educators are familiar with them.[2]

Nearly all of these studies, from Powers and Witmer[3] through Meyer, Borgatta, and Jones,[4] to Brown[5] and to Blenkner, Bloom, and Nielsen,[6] have produced consistent findings. These studies show that persons receiving the services of professional social workers did not fare better than those who did not receive them. In nearly half these studies, persons receiving professional social work services appeared to fare worse than those who did not. In the Blenkner, Bloom, and Nielsen study of services for the aged, persons in the treated group had significantly higher rates of institutionalization and death than did persons in the control group.[7]

The Professional Rationale

The first obstacle that confronts us if we try to deal constructively with the effectiveness issue is that the profession and the educational establishment have not yet fully faced the reality of these findings and their implications partly because they do not seem to believe these studies. It seems, for example, that many practitioners do not recognize themselves and their practice in these studies. They are sure that their *own* practice and that of their immediate colleagues *is effective,* so they conclude that the researchers must have studied the wrong social workers. Moreover, some of these studies were conducted with clients—the aged, delinquents, and multi-problem families—whom many practitioners rarely see. On that basis many practitioners say that these findings do not apply to their own work.

If we look to the much larger number of studies dealing with psychotherapy, many of which have examined client populations and methods that are similar if not identical to the practice of many social workers, the results are similar.[8] Yet schools of social work still teach approaches to direct practice that outcome studies have found to be ineffective. It appears that some educators do not believe these findings either.

Do the findings of the available outcome studies accurately reflect the effectiveness of the direct services provided by professional social workers? We cannot know for sure, of course, but every additional study increases the plausibility of their accuracy. Moreover, over a period of time, evaluative studies have become increasingly sophisticated. In fact, the cumulative evidence is now sufficient to put the burden of proof on those who would argue that practice is more effective than the research studies indicate.

The Professional Reaction—Varieties of Response

Thus far, the general reaction of the profession to these realities has not been conspicuously promising or constructive. One response has been

9

to ignore the research on effectiveness and try to preserve the faith and confidence that once prevailed. For example, organizations called Societies for Clinical Social Work have sprung up in a number of states and appear to be growing rapidly. Recently they held their first national conference and I was struck by the fact that many of the topics and practice approaches represented on the program were nearly identical to those that appeared on programs of this sort when I first entered social work a long time ago. Among other things, these groups seem to want to preserve the faiths, theories, and practices of the past.

A second response is one that says essentially that the problem is not important. It comes from practitioners who are willing, even eager to change their practice methods. They shift, sometimes abruptly, from one approach to another—from ego-oriented casework, to crisis intervention, to reality therapy, to transactional analysis, to gestalt, or to whatever new method appears next. They move on without ever asking whether the new method is more effective for their *clients* than the one they have just abandoned.

I can understand that perspective. I know, for instance, that during the years when I progressed from student to psychiatric social worker, to supervisor, to field instructor, and to private practitioner, my advancement was based on evaluation of my practice *style*—on how I handled myself within specific situations—not on my success rate in helping clients. The kind of exchange between social worker and supervisor that comes to mind probably has a familiar ring to many social workers.

The social worker reports that the client said, "I am not sure I should continue to come to see you." The supervisor asks, "And what did you say?" The worker reports what was said, and the supervisor then signals, gently and subtly, that it was a good response worthy of reinforcement—perhaps by saying, "Yes, and then how did the client respond?" Or the supervisor might indicate that it was a questionable response, one that merits a "Well, let's look at that together."

Over all those years, no one ever asked me what percentage of my clients improved, and to my knowledge, that question was never asked of my colleagues. I am not sure that this has changed very much today. If a client walked into a gathering of social workers, presented his problem, and asked for the social worker who could deal most effectively with it, how would he be answered? We rarely look at the situation in this way, but it is a natural and sensible question for a client to ask. I remember that I was trained to respond to that sort of question from my clients by treating it as a form of resistance.

Explaining Away the Research Results

A third, widespread response has been to recognize the research findings but then try to explain them away. One major study of effectiveness appeared in book form. The format consisted of chapters written by different people, many of whom tried to explain why they thought the findings were invalid. But the study and its findings were *relegated to the appendix*.[9]

To be sure, when the earliest studies appeared, there was little response the practitioners could make, because at that time there were no alternative approaches known to be more effective. Consequently, when practitioners were told that their work was ineffective, there was not much they could do, other than to continue what they had been doing, or to try something else for which results were not predictable.

That situation has since changed, in the sense that there are now alternatives known to be more effective for *some* problems. The behavior of many practitioners, however, has not changed accordingly. Let me mention just one example. Over fifteen years ago, Virginia Satir and her colleagues began the work that led to the family-therapy approach now identified with her name. The influence of that school of family therapy on social work practice has been enormous and continues to spread. If social work practitioners were asked to name the most important figures in the family treatment field, Satir's name undoubtedly would head the list. Yet in all that time, during much of which the work of Satir and her colleagues was supported by federal research and demonstration funds, not one report was issued providing a systematic assessment, no matter how crudely measured, of the relative effectiveness of her approach.

Meanwhile, in the early 1960s, MacGregor and his colleagues developed a very different approach to family treatment. Moreover, every family was carefully followed up at six- and eighteen-month intervals. The results showed an impressive success rate and revealed that none of the families needed to seek further help during the eighteen-month follow-up period.[10] All that based on a treatment approach that extended over only two days! But the project died for lack of continued funding, and as far as I know, this approach is not being used anywhere today. The use of other family treatment approaches of unknown effectiveness, however, continues to spread. This is one example, but by no means an isolated one.

The Response of Despair

A fourth response, and probably the most insidious, is that of cynicism and despair associated with a feeling that social workers are useless.[11] The issue—Are social workers useful?—is neither inappropriate nor destructive in itself. In fact, as part of a constructive search for improvement, it is necessary. But the criticism can be corrosive, both for the profession and for the profession's relations with the public, when it is pressed without a commitment to improvement that is coupled with a call for social work to abandon the direct-service field. In my view, abandonment of direct service would destroy the heart and soul of the profession. To learn that we are not as effective as we need to be should be a stimulus to develop ways of becoming more effective.

Finally, I want to recognize that there is a growing group of social workers who take seriously the question of effectiveness; I will have more to say about their work later.

The Pursuit of Effectiveness

If we are going to be serious about the pursuit of effectiveness and are going to list its achievement as a very high priority in the profession, it will require a substantial and sustained effort on our part. The first task will be to develop ways of defining what we are attempting to accomplish in particular situations or cases in terms that have tangible, observable referents to those situations.[12] If we seek better lives for our clients what do we mean, precisely and empirically, by a better life in this or that situation? Put differently, we must be able to articulate what we are trying to accomplish concretely enough for us and others to determine whether or not we got there.

As you know, one of the criticisms of some of the evaluative studies is that the researchers, not the practitioners, defined the outcome criteria.[13] The problem is that researchers often had to define the criteria because practitioners could not or would not define their goals in specific, observable terms. And systematic evaluation is impossible unless the desired outcome can be stated in observable terms.

This will not be an easy task. The overall objectives of social work are vague and abstract. That is all right. Health and justice are vague objectives also. The problem is not that our general objectives are vague, but that we have not been able to work out the meaning of those objectives in particular cases and situations in terms that have tangible meaning in the real world. When we do talk about what we are trying to do in specific cases, we use terms as vague and abstract as those we use when we talk about the general purposes of the profession.[14]

We move from broad statements about such matters as the development of individual potentialities and self-determination to specific situations while continuing to use the same language. We actually talk in individual cases about helping the person develop his potentialities as a service objective. That kind of vagueness makes evaluation of effects and effectiveness impossible.

12

The Movement Away from Vagueness

It will be painful to replace a language that has become comforting in its vagueness with one that is empirical and more mundane, for it will require us to make choices among specific outcome alternatives that we often would rather not make. We have to begin to make explicit the specific behaviors we are trying to change in a person or the specific changes we are trying to accomplish in his situation.

When I entered social work, and during my early years as a practitioner, the most prevalent term used by caseworkers to talk about what they were trying to accomplish was "ego-strength." We were trying to strengthen weak egos, shore up ego defenses, support ego strengths, and so on. I became as good as the next one in this activity; I could spot an ego weakness or strength when I saw one. But gradually I found the concept becoming slippery.

I participated in interminable case conferences in which a multiplicity of perceptions of a client's ego state were expressed with equal confidence and assurance. It was only much later that I realized what the problem was. At the time it just seemed that we were adrift in a dense fog on a bottomless sea. Like many of my colleagues groping in that situation, I cast about for another chart to take me out of the fog—family therapy, transactional analysis, gestalt and existential therapy, the whole gamut.

Consider existential therapy, for example. It has this great, central concept called *authenticity,* which is a sort of goal. The concept sounds basic, substantial, even "authentic." But what is it? How does one recognize it? Does the person himself actually know when he is being authentic and when he is not? Well, not always. In any event, he is not a good judge because he is, of course, prone to self-deception and game playing. Who does know? Existential therapists do. And how do they tell? It's not something they can explain; they just *know* authenticity when they see it. I began to realize that I had not gotten out of the fog; I had just drifted from one fog to another.

I realized that the problem is that all these orienting concepts (and I could give a *very* long list) have no tangible, observable referents in the real world. Their only referents are to their definitions which are stated in words that are also without tangible meaning in the real world, the definitions often being only descriptive analogies. Efforts have been made, of course, to give concepts such as "ego strength" some meaning in the real world. However, even very sophisticated efforts have been unsatisfactory, because this concept, and others like it, were never anchored in the real world in the first place.

Continuing Problems of the Profession

These problems were, and still are, manifest in the profession at large. Several years ago, social work embarked on a veritable orgy of "theory building."[15] This took several forms, but always required one to engage in theory collecting. If a particular psychological theory was not precise enough for action, then one should add on a second or preferably a third or fourth. Moreover, if psychological theories were inadequate to provide sufficiently specific directions for practice, one was supposed to add on a social theory, or perhaps two or three. This impulse is sound and, in some important respects, is a good one. The problem is that this approach brought along with it an enormous increment in our list of vague, fuzzy terms—concepts such as homeostasis, anomie, general systems, and pattern variables.

Let me add that I am not suggesting that vague, hypothetical constructs have no value for us. They may, in fact, have considerable sensitizing and heuristic value. The problem comes in failing to recognize that so long as such concepts remain empirically unanchored they will remain unsatisfactory for the world of action, which is the world in which practitioners work. Concepts or propositions that cannot generate tangible, testable implications for action not only are not helpful to the practitioner, they tend to add to his burdens, like so much unused baggage on a trip. Such concepts and propositions appear to suggest that there is something different that practitioners should do, but the concepts are incapable of indicating what that something is because they are not empirically grounded.

We need to set about immediately to acquire and use a vocabulary grounded in the real world. Our educational efforts need to stress the importance of raising these questions about the concepts and propositions of theories we consider for use. This will be a difficult task, but it now is clear that it can be done, even for our most vague and general objectives.[16]

Collecting Information About the Effects of Interventions

There is a second, equally pressing task required by the pursuit for effectiveness. Once we are able to define what we are trying to accomplish in individual situations, the next question is, How can we most effectively accomplish these objectives? To answer this question, we need to accumulate and codify the known effectiveness of the variety of possible interventions. And we can do that, of course, only for those interventions that can be described in observable terms. We cannot determine the effectiveness of interventions such as "environmental manipulation," "psychological support," or "crisis intervention" unless they are defined more precisely. We must develop a language that makes it possible to talk about interventions in observable terms.[17]

The task of collecting information about the known effects of particular techniques and about the effectiveness of intervention methods will be an enormous one. This task cannot wait upon the occasional, expensive major outcome study. Fortunately, this is not necessary. Until recently it seemed that the only way to study service outcomes rigorously was with the large sample—the control group design. Methodologies, however, are now being developed that make possible reasonably rigorous studies of effectiveness using few or even single cases.[18]

These methodologies, such as the multiple baseline and ABAB designs, will require alterations in our assessment techniques, and to use them it will be absolutely necessary that our intervention goals and methods be stated in observable terms. An important advantage of these methodologies is that they make it possible for practitioners to conduct such research as an integral, routine part of their practice, which is a necessity if we are to accumulate rapidly information about intervention effects and effectiveness.

There has recently appeared a vast body of literature, not widely read by social workers, containing a substantial amount of tested information about the effects and effectiveness of a variety of intervention methods and techniques. Equally important, this literature shows how goals and interventions can be described in observable terms and how effectiveness research can be incorporated routinely into practice.[19]

Implications for Direct Practice

It probably is clear that the pursuit of effectiveness would require a substantial investment of time, energy, and resources—resources which, for the most part, we will not be able to obtain externally. Consequently, as I have proposed elsewhere, social agencies, social work organizations, and schools of social work should reallocate at least 20 percent of their current resources to the pursuit of effectiveness. My only hesitation about the 20 percent figure is that I doubt that it is enough. By resources I do not necessarily mean money; I mean time and effort.

Curriculum Modifications

The core curriculum for training direct service practitioners would need to be changed radically. The modified core curriculum would focus on four basic areas. The *first* would be goal-setting, or how to set specific intervention objectives in observable terms. This would include what we

15

now call assessment and diagnosis. The study of goal-setting should be conducted within the context of a sophisticated analysis of the value, moral, and cultural dilemmas involved in establishing goals.[20]

The *second* basic area would be the study of intervention methods and techniques and their known effectiveness. The foundation here would be the known effectiveness of various interventions. Everything taught about practice interventions should be clearly labelled according to whether the method or technique has been tested and found to be effective or ineffective, or has not yet been systematically tested. The student should know when he is experimenting on a client with an untested method or using a method that so far has been found to be ineffective. It may be that ethical considerations would also require the practitioner to share that information with the client. Whether we would want to continue to teach ineffective methods or teach untested methods for general, rather than experimental use, would become an issue to be examined.

The fundamental knowledge base for these two core areas would be what is known about the effectiveness of intervention methods and the effects of intervention techniques. Theory and other speculative materials would play an important supplementary and heuristic role but not a central one, and theories that do not generate concepts or propositions with observable referents would be little used, except perhaps for their historical interest. The approach would be empirical and inductive, not deductive. In the event that some may fear that these constraints would leave little of substance to teach, let me emphasize that the body of literature and research that meets these criteria is already so vast that it would be impossible for a student to master all of it in two years.

Specialization would be necessary even if we were to construct such a curriculum tomorrow. I want to be sure that this point is clearly understood. I am suggesting that over the past five to ten years a fundamental breakthrough has been occurring in the knowledge base for direct practice. As a result, there is now available a very substantial body of tested knowledge about the effects and effectiveness of a variety of methods and techniques applied to a large array of problems. As yet, this body of knowledge is infrequently used by social workers, because most of them are not familiar with it. This knowledge requires some translation and considerable extension to meet the specific conditions of social work practice, but the means to do both are available.

The *third* area in the core curriculum would be methods and techniques of evaluative research, with primary emphasis on single case and small sample designs, and on how to integrate research into the routine of every-day practice. This material is sophisticated and exacting, and will require considerable time and practice. These developing advances in

16

methodology appear to represent a second major breakthrough of fundamental significance for direct practice and practice research.

I do not mean to imply that these three areas should be taught in separate courses. On the contrary, the introduction to them should involve an integrated approach. The student should also study, as the *fourth* core area, the field of social welfare and social welfare policies and programs.

In field instruction, students would be expected to demonstrate their ability to set specific goals in individual cases with appropriate recognition of the moral and cultural dilemmas involved, and with respect for the client as the principal definer of what, if anything, should be changed. The student also would be expected to demonstrate the ability to appropriately select and successfully apply methods of known effectiveness, and to demonstrate the relative effectiveness of his practice, thereby demonstrating his ability to incorporate systematic evaluation procedures into his practice routines. In addition, the student might be expected to test and evaluate a previously untested intervention method or technique, thus making a direct contribution to the knowledge base of practice. Needless to say, the development of field settings in which this kind of field experience is possible will require a considerable amount of work.

This is one prescription for education to prepare social workers for effective direct service practice. I would argue that such an educational program is now entirely feasible if we are willing to invest the effort to bring it about. Basically, I am simply arguing that social workers will be more effective if they are trained to know and use methods of known effectiveness.

Anticipating the Critics

Even if we were to start down this pathway today, it would take some time to fully achieve what I have outlined here. The reorientation required on the part of practicing social workers, agencies, and schools is considerable. I do not believe, however, that the difficulty of the task should deter us. On the contrary, I think we must begin to move in this direction.

A frequent objection to some of these ideas is that the most important things in life are intangible and cannot be observed or measured. I really do not believe that the important things in life are intangible. But the best way to settle that question would be to try to find out. The love of a mother for her child or of a man for his wife can be observed and described. Feelings can be reported, described, and in some instances even measured on a meter. Observing and describing such phenomena does not destroy or do harm to them, as anthropologists have demonstrated.

17

It may be pointed out that the body of social and behavioral science knowledge is not organized in a way that easily lends itself to the kind of curriculum I have outlined. That is true for much of the social and behavioral science material, but there is no reason to think that it ever will be properly organized by others for our purposes. My point is that eventually *we* will have to organize the available, pertinent knowledge to fit our specific needs and programs. Moreover, the available knowledge on the known effectiveness of intervention methods and techniques already is organized or easily could be in ways that are useful and accessible for teaching. This could be the central knowledge base for the training of direct practitioners.

Finally, it will be noted that if we are to move in the direction I have proposed, it would entail a shift away from identification with particular theories and toward a commitment to discovering and determining empirically what is effective practice, letting the theoretical chips fall where they may. Such a commitment imposes two requirements on practice, namely that there be systematic and rigorous evaluation of outcomes and, second, that the outcomes sought and the methods used be observable or describable. It does not require that practitioners surrender humanistic values. .

Conclusion

Direct services for a variety of human problems are here to stay; even the most conservative in our society will concede that. But there is a growing insistence that the survival of particular services should depend on their effectiveness. Now it is the cost-benefit analysts who are asking embarrassing questions about effectiveness, but it is only a matter of time before consumers of service ask the same questions—they already are doing so in other areas of direct concern to them.

Under these circumstances it seems reasonable to expect that only those professions that take these questions as a serious responsibility *and do something* about them will survive. The historical record shows that the mainstream of social work has always been concerned about effectiveness, although we have lacked the means to do much about it. What is different now is that the means to increase the effectiveness of direct practice are becoming available. I hope and trust we will use them.

Notes

1. Scott Briar, "Money, Politics and Social Services," *Social Work*, Vol. 17 (November 1972), p. 2.

2. See, for example, Scott Briar, "Family Services," in Henry S. Maas, ed., *Five Fields of Social Service: Review of Research* (New York: National Association of Social Workers, 1966), pp. 9–50; Scott Briar, "Family Services and Casework," in Henry S. Maas, ed., *Research in the Social Services: A Five Year Review* (New York: National Association of Social Workers, 1971), pp. 108–129; Joel Fisher, "Is Casework Effective? A Review," *Social Work*, Vol. 18 (January 1973), pp. 5–20; Edward J. Mullen and James R. Dumpson et al., *Evaluation of Social Intervention* (San Francisco: Jossey-Bass, 1972); William J. Reid and Ann W. Shyne, *Brief and Extended Casework* (New York: Columbia University Press, 1969); Steven Paul Segal, "Research on the Outcome of Social Work Therapeutic Interventions: A Review of the Literature," *Journal of Health and Social Behavior*, Vol. 13 (March 1972), pp. 3–17; and Martin Wolins, "Measuring the Effect of Social Work Intervention," in Normon A. Polansky, ed., *Social Work Research* (Chicago: University of Chicago Press, 1960), pp. 247–272.

3. Edwin Powers and Helen Witmer, *An Experiment in Prevention of Delinquency—The Cambridge-Summerville Youth Study* (New York: Columbia University Press, 1951).

4. Henry J. Meyer, Edgar Borgatta, and Wyatt Jones, *Girls at Vocational High: An Experiment in Social Work Intervention* (New York: Russell Sage, 1965).

5. Gordon E. Brown, ed., *The Multi-Problem Dilemma: A Social Research Demonstration with Multi-Problem Families* (Metuchen, N. J.: Scarecrow Press, 1968).

6. Margaret Blenkner, Martin Bloom, and Margaret Nielsen, "A Research and Demonstration Project of Protective Services," *Social Casework*, Vol. 52 (October 1971), p. 489.

7. *Ibid.*

8. See, for example, Allen E. Bergin and Sol Garfield, *Handbook of Psychotherapy and Behavior Change: An Empirical Analysis* (New York: John Wiley and Sons, 1971); Hans J. Eysenck, *The Effects of Psychotherapy* (New York: International Science Press, 1966); Julian Meltzoff and Melvin Kornreich, *Research in Psychotherapy* (New York: Atherton Press, 1970); Gary E. Stollak, Bernard G. Guerney and Meyer Rothberg, eds., *Psychotherapy Research* (Chicago: Rand McNally, 1966); and Hans H. Strupp and Allen E. Bergin, *Research in Individual Psychotherapy—A Bibliography* (Chevy Chase, Maryland: National Institute of Mental Health, 1969).

9. Brown, *op. cit.*

10. Robert MacGregor, Agnes M. Ritchie, Alberto Serrano, and Franklin P. Schuster, Jr., *Multi Impact Therapy With Families* (New York: McGraw Hill, 1964).

11. Harry Specht, "The Deprofessionalization of Social Work," *Social Work*, Vol. 17 (March 1972), pp. 3–15.

12. Scott Briar and Henry Miller, *Problems and Issues in Social Casework* (New York: Columbia University Press, 1971), pp. 160–172.

13. Helen Harris Perlman, "Casework and the Case of Chemung County," in Gordon E. Brown, *op. cit.*, pp. 47–71.

14. Richard B. Stuart, *Trick or Treatment* (Champaign, Ill.: Research Press, 1970), pp. 169–196.

15. For one example, see Gordon Hearn, *Theory Building in Social Work* (Toronto: Toronto University Press, 1958).

16. See especially, H. A. Wallin, *Evaluating Effectiveness in the Social Services: A General Discussion of Problems, Models, Methods, and Recent Efforts* (Vancouver: United Community Services, 1972); and H. A. Wallin, *Family and Individual Counseling* (Vancouver: United Community Services, 1972). Other useful sources include: Albert Bandura, *Principles of Behavior Modification* (New York: Holt, Rinehart & Winston, 1969), pp. 70–117; John H. Kunkel, *Society and Economic Growth: A Behavioral Perspective of Social Change* (New York: Oxford University Press, 1970); Stuart, *op. cit.*, pp. 65–102; Leonard P. Ullman and Leonard Krasner, *Case Studies in Behavior Modification* (New York: Holt, Rinehart & Winston, 1969), pp. 9–13; and Hugh B. Urban and Donald H. Ford, "Some Historical and Conceptual Perspectives on Psychotherapy and Behavior Change," in Bergin and Garfield, *op. cit.*, pp. 3–35.

17. Frederick H. Kanfer and George Saslow, "Behavioral Diagnosis," in Cyril Franks, ed., *Behavior Therapy: Appraisal and Status* (New York: McGraw Hill, 1969), pp. 417–444.

18. General treatments of the single organism design can be found in: Robert M. Browning and Donald O. Stover, *Behavior Modification in Child Treatment* (Chicago: Aldine-

Atherton Press, 1971), pp. 1–17, 42–110; Donald T. Campbell and Julian C. Stanley, *Experimental and Quasi-Experimental Designs for Research* (Chicago: Rand McNally, 1963); Donald J. Kiesler, "Experimental Designs in Psychotherapy Research," in Allen E. Bergin and Sol L. Garfield, *op. cit.*, pp. 36–74; Gordon L. Paul, "Behavior Modification Research: Design and Tactics," in Cyril M. Franks, ed., *Behavior Therapy: Appraisal and Status* (New York: McGraw Hill, 1969), pp. 29–62; and S. H. Revusky, "Some Statistical Treatments Compatible with Individual Organism Methodology," *Journal of Experimental Analysis of Behavior*, 10 (May 1967), pp. 319–330. Further illustrations and discussion of these designs can be found in: Donna Gelfand and Donald Hartman, "Behavior Therapy With Children," *Psychological Bulletin*, Vol. 69 (March 1968), pp. 204–215; R. Vance Hall *et al.*, "Teachers and Parents as Researchers Using Multiple Baseline Designs," *Journal of Applied Behavior Analysis*, Vol. 3 (Winter 1970), pp. 247–255; Robert M. Leff, "Behavior Modification and the Psychoses of Childhood: A Review," *Psychological Bulletin*, Vol. 69 (March 1968), pp. 396–409; Gordon L. Paul, "Strategy of Outcome Research in Psychotherapy," *Journal of Consulting Psychology*, Vol. 31 (April 1967), pp. 109–118; Todd R. Risley, "Behavior Modification: An Experimental-Therapeutic Endeavor," in Leo A. Hamerlynck, Park O. Davidson and Loren E. Acker, *Behavior Modification and Ideal Mental Health Services* (Calgary, Alberta: University of Calgary, 1969); Roland G. Tharp and Ralph J. Wetzel, *Behavior Modification in the Natural Environment* (New York: Academic Press, 1969).

19. The literature on the known effects and effectiveness of various intervention methods and techniques is substantial and growing rapidly. While much of this literature has been associated with the "behavioral" approach, the common denominator in this literature is not any particular theory, but a commitment to a rigorous, empirical approach to evaluation of effects and effectiveness. Some examples of the numerous summaries and bibliographies on this literature in the behavioral field include: Allen E. Bergin and Sol L. Garfield, *Handbook of Psychotherapy and Behavior Change, op. cit.;* Cyril M. Franks, ed., *Behavior Therapy: Appraisal and Status* (New York: McGraw Hill, 1969); Leonard Krasner and Leonard Ullman, *Research in Behavior Modification: New Developments* (New York: Holt, Rinehart & Winston, 1965); and Aubrey J. Yates, "Assessment of Results," in *Behavior Therapy* (New York: John Wiley & Sons, 1970), pp. 371–387. Examples from other areas include: Irving Piliavin and Joel Handler, *Lay Advocacy* (Madison: University of Wisconsin, Processed, 1973); Ruth Middleman and Gale Goldberg, *Social Service Delivery: A Structural Approach to Social Work Practice* (in press); and William J. Reid and Laura Epstein, *Task-Centered Casework* (New York: Columbia University Press, 1972).

20. Scott Briar and Henry Miller, *op. cit.*, pp. 32–52, 160–172; Frederick H. Kanfer and Jeanne S. Phillips, "Some Issues in Ethics Training and Theoretical Foundations of Behavior Modification," in *Learning Foundations of Behavior Therapy* (New York: John Wiley & Sons, 1970), pp. 521–574.

A LABORATORY APPROACH TO GROUP WORK INSTRUCTION

Morley D. Glicken

If one is to believe the social work literature as it evaluates success of treatment, the profession appears not to be providing a type of service most workers should take pride in. Research evidence indicates that social work practice, on the whole, has failed to show effectiveness, and in some studies, marked deterioration inclients receiving services over those not helped has been noted.[1] While the reasons for this apparent lack of success are, of course, complex, this paper proposes a learning approach which may be of use in improving worker effectiveness.

Traditionally, the educational process in social work has been approached on two levels: one, in the classroom where didactic material is provided, hopefully allowing for some semblance of an academic experience useful to future practice. The other level, field experience, provides the raw exposure to clients, hopefully in the context of a highly structured and closely supervised nature. Throughout this process, growth is seen in a somewhat abstract manner and is often unrelated to practice. Which is to say that a bright but not particularly warm or genuine student can often survive the educational process in that one level in the educational experience often negates the other. And as we know too well, the field is often reluctant to remove a student who lacks basic people skills because of intimidation by classroom faculty.[2]

Social work prides itself on the importance of the worker-client relationship and of the pioneering use of supervision in training workers. And yet, precious little has been done to systematically look at just what is necessary to effect change in the way workers relate to clients. We have assumed that some workers possess basic people skills and that some don't but the assumption is largely considered a predisposition or attribute inherent in the worker prior to the educational experience. Consequently, social work education often approaches the student from the point of view of providing didactic information and techniques of practice, assuming that basic people skills are not necessarily open to growth, or worse, that the cool, aloof, ill at ease worker will: a) Leave social work or better, be unable to find a job. b) Go into research or c) Become (God save us) a supervisor.

Paper presented at the 20th Annual Program Meeting of the Council on Social Work Education, March 1974, in Atlanta, Georgia.

The problem with this process is that considerable research evidence does exist supporting the notion that the most effective change agent providing help to individuals, families, and small groups has a high degree of warmth, genuineness, and empathy in relationships with clients.[3] Further, considerable evidence suggests that without these characteristics not only is there lack of change or movement in clients, but that considerable numbers regress or deteriorate. Truax and Carkhoff for example, in their research on the effectiveness of treatment report that on the whole, treatment is no more effective than no treatment at all.[4] Taken on a continuum, this would indicate that a third of clients treated improve, a third stay about the same, and a third get worse.[5] The social work literature reports essentially the same findings, but in some studies the deterioration process shows itself in higher death rates and institutionalization than clients in the control group.[6]

Further, Truax and Carkhoff report what many social work educators have suspected: essentially similar levels of warmth, genuineness, and empathy in untrained volunteer undergraduate involved in visiting patients or providing professional help to similar client groups.[7] In fact, in several minor studies, untrained volunteers showed substantially higher levels of facilitative skills in effecting change than did professionally trained workers.[8]

This is not to say that other problems in providing effective service are not present. Certainly we have been less than progressive in developing approaches which have some level of success. Further, we continue to operate in settings which are often anti-people, involuntary, and harmful. However, it would appear that improvement in people related skills marks a beginning attempt to increase worker effectiveness, and that if one is to judge from research findings, there appears to be a definite connection between effectiveness and high facilitative levels of those characteristics necessary for an open and meaningful client-worker relationship.

There is substantial evidence in the literature that it is possible to provide conditions in the learning experience which have direct impact on improving facilitative effectiveness in relationships. Further, these conditions are readily available for use in the classroom. For example, McKeachie reports that students in classes using a group discussion method as compared to those in classes relying on the lecture approach develop greater insight into personality dynamics and seem better able to apply what they've learned to new problems.[9]

Zeleny conducted two studies of college students in a Sociology course who were taught by the same instructor. One class was lecture-recitation; the other consisted of small discussion groups. The amount of factual material learned by both groups was essentially the same (a finding in all studies evaluated). However, those in the group discussion class were superior in mutual tolerance of each others views, participation with other group members, and in "personality development, social adjustment and cooperation".[10]

Asch compared the learning achieved by college students in a non-directive classroom with classrooms in which the teacher assumed a directive role. The group in the non-directive classroom showed increased emotional stability as measured on the M.M.P.I. Students in the non-directive classroom also did more independent reading than did those in the directive classroom.[11]

Truax and Carkhoff report that lay workers can be brought to a level of facilitative effectiveness in contact with clients comparable to highly effective professionals in approximately 100 hours using role playing, videotaped material, peer evaluation of interviewing techniques and discussion material all introduced in an essentially experiential model of learning.[12]

These studies and others tend to show that conditions in the learning experience can be developed to enhance and increase those characteristics shown to be necessary for effective work with clients at no loss in specific factual information learned by the student. Which is to say that neither the directive nor the non-directive method of teaching has inherent superiority over the other in the amount of specific information learned. However, the non-directive or experiential method allowing for substantial class interaction, appears to result in a student more highly motivated to continue learning after the class ends, one who seems more interested in applying his knowledge, and one with significantly higher levels of those personal characteristics considered necessary for effective work with clients.

In an attempt to test out alternative approaches to instructing an academic subject, but one which would hopefully increase openness and improve relationship skills as well, the Graduate School of Social Service Administration at Arizona State University has taught its group process classes exclusively from the laboratory point of view.

The labortory approach teaches from an experience-based frame of learning. Students are brought together in an informally structured group, and with little preparation, are asked to "come to terms with the task of becoming a

23

group and increasing understanding of group process."13
In this informal setting, the classroom takes on the appearance of a seminar or workshop. The instructor assumes a rather passive role. While he may introduce readings or convey his impression of group development and interaction from time to time, his is largely the role of a facilitator - one who allows the group to develop its own unique personality, traditions, and goals. As these traditions and interactions come into focus, the group periodically processes what it sees, hears, and feels taking place in the group. While the instructor may provide initial structure for this to take place, he largely allows the group to process when it feels closure has been achieved around a specific set of interactions.

Processing attempts to identify group interaction, verbal and non-verbal behavior, levels of group development, individual behavior in the group, and numerous other relevant group functions.

For the group to develop a degree of cohesion and success in interaction, a rather free and permissive atmosphere is useful. This open class atmosphere permits freedom to "prove, to ask, to challenge, to contribute, to listen, and to explore."14 Further, the freedom in the group allows group members to begin to feel comfortable enough to share observations with others and to then accept or reject differing perceptions of his behavior. Our experience is that free of psychological threat, the group provides an atmosphere readily conducive to looking openly at ones own behavior as well as the behavior of others.

An important belief of the laboratory approach is that one learns considerably more about the reality of groups when asked to participate in group decision making, to react to criticism or confrontation, to deal with ones feelings of isolation and anger than one learns theoretically in a structured-didactic learning experience. The difference relates less to objective-factual information than it does to information necessary for the student to lead and understand groups.

The laboratory approach allows the student to experience those intangibles not experienced in a more formal structured learning approach. He experiences, for example, how it feels to relate to someone in a group as compared to theoretical information which may have little actual impact. He larns the difference between what small group theory suggests about groups as compared to what actually happens. He begins, in essence, to put theoretical information into perspective and to relate theory more realistically to his own definition of group behavior gained in part in the laboratory.

The laboratory approach has allowed us to experiment with some interesting and useful assignments. Students in small groups of three or four are asked to design and implement research, probing various aspects of group process. Findings are then reported back to the group for purposes of discussion always, however, in such a way as to stimulate awareness of group process and individual growth. Several projects used include:

 a) A rating scale measuring empathy in the early and later stages of the group.
 b) A study comparing assertiveness with frequency and duration of individual responses in the groups.
 c) A study of whether changes in settings have any affect on assertiveness and verbosity.
 d) A measure of who spoke to whom during specific group meetings.

The reaction to this method is largely very positive. Our findings closely parallel those in the literature. Glicken and Mathews attempting to find if those students taking the second semester group process class (approximately 40% of the class) gained in openness over their peers not taking the class, found significant positive increases in openness in those taking the second semester class which appeared to have carry over to other graduate classes.[15] They defined openness as the "verbalization of what one thinks, feels, sees and hears in a clear, direct and specific way."

Students asked at the end of the first semester if they would prefer a return to a less experiential and more traditional approach to group work overwhelmingly chose the laboratory approach. This came about even though assignment loads are considerably heavier than in other more traditional classes and that group interaction is often supercharged with emotionally draining and upsetting material.

Alumni of the School have indicated that the group process class is one of the most important experiences in their graduate training as it related to professional growth.

While the second semester class is an elective and the assignment load extremely heavy and time consuming, 2/3 to 3/4 of our first year class chose to take it.

Both instructors teaching the group process class have taught it in the more traditional manner (lectures, observations of groups, assigned readings, case material, films and audio tapes, role play etc.) and feel strongly that students are better prepared theoretically and technically to lead groups. But more significantly, both

25

instructors see real change in those characteristics of
warmth, empathy and genuiness between those who continue
on in the second semester class and those who do not take
it.   In that both instructors teach other subjects, they
have an opportunity to view growth over the year and
believe their observations to be objective.

This is not to say that the laboratory approach
has been completely successful or accepted. To begin with
there has been less than complete acceptance by faculty of
the course, many feeling it to be used more therapeutic
than educational. Furthermore, in the course on group
interaction considerable negative material is expressed
concerning the total learning experience as well as
individual instructors. Consequently, some instructors
believe the class to be dangerously cathartic and feel that
instructors teaching the class encourage negative comments
about faculty and the school.

Additionally, material discussed in the class is
often highly personal, coming as it does at a time when
students are often at the heighth of feeling their most
negative about the school and its individual components.
Consequently, concerns over confidentiality are realistically a problem not only as they relate to peers, but more
importantly, as they relate to instructors teaching the
class. While the instructors have stressed the importance
of confidentiality and have guaranteed that problems of
feelings shared in the group will not be shared with
other members of faculty, still the concern remains. And
more upsetting is the process of opening up and divulging
emotionally traumatic experiences to a group whose charge
is not directly therapeutic and, who in fact, are possibly
inclined toward rejections and ridicule.

Those concerns have not been felt to be a problem of
significance as they relate to students. In fact, seldom
have we found groups unsupportive or inclined to misuse
information. Quite the contrary, we note increased acceptance of those who risk themselves and development of a warm,
therapeutic, supportive atmosphere which helps students
feel at ease with themselves, the instructors, and the
other members of the group.

The concerns of colleagues are quite another story
How functional it is to define a specific class as out of
the main stream is of course, difficult to say. But
doubtless the process of allowing students to share their
dislikes and their concerns for the competence of colleagues
wins few friends. Furthermore, instructors teaching from
the laboratory approach are placed in a largely inaccurate
position of being more open, trustworthy, and progressive
by students.

26

At the heart of a dicision to use experiential learning, however, is the question of whether instructors see the student as needing a classroom experience which enhances growth in those areas directly related to people skills. If the primary function of classroom learning is to impart objective information with minimal concern for the student's emotional growth, the laboratory approach or a variation is not specifically recommended. If, however, one can see it as a beginning step to enhance and develop important people skills here-to-fore neglected or dismissed as not part of the classroom experience, the laboratory approach has potential for future learning directions in social work education.

1. Joel Fisher, "Is Casework Effective? A Review", Social Work, Vol. 18 (January 1973), pp. 5-20.

2. Willard Richan and Allan Mendelsohn, Social Work: The Unloved Profession (New York: New Viewpoints, 1973), pp. 66-94.

3. Charles Truax and Robert Carkhoff, Toward Effective Counseling and Psychotherapy (Chicago: Aldine Publishing Company, 1967).

4. Ibid. pp. 4-22.

5. Ibid.

6. Margaret Blenkner, Martin Bloom, and Margaret Nielsen, "A Research and Demonstration Project of Protective Services", Social Casework, Vol. 52 (October 1971), p. 489.

7. Truax and Carkhoff, op. cit. pp. 110-111.

8. Ibid. pp. 224.

9. W. J. McKeachie, "The Instructor Faces Automation," Improving College and University Teaching, 8:91-95, 1960.

10. I. L. Lorge, D. Fox, J. Davitz, and M. Brenner, "A Survey of Studies Contrasting the Quality of Group Performance and Individual Performance," Psychological Bulletin, Vol. 55 (1958) pp. 337-372.

11. M. J. Asch, "Nondirective Teaching Psychology: An Experimental Study", Psychological Monographs, Vol. 65 (1951) p. 4.

12. Truax and Carkhoff, op. cit., p. 226.

13. Joseph Luft, Group Processes (Palo Alto: National Press Books, 1970) p. 7.

14. Ibid., p. 9.

15. Virginia Glicken and Claudia Mathews, A Study of Degree of Change in Openness Between Group Dynamics Enrollees and Nonenrollees. (unpublished Masters Thesis, Arizona State University, 1972).

Is casework effective? a review

by Joel Fischer

The core of professional practice is a commitment to competence—a commitment that most directly refers to a concern with the effective carrying out of professional services. Unfortunately, social casework, the largest segment of the social work profession, has been criticized consistently and most dramatically for its failure to demonstrate clearly effectiveness in helping clients.[1] Much of the criticism leveled at casework, however, has been based either on ideological grounds, with little apparent concern for research data to support such criticism, or on an inadequate review of research, for example, using only one study, from which the critic attempts to draw conclusions for the entire profession. One can hardly be confident in conclusions derived from such methods of evaluation.

Although there was a flurry of interest in the question of casework effectiveness raised by the publication of *Girls at Vocational High*, the issues raised at that time are far from settled.[2] In fact, they never have been thoroughly discussed. It seems as if, by some tacit arrangement, major contenders in the issue of effectiveness had agreed to let the matter drop.

The thesis of this paper is that the issue of effectiveness of practice always must be of paramount concern to the profession and cannot be brushed aside. A convergence between the professional values of commitment to the scientific method and the desire to promote capably the well-being of our clients demands such a stance.[3] It is surprising then that although the issue of effectiveness frequently is a topic of discussion, and there have been some attempts to examine aspects of the research on this subject, no comprehensive review of all the available major evaluative research on casework effectiveness is available in the social work literature.[4]

This article is an attempt to provide such a review. Its aim is to examine casework effectiveness in such a way as to generate reliable conclusions that can be scrutinized and tested through independent investigation. Utilizing analytic criteria of demon-

The author is indebted to Harvey Gochros for suggestions on an earlier draft of this paper and to the following for their help in collecting and analyzing the data included in this article: Eugene Fisher, Sally Leisen, Phyllis Morrison, Howard Sur, and Joy Valentine.

Reprinted with permission of the National Association of Social Workers, from SOCIAL WORK, Vol. 18, No. 1 (January 1973), pp. 5-20.

strated validity, this review will present the findings of major extant evaluative research and will extrapolate from these studies conclusions as to whether professional casework practice has indeed been found to be effective.

WHAT IS SOCIAL CASEWORK?

To draw conclusions about how effective casework is, it is first necessary to consider just *what* casework is, that is, what is to be examined. Hartman poses this well:

> Because people who define themselves as caseworkers define the practice so differently, and because no one has been elected to determine the definition, I assume that we can all carve out our area, practice it, teach it and write articles about it as long as the community, clients, universities and editors will support us.[5]

She also reviews a number of definitions of social casework that reflect the major streams of casework since its earliest days.

However, for research purposes, the definitions reviewed by Hartman neglect a most crucial variable—exactly what it is that caseworkers do. Complicating this problem is the increasing recognition that caseworkers do many things in many ways, all of which legitimately can be called casework.[6] This confusion in specification of casework methodology, to paraphrase Raimy's definition of psychotherapy, points to a view of casework as a set of undefined techniques, applied to unspecified problems, with unpredictable outcome. For this approach, rigorous training is recommended.[7]

In a most general sense, then, casework could be defined—at least for the purpose of reviewing studies that evaluate casework —as the services of professional caseworkers. Specification of the details of these services generally has been held to be less important than agreement that the services should be provided by persons whose educational qualifications have met the standards of the profession. And these qualifications traditionally have consisted of a master's degree from an accredited graduate school of social work (MSW).

The implication is that educational criteria relate to a presumed basic minimum competence in the practice of casework for all those who have been educated as caseworkers, but that it is not necessary to specify the exact nature or kind of casework. Thus any conclusion about the general success or failure of casework reached from reviewing the research can be made only if two conditions are met: (1) the services evaluated are performed by professional caseworkers and can be shown to have some central core of relevance to casework practice and (2) success or failure is the *rule* in the studies evaluated, cutting across a variety of clients, approaches, and situations. Although the issue of specification of practice methodology is important, lack of specification does not preclude drawing conclusions on a broader level— the level that examines the effectiveness of services offered by professional caseworkers, no matter which techniques and methods have been used in these services.

Almost as difficult as defining casework, however, is the problem of specifying just what is meant by "effectiveness" (or "success" or "improvement"). Obviously, the effects of intervention can show up in a number of ways, from subtle psychological changes to objective, observable changes in school grades, delinquency rates, and other performance dimensions. There might be some validity in drawing general conclusions about the effectiveness of casework from changes in only a few measures of outcome, since those few measures might really be the only appropriate indicators of the kinds of changes casework services are capable of producing. However, the scope of potential changes resulting from casework intervention would suggest that one would have more confidence about conclusions when positive changes can be demonstrated using varying types of criterion measures in one study and across several studies.

Actually, the selection of outcome indicators is a task that must be determined in

"In a high proportion of psychotherapy studies, as many clients receiving professional services deteriorate as improve . . . . the studies in this review show a parallel phenomenon."

advance in each study.[8] Effectiveness would then mean that differences in scores significantly favor one group over another in achieving a goal specified in advance by the researcher. Thus this review is constrained by the fact that results can only be reported in relation to the measures included in the primary investigations, even though there may have been other unknown, potentially important effects of the services.

SELECTION OF STUDIES

The purpose of a study of casework effectiveness is to examine whether the services were successful in helping clients.[9] A minimum requirement for establishing that whatever changes in clients could be found were actually a result of the specific services provided is the use of a control procedure. So evidence of change in clients is not necessarily evidence that the changes came about because of the casework services, and evidence of no change cannot be taken as a demonstration that the services had no effect (e.g., that intervention might have prevented deterioration). In either situation the researcher cannot draw definite conclusions unless some form of control has been introduced to minimize alternative explanations. As Nagel points out succinctly:

> . . . data must be analyzed so as to make possible comparisons on the basis of some *control* group, if they are to constitute cogent evidence for a causal inference. The introduction of such controls is the minimum requirement for the reliable interpretation and use of empirical data.[10]

Therefore, a minimum requirement for selection of studies for this review was that some form of control group of clients was utilized in the study.

Beginning with recent reviews, major social work journals, dissertation abstracts, and unpublished agency reports were surveyed from the 1930s to the present. Over seventy studies were located that purported to examine the effectiveness of casework services. However, although these studies contained much valuable information, most neglected to include a control group in their design. Because of the difficulty in drawing a valid conclusion regarding cause and effect without a control group for comparison, the bulk of these studies had to be excluded from this review.

Two major types of control were utilized in the studies eventually selected: (1) untreated control—a group that purportedly received no treatment at all and (2) a specific form of "other-treated control." In the second type of study the experimental group received the services of professional MSW caseworkers and the control group received services from nonprofessionals (e.g., non-MSW public assistance or probation workers). Despite obvious differences in the two categories of studies, certain assumptions basic to professional education and practice are utilized in this review.

Essentially, these assumptions are as follows: given client groups with similar problems appropriate for social work intervention (1) caseworkers with professional degrees should achieve more successful results than nonprofessional workers and (2) a program of professional intervention should achieve more successful outcome with clients than either no treatment at all or nonspecific or haphazardly selected treatment. Considerable research points to the fact that there are few pure control groups. Even when nominally in a control group, people often seek help from a variety of sources, such as family, friends, the clergy, and so forth. In such cases it is assumed that a program of professional intervention should, on the whole, achieve more efficacious results.[11]

Thus in line with the definition of casework as the services offered by professional caseworkers, this review will attempt to ascertain whether such services have been found to be more effective than no treatment or other nonspecific or nonprofessional services with which they have been compared.

Several other types of studies were excluded from this review in the hope that their omission would permit greater precision in drawing conclusions by minimizing potential biasing and the confounding effects which could have occurred if they had been included. Studies examining casework services outside the United States proper were not included.[12] Since the effectiveness of MSW caseworkers was the object of attention, several well-known studies examining only the services of nonprofessionals also were not reviewed.[13] Those studies that examined variations in types of professional casework without utilizing an untreated or nonprofessionally treated control group were excluded as well.[14] Further, those studies in which it appeared that caseworkers were only a small minority of the treatment team providing services to clients in the experimental group were omitted.[15] However, when there was lack of clarity in the text of the report as to certain characteristics of the study (e.g., number or proportion of caseworkers involved or the exact nature of their training), such studies were included. This was done because it was thought that the chance rejection of an appropriate study could detract more from the generality of conclusions than the chance inclusion of an inappropriate study.

Eleven studies were located that met the minimum criteria for inclusion in this review: (1) services were provided by professional caseworkers for the experimental group and (2) an "untreated" or nonprofes-

sionally treated control group was used. The criteria used to analyze these studies were derived from available texts on the evaluation of research.[16] In general, the studies were analyzed along the following dimensions: (1) formulation of the problem, (2) research design and method of data collection, (3) methods of data analysis, and (4) the authors' conclusions. Because of space limitations, detailed analysis of each study is not included here, except when problems in design either obscured potential findings or produced incomplete conclusions.

Except for a few situations in which methods traditionally defined as group work or community organization were used, the studies reviewed here ". . . addressed the practice of social casework . . . for the most part practiced 'classically.'"[17] Thus it could be assumed, and the studies themselves demonstrate, that each examines the practice of professional caseworkers, that there is indeed in all of the studies a central core of relevance to casework practice.

Since many readers may be unfamiliar with the results of these studies, the following sections present brief summaries, detailing the types of clients included, the nature and length of service, crucial aspects of the research method, and, of course, the findings. These summaries are so presented because such a review of the content of the studies is a necessary substantive basis for forming conclusions regarding the state of casework practice. For clarity of exposition, the studies are grouped into two categories according to whether they used one or the other of the two types of control groups already described.

UNTREATED CONTROLS

Berleman and Steiner. This study attempted to measure the impact of a service program on the prevention of juvenile delinquency.[18] The researchers studied 167 black seventh-grade boys to determine past evidence of acting out and to predict future acting-out behavior. Four "high-risk" categories were formed from this group, and

"Not only has professional casework failed to demonstrate it is effective, but lack of effectiveness appears to be the rule rather than the exception across several categories of clients, problems, situations, and types of casework."

the boys were randomly assigned from these categories to experimental and control groups. Owing to attrition and other factors, the experimental group eventually consisted of twenty-one boys and the control group of twenty-six. Three trained social workers provided intensive individual and group services to the experimental group for five months. The dependent variable of juvenile delinquency was operationally defined as acting-out behavior and measured by school and police disciplinary records. Outcome was assessed between the preservice and service periods and at two postservice periods. No significant differences were found between the groups on the criterion measures of acting-out behavior at any of the service or postservice periods.

Craig and Furst. This study was also designed to influence delinquency rates.[19] It included boys who rated high in predictions of probable delinquency (according to the Glueck Social Prediction Table, designed to predict future delinquency) as well as a small group of referrals from teachers. On the basis of matching, twenty-nine first-grade boys were assigned to an experimental group and twenty-nine to a control group. The boys in the treatment group were given intensive child guidance therapy by psychiatric social workers and other clinic professionals. The median length of clinic contact was fifty months. Delinquency records (presumably police and court records) were inspected over a ten-year interval and revealed the same number of delinquents in the experimental and control groups. In addition, school behavior reports, based on teacher evaluations, for nondelinquent boys were compared. These reports also revealed that the groups were not significantly different.[20]

McCabe. This study attempted to use social work intervention to diminish the deleterious effects of a "pathological environment" on intellectually superior children.[21] From a larger group of predominantly black and Puerto Rican children in the second to fourth grades, who had demonstrated superior ability on IQ tests, sixty-seven children were matched and randomly assigned to treatment and control groups. Forty-two children were placed in treatment groups and twenty-five in control groups. Social workers conducted a program of intervention grounded in principles of ego psychology. They concentrated most of their efforts on small-group services to both the children and their parents.

Outcome was operationalized in terms of the children's intellectual functioning, the parents' functioning, and the family's overall functioning and measured fifty-eight indicators of change. These measures included items from intelligence and school achievement tests, behavior rating scales, and scales of parental and family functioning. The researchers compiled an overall index of outcome that showed no significant differences between the experimental and control groups. In addition, of fifty-eight measures, only one statistically significant difference—reading achievement—favored the experimental group. The overall impact of this intensive service program, even if the one significant difference was not just a statistical artifact, was negligible.

Meyer, Borgatta, and Jones. The purpose of this large-scale study was to examine "the extent to which social casework is effective in prevention" with potentially

> *"Caseworkers do have to act, even in the face of such discouraging evidence, since practice can never be painted in terms of absolute success or failure."*

problematic subjects.[22] The study subjects were four cohorts of high school girls, selected from the entire population of one school and identified on the basis of school records as "potential problem cases." Eventually, by random assignment, 189 were referred to the experimental group and 192 to the untreated control group.

Services were provided by trained social workers from an agency specializing in the problems of adolescent girls. Both individual and group services were provided, although after the first year of the three-year program, group treatment was the primary mode of service. Three of the cohorts were included in analyses of all the data, while the last cohort, which had been exposed to treatment for two instead of the normal three years, was included only on selected measures.

Measures of outcome included a variety of subjective and objective criteria: school achievement and behavior ratings, personality and sociometric data, and client and worker ratings. Of the dozens of criteria by which experimental and control groups were compared, there were significant differences between the groups on only one of twelve factors of the Junior Personality Quiz. Although several other criteria tended to favor the experimental groups, no other between-group differences were statistically significant. To quote the authors: ". . . the conclusion must be stated in the negative when it is asked whether social work intervention with potential problem high school girls was . . . effective." [23]

Miller. The goal of this study was to prevent adolescent delinquency—operationally defined as the amount of law-violating behavior—in a lower-class urban district.[24] As part of a large-scale "total

community delinquency control project," an experimental group of 205 gang members was matched with a control group of 172 gang members. Over a period of three years, the experimental group received both individualized and group services, with emphasis on group services. Although data on several outcome indicators were reported, the only clear comparison between experimental and control groups was on the number of court appearances. On this measure, there was no discernible difference between the groups. Reviewing the overall impact of the project, the author asked rhetorically: "Was there a significant measurable inhibition of law violating . . . behavior? The answer . . . is 'No.' " [25]

Powers and Witmer. This was the first controlled study to examine the effects of casework intervention.[26] A well-designed delinquency prevention project, it matched and then randomly assigned 325 "predelinquent" boys to an experimental group and 325 to a control group. Direct individualized services were provided predominantly by caseworker-counselors. The mean length of contact per boy was four years and ten months.

Outcome was measured by court and police records, ratings of social adjustment, and psychological inventories. No significant difference was found between experimental and control groups on all major methods of evaluation. As frequently happens in the evaluation of services, the workers involved believed they had substantially helped a greater proportion of their clients than the more objective outcome measures revealed. This is an important indicator of the need for control groups and objective criterion measures.[27]

Of the six studies utilizing untreated control groups reviewed so far, all dealt primarily with children and adolescents, most in preventive rather than remedial terms. However, although most of the studies were conceptualized as prevention efforts, outcome indicators (e.g., personality measures, school achievement) are mainly the same as would be used in evaluating the effectiveness of remedial efforts. The overall outcome was clear: none of the studies revealed that their program had any significant effect on the clients when outcome measures for experimental and control groups were compared.

OTHER-TREATED CONTROLS

Blenkner, Bloom, and Nielsen. This study evaluated the effects of a program of services for the aged. A group of 164 aged persons were referred to community agencies for protective services because they had difficulty in caring for themselves. From this group 76 were randomly assigned to an experimental group and 88 to a control group. For one year the experimental group received intensive individualized services from experienced caseworkers; the goal was to do "whatever is necessary to meet the needs of the situation."[28] The control group received ordinary community services from a variety of agencies. Outcome was operationalized in terms of four major aspects of the clients' lives and situations: competence, environmental protection, affect, and effect on others.

Data were collected through structured interviews and ratings by observers. There were no significant differences between the experimental and control groups on most measures. Measures of "physical environment" and "concrete assistance" (both in the area of protection and not further delineated) and relief of stress on collaterals significantly favored the experimental group. However, most of the apparent gains in relation to these variables were explainable by a higher rate of institutionalization for experimental group subjects. In fact, overall findings from the initial part of the study led the project staff to

consider the hypothesis that intensive service actually accelerates decline and to further examine follow-up data.

When data were examined at a five-year follow-up, there were significant differences between the experimental and control groups. That is, the experimental group members were found to have significantly higher rates of institutionalization and death than the control group members. Thus with survival being the ultimate outcome criterion, the effects of this intervention program favored the control, rather than the experimental group.

Brown. Brown reported the findings of a program intended to evaluate the effectiveness of intervention with low-income multiproblem families.[29] Fifty multiproblem families receiving Aid to Families with Dependent Children (AFDC) were randomly assigned to an experimental group and fifty to a control group. The experimental group received intensive family-centered services from professional caseworkers with reduced caseloads, while the control group received the usual services of the public assistance agency. The program lasted thirty-one months, and the dependent variable of family functioning was operationalized as movement on the Geismar Scale of Family Functioning and the Hunt-Kogan Movement Scale. There were no significant differences between the groups, which led the researchers to conclude as follows: "Whatever was done by these workers for these clients cannot be demonstrated to have had a beneficial effect. . . ."[30]

Geismar and Krisberg. This was another study dealing with the effect of reaching-out family-centered casework on low-income multiproblem families.[31] The treatment group consisted of thirty of the most "seriously disorganized" families in one housing project. The control group was composed of fifty-one families from another housing project, all of whom were receiving AFDC and associated services. The control group differed from the treatment group on several variables. That is, it contained a far higher percentage of black families and families with absent fathers and demonstrated higher levels of family functioning at the pretest on the main criterion measure, the Geismar Scale of Family Functioning. In addition, the control and experimental groups lived in different geographic areas.

Services to the treatment group utilized various methods, primarily intensive direct services and use of environmental resources. Outcome was assessed on the Geismar scale twice for the control group and three times for the experimental group over the eighteen-month experimental period. At the conclusion of the project, the experimental group showed a gain of just under seven steps in mean "total family functioning," while the control group gained less than one scale step. The authors concluded that this demonstrated a significant effect of treatment.

Unfortunately, the data do not support this conclusion. The initial differences previously noted between the experimental and control groups—several possibly crucial variables for which the two groups were not comparable—makes any conclusion of effectiveness or noneffectiveness potentially misleading. With neither matching nor the more preferable randomization of assignments to the experimental and treatment groups, and such obvious noncomparability, any gain for the experimental group can be explained as a "selection-maturation" artifact.[32]

The treatment workers supplied information on the families' social functioning for the experimental cases, and a different group of trained researchers supplied this information for the control group, which introduced an obvious and critical source of bias. And since the scores at pretest were more extreme in a negative direction for the experimental than for the control group, any positive change from pre- to post-test may be a product of statistical regression, independent of the effects of the experimental variable.[33] In fact, the mean total family functioning score for the experimental families at the conclusion of treatment was still more than three steps below the pretest scores of the control group.[34] Thus the only conclusion that can be drawn from this study is that no definite conclusion about the effectiveness of the intervention program is possible.

Mullen, Chazin, and Feldstein. This study utilized more satisfactory design procedures.[35] Eighty-eight new public assistance families were randomly assigned to an experimental group and sixty-eight to a control group. The experimental families received intensive professional casework services aimed at decreasing rates of family disorganization and enhancing family functioning. Control families received standard public assistance services. Eleven areas of family functioning, based on ratings of structured interviews, were used as criterion measures. At the conclusion of up to two years of service, no significant differences in family functioning were found between the experimental and control groups.

Webb and Riley. The last study to be reviewed here was an attempt to affect the "life adjustment" of female probationers, aged 18 to 25.[36] Using random assignment, twenty-six recent probationers were assigned to an experimental group and thirty-two to a control group. The experimental group received intensive individualized services from family agency caseworkers for one year, and the control group received the usual probation services.

The dependent variable of life adjustment was operationalized as several dimensions of the Minnesota Multiphasic Inventory and a form of semantic differential. Subjects were also rated on sixteen "behavior correlates" by probation officers. The authors reported that the project was successful because six of twelve psychological measures showed significant improvement in the experimental group and only one of twelve showed significant improvement in the control group. In addition, five of sixteen behavior correlates "reflected markedly improved ratings of the experimental group as compared to the control group."[37]

These conclusions cannot be sustained, however, because Webb and Riley, at least on the psychological dimensions, did not include between-group statistical measures. They only reported that the experimental group improved significantly on selected measures and that the control group did not. However, if the authors had utilized a more appropriate statistical test—an analysis of covariance with pretest scores as the covariate (or even a t-test between the experimental and control group means if the pretest scores were equivalent)—the difference *between* groups, which is the crucial measure in evaluating overall impact of an experimental variable, may not have been significant. This is especially true in the several instances in which the differences between the groups were so slight. Again, the only conclusion that can be reached in this study is that the data were not presented in such a way as to justify a conclusion either of no effect or of significant effect.

The studies reviewed in this section contained a wider variety of clients and programs than those studies reviewed in the previous section. However, of the five studies, three clearly revealed little or no significant differences between the experimental and control groups and two provided inconclusive results.

SUMMARY ANALYSIS OF STUDIES

Tables 1 and 2 provide a summary of all the studies reviewed. Six of the eleven studies dealt primarily with children as clients, three with low-income multiproblem families, one with the aging, and one with female probationers, aged 18–25. Most studies dealt with predominantly low-income subjects, although this was not uniformly the case. Both sexes and several ethnic groups were represented. Over two thousand separate cases, including a high percentage of families with multiple members, were involved. The group of studies reviewed here demonstrated a great diversity in criterion measures, ranging from subjective to objective measures that deal with several aspects of both personal and social functioning. Judgment, descriptive,

and performance data were utilized and collected in a variety of ways, from psychological inventories and questionnaires, to worker and client ratings, to observed behaviors. While these measures individually could be faulty as indicators of change resulting from casework services, together they provide a wealth of information about the effects of casework services. More than one source of data was used to draw conclusions in almost all the studies. A wide variety of services was offered, although perhaps because many of the studies were conducted in the same time period, they reflect some uniformity in caseworker orientation, which is related to psychodynamic theoretical perspectives and/or "family-centered reaching-out" approaches.

Most of the studies provided at least minimally acceptable designs wherein experimental and control groups were assigned either through matching, randomization, or a combination of the two.[38] Frequently, however, the independent variable was inadequately defined, so that the precise nature of the casework techniques used was unknown. This, however, may be less a fault of the research than, as noted earlier in this paper, of the theory and field that spawned it. There were no attempts to control for various traits and characteristics of the caseworkers (e.g., style, personality, techniques) and few attempts to examine differential characteristics of clients, especially in relation to differential responses to treatment.

Although these last flaws detract somewhat from the ability to analyze comprehensively all aspects of the results of these studies, they do not detract from the more general conclusions that can be drawn from this review. Of all the controlled studies of the effectiveness of casework that could be located, nine of eleven clearly showed that professional caseworkers were unable to bring about any positive, significant, measurable changes in their clients beyond those that would have occurred without the specific intervention program or that could have been induced by nonprofessionals dealing with similar clients, often in less-

TABLE 1. SUMMARY OF STUDIES REVIEWED: UNTREATED CONTROL GROUPS ^a

Author and Year	Clients			Caseworkers		
	Number	Characteristics	Method of Selection	Orientation	Major Approach	Setting for Services
Berleman and Steiner (1967)	E=21 C=26	Black seventh-grade boys with school disciplinary problems and police records	Matching, random	Undetermined	Intensive, direct individualized, and group services	Settlement house, home, and school
Craig and Furst (1965)	E=29 C=29	First-grade boys rated as "probable delinquents" on Glueck Social Prediction Scale	Matching	Undetermined, possibly psychodynamic	Intensive child guidance therapy	Child guidance clinic
McCabe (1967)	E=42 C=25	Mainly "intellectually superior, socially disadvantaged" black and Puerto Rican children	Matching, random	Ego psychology	Groups, some individual services	Office
Meyer, Borgatta, and Jones (1965)	E=189 C=192	High school girls, varied races and socio-economic statuses, identified as "potential problems"	Random	Ego psychology, diagnostic casework	Group services, individualized services	Office
Miller (1962)	E=205 C=172	Lower-class gang members, varied ethnic backgrounds, both sexes	Matching	Psychodynamic, group dynamics	Group and individualized services	Streets, homes, schools
Powers and Witmer (1951)	E=325 C=325	Predelinquent boys aged 10–17, screened through teacher reports and test data. A variety of socioeconomic classes and ethnic groups	Matching, random	Dynamic psychology	Direct individualized services	Homes, school, office

^a In this table "L" stands for length, "A" stands for amount of contact, "E" stands for experimental group, and "C" stands for control group.

intensive service programs. In the two additional studies, the results were obfuscated by deficiencies in the design or the statistical analysis. Thus not only has professional casework failed to demonstrate that it is effective, but lack of effectiveness appears to be the rule rather than the exception across several categories of clients, problems, situations, and types of casework.

DETERIORATION OF CLIENTS

One of the most disturbing conclusions from the field of psychotherapy research is the finding that in a high proportion of psy-

| Length and Amount of Contact | Assessment Procedure | | Outcome |
	Dependent Variable	Criterion Measures	
L=5 months A=median—75 hours per client	Acting-out behavior	School disciplinary records, police records	No significant difference between E and C groups
L=5 years (median 50 months) A=Unknown	Delinquency rates	Teacher's behavior reports, delinquency records	No significant difference between E and C groups
L=3 years overall A=90.5 meetings	Intellectual functioning of children, parental functioning, family functioning	Intelligence tests, school achievement, behavior rating scales, ego functioning scales, ratings of parental and family functioning	No significant difference between E and C groups
L=1 contact to 3 years A=median—17 contacts	School behavior, social functioning	Client and worker ratings, school grades, school-related behaviors, teacher ratings, personality and attitude inventories	No significant difference between E and C groups
L=3 years A=3.5 contacts per week	Law-violating behavior (delinquency)	Number of court appearances	No significant difference between E and C groups
L=8 years (mean of 4 years, 10 months per boy) A=27.3 contacts per year	Frequency and seriousness of delinquency, social adjustment	Court records, police statistics, ratings of seriousness of offenses, ratings of social adjustment, psychological inventories	No significant difference between E and C groups

[a] In this table "L" stands for length, "A" stands for amount of contact, "E" stands for experimental group, and "C" stands for control group.

chotherapy studies, as many clients receiving professional services deteriorate as improve.[39] Averaged together and compared with a control group, the experimental group would therefore show no differences; thus the true effects of the experimental variable would be concealed. A reanalysis of the studies in this review shows a parallel phenomenon. In over 50 percent of the studies, six out of eleven clients receiving services in the experimental group were shown either to deteriorate to a greater

TABLE 2. SUMMARY OF STUDIES REVIEWED: OTHER-TREATED CONTROL GROUPS [a]

Author and Year	Clients				Caseworkers	
	Number	Characteristics	Method of Selection	Orientation	Major Approach	Setting for Services
Blenkner, Bloom, and Nielsen (1971)	E=76 C=88	Mentally impaired aged in need of protective services; noninstitutionalized	Random	Undetermined, probably psychodynamic, "social therapy"	Intensive direct services, use of environmental resources	Office and home
Brown (1968)	E=50 C=50	Multiproblem families receiving AFDC	Random	Multiproblem, family centered	Intensive direct services, use of environmental resources	Office and home
Geismar and Krisberg (1967)	E=30 C=51	Low-income multiproblem families, predominantly white	Unclear, mainly post-hoc matching	Reaching-out, family centered	Intensive direct services, use of environmental resources, multimethod	Office, home, neighborhood
Mullen, Chazin, and Feldstein (1970)	E=88 C=68	Newly dependent public assistance recipients, mixed ethnic group, families with at least 2 members	Random	Psychodynamic	Direct individualized services	Undetermined, probably office, home
Webb and Riley (1970)	E=26 C=32	Female probationers aged 18–25; variety of ethnic groups	Random	Psychodynamic	Direct individualized services	Office

[a] In this table "L" stands for length, "A" stands for amount of contact, "E" stands for experimental group, and "C" stands for control group.

degree than clients in the control group or to demonstrate improved functioning at a lesser rate than control subjects.

For example, Berleman and Steiner, in examining the percentage of boys with school disciplinary records, concluded that there was no overall difference between the groups.[40] However, further analysis reveals that the percentage of boys in the experimental group with school disciplinary records was far higher (X^2 was significant beyond .01) than the percentage of boys in the control group. The study of Blenkner, Bloom, and Nielsen was already reviewed with regard to the deterioration of clients in the experimental group. That is, the experimental group subjects had a significantly higher death rate than those in the control group.[41]

The study by McCabe of educationally

| Caseworkers | | Assessment Procedure | | |
Control Group Workers	Length and Amount of Contact	Dependent Variable	Criterion Measures	Outcome
Variety of community workers, generally not social workers or not MSWs	L=1 year A=mean of 31.8 per case	Competence, environmental protection, affect, effect on others	Ratings from structured interviews, observer ratings, clinical ratings, death and institutionalization rates	Experimental group had higher death and institutionalization rates. Also higher on "physical environment," "concrete assistance," and relief of collateral stress
Public assistance workers—BAs	L=31 months A=median of 2+ per month	Family functioning	Geismar Scale of Family Functioning, Hunt-Kogan Movement Scale	No significant difference between E and C groups
Public assistance workers—BAs	L=18 months A=mean of 4.4 direct contacts per month	Family functioning	Geismar Scale of Family Functioning	Major movement within E group. Major differences between E and C groups at pretest not handled statistically
Public assistance workers—BAs	L=up to 2 years A=median of 15 direct interviews	Individual and family disorganization, family functioning	Ratings of structured interviews with clients in 11 areas of family functioning	No significant differences in family functioning between E and C groups
Non-MSW probation workers	L=1 year A=median of 6 to 9 interviews	Life adjustment	MMPI, Semantic Differential, behavior ratings	No between-group measures reported. Reported "improved" scores on 5 of 16 behavior ratings favoring E group and on 5 of 12 psychological measures favoring E group

[a] In this table "L" stands for length, "A" stands for amount of contact, "E" stands for experimental group, and "C" stands for control group.

superior children revealed several areas in which experimental group members declined at a higher rate than control group members or in which control group members improved at a higher rate than experimental group members.[42] On the overall index of functioning, 50 percent of the experimental group members declined, compared to only 38 percent of the control group members. The greatest decline was found in the black clients: eight out of fourteen in the experimental group deteriorated—presumably as a result of treatment—whereas only one black control group member did so. The outcome pattern was reversed for Puerto Rican clients. Thus the overall effect was that the black and Puerto Rican clients canceled each other out so that no significant differences could be observed. McCabe further reported that means on both ego and family functioning indicators for black subjects tended to increase (indicating more positive outcome) to a greater extent for control group members than for experimental group members. This suggests treatment may have retarded normal improvement.

The delinquency control project by Miller also showed evidence of this phenomenon. In several areas related to trends in disapproved behavior and in illegal acts, the experimental group showed statistically significant increases rather than the hypothesized desired decreases.[43] However, since no figures were reported for the control group, there is no way of knowing whether such deterioration was an effect of treatment or of other circumstances.

The Powers and Witmer study showed that although some of the clients in the delinquency program seemed to benefit from treatment, a substantial proportion actually were handicapped by it. The authors concluded that "the apparent chance distribution of terminal adjustment ratings . . . was due to the fact that the good effects of the study were counterbalanced by the poor." [44]

Geismar and Krisberg revealed that 10 percent of the experimental group members in their study deteriorated in social functioning over the course of the project. A comparable breakdown was not available to examine such possible decline in the control group.[45]

In four of the six studies (Berleman and Steiner; Blenkner, Bloom and Nielsen; McCabe; and Powers and Witmer) control procedures made it appear likely that decline in the experimental group was actually a result of the treatment, while in two studies (Miller and Geismar and Krisberg) there is evidence to suggest that such deterioration took place. It was not always clear that the deteriorated group was sufficient in number to offset statistically the number of clients who may have improved and thereby produce a finding of no significant difference between experimental and control groups. However, even the evidence presented here is strong enough

to suggest that, as with psychotherapy, the results of casework may be for better or for worse! [46] At the least, future research should attempt to specify the influence, whether personal (e.g., personality characteristics of caseworkers) or situational, that might account for this variation in effects.

CONCLUSION

This article has been concerned primarily with a presentation of research findings related to practice, rather than with an analysis of practice per se. But the disturbing nature of the results of these studies does suggest some areas for further questioning.

It is possible that the type of casework used in these studies really was not representative of the mainstream of casework practice. There appeared to be, for example, a disproportionate number of studies concentrating on work with children, especially with juvenile delinquents. Also since most of the studies dealt with low-income clients and few with middle-class clients, it might be argued that the high rate of failure was merely an artifact of the general inability of caseworkers to help clients when other more powerful environmental forces hold sway. And, although the nature of the problem is important, the methods used may reflect outdated forms of casework.

Most of the studies were conducted in the 1950s and 1960s and reflect the dominant modes of practice in those decades. Compared at least to the services offered in the earlier studies, the nature of casework practice has undergone many alterations, although there is as yet no controlled evidence that newer schools of casework have been able to demonstrate success in helping clients.[47]

But caseworkers do have to act, even in the face of such discouraging evidence, since practice can never be painted in terms of absolute success or failure. Making judgments in the face of uncertainty of knowledge has long been a characteristic of most of the helping professions. A variety of emerging approaches to practice are available as the search for more effective methods of intervention continues.[48] Perhaps future research will be able not only to validate new methodologies, but, as in the studies in which client deterioration was evident, more clearly define the elements of the old forms that enhance effectiveness.

Nevertheless, this review of the available controlled research strongly suggests that at present lack of evidence of the effectiveness of professional casework is the rule rather than the exception. A technical research corollary to this conclusion, and a comment frequently appearing in the social work literature, is that "we also lack good scientific proof of ineffectiveness."[49] This assertion, however, taken alone, would appear to be rather insubstantial grounds on which to support a profession.

Notes and References

1. See, for example, Scott Briar, "The Current Crisis in Social Casework," *Social Work Practice, 1967* (New York: Columbia University Press, 1967), pp. 19–33.
2. Henry J. Meyer, Edgar Borgatta, and Wyatt Jones, *Girls at Vocational High: An Experiment in Social Work Intervention* (New York: Russell Sage Foundation, 1965). For examples of the issues raised at that time, see Earl Ubell, "Social Casework Fails the Test," *New York Herald Tribune* (October 4, 1964); and Briar, op. cit.
3. Scott Briar and Henry Miller, *Problems and Issues in Social Casework* (New York: Columbia University Press, 1971).
4. Attempts to examine aspects of this research have been made by Scott Briar, "Family Services," in Henry S. Maas, ed., *Five Fields of Social Service: Reviews of Research* (New York: National Association of Social Workers, 1966); Briar, "Family Services and Casework," in Maas, ed., *Research in the Social Services: A Five-Year Review* (New York: National Association of Social Workers, 1970); and Ludwig L. Geismar, "Implications of a Family Life Improvement Project," *Social Casework*, 52 (July 1971), pp. 455–465.
5. Ann Hartman, "But What Is Social Casework?" *Social Casework*, 52 (July 1971), p. 419.
6. Robert W. Roberts and Robert H. Nee, eds., *Theories of Social Casework* (Chicago: University of Chicago Press, 1970).
7. Victor Raimy, ed., *Training in Clinical Psychology* (Englewood Cliffs, N.J.: Prentice-Hall, 1950), p. 93.
8. Elizabeth Herzog, *Some Guide Lines for Evaluative Research* (Washington, D.C.: U.S. Department of Health, Education & Welfare, 1959).

9. This type of study should be distinguished from other types of outcome research that might examine the *effects* of services (e.g., along such dimensions as continuance-discontinuance) which may be unrelated to the question of whether the services were *effective*.
10. Ernest Nagel, "Methodological Issues in Psychoanalytic Theory," in Sidney Hook, ed., *Psychoanalysis, Scientific Method and Philosophy* (New York: New York University Press, 1959), p. 53.
11. See Allen E. Bergin, "The Evaluation of Therapeutic Outcomes," in Bergin and Sol L. Garfield, eds., *Handbook of Psychotherapy and Behavior Change: An Empirical Analysis* (New York: John Wiley & Sons, 1971).
12. See, for example, E. Matilda Goldberg, *Helping the Aged* (London, England: Allen & Unwin, 1970); Rosa A. Marin, *A Comprehensive Program for Multi-Problem Families: Report on a Four-Year Controlled Experiment* (Rio Piedras: Institute of Caribbean Studies, University of Puerto Rico, 1969); and P. M. Kuhl, *The Family Center Project and Action Research on Socially Deprived Families* (Copenhagen: Danish National Institute of Social Research, 1969).
13. See, for example, John H. Behling, "An Experimental Study to Measure the Effectiveness of Casework Service" (Columbus, Ohio: Franklin County Welfare Department, 1961) (mimeographed); Geismar, op. cit.; Alvin Rudoff and Irving Piliavin, "An Aid to Needy Children Program: A Study of Types and Responses to Casework Services," *Community Mental Health Journal*, 5 (January 1969), pp. 20–28; and Edward E. Schwartz and William C. Sample, "First Findings from Midway," *Social Service Review*, 41 (June 1967), pp. 113–151.
14. See, for example, Margaret Blenkner, Julius Jahn, and Edna Wasser, *Serving the Aging: An Experiment in Social Work and Public Health Nursing* (New York: Community Service Society, 1964); and William J. Reid and Ann W. Shyne, *Brief and Extended Casework* (New York: Columbia University Press, 1969).
15. See, for example, Donald G. Langsley, Frank S. Pittman III, and Kalman Flomenhaft, "Family Crisis Therapy—Results and Implications," *Family Process*, 7 (September 1968), pp. 145–158.
16. See Donald T. Campbell and Julian C. Stanley, *Experimental and Quasi-Experimental Designs for Research* (Chicago: Rand McNally Co., 1963); Herzog, op. cit.; Julian Meltzoff and Melvin Kornreich, *Research in Psychotherapy* (New York: Atherton Press, 1970); and Tony Tripodi, Philip Fellin, and Henry S. Meyer, *Assessment of Social Research* (Itasca, Ill.: F. E. Peacock Publishers, 1969). For a summary of the criteria used in these texts *see* Joel Fischer, "Framework for the Analysis of Outcome Research" (Honolulu: School of Social Work, University of Hawaii, 1971), (Mimeographed.)
17. Carol Meyer, "Implications of Evaluative Research Findings for Curriculum Concerned with Intervention on the Micro-System Level." Paper prepared for the Symposium on the Effectiveness

of Social Work Intervention, Fordham University, New York, New York, January 14–15, 1971.

18. William C. Berleman and Thomas W. Steiner, "The Execution and Evaluation of a Delinquency Prevention Program," *Social Problems*, 14 (Spring 1967), pp. 413–423.

19. Maude M. Craig and Philip W. Furst, "What Happens After Treatment? A Study of Potentially Delinquent Boys," *Social Service Review*, 39 (June 1965), pp. 165–171.

20. The statistics used were not specified in the report.

21. Alice McCabe, *The Pursuit of Promise* (New York: Community Service Society, 1967).

22. Meyer, Borgatta, and Jones, op.. cit., p. 3.

23. Ibid., p. 180.

24. Walter B. Miller, "The Impact of a Total Community Delinquency Control Project," *Social Problems*, 9 (Fall 1962), pp. 168–191.

25. Ibid., p. 187.

26. Edwin Powers and Helen Witmer, *An Experiment in the Prevention of Delinquency—The Cambridge–Somerville Youth Study* (New York: Columbia University Press, 1951).

27. See, for example, Harvey Gochros, "The Caseworker–Adoptive Parent Relationship in Post-Placement Services," *Child Welfare*, 46 (June 1967), pp. 317–326.

28. Margaret Blenkner, Martin Bloom, and Margaret Nielsen, "A Research and Demonstration Project of Protective Services," *Social Casework*, 52 (October 1971), p. 489.

29. Gordon E. Brown, ed., *The Multi-Problem Dilemma* (Metuchen, N.J.: Scarecrow Press, 1968).

30. Ibid., p. 127.

31. Ludwig Geismar and Jane Krisberg, *The Forgotten Neighborhood* (Metuchen, N.J.: Scarecrow Press, 1967).

32. Campbell and Stanley, op. cit. A selection-maturation artifact refers to an interaction that occurs when the selection of subjects for experimental and control groups results in groups with different potentials for rates of change.

33. Statistical regression refers to a general tendency for those groups selected for treatment because of extremely negative scores to show evidence of improvement at a later point in time, irrespective of the treatment.

34. Although a design using analysis of covariance techniques for equating experimental and control groups on pretest measures might have reduced uncertainty, such a design is hampered when the covariate is not perfectly reliable and when the samples are drawn from such obviously disparate populations. See F. M. Lord, "Large-Sample Covariance Analysis when the Control Variable is Fallible," *Journal of the American Statistical Association*, 55 (1960), pp. 437–451.

35. Edward Mullen, Robert Chazin, and David Feldstein, *Preventing Chronic Dependency* (New York: Community Service Society, 1970).

36. Allen P. Webb and Patrick Riley, "Effectiveness of Casework with Young Female Probationers,"

Social Casework, 51 (November 1970), pp. 113–115.

37. Ibid., p. 569.

38. Randomization is an attempt to ensure that every potential subject has an equal chance of being assigned to an experimental or control group and is the preferable approach in attempting to avoid bias. Matching of subjects is often used when randomization is not possible. Since it would be desirable to have experimental and control groups demonstrate pretest equivalence on outcome measures (and perhaps other relevant life measures such as age) and also have an equal chance of being assigned to treatment or control groups, the optimum design would include both matching and randomization procedures. Randomization alone often produces equivalence, but this still must be examined separately by the researcher to determine whether equivalence between groups has in fact been attained.

39. Bergin, op. cit.

40. Berleman and Steiner, op. cit., p. 421.

41. Op. cit.

42. Op. cit.

43. Op. cit., pp. 180–183.

44. Op. cit., p. 455.

45. Op. cit.

46. Charles Truax and Robert Carkhuff, *Toward Effective Counseling and Psychotherapy* (Chicago: Aldine Publishing Co., 1967).

47. Roberts and Nee, op. cit.

48. See Joel Fischer, *Interpersonal Helping: Emerging Approaches to Social Work Practice* (Springfield, Ill.: Charles C Thomas, 1972).

49. Mary E. MacDonald, "Reunion at Vocational High: An Analysis of 'Girls at Vocational High'" *Social Service Review*, 40 (June 1966), p. 188. *See also* Cooper and Krantzler, op. cit.

The high cost of delivering services

by Alan R. Gruber

Social welfare financing has traditionally been based on the concept of providing enough money for an agency to employ enough staff to carry out the functions set forth in its charter. The important element has been the provision of funds so that staff would be available to carry the necessary responsibilities. Whether or not they efficiently did so has almost never been directly related to the funding picture.

United Way organizations, for instance, have not provided grants to agencies based on actual time that staff spent delivering services directly to recipients. Rather, they have based allocations on aggregate data, that is, the number of cases (even though some cases may not have been seen for months), budget, number of staff, and so on. Worse, of course, has been funding based on who on the requesting agency's board knew whom on the funding agency's budget review committee. The accepted and typical procedure has been for the agency executive and a selected board member to go into the budget hearing with colorful charts, the agency's annual budget sum-mary, and most important, a few good case examples designed to tear at the purse strings of budget review committees.

Collecting and transforming data into usable information has been at best a haphazard activity in most health and social welfare organizations. Gathering information has been largely construed to mean compiling case records, often without even a standard outline, or completing forms such as face sheets and sometimes employee time forms. Traditionally, the social worker's sophistication in this area has not gone beyond counting or categorizing client contacts, counting cases, and tracking cases that are new, opened, reopened, or closed.

It has, then, been on the basis of such information that important administrative and program decisions have been made—or just as often not made. Terms such as cost analysis, cost benefit, service and overhead ratios, service accounting, and others denoting concepts common in business and industry have seldom been relevant to social welfare administration.

Reprinted with permission of the National Association of Social Workers, from SOCIAL WORK, Vol. 18, No. 4 (July 1973), pp. 33-40.

ACCOUNTABILITY

Thomas has made the point that a system of collecting statistics about an organization must serve as an administrative tool to expedite accountability. He has further pointed out that it also can serve to monitor program development, maintain program control, check and guide staff development and evaluation, and provide a basis for research.[1]

It is primarily the first issue—accountability—that supports the need for more knowledgeable, accurate collection of information than the vast majority of public and private nonprofit organizations currently do. Accountability has always been espoused as an extremely important component of the social work profession, and yet most social agencies have not implemented it enough so that it has become an ongoing element in their pattern of work. Sanction has often replaced accountability in that as long as funding and other mechanisms permitted an organization to function, it was assumed to be fulfilling its stated purposes.

Accountability becomes all the more imperative for the private, nonprofit service organization when it depends on the public dollar—and to many persons in the business of delivering health and welfare services from the voluntary sector it is agonizingly clear that such dependence will grow in the next few years.

Over the last decade, for instance, private philanthropic giving to support social welfare services has substantially decreased while giving to other endeavors of nonprofit organizations—except religious work—has substantially increased.[2] Large donors particularly have created this situation by generally providing more support to cultural, educational, and health facilities and assuming that the federal and state governments would support the social services.

Added to this—assuming that Boston is typical of large metropolitan areas—support of social agencies by United Way has decreased appreciably in the last decade: a reduction in Boston from 28 percent of the annual operating budgets in 1962 to 18 percent in 1972.[3] This loss has largely been made up through public funds, that is, purchase-of-service contracts. In agencies of the Child Welfare League of America, for example, government payments for services increased by 33 percent between 1968 and 1971.[4] Social agency executives are no longer shocked to hear at their gatherings someone from funding agencies state that in five years approximately 25 percent of the voluntary agencies will no longer exist. Even today, news is often heard of the closing or radical restructuring of a private agency because of its lack of funds.

To counter this trend and attempt to strengthen public faith in private agencies, farseeing agency administrators have recently been turning to service accounting and cost accounting. By using these systems, they are hoping to find the answers to questions that taxpayers are asking about services, costs, benefits, and the wise use of funds.

SERVICE ACCOUNTING AND COST ACCOUNTING

The primary objective of a system of service accounting (sometimes called management information) is the collection of systematic data that will enable an organization to improve its decision-making processes and thereby allocate its resources more efficiently—that is, its funds, personnel, space, and so on. Thus in a social welfare organization, with greatly improved management, the delivery of social and health services should become considerably more efficacious. Specifically, with regard to service delivery, an effective system of service accounting allows for collecting and measuring data related to recipients and provides information from which programs and techniques can be developed and refined.

No system of service accounting has yet been devised that will, in itself, make the decisions required. The function of such a system is to define and illuminate the issues so that appropriate personnel may take rational and informed action. Given our increased technological abilities, service accounting in a social welfare organization aims not only to improve the administrative operation but to reinforce existing information sources and strengthen current practices so that they effectively promote the attainment of social welfare goals.

Cost accounting is a long-accepted practice in commerce and industry. Its objective is simply to determine how much it costs an organization to produce, market, and deliver a product. Knowing that, management is able to make decisions regarding the utilization of manpower, space, and other resources. Management then knows how much it is making—or losing—on its various endeavors and is able to decide whether or not the organization will continue certain practices and products, according to the resulting benefit.

One must remember that benefit need not always be financial reward. Many organizations continue to produce and deliver products on a break-even basis—perhaps even at a loss—because of other benefits derived, such as favorable public relations, worthwhile service to the community, or professional acclaim.

Cost accounting has not been utilized extensively in social welfare. By and large, administrators have taken the position that it is irrelevant since there is no product, that it is impossible to implement, or simply that no one in the organization knows how to do it. However, the thesis of this article is that a specific unit of service rendered by an organization can be considered to be synonymous with a product; therefore, cost accounting and service accountng can be quite readily implemented.

A service unit may be arbitrarily defined in whatever way the administration chooses. For instance, a service unit for an entire day of day care may be defined as (1) a full day of day care for a child, (2) two half-days of day care for a child, (3) nine hours of day care for a child, or (4) any suitable period. The number of administrators who have recognized the feasibility of using service

accounting and cost accounting in social welfare has been growing in recent years. Increasingly, social agencies are combining cost accounting functions with service accounting systems and beginning to implement them.

As a result of such implementation, administrators and board members are being forced to deal with some embarrassing and revealing facts. Why, for instance, does it cost some social agencies or clinics so much

---

"Why does it cost some agencies so much more than $1 to support delivery of $1's worth of service?"

---

more than one dollar to support the delivery of one dollar's worth of service? Why do some administrators estimate that it costs forty to sixty dollars or more per hour to deliver casework/psychotherapy services to individuals or families, although these services are often delivered by students or paraprofessionals? Why do professional personnel, on an average, deliver only about twenty hours a week of direct service, including travel and collateral contacts?

It is important to note that the most progressive and competent administrators are the ones likely to be caught in the squeeze of these issues. Quite obviously, the board members and other decision-makers who are able to ask such questions in the first place are those in organizations that have instituted and implemented service and cost accounting systems. These systems have provided the controversial data. Administrators who continue to use traditional accounting procedures tend to remain blissfully ignorant of such issues.

PURCHASE-OF-SERVICE CONTRACTS

The beginning of a system of service and cost accounting has recently been introduced in Massachusetts for purchase-of-service contracts. Since both federal and state funds are involved, this is a situation in which the significance of accountability cannot be overemphasized.

The author chaired a task force responsible for developing procedures of cost determination, monitoring, and evaluation to utilize Title IV-A funds for purchase-of-service contracts with the Massachusetts Department of Public Welfare. Title IV-A is a part of the social security law, which provides that the federal government under certain conditions will match each dollar supplied by the state with three dollars when the funds are expended for certain social services.

Through this mechanism, the Commonwealth of Massachusetts expects to spend approximately $12 million each year on day care, homemaker services, protective services, services to unmarried mothers, and counseling and emergency services. A large portion of these funds will be spent through purchase-of-service contracts with private agencies.

Purchase-of-service contracting is of course not a new concept in social welfare. In the past, however, such contracts have almost always been based on arbitrary cost figures—for example, twenty-five dollars per week per case, even though generally neither the contracting organization nor the contractor knew how much it would actually cost to deliver the services requested. In most such contracts, grants are given to the contractor, who agrees to provide certain defined services. Then the funds are used, for instance, to hire social workers who theoretically will provide the services. Generally, there is no provision requiring a contractor to account for what has actually been done on the case, how much of the service specified has been rendered, and what benefit has accrued from delivering the service.

In a situation like this, the less a contractor does while still meeting the basic although loose provisions of the contract, the more money he makes. In essence, this type of loose contracting rewards organizations that do the least, beyond an established minimum. From a practical viewpoint, there is a financial disincentive that prevents an organization from doing too much.

On the other hand, organizations working on some contracts found, after they had instituted systems of cost and service accounting, that they were losing literally tens of thousands of dollars. With that in mind, the cost determination system for use of Title IV-A funds in Massachusetts was established with two primary principles: (1) the contractor must be assured of being reimbursed one dollar for each dollar he spends on a contract, including administration and overhead expenses, and (2) the contractor must be assured of maintaining his autonomy and his freedom to design the service delivery system in the way he feels is most efficient and effective.

In line with the latter principle, the system was planned in a way to assure that contracts were not let simply on the basis of price. If they had been, then there would have been a simple, competitive bid system, which again would have rewarded those who delivered the least possible service beyond the established minimum. It was even more important, however, to make sure that contractors were paid dollar for dollar for what they actually delivered, not for the staff they hired, who might or might not deliver the requested services.

To assure attaining these results, a rather tight system of cost determination evolved. It benefits both parties to the contract by assuring that the agreed-upon services are in fact delivered and that the contractor is totally reimbursed. The client obviously is the ultimate beneficiary, and at the same time, the taxpayer is happy because of the maximized accountability and cost benefit.

This system was presented by the Massachusetts Department of Public Welfare at seventeen meetings across the state, which were attended by executive directors of private agencies. At one meeting, the director of a relatively large family counseling agency, clearly recognizing the implications of establishing direct service costs versus general costs, brought up an important issue.

"I'm in private practice," he said, "with a group of social workers and other well-trained and experienced professionals. We could deliver services, say, to unmarried mothers at a price of about twenty-five dollars an hour and make quite a bit of money for ourselves. I could never do it at that price in my agency, however, because of the cost of meetings, training, fringe benefits for my staff, and all the other elements that go into my overhead." Therein lies the issue: he was probably right. In private practice such as he described, he could offer services, delivered by exceptionally well-trained and experienced personnel with full credentials, at a lower rate than his own agency could offer these services with delivery by much less qualified persons. Why?

USE OF TIME

To answer that question, it will be helpful to look at social workers' use of their time. When an agency with a thirty-five-hour working week employs a social worker to deliver services, theoretically that worker is being paid to deliver thirty-five hours of services each week. But it is obvious that he will not do so—and no one expects him to.

Table 1 shows how an average social worker in a large multifunctional agency, Boston Children's Service Association (BCSA), spent his time in 1971. The data for this table were collected for more than a year by the BCSA service and cost accounting systems. Continued use of the systems led to the development of improved administrative procedures that made it possible to redistribute the proportions of time and subsequently reduce the costs of service delivery. The BCSA service and cost accounting systems have also been used to test costs in other agencies, and the figures from those tests are consistent with the data shown in the table.

Costs are figured on the basis of a thirty-five-hour week, an annual salary of $10,000, and thus an hourly rate of $5.49. Time is distributed according to the way the agency's total professional staff—excluding top administrators—spent their working hours.

As Table 1 indicates, an average social worker spends only 19.5 percent of his time delivering services directly to clients. Adding collateral services to the direct services accounts for only 29.5 percent of his time. When all the activities are combined that

TABLE 1. DISTRIBUTION OF TIME FOR A TYPICAL SOCIAL WORKER

Activity	Hours[a]	Percent of Time	Cost[b]
Charged directly to specific cases			
Face-to-face services to clients[c]	354.9	19.5	1,950
Collateral services on behalf of clients[c]	182.0	10.0	1,000
Dictation, administration, and supervision	236.6	13.0	1,300
Travel	127.4	7.0	700
Charged to overhead			
Fringe benefits (vacations, holidays, etc.)	182.0	10.0	1,000
Community activity	72.8	4.0	400
Agency activity (staff meetings, staff development, etc.)	309.4	17.0	1,700
Unspecified and unaccounted-for time [d]	354.9	19.5	1,950
Total	1,820.0	100.0	10,000

[a] Hours per year based on a 35-hour week.
[b] Dollars per year based on an annual salary of $10,000.
[c] These figures include time on the telephone.
[d] It is estimated that, at best, approximately 20 percent of the unspecified and unaccounted-for time (71 hours, for a cost of $390) is used for general administrative purposes such as completing statistical forms, program reports, etc. At least $1,560, therefore, is spent to support activity irrelevant to the agency but important to the worker, e.g. coffee breaks, short shopping trips, etc. Note that all social action, education, and other important noncase costs would be accounted for under the categories of community activity and agency activity.

SOURCE: The figures in this table were obtained at Boston Children's Service Association (BCSA), Boston, Massachusetts, through the use of the BCSA service and cost accounting system.

can be charged directly to specific cases—that is, direct and collateral services, plus the reporting, administrative and supervisory responsibilities, and travel related to cases—they still take up only 49.5 percent of his time. Thus slightly more than half that social worker's salary should in reality be charged to overhead.

These ratios have significant operational implications for agency administrators. Seemingly, however, most administrators have not been concerned about the problem—at least, if they have, not many have allowed their concern to become public knowledge.

EXEMPLAR AGENCY

The data in Table 1 showing how the average social worker in a large agency spends his time—along with other data based on analyses of actual agency budgets—are used in demonstrating how an exemplar agency establishes costs. For purposes of illustration, it is assumed that the agency renders casework services only; therefore, the service unit (product) is one hour of casework services delivered.

The exemplar then is a large casework agency that carries responsibilities for approximately 2,000 active cases and has an annual budget of $2 million. A traditional system of case costing—simply dividing the budget total by the number of cases—yields a figure of $1,000 per case. That figure, however, provides little if any usable information.

Most social welfare organizations are more sophisticated about case costing and, therefore, figures are not constructed in this traditional way as often now as in the past. Instead, increasing attention is being paid to the overhead rate, which can be defined simply as the portion of the agency budget that is used to enable the agency to deliver its services, as opposed to the portion used for actually delivering them. Services obviously differ from organization to organization. A community organization agency delivers services that a family service agency might carry as overhead—for example, organizing tenants.

It is usually assumed, in considering personnel needs and estimating costs, that staff who deliver services are using their time efficiently to do so. Granted that this assumption is correct, how does an administrator proceed to figure costs of services, costs of overhead, and overhead rate?

First, he recognizes that, out of the agency's $2 million budget, a considerable sum must be set aside for reimbursables. Reimbursables make up the portion of the budget that is essentially cash flow; they include, for example, expenditures for foster care or for a child's residential treatment.

After allocating $600,000 for reimbursables, he subtracts from the balance of $1.4 million the amount required for salaries of workers who are theoretically devoting all their time to the delivery of services to clients—that is, the social workers who are not administrators. He decides on $600,000 for these salaries. The remainder, $800,000, is the overhead.

Next, the overhead rate is calculated by establishing the percentage by which $600,000 must be increased to get $1.4 million. The rate is found to be almost 234 percent.

There may be legitimate reasons that justify an overhead rate of this size. The agency, for instance, may be performing many functions in the community that cannot be charged to specific cases. Action geared to solving problems of racism, housing, poverty, and so on are not always or even usually based on circumstances or events that can be dealt with on a case-to-case basis. Thus the overhead rate for these agencies is generally higher.

As a rule, however, agencies that attempt to deal with social conditions affecting the lives of their clients make more significant contributions to their communities than those that do not. The costs of such efforts, as well as those for education and consultation, are usually justifiable and warrant support from funding sources. Because of these factors, the simple comparison of costs per unit of service in a large multifunctional agency and in private practice may be inappropriate and unfair.

SERVICE COSTS PER HOUR

Looking at Table 1 from another viewpoint, it can be seen that the typical social worker spent 354.9 hours during the year delivering face-to-face services to clients. Dividing his salary of $10,000 by those hours yields a cost of $28.18 per hour. However, considering only direct services as relevant is a rather regressive concept in social work practice. Including also the hours spent on collateral services, the total comes to 536.9 hours and the resulting cost is $18.63 per hour of service.

Since this worker was theoretically hired to work full time (1,820 hours) delivering services, those services are being delivered at a salary rate of approximately $34,000 per year. Even so, the major problem is yet to be addressed. These costs reflect only salary; how does one allocate the overhead?

It must be remembered that the issue here is cost per service unit. If that service unit is defined as one hour of service delivered directly to a client, then as Table 1 indicates, only 19.5 percent of the worker's time was actually devoted to such functions. Consequently, only 19.5 percent of the $600,000 that the agency spent for salaries of direct service workers (or $117,000) actually represented services delivered directly to clients. Therefore, 80.5 percent of $600,000, or $483,000 should be transferred to overhead costs. Adding this to $800,000 already allocated to overhead means that it has taken $1,283,000 to deliver $117,000 worth of direct worker-to-client services. That represents an effective overhead rate of almost 1,200 percent. Put yet another way, it has taken almost twelve dollars to deliver one dollar's worth of service!

Using the more progressive model—including collateral services as a legitimate part of a service unit—means that 70.5 percent of $600,000 should be transferred to overhead. Then it would take $1,223,000 to deliver $177,000 worth of services with an overhead rate of almost 800 percent—that is, a ratio of almost eight dollars for one dollar's worth of service! Even including dictation, administration, supervision, and travel, the overhead rate would still be approximately 472 percent.

Using the latter ratio, for each dollar that the agency is spending for service directly chargeable to a case, it is spending four to five dollars for overhead. This covers costs of staff meetings, vacations, staff development, conferences, secretarial and clerical assistance, fringe benefits, administration, record-keeping, accounting, and a whole host of other elements—including a significant amount of unaccounted-for time.

SOURCES OF PROBLEMS

It should be pointed out that the data in Table 1, showing the number of hours and the percentage of time devoted to various activities, are based on the records of how working hours were spent in a large agency by the entire professional staff, excluding top administrators. The costs of direct services, costs of overhead, and overhead rates are of course calculated on the same time distribution.

When the time distribution for social workers in *direct service positions* was analyzed, the findings indicated that they spent about 70 percent of their time on activity that could be charged directly to specific cases. Thus the picture regarding overhead costs and overhead rate would be much brighter in an agency having a high proportion of its professional staff in direct service positions.

The data revealed, however, that some workers averaged only twenty or twenty-five

51

client contacts per month. And in the average bureaucratic agency there are whole groups of workers who deliver virtually no case services, but rather spend the greater part of their time on such functions as liaison with other organizations, supervision, and the processing of information.

The proportion of time that must be charged to overhead is of vital significance to the private practitioner. Suppose that a social worker in private practice, full time, is spending only 29.5 percent of his time actually seeing clients or providing collateral services to them. Then less than one-third of his time is generating income, and he is in serious financial difficulty. To stay in business, he must devote a larger proportion of his time to direct and collateral services. Does this perhaps help to explain why the director of the family counseling agency previously referred to could offer services through his private practice at a lower rate than his nonprofit agency could offer them?

It should also be noted that the overhead rate is of paramount importance when a purchase-of-service contract is involved. It is from that segment of the payment that an agency will obtain its general fiscal support.

CONCLUSIONS

Data collected for more than a year in a number of private social agencies indicate that, in general, the ratio of service costs to overhead costs is quite unreasonable. The author believes that the main reason for uncontrolled costs and minimal benefits lies in the system itself, in that organizations are too heavily staffed by bureaucratic personnel who spend little if any time in actual service delivery—and the larger the organization, the more frequently this occurs.

Although line workers seem to be spending most of their time on services, some deliver little, and this is undetected because of the loose or nonexisting procedures of service accounting. Thus it is probably true that the unproductive line workers account for a small proportion of the uncontrolled costs.

The inevitable and disturbing conclusion, however, is that the costs could be much less and the benefit could be much greater. The real issue is probably more visible when seen in terms of Parkinson's Law, i.e., people fill time with work, whether the work is necessary or not.

Evaluation is certainly not a new concept in social welfare organizations. Combining general program evaluation with cost and service accounting leads to the analysis of cost benefit. Only when more agency administrators and board members recognize that they must know what is actually occurring in their organizations—that is, how time is being spent and what service delivery costs—will more efficient and efficacious services begin to appear.

NOTES AND REFERENCES

1. Thomas Marvin, "Service Accounting for the Large Multi-Purpose Family Agency" (Seattle, Washington: Family Counseling Service of Seattle, 1968). (Mimeographed.)

2. See *Giving U.S.A.*, annual reports (New York: American Association of Fund-Raising Counsel).

3. Personal communication with Dr. Howard Demone, Director, United Community Services, Boston, Mass.

4. *See* Michael J. Smith, *Child Welfare Agency Income: Amount and Source, 1970–1971* (New York: Child Welfare League of America, 1971), p. 5.

5. Keeping in mind that the reimbursables are simply cash flow for the agency, the following formulas show how to calculate an effective overhead rate. Given:

S = salaries for providing direct services to clients.

R = reimbursables, that is, funds returned to the agency by third parties for costs of foster care, residential treatment, hospitalization, and so on.

O = overhead, that is, cost of space, telephone service, heat, light, and the like; also, salaries of administrators, secretaries, maintenance personnel, and so on.

T = total operating budget of agency.

C = cost of delivering service.

We know that $S + R + O = T$.

We also know $C = S + O$ or $C = T - R$.

The formula used to calculate the overhead rate (OR) is, therefore:

$$OR = \frac{S + O}{S} \times 100.$$

Morley Glicken

The Troubled Child in Foster Care

Something very wrong exists in our Society today which combines numerous elements of social pathology to produce alarming numbers of children so troubled they must be removed from their homes. Very often this type of child has been deprived of consistent affection, confused over his position in and identification with his family, brutally mistreated by parents, neglected, uncared for, ridiculed or just ignored. He is a child who, to the core of his soul, suffers.

And yet one finds this profession doing something as deplorable to the child. One finds placements in foster situations of minimal and poorly evaluated nature. One finds a society allowing so little in the way of concrete help to the child that it constitutes a national tragedy. One finds agencies not attracting professionally trained workers because they fear innovation and change. One finds social workers sincerely offering to help families when, by the very fact they have the power to take the child away, families will not trust them and therefore cannot involve themselves in treatment.

Such is the nature of the problem social work has to face. We have handled it rather badly. Turnover rates as high as 30% to 40% a year in foster homes are common throughout Canada. Children moved five, ten and fifteen times are far from uncommon. Monthly payments of $65 to $75 for the care of a child are legally prescribed, even though it is incomprehensible how a normal child, let alone a troubled child, can be cared for on such a sum.

The use of foster homes as the primary facility for the care of children goes against evidence that most foster parents cannot cope with the troubled child. A Saskatchewan Welfare Department Survey in 1968 points out that

JOURNAL, Ontario Association of Children's Aid Societies, October 1970, pp. 10-14.

most foster parents are ill-equipped to handle most problems, even the normal problems of children. It found that many opt out in times of crisis and that few can invest anywhere near the degree of time and concern required. Few of the foster parents surveyed experienced much reaction to a child leaving the home. Only six percent expressed any concern for the child's future and as few as 17% said they felt some loneliness.

The literature of the past 10 years in North America abounds with similar material. Zira de Fries calls the foster family an inappropriate way of caring for neglected children, one in which rejection by the foster parents is a possibility too great to risk. Catholic Children's Aid Society of Toronto found that it lost 86% of its newly found homes in 1964 and that one third of the children in care had to be removed. The Director of Child Welfare (Ontario) stated in the JOURNAL that too many children are moved too rapidly from home to home without adequate preparation and wonders if it is because children are placed "like square pegs in round holes." Vincent Bocchini calls foster homes "jungles" where the child is shuttled about so often he rapidly learns to distrust strangers, to see himself as unwanted — to barely survive.

Clearly, today's foster homes represent little more in many cases than an economical place for the child to live and a naive belief that enough people with warm hearts exist in the community to do the job.

Lest this sound like an attack on foster parents, my concern is for the use of foster homes as a primary treatment device. It's most ironic that we should spend considerable time evaluating a pathological home situation before removing the child, only to place him in a home ill-prepared to receive him. We then keep our fingers crossed that the home will stay intact with minimal supervision because we haven't the staff or time to spend with foster parents. The foster parent role is a complex one. It requires training, supervision, continued contact, and above all, role definitions which are precise and clearly understood by all involved. To assume that a foster parent can care for troubled children in most situations is naive. To assume further that he can do it with little in the way of preparation is cruel to the foster parent and to the child. The fact is that most people have not the depth of understanding or the theoretical preparation to care for troubled children. How can they understand the amount of time and care necessary to work through feelings of rejection? How can they understand that a child often fears involvement with his substitute family because, bad as his parents were, they still were his own and any act of affection for his foster parents may be seen as disloyalty to his own parents?

I would suggest that we consider the following as basic to the care of the troubled child:

1. Every effort should be made to keep the child in his home. Only where dangerous physical abuse exists should the child be immediately removed

and then with an eye toward helping the parents so that the child can return home. This suggests that the present role of authority to remove the child be eliminated so that the worker exists entirely to treat in an atmosphere free of tension.

Agencies should develop progressive treatment approaches to serve the family and the child in realistic ways to improve functioning. Such approaches as behavior modifications, family therapy, and group therapy to mention a few should be integral parts of an agency's repertoire of approaches. Aggressive seeking of professionally trained workers through a salary scale and freedom commensurate with their ability should be offered.

Short term treatment facilities for the child with intensive help offered to families while the child is in treatment is another suggested service.

2. If removal of the child is necessary, we should have diagnostic centers for evaluative purposes so that placement can be done in a professional manner with the child situated in the setting most conducive to growth.

3. Small group homes staffed by professionally trained workers and experienced foster home parents should provide the basic unit of care for the child. The situation is much more neutral to the child than a foster home and provides elements of family life while not demanding of him involvement in the tenuous atmosphere of the foster home. The group home can be seen as a long or short term setting depending on the child's needs where agency and foster group parents work together in a joint and co-operative approach to helping the child. The home should be seen as an agency facility with appropriate treatment services provided on a regular basis. The philosophy of the home should be democratic with the child given responsibility for many aspects of the home just as he would if he were living with his parents. To approximate family living, boys and girls should live in the home together so that some semblance of normal heterosexual development can be achieved. One can only look at the segregated nature of some homes with a jaundiced eye. This often reflects moralistic fears and judgements which are based on concerns for illegitimate births -- an attitude which says little for the integrity of the child.

4. Foster parents should be used sparingly. They represent a service of a limited and sometimes harmful nature. If foster homes are recruited, it should be on the following basis:

- Intensive evaluation of the foster home's potential.

- A training period which includes intensive in-service education and short term placement of children in the home to provide a controlled learning experience.

- A clear definition of roles for the parents, the child, and the agency.

- A realistic payment for services beyond the meagre sum offered today.

- On-going contact with the agency for in-service purposes.

5. General treatment issues with the foster child should concern themselves with how to overcome past deprivation and abuse. The foster child can be thought of clinically as existing in the midst of an identity crisis.

This suggests that feelings around rejection by his parents should be a primary focal point. Rather than severing contact with parents or making it difficult for parents to see their child, we should try to involve them in continued therapeutic contact. It's often tempting to eliminate the child's involvement with his parents considering the past abuse suffered at their hands. This does however negate the possibility of change by the parents. Further, it fails to understand the child's continuing affection for his parents even though he might verbalize hostility. To emphasize this point one need only think of the numbers of children in our caseloads who return home to live with their parents after care is terminated. One should not misjudge the tie between child and parent even when severe pathology exists. It is one of our most valuable treatment motivators.

One of the most frequent mistakes of well intentioned foster parents is their attempt to protect the child from his parents or in other ways remove the memory of parents from the child's mind. To help the child, realistic discussion of feelings toward parents should be worked through by worker and foster parent in an atmosphere free of moral judgment about past behavior of the parents. If we moralize, the child will more fiercely than ever hold onto his image of the worker and the foster parents as being the bad guys and the parents no matter how bad the situation, without blame. It is continually intriguing to this writer that children often see a home situation we couldn't begin to accept as tolerable as not only acceptable, but much better than their life in foster care.

The adolescent is, of course, another matter. He leaves home on a much more voluntary basis. Before we accept his desire to leave, we should be sure that we've explored all possibilities for his continued stay. It's not unusual for the child to test parents by threatening to leave or for parents to test the child by suggesting that he go. The decision to leave should be based upon a rational diagnostic judgment and not upon the emotions of the moment.

The adolescent in care is one of our primary treatment problems. His difficulties do not end when he leaves home. Normal adolescent problems combine themselves with whatever his difficulties might have been at home – normally rebellion against authority. This should be met with consistent limit setting, democratic involvement in decision making, responsibilities commensurate with ability, psychological room to grow including privacy and acceptance of the adolescent's need to be alone, realistic and open discussion of sex, concern for his adjustment to life discussed in a warm and sensitive way, avoidance of red herring issues such as dress and hair styles which only alienate the adolescent, and above all, honesty and involvement.

The foster parent's role with the troubled child is a vital one – beyond the reach of most people. The parents must accept a child who often does not want to be there, and who reacts negatively under the belief that if he fights it enough he'll be sent back to his parents. This child is either passively or actively rebellious. He'll go out of his way at times to test the foster parents or to make them believe that they're failing with him. The foster parents must give the child time to work through his feelings about his new home. They must not demand responses that the child may be incapable of. Further foster parents have to respond as more than disciplinarians or guardians of the child's physical wants. They must be willing to accept frequent crises – crises which may affect the continuity of the home. Foster parents will have to accept habitually anti-social or embarassing activities in the initial stages of placement. It suggests that parents possess patience, tact, understanding of the child's inner needs, knowledge of what to do when the child hurts, and above all, a concern for him which reaches the child's heart and forms itself as the beginning of a positive relationship.

6. The worker in child care has a social action responsibility. This implies a need to inform the public about the real needs of children, about the crisis in child care of too many children, too few staff, and too little money, and about the situations in homes which cause such a wide range of pathology that our agencies are flooded with requests for help. It implies that workers should be involving themselves in institutional change so that children disturbed by family life can at least be maintained and helped without need to remove them. Schools, churches, recreational facilities and many others can provide this type of institutional concern if we insist that they begin assuming their share of the responsibility for change. The social action component further suggests that we begin informing the public that the cost of decent and effectice services for the troubled child in foster care is a large one. We ought not be in the position of making do with what we have, when that represents only the barest and least expensive type of service one could offer.

Foster care is a most important area of social work. As society continues producing children with large degrees of pathology, it becomes incumbent upon us to present care which is truly effective. Our present approach has been found wanting. Not to change it would be to ignore the pain large numbers of children feel.

BY JONATHAN KRAUS

Predicting Success of Foster Placements for School-Age Children

■ Although the need for objective criteria in selecting foster homes has been stressed repeatedly in the literature, social workers continue to select foster homes on the basis of their subjective judgments. This article attempts to relate certain objective characteristics of foster parents and foster children to the success or failure of foster home placements. ■

THE SUCCESS OF foster home placements is often defined in the literature in terms of judgments made by caseworkers that are based on some idealized norms. It is true, however, that the ultimate criterion of success is the survival of a placement for the length of time needed to provide substitute parental care for a child. The stability of a placement is important not only for the child's social and emotional adjustment but also from the administrative point of view. Placements that break down put an additional strain on the already overtaxed human and economic resources of social agencies concerned with foster placements and discourage foster parents from further involvement in foster care.

Despite the obvious conclusion that survival of a foster placement is the basic criterion for its success, Taylor and Starr found in reviewing the literature that most studies used the social worker's judgment as the criterion. Even more surprising was

the realization that "there is considerable evidence that the social and psychological distance between social workers and foster parents tends to bias those judgments." They also found that a sound empirical approach to foster home selection was generally lacking. Most authors advocated selection on the basis of "generalizations from [their] thoughts and feelings . . . informal observations and experiences with foster parents . . . [and] results of descriptive and exploratory studies. . . ." In addition, they had conflicting opinions on such fundamental issues as the need for matching children with foster parents, and their definitions of an "adequate" foster home reflected the middle-class values of social workers.[1] This lack of empiricism and objectivity in the approaches to foster home selection appeared to stem from the relatively common attitude among social workers that casework is an art, not a science—an attitude that in its extreme form advocates the use of intuition and imagination and asserts not only that casework is not a science but that it "cannot be a

JONATHAN KRAUS, MA, is Senior Research Officer, Department of Child Welfare and Social Welfare of New South Wales, Sydney, Australia. The author thanks A. C. Thomas, Under Secretary of the Department of Child Welfare and Social Welfare of New South Wales, for permission to publish this paper.

[1] Delores A. Taylor and Phillip Starr, "Foster Parenting: An Integrative Review of the Literature," Child Welfare, Vol. 46, No. 7 (July 1967), pp. 371–385.

Reprinted with permission of the National Association of Social Workers, from SOCIAL WORK, Vol. 16, No. 1 (January 1971), pp. 63-72.

science; nor should it harbour the design to be a science even if that were possible."[2]

The reluctance to modify the intuitive and judgmental approach to foster home selection persists despite its inefficacy, lack of validity, and the demonstrated superiority of statistical over clinical prediction.[3] Although the need for practice-derived research has been discussed repeatedly in the literature, the number of empirical studies relevant to foster home selection is small.[4] It is also worth noting that the value of a study by Wolins, which appeared to be the most extensive and thoroughly conducted of these investigations, was seriously questioned on both methodological and theoretical grounds by Macdonald and Ferguson.[5] Consequently, as Foy points out, it is not surprising that existing guidelines for decision-making in foster home placements are unpragmatic, atomistic, and consist mainly of abstract norms that are difficult to apply in practice. Foy argues that the guidelines needed by social workers for matching children with foster parents should be founded in practice; should be interpreted in relation to each other, not in isolation; and

should be based on verifiable criteria of success. He suggests that such guidelines could be provided by "experience tables" with practice-derived typologies defining the matrix categories.[6] In this context the obvious verifiable criterion for successful placement would be its survival over a specified period of time.

THE STUDY

The present study was designed to implement some of the suggestions made by Foy, and its specific purpose was (1) to investigate the relationship of selected objectively definable characteristics of children and foster parents to the success of foster home placements, (2) to establish a taxonomy of children and foster parents based on these characteristics, and (3) to construct experience tables that could be used as guidelines for successful matching of children with foster parents.

The sample was restricted to children 6 years of age or older who were in their first foster home placement, had no siblings living in the same foster home, and could have been living in the foster home for at least twenty-four months by March 31, 1969. The Department of Child Welfare and Social Welfare of New South Wales made 268 such foster home placements between March 1, 1965, March 31, 1967. The minimum information required for the study was only available for 214 placements, however. These 214 placements consisted

[2] Morton I. Teicher, "Social Casework—Science or Art?" *Child Welfare*, Vol. 46, No. 7 (July 1967), pp. 393–396.

[3] J. McVicker Hunt, "On the Judgment of Social Workers as a Source of Information in Social Work Research," in Ann W. Shyne, ed., *Use of Judgments as Data in Social Work Research* (New York: National Association of Social Workers, 1959), pp. 38–54; Martin Wolins, *Selecting Foster Parents* (New York: Columbia University Press, 1963), pp. 147–151; Edward Foy, "The Decision-Making Problem in Foster Care," *Child Welfare*, Vol. 46, No. 9 (November 1967), pp. 498–503; Daniel Glaser, "Automated Research and Correctional Practices," *California Youth Authority*, Vol. 18, No. 4 (Winter 1965), pp. 24–31; Jack Sawyer, "Measurement and Prediction, Clinical and Statistical," *Psychological Bulletin*, Vol. 66, No. 3 (September 1966), pp. 178–200; and D. V. Babst, D. M. Gottfredson, and K. B. Ballard, "Comparison of Multiple Regression and Configural Analysis Techniques for Developing Base Expectancy Tables," *Journal of Research on Crime and Delinquency*, Vol. 5, No. 1 (January 1968), pp. 72–80.

[4] Robert K. Merton, *Social Theory and Social Structure* (New York: Free Press, 1949); Joseph F. Meisels and Martin B. Loeb, "Unanswered Questions about Foster Care," *Social Service Review*, Vol. 30, No. 3 (September 1956), pp. 239–245; Foy, op. cit.; and Taylor and Starr, op. cit.

[5] Mary E. Macdonald and Marjorie F. Ferguson, "Selecting Foster Parents: An Essay Review," *Social Service Review*, Vol. 38, No. 3 (September 1964), pp. 316–327; Taylor and Starr, op. cit.; and Wolins, op. cit.

[6] Foy, op. cit.

of 172 placements in foster homes and 42 placements with relatives acting as foster parents. Of the 172 children in foster homes, 15 were restored to their natural parents before twenty-four months had elapsed. Consequently, the size of the actual sample was 157. In this group, 79 placements survived for at least twenty-four months and thus were classified as successful. Seventy-eight placements broke down before twenty-four months had elapsed and were classified as failures. The size of each of the two populations ($n=78$) had a distribution-free sample tolerance limit of 95 percent with $p=0.90$ confidence probability.

The number of characteristics of the sample was restricted to increase the power of statistical analysis of the relevant variables. The rationale for restricting the ages of the children was that the rate of breakdown for placements involving preschool children was so low in the experience of this department that it was not considered a problem. This experience is also consistent with the findings reported in the literature.[7] The restriction to first foster placements was based on indications that failure rates increase with each successive placement.[8] The restriction on the child's siblings being placed in the same home was based on findings that there is a significant positive relationship between the success of foster placements and the presence of siblings in these placements.[9] Length of residence was restricted because, in this study, success is defined as the survival of a foster home placement for a minimum of two years.[10]

RELEVANT DATA

The relevant data collected for foster children consisted of the following: sex, chronological age, intelligence level (Wechsler Intelligence Scale for Children or Wechsler Adult Intelligence Scale, full-scale IQ), date of placement, and date of termination (if a breakdown occurred). For foster parents the data included religion(s) of the foster parents; chronological ages; occupations; number of natural, adopted, or foster children (excluding the present foster child); combined weekly income; reasons for wanting a foster child; preference in sex and age; number of children in the household who were within two years of the current foster child's age; number of persons living in the house (including the foster child); number of rooms in the house; and the caseworker's assessment of the foster parents' ability to cope with a child's behavior problems (e.g., enuresis, emotional disturbances, mental retardation, and so on). In addition, a crowding index was calculated for each foster home by dividing the number of residents into the number of rooms in the house.

For purposes of analysis, the motives for becoming foster parents were classified into the following four categories:

1. "Generally interested." This category comprised foster parents who had no clearly stated motives except an interest in caring for a child, including underprivileged or handicapped children; sharing their home with a child; helping a child because one of the foster parents had been orphaned, underprivileged, or had grown up in an intitution, and so forth.

2. "Know child." The foster parents expressed an interest in a specific child for a

[7] G. Trasler, *In Place of Parents* (London, England: Routledge & Kegan Paul, 1960), p. 215; and M. O. Oswald, "An Analysis of Some Factors Associated with Success and Failure in Foster Home Placements," *Australian Journal of Social Work*, Vol. 17, No. 2 (May 1964), pp. 17–21.

[8] Oswald, op. cit.

[9] Trasler, op. cit.

[10] "Breakdown of Foster Home Placements." Unpublished paper, Department of Child Welfare, New South Wales, Australia, 1966. This definition was based on the findings that 50 percent of foster placements break down within two years and 54 percent within six years. Thus the chances of a placement breaking down after two years are small.

Table 1. Prediction of Successful Placement When Combined Characteristics of Foster Home Include Foster Parents' Motivation, Number of Residents, and Foster Mother's Age (statistical probabilities and standard errors)

Motivation of Foster Parents	Four Persons in Home [a]		Other than Four Persons in Home [a]	
	Age of foster mother		Age of foster mother	
	46 or older	45 or younger	46 or older	45 or younger
Generally interested	—	.67±.19	.82±.12	.70±.08
Know child	—	.33±.19	.83±.14	.55±.11
Want company for own child	—	.14±.08	—	.26±.10

[a] Includes current foster child.

variety of reasons (e.g., they had spent one or more holidays with the child, had known the child before he had become a ward of the state, and so on).

3. "Want company for own child." This motivation was often inferred from the family situation or from comments made by the foster parents (e.g., foster parents had four preadolescent daughters and one small son and had applied for a foster child of the son's age).

4. "Want a child." A variety of reasons were included in this category (e.g., the foster parents were interested in taking a foster child as a preliminary to adoption, wanted to replace a lost child of their own, and so on).

As mentioned earlier, a successful foster placement was defined as one that survived for a continuous period of twenty-four months or longer and a failure was defined as a placement that broke down before twenty-four months had expired.

ANALYSIS OF THE DATA

The relationship of the characteristics of children and foster parents to successful placement was analyzed statistically.[11] The following characteristics were found to have

a significant positive association with success: (1) foster mother is 46 years of age or older, (2) foster parents have two children of their own, (3) another foster child is already present in the home, (4) number of persons (including current foster child) residing in the home is greater or less than four, (5) foster parents' motivation is "generally interested" or "know child." In addition, the motivation "want company for own child" was found to have a significant negative association with success.

When the data were reanalyzed to find the net relationship between successful placement and individual characteristics, however, the positive association was found not to hold. (While individual characteristics were being analyzed, the others were controlled by excluding them or holding them constant.) Therefore, the findings indicate that successful placement does not depend on the presence of a single characteristic but on the interaction of a number of them. Thus the need for multidimensional experience tables is confirmed.

In the actual construction of these experience tables, no more than three variables could be used at one time because the number of individual cases was relatively small. Because motivation had the strongest association with success of placement, it was included in all tables, while the remaining four variables were tabulated with motivation in all possible combinations of two variables at a time (except for the combination of "number of own children" and "number of persons residing in foster home" because one variant of it was repre-

[11] The data were analyzed by calculating overall chi-squares for contingency tables and, when appropriate, the chi-squares were partitioned into components (A. E. Maxwell, *Analyzing Qualitative Data* [London, England: Methuen & Co., 1961], pp. 56–60). Yates Correction for Continuity was used in fourfold tables in which any cell had $n=5$.

sented by only two cases). The motivational category "want a child" was not used at all because it was represented by only thirteen cases. The probabilities of successful placement, based on various combinations of three variables, are shown in Tables 1 through 5.

On visual inspection the interrelationships (correlation matrix) of characteristics associated with success did not show any clusters that could serve as a basis for a taxonomy (the matrix was too small for a formal cluster or factor analysis). A taxonomy of foster homes was made, however, by arbitrarily using the four motivational classifications as axes for the correlation clusters on which four descriptive categories of foster homes are based (see Table 6).

DISCUSSION

It was found in this study that no relationship existed between the outcome of foster home placements and the sex, age, and intelligence of foster children. Thus the need for parent-child matching that is frequently advocated in the literature seems questionable.[12] This finding also defeated one of the main purposes of the study—to establish a taxonomy of children that could be used in such matching.

The negative finding regarding the sex of foster children is consistent with the results of a study by Oswald.[13] The negative

---

[12] Taylor and Starr, op. cit.
[13] Oswald, op. cit.

TABLE 2. PREDICTION OF SUCCESSFUL PLACEMENT WHEN COMBINED CHARACTERISTICS OF FOSTER HOME INCLUDE FOSTER PARENTS' MOTIVATION, FOSTER MOTHER'S AGE, AND PRESENCE OF OTHER FOSTER CHILDREN
(statistical probabilities and standard errors)

Motivation of Foster Parents	Foster Mother 46 or Older		Foster Mother 45 or Younger	
	Foster children present	No foster children	Foster children present	No foster children
Generally interested	—	.70±.14	.95±.07 [a]	.59±.09
Know child	—	.86±.09	—	.52±.09
Want company for own child	—	.43±.19	—	.21±.07

[a] $p=1.00$ was arbitrarily changed to .95 so that the standard error could be computed.

TABLE 3. PREDICTION OF SUCCESSFUL PLACEMENT WHEN COMBINED CHARACTERISTICS OF FOSTER HOME INCLUDE FOSTER PARENTS' MOTIVATION, FOSTER MOTHER'S AGE, AND NUMBER OF FOSTER PARENTS' OWN CHILDREN
(statistical probabilities and standard errors)

Motivation of Foster Parents	Foster Mother 46 or Older		Foster Mother 45 or Younger	
	Two own children	Other than two own children	Two own children	Other than two own children
Generally interested	.83±.15	.63±.17	.67±.14	.71±.09
Know child	—	.83±.11	.71±.17	.43±.11
Want company for own child	—	—	.33±.19	.18±.07

TABLE 4. PREDICTION OF SUCCESSFUL PLACEMENT WHEN COMBINED CHARACTERISTICS OF FOSTER HOME INCLUDE FOSTER PARENTS' MOTIVATION, NUMBER OF OWN CHILDREN, AND PRESENCE OF OTHER FOSTER CHILDREN
(statistical probabilities and standard errors)

Motivation of Foster Parents	Two Own Children		Other Than Two Own Children	
	Foster children present	No foster children	Foster children present	No foster children
Generally interested	—	.64±.13	.89±.10	.61±.10
Know child	—	.75±.15	—	.61±.08
Want company for own child	—	.38±.17	—	.22±.07

TABLE 5. PREDICTION OF SUCCESSFUL PLACEMENT WHEN COMBINED CHARACTERISTICS OF FOSTER HOME INCLUDE FOSTER PARENTS' MOTIVATION, NUMBER OF RESIDENTS,[a] AND PRESENCE OF OTHER FOSTER CHILDREN
(statistical probabilities and standard errors)

Motivation of Foster Parents	Four Persons Reside in Home [a]		Other Than Four Persons [a] Reside in Home	
	Foster children present	No foster children	Foster children present	No foster children
Generally interested	—	.50±.20	.95±.07 [b]	.65±.09
Know child	—	.57±.19	—	.65±.08
Want company for own child	—	.21±.08	—	.29±.10

[a] Including the current foster child.
[b] $p=1.00$ was arbitrarily changed to .95 so that the standard error could be computed.

relationship regarding age, however, is not in line with the inverse relationship between the ages of foster children and rates of success for foster placements as reported in the literature.[14] Although "good" foster homes were reported to be equally successful with retarded and normal children,[15] and intelligence was not found to be related to success in the present study, it must be noted that the difference between the failure rates of the mentally deficient children (IQs of 69 or less) and normal children found in this study would have been statistically significant but for

the small size of the sample. Therefore, although the results of this study indicated that placements of children with borderline intelligence are as successful as those of normal children, in a larger sample mentally deficient children possibly could have significantly higher rates of failure.

Of particular interest was the absence of a relationship between successful placement and agreement between the foster child's sex and age with those desired by the foster parents. The finding relating to placements of children of the opposite sex to that desired by foster parents must be viewed with caution because the number of such placements was small, but placements of children two or more years older than the age desired were common (41 percent of all placements), and such placements did not have higher failure rates than those in which foster parents' age preferences were met.

[14] See Walter J. Ambinder, "The Extent of Successive Placements Among Boys in Foster Family Homes," *Child Welfare*, Vol. 44, No. 7 (July 1965), pp. 397–398; Leslie W. Hunter, "Foster Homes for Teenagers," *Children*, Vol. 11, No. 6 (November–December 1964), p. 234; and Oswald, op. cit.

[15] Mabel Rich, "Foster Homes for Retarded Children," *Child Welfare*, Vol. 44, No. 7 (July 1965), pp. 392–394.

TABLE 6. FOUR DESCRIPTIVE CATEGORIES OF FOSTER HOMES AND THE PROBABILITY OF SUCCESSFUL PLACEMENT WHEN AT LEAST FOUR OR ALL FIVE CHARACTERISTICS FOR EACH CATEGORY ARE PRESENT

Description of Foster Home	Characteristics of Home [a]	Probability of Success and Standard Errors
Very successful	Foster mother 46 or older Two own children One or more foster children Other than four residents [b] Motivation "generally interested"	.92 ± .08
Moderately successful	Foster mother 46 or older Other than two own children No foster children Other than four residents [b] Motivation "know child"	.70 ± .08
Moderately unsuccessful	Foster mother 46 or older No own children, or any number One or more foster children Other than four residents [b] Motivation "want a child"	.50 ± .20
Very unsuccessful	Foster mother 45 or younger Other than two own children No foster children Four residents [b] Motivation "want company for own child"	.21 ± .07

[a] When four characteristics are used for prediction, foster parents' motivation must be included.
[b] Including current foster child.

What was the rationale for investigating the socioeconomic characteristics of foster homes, apart from the pragmatic consideration that such data are invariably collected by social agencies dealing with foster placements? The accessibility and objective character of the data do not justify its use unless the data is known or expected to be relevant to the study. The answer is that certain objective characteristics of foster homes are known to be related to the outcome of foster placements (e.g., foster mother's age, presence of other children, and so on).[16] In the light of social role theory, all such characteristics could represent indexes of attitudes, values, and secondary traits that have attained a degree of functional autonomy and thus could be factors in foster parent–child relationships. Such objective indexes, if found to be related to the outcome of foster placements, would be of greater practical value to the caseworker when selecting a foster home than the subjective procedures advocated in the literature, such as understanding the emotional makeup of the foster parents, the vulnerable areas in the emotional makeup of the child, and other time-consuming psychoanalytic-type assessments.[17] In this context it was interesting to note that placements with foster parents assessed by the social workers as having the ability to cope with a child with behavior problems were no more successful than other foster placements.

Of the fifteen characteristics of foster homes investigated in the present study, six had a significant or nearly significant relationship to outcome of placement when they were associated with other characteristics, but none were related to outcome

[16] Trasler, op. cit.

[17] Taylor and Starr, op. cit.

when considered individually (although two showed a trend toward such a relationship). These findings support Foy's contention that in making placement decisions it is necessary to consider the dynamic interplay of many factors, not the individual elements of a situation in isolation.[18]

It was found that a significantly greater number of placements survived when the foster mother was 46 years of age or older.[19] This finding is consistent with those reported by Trasler and Rich, and Trasler's explanaton that higher failure rates occur among younger foster mothers because they seek a companion for their own child agrees with the finding in the present study that there is a significant negative correlation between the foster mother being age 46 years or older and the motivation to take a foster child as a companion for her own child.[20]

The variables reflecting the foster parents' socioeconomic status (occupation, income, number of rooms in the house, crowding index) were found to be unrelated to the outcome of placements. Because in this case the variables were to serve as indexes, these negative findings can be interpreted to show that social roles imposed on foster parents by their socioeconomic status do not comprise values and attitudes, nor do they generate traits that are relevant to foster care. Also important was the finding that foster mothers who worked full time were as successful as those who did not work, which indicates that the usual reluctance of social agencies to place a child in a foster home when the mother works is unwarranted.

There was a trend for a greater number of successful placements in homes in which the foster parents had two children of their own or in which one or more foster children were already residing. No relationship was found between the presence of adopted children or children near to the age of the current foster child and the outcome of placement. The finding that a significantly greater number of placements failed when there were four residents in the foster home (including the current foster child) is meaningful only when examined in relation to the foster parents' motivation and the number of their own children. It can be inferred that in the homes with a high failure rate and in which there are four residents, the residents are the foster parents, their natural, adopted, or foster child, and the current foster child and that the foster parents were motivated to take the current foster child as a companion for their own child. As noted in the literature, this type of foster home is a poor prospect for successful placement.[21]

The finding that placements tend to be more successful when foster parents have two children of their own is difficult to explain and does not appear to have a counterpart in the literature. Obviously such foster parents are not looking for a companion for their own child, but neither are those who have more than two children; yet they are not as successful. Wolins reported that a greater number of "superior" foster homes had two or three children than did "inferior" homes, and Hunter found the greatest number of failures occurred when foster parents had four or more natural children and the least failures occurred when there was no natural child in the home.[22] The trend for more successful placements in homes in which a foster child is already present agrees with Trasler's findings, but inconsistent with his findings and with the assertions made by Charnley was the lack of relationship found in the present study between the presence

[18] Foy, op. cit.

[19] The foster fathers' ages were disregarded for the purposes of analysis and prediction because of their obvious correlation with the ages of foster mothers.

[20] Trasler, op. cit.; and Rich, op. cit.

[21] Neil Kay, "A Systematic Approach to Selecting Foster Parents," Case Conference, Vol. 13, No. 2 (June 1966), pp. 44–50; and Trasler, op. cit.

[22] Wolins, op. cit.; and Hunter, op. cit.

of natural children of an age close to that of the foster child and the failure of foster placements.[23]

MOTIVATION AND SUCCESSFUL PLACEMENT

It was found in this study that there are highly significant differences among the rates of successful foster placements associated with the various categories of motivation on the part of foster parents. The motivation "generally interested" was most successful, with "know child," "want a child," and "want company for own child" following in that order. Of the four categories of motivation, "generally interested" and "want company for own child" were significantly correlated with success (the former positively and the latter negatively). The "know child" category showed a trend toward significance, and no trend was shown for "want a child."

Because the basic data for the investigation of motives seemed inadequate in both content and method of collection, the finding that the motivation of foster parents had a closer association with the outcome of placements than any of the other variables investigated was unexpected. However, the validity of this finding is supported by the fact that it occurred despite the inadequate data. Furthermore, had the data been collected with the express purpose of assessing motivation, the statistical significance of the results probably would have been even higher.[24]

There appears to be agreement among the experts that the motives categorized as "want company for own child" and "want a child" indicate poor chances for a successful foster placement,[25] whereas the motives categorized as "generally interested" and "know child" indicate the likelihood of a successful placement.[26] The present finding that motivation alone is not related to the outcome of a foster placement highlights a crucial facet of motivation that is mentioned explicitly or implicitly only by a few authors—namely, the motives of foster parents cannot be viewed in isolation; they must be examined in the context of other factors (e.g., those shown in experience tables) in the foster parents' lives.[27] In fact, the findings indicate that motivation is a product of the interaction of such factors and that they alone could be used for predicting outcome of placements. Thus motivation could remain an unidentified intervening variable.

Although it was impossible to construct prediction tables based on more than three variables at a time, a taxonomy of foster homes was derived from the correlation matrix in Table 6, which allows predictions based on the most typical combina-

---

[23] Jean Charnley, *The Art of Child Placement* (Minneapolis: University of Minnesota Press, 1955), pp. 177–178.

[24] Another procedural facet that supports the validity of this finding is that the categorization and designation of the categories were done by two psychologists who had no background in foster care or the motivations of foster parents. The designations that emerged, however, are almost identical to those reported in the literature. Equally important, the relationship between the categories of motivation and successful placement found in this study is generally consistent with the findings or observations of other investigators.

[25] Charlotte G. Babcock, "Some Psychodynamic Factors in Foster Parenthood—Part I," *Child Welfare*, Vol. 44, No. 9 (November 1965), pp. 485–493; David Fanshel, *Foster Parenthood: A Role Analysis* (Minneapolis: University of Minnesota Press, 1966), pp. 5–7, 142–152; Charnley, op. cit.; Trasler, op. cit.; and Kay, op. cit.

[26] R. W. Colvin, "Towards the Development of a Foster Parent Attitude Test," *Quantitative Approaches to Parent Selection* (New York: Child Welfare League of America, 1962); H. B. M. Murphy, "Foster Home Variables and Adult Outcomes," *Mental Hygiene*, Vol. 48, No. 4 (October 1964), pp. 587–599; Rich, op. cit.; and Kay, op. cit.

[27] Irene Josselyn, "Evaluating Motives of Foster Parents," *Child Welfare*, Vol. 31, No. 1 (January 1952), pp. 3–9, 13–14; Eugene A. Weinstein, *The Self-Image of the Foster Child* (New York: Russell Sage Foundation, 1960), pp. 7–8; and Foy, op. cit.

tions of four or five variables. In constructing the taxonomy, because motivation had the strongest association with success, the four categories of motivation were used as axes for the correlation clusters on which the types of foster homes were based. Their use as axes makes them comparable with factors, but while factors derived by factor analysis are usually assumed to have a causal significance, the motivational categories are without doubt the effects of interaction of the variables correlated with them.

Prediction tables probably provide the most graphic illustration of the dependence of motivation on the context in which it occurs. For example, Table 3 shows that when the foster mothers are 46 years of age or older and have two natural children, the motive for becoming a foster parent is almost exclusively "generally interested," whereas in the homes with younger foster mothers and the same number of natural children, the motives are varied. The interaction effects, which make the overall context of a foster home more than the sum of its parts in terms of its relationship to motivation and the outcome of placements, make it necessary to construct prediction tables based on the greatest possible number of relevant factors. However, tables constructed on many factors are usually impracticable because of the size of the samples they require. When the sample is too small to represent all combinations of a number of variables, one method of bypassing the difficulty of prediction is to find the combinations that occur most commonly in practice and establish the probabilities of the wanted events associated with them. This procedure was adopted in the construction of Table 6, which allowed predictions to be made using four or five variables at the same time.

CONCLUSION

The purpose of this study was to relate selected characteristics of foster parents and foster children to the success or failure of foster home placements. Significant relationships were found to be contingent upon the interactions of various characteristics—no individual characteristic was significantly correlated with outcome of placement when other relevant characteristics were controlled. The successful placement, defined as one that survived for twenty-four months or more, was found to be related positively to the following factors: the foster mother was 46 years of age or older, the foster parents had two children of their own, a foster child was already present in the home, the number of persons residing in the home was other than four (including the current foster child), the foster parents were motivated by a general interest in helping a child or by knowing a specific child (rather than wanting a companion for their own child or wanting to satisfy their own emotional needs).

Prediction tables were constructed that indicate the probabilities of success associated with the various combinations of the relevant characteristics of foster homes. It should be noted that prediction tables are meant to help, not substitute for, the caseworker's placement decisions. Because the present findings indicate that the success of placements involving school-age children depends on the selection of foster homes, not on matching homes and children, the use of prediction tables could be questioned on the grounds that the problem of selection is irrelevant in practice because there is a chronic shortage of foster homes. The answer to this is that although comparative studies of the long-term adjustment of those children brought up in institutions and those brought up in a series of foster homes are lacking, there is little doubt that a school-age child's socialization, self-concept, and emotional stability are more adversely affected by frequent changes in foster homes. Consequently, prediction tables could be used to eliminate potential foster homes that have a low probability for successful outcome.

BY ALFRED KADUSHIN

Diagnosis and Evaluation for (Almost) All Occasions

A SURPRISINGLY LARGE number of people in need of personal counseling tend to take their problems to astrologers, palm readers, pseudopsychologists, and professional charlatans.[1] Even more surprising are the frequent testimonials offered by the clients of such practitioners to the psychological astuteness of the "counselor." Perhaps most surprising is that such testimonials are not always unwarranted.

The charlatan "counselor," whether he recognizes it or not, generally tends to operate in terms of what has been called the "Barnum effect."[2] In giving a character reading of the client he selects diagnostic statements that, because they are universally valid or nearly so, tend to be accepted as perceptively correct.

Forer tested this procedure with a class of 39 beginning psychology students.[3] Each was asked to complete a psychological test —the Forer Diagnostic Interest Blank—and was told that on the basis of his responses to the diagnostic form an individual personality sketch was to be written. Forer, however, wrote a single diagnostic statement, which was composed of "Barnum effect" phrases culled from a newsstand astrology book. The following are typical of the comments that constituted this statement: "You have a tendency to be critical of yourself." "At times you are extroverted, affable, sociable, while at other times you are introverted, wary, reserved." "Disciplined and self-controlled on the outside, you tend to be worrisome and insecure inside." "Your sexual adjustment has presented problems for you."

Forer then returned the supposedly individualized sketch to each of the students and asked them to rate the diagnostic summary in terms of the degree to which each thought the "personality description reveals the basic characteristics of your personality." On a scale of 0 (poor) to 5 (perfect), Forer's students gave the statement a mean rating of 4.26—almost perfect.

Bachrach and Pattishall replicated Forer's experiment with a group of 64 undergraduate and graduate students in advanced psychology courses and 9 psychiatric residents in training.[4] Instead of the Diagnostic Interest Blank, they asked their respondents to complete a standardized psychology test —the Taylor Manifest Anxiety Scale. For this somewhat more sophisticated group, the mean rating of the degree to which the respondents thought the personality description revealed basic characteristics of the subject's own personality was 3.78 on a 5-point scale.

"AUNT FANNY DESCRIPTION"

The professionally trained counselor is prone to an approach somewhat similar to the "Barnum effect" in writing diagnostic reports. This has been identified as the "Aunt Fanny description." The statement is diagnostically valid for the client but would be equally true of his—or anybody's —"Aunt Fanny."

[1] L. R. Steiner, *Where Do People Take Their Trouble?* (Boston: Houghton Mifflin, 1945).

[2] P. E. Meehl, "Wanted—A Good Cookbook," *American Psychologist*, Vol. 11, No. 6 (June 1956), p. 266.

[3] B. R. Forer, "The Fallacy of Personal Validation: A Classroom Demonstration of Gullibility," *Journal of Abnormal and Social Psychology*, Vol. 44, No. 1 (January 1949), pp. 118–123. *Also see* "Psychological Test Reports: Universal or Discriminating," *The Journal of Nervous and Mental Disease*, Vol. 129, No. 1 (July 1959), pp. 83–86.

[4] A. J. Bachrach and E. E. Pattishall, "An Experiment in Universal and Personal Validation," *Psychiatry*, Vol. 23, No. 3 (August 1960), pp. 267–271.

ALFRED KADUSHIN, Ph.D., *is professor, School of Social Work, University of Wisconsin, Madison.*

Reprinted with permission of the National Association of Social Workers, from SOCIAL WORK, Vol. 8, No. 1 (January 1963), pp. 12-19.

Tallant cites, as examples of the "Aunt Fanny description" frequently used in psychological reports, such diagnostic statements as: "The client has difficulty in performing at optimal capacity when under stress." "The client has unresolved dependency feelings." "The client has unconscious hostile urges." [5] To each, one can justifiably respond, "So has your Aunt Fanny."

Sundberg has formulated an example of a faked psychological test report that has high face validity because it contains many Aunt Fanny statements—statements that have nearly universal validity for a particular group, in this case schizophrenic veterans recently admitted to a veterans hospital. Some excerpts from the report follow.

This veteran approached the testing situation with some reluctance. He was cooperative with the clinician but was mildly evasive on some of the material. Both the tests and the past history suggest considerable inadequacy in interpersonal relations, particularly with members of his family. Although it is doubtful whether he has had very close relationships with anyone, the few apparently close relationships which he had had were tinged with a great deal of ambivalence . . . . He tends to be basically passive and dependent though there are occasional periods of resistance and rebellion against others . . . . His intelligence is close to average but he is functioning below his full capacity. In summary, this is a long time inadequate or borderline adjustment pattern. Test results and case history, though they do not give a strong clear-cut diagnostic picture, suggest the diagnosis of schizophrenic reaction, chronic undifferentiated type. Prognosis for response to treatment appears to be poor.[6]

Similar, equally valid diagnostic statements have been written regarding TAT test results, before examining the test results; [7] "faked" Minnesota Multiphasic Personality Inventories have received as much acceptance as bona fide statements based on the actual MMPI results; [8] and Rorschach reports have been compared with astrology horoscopes in demonstrating some of the similarities.[9]

One might suspect that many diagnostic summaries in social work contain some "Aunt Fanny" component. To test this, the following experiment was conducted: a diagnostic statement designed to have near universal validity was formulated. Three case summaries were then selected from the literature. The cases chosen were widely different as to age range: one client was a boy of 5,[10] another a girl of 15,[11] the third a woman in her late 30's.[12] The case summaries were edited somewhat so that they would be of nearly uniform length. To each was appended the same diagnostic statement, formulated before the case material was selected.

The material was distributed to 60 student supervisors during the course of an institute on supervision conducted by a graduate school of social work. All respondents were master's degree graduates of a school of social work. All but one had

[5] N. Tallant, "On Individualizing the Psychologist's Clinical Evaluation," *Journal of Clinical Psychology*, Vol. 14, No. 3 (July 1958), pp. 243–44.

[6] Quoted in F. C. Thorne, *Clinical Judgment* (Brandon, Vt.: Journal of Clinical Psychology, 1961), p. 37.

[7] E. S. Shneidman *et al.*, "The Case of Jay: Interpretations and Discussion," *Journal of Projective Techniques*, Vol. 16, No. 4 (December 1952), pp. 457–461.

[8] N. D. Sundberg, "The Acceptability of 'Fake' Versus 'Bonafide' Personality Test Interpretations," *Journal of Abnormal and Social Psychology*, Vol. 50, No. 1 (January 1955), pp. 145–147.

[9] D. M. Kelley, "Clinical Reality and Projective Technique," *American Journal of Psychiatry*, Vol. 107, No. 10 (April 1951), pp. 753–757.

[10] G. E. Blom, "Ulcerative Colitis in a Five-Year-Old Boy," in *Emotional Problems of Early Childhood*, G. Caplan, ed. (New York: Basic Books, 1955), pp. 169–191.

[11] V. S. Margolis, "Ego-Centered Treatment of an Adolescent Girl," in *Casework Papers 1956* (New York: Family Service Association of America, 1956), pp. 91–106.

[12] F. M. Hunt, "Initial Treatment of a Client with Anxiety Hysteria—A Case Presentation," in *Ego Psychology and Dynamic Casework*, H. J. Parad, ed. (New York: Family Service Association of America, 1958), pp. 174–182.

experience in supervising and evaluating the work of graduate students. The supervisors came from a wide variety of settings: mental hospitals, family service agencies, child guidance clinics, probation and parole, child welfare agencies, medical social work agencies, school social work units, and the like. They were given the following explanation and directions:

We are concerned with establishing standards regarding the diagnostic competence of students. You are being given two items: (1) A resumé of the essential information on a particular case. (2) The diagnostic summary, based on this case material, written by a student. The student is in the last semester of the second year of graduate training.

You are asked to *read* the case material and *evaluate* the diagnostic summary which the student has written based on this case material. Thank you very much for your help with this. Do not sign your name.

The 60 supervisors were then given one or another of three case summaries, so that each case was rated by 20 different supervisors.

CASE 1

Larry was a 5-year-old boy who was referred to a child guidance clinic for casework. He had recurrent bloody diarrhea of one-and-a-half-years duration, diagnosed as ulcerative colitis. The mother thought that episodes of diarrhea often occurred at times of emotional stress.

The family, consisting of mother, father, and two children (Larry and Carol, two years older), is of the Jewish upper middle class. They own their home, which is in a suburb of ————.

Larry's mother, the oldest of three children, described her childhood in ———— as an unhappy one; she had strongly objected to being a girl. Her parents had had violent arguments and eventually were divorced. The maternal grandmother, who was devoutly religious and took hardships with an attitude of martyrdom, died of cancer of the stomach after a three-year illness. The maternal grand-

father had a recurring depressive illness and committed suicide during a depressive state. Both deaths occurred when the mother was fifteen. A younger brother suffered from eczema and asthma, and Larry's mother had had vasomotor rhinitis for many years.

Larry's father was brought up under circumstances of poverty and financial struggle, and began to work at the age of seven or eight. The paternal grandfather was described as a powerful man. The paternal grandmother has hypertension. During episodes of emotional stress Larry's father had developed gastrointestinal disturbances. A stomach X-ray at one time revealed a healed peptic ulcer. Larry's father slept in a room by himself and had little contact with his wife.

Pregnancy was planned because the mother was afraid that she was old. She had mild nausea at times. Birth came at full term and was a normal delivery following labor of six hours' duration. The mother spoke of the pain being so intense she could not move, and said that while under medication, she tore the uniform of a nurse and called for her mother. Birth weight was 7 pounds, 2 ounces, with no neonatal distress.

On her return home from the hospital, the mother was nervous and depressed for six months before she finally began to have feeling for Larry. An elderly maid took care of him during this time.

Larry was a healthy, handsome baby who was particularly admired by others. As a result, his mother felt sorry for the first child, gave her more attention, and let maids care for Larry. When the colitis began, however, she gave much more attention to him.

Because Larry's mother did not want to slight her older child, she did not nurse Larry and he was bottle-fed. From early infancy both he and his sister sucked two fingers, but later on did this only when they were tired.

Larry was toilet trained at two years, four months, in a supposedly permissive way. He did not like to be wet and would become upset if a child soiled his pants at school.

Motor development was normal. He

lifted his head at one month, sat at seven months, stood at nine months, and walked at a little over a year. Teeth developed slowly, the first at ten months, but the others followed rapidly. He said words at a little over a year, and sentences at nineteen months. At the age of three there was some stuttering.

Larry had considerable sleeping difficulty during his first three years. He became fearful of the dark during his second year, had nightmares, and would get out of his bed at night and come into the parents' room. When a rod was put up on his crib to obstruct him, Larry would climb over this.

In the summer of ———— when Larry was about two years old, his sister developed cyclic vomiting, and the mother gave much more attention to her. There followed a time when the competitive demands of both siblings on the mother were extreme, and Larry often wandered away from home. At the age of two and a half, Larry was sent to nursery school for the whole day. Three changes in schools were made before a satisfactory adjustment was achieved. Larry ran away from one school, going through a hole in the wall.

At the time of referral he was described as high-strung and hyperactive, a "hellion," and extremely negativistic at home, but well behaved outside. He would not cry when upset, but bottled up his feelings. He had very few friends, preferred older children and adults, was in an intense rivalry with his older sister, and would become upset about children fighting. Larry seems unhappy about his relationships with his family.

CASE 2

Sylvia's problem was brought to the attention of a family service agency by the group worker in the recreational agency to which she belonged. The other youngsters in the group had made it plain that they disliked her. Sylvia, at 15 years of age, was bright and able, but tried to win recognition by aggressive, intellectual behavior that antagonized the group into frank hostility. On several occasions Sylvia had expressed to the group leader her deep feelings of rejection and isola-

tion, and eventually she accepted the suggestion that she needed individual help. She also suffered from frequent headaches. She had discussed this with her parents, who had telephoned the family service agency to ask for an appointment.

Mrs. G was seen first, at her request. She was a good-looking, trim woman. She seemed capable, efficient, and self-contained, but there was a sad quality about her. She said that Sylvia's problems had begun six years previously when the family had moved to ———— from Montreal. The family had settled in what she felt to be a snobbish neighborhood where they did not feel accepted. Mrs. G recalled that her life in Montreal had been happy. She had not made a good adjustment in ———— where they had remained because Mr. G had a secure but low-salaried job as a draftsman. His work history had been characterized by frequent unemployment and consequent financial insecurity. Mrs. G's "self-confidence" had ebbed because of the family's economic privation and the radical change in social activities that had resulted from her husband's withdrawn personality. She had never had much self-confidence since, in her own adolescence, she had had no help from an indecisive mother and a dominating, rigid father. She expressed humiliation that, although past middle age, she and Mr. G were still trying to furnish a modest home. They had had only one child, after seven years of marriage, because of the continuous financial struggle. She herself was working part time to add to the family income.

Sylvia was a planned child; pregnancy and delivery were normal. Mrs. G had breast fed Sylvia for five months but she had not found this a pleasurable experience. Sylvia's infancy had been uneventful and Mrs. G did not spontaneously reveal any affectionate memories of Sylvia's childhood. She blocked when the caseworker led her to discuss dynamic developmental history, and indicated that feeding, toilet training, and so on were dealt with by rigid scheduling. She described Sylvia as a good, conforming child who had given her absolutely no trouble and who had always done well in school.

Thus, Sylvia's present behavior at home was particularly hard to bear, since she was so moody, angry, unco-operative, and selfish.

Mr. G was a short, gray-haired, timid man. His attitude was apologetic in regard to his job, his salary, and his ability to be a good father. He corroborated the material presented by his wife, but conveyed to the caseworker a warmer feeling for his daughter than did Mrs. G.

First interview of the caseworker with Sylvia:

Sylvia was tall, stoop-shouldered, awkward, tense, and frightened. Her bright blue eyes were filled with panic at the start of the first interview, and she looked at the caseworker furtively and fearfully. She licked her lips, shredded facial tissue, bit her nails, and poked in her purse. There was no softness or femininity about her. Sylvia was led to tell of her efforts to make friends. She mentioned many groups to which she belonged, but in none of them did she feel comfortable. She felt "pushed around," especially by girls. She believed they laughed at her behind her back, gossiped about her, were maliciously mean, and thought her queer and different. As a result she felt frozen with self-consciousness. She dealt with these seeming attacks through angry retort, haughty attitude, sarcastic repartee, and fierce intellectual competition. She said that she hated and despised the popular crowd but she obviously tried hard to be one of them. She yearned for dates and invitations to parties. Of her parents she had little to say—she and her folks had no difficulties, and she thought them reasonable, sensible parents.

CASE 3

Early in June, Mrs. L was referred to the family service agency by a psychiatric clinic in which she had been interviewed once. When she first came to the office Mrs. L was extremely tense and frightened. She was an attractive woman in her late 30's, neatly dressed but very thin and pale. Her symptoms were a feeling of tension and panic which became particularly acute at times, a fear that she was "going to crack up," and phobic reactions when she was away from the house,

particularly on public transportations. When she had the nervous spells—which she could describe only as a terrible feeling—she became very frightened that something awful was going to happen to her and that she could not continue to carry on.

Mr. L was her second husband and the father of her two younger children, Betty, 5, and Anne, 3. There were also three children by her first marriage, Richard, 16, Donald, 13, and John, 8. For a year and a half Mr. L had been ill with cancer, although he had not been told this. After a series of X-ray treatments he had been able to return to his job, as a government clerk, but he had not felt well and had been exceedingly irritable and increasingly dependent on Mrs. L. As he became sicker there was increasing friction between him and the children, especially the two oldest boys. Mrs. L was also disturbed by the uncertainty about the future because of the nature of her husband's illness.

In talking about her marriage, Mrs. L spontaneously brought out a good deal of background material. She felt that she had never had much in her early life, and except for the few brief happy years before her husband's illness, it looked as if she never would. She was the oldest of three children and had two younger brothers. She described her childhood as upset and deprived. Her father was alcoholic and very abusive toward her mother although he worked steadily. She remembered being very much frightened for her mother and trying to protect her. From the time Mrs. L was 8 or 9, her mother would sometimes leave the home for several days after a particularly violent upset with the father because she could not take it any longer. Mrs. L would manage as best as she could to care for herself and the two younger children. Sometimes the father would take them to the paternal grandmother's home. Mrs. L recalled her grandmother as kindly and warm but she did not give the impression that the grandmother was a very important figure in her early life. She could express no hostility toward her own mother for these periodic desertions, but only identification with her suffering.

She felt that her mother had never been a strong person but did not say this in a critical manner. Rather, she herself had assumed a protective role on behalf of her mother. It was interesting that, although Mrs. L's mother was now living in the home with her, she did not regard her as any sort of help. Mrs. L did not want her mother to stop working because, if her mother were at home all the time, Mrs. L thought she would just sink into a state of apathy and become dependent.

When Mrs. L was 17 she went to live with a friend. However, she worried about what was happening to her mother at home and could not sleep at night, feeling that she was comfortable while her family was not. It was at this time that she first had experienced symptoms of panic and a feeling that something dreadful was going to happen.

DIAGNOSTIC SUMMARY

The following "universal" diagnostic summary, supposedly written by a student, was appended to *each* case summary:

Larry [or Sylvia or Mrs. L] is reacting to a difficult life situation. The situational problem is, however, superimposed on the trauma of emotional deprivation during earlier, crucial periods in the client's developmental history. There is ambivalence toward parental figures and while the client shows some capacity to develop healthy object relationships, potentialities in this regard show some impairment. There is tendency to convert emotional difficulties into physical symptoms as a mechanism of defense. The client's tendency toward anxiety is evident in relation to dependency needs and in the area of sexual identification. Aggressive drives are turned away from the more significant figures in the client's environment and directed toward self either through self-punishment or in masochistic instigations of punishment by others.

There is limited capacity to control unacceptable impulses and reactivation of guilt when such impulses break through the barrier of superego control. A considerable amount of emotional energy is being absorbed in internal conflicts so that limited energy is available to deal constructively with environmental difficulties.

The client is basically insecure, having experienced some rejection by parents and peers.

The fact that the client seems disturbed about the situation would indicate that there is reasonably good motivation toward acceptance of treatment at this time. A supportive relationship with a warm, accepting worker would be of therapeutic value. In such a permissive atmosphere that would permit the expression of negative feelings without condemnation, the client can be helped to gain some understanding of the problems faced. Resolution of the marital problem, implied in the material, would likewise be helpful in reducing stress on the client's ego.[13]

The supervisors were then asked to evaluate this summary in terms of a 7-point scale in accordance with the instructions:

Please evaluate the student's summary in terms of the following scale: Check one of the following: (Remember there is no right or wrong answer. In terms of your own judgment, whatever item you choose to check is correct.)
This diagnostic summary is:

7 ——— Definitely superior
6 ——— Excellent
5 ——— Slightly above average
4 ——— Average
3 ——— Slightly below average
2 ——— Poor
1 ——— Definitely inadequate

Table 1 summarizes the results of the supervisors' evaluation of the identical diag-

---

13 The summary is, admittedly, psychoanalytically oriented. A similar, but somewhat more sociologically *au courant*, statement might have included universally valid generalizations such as: "There is, on the part of the client, some failure to effectively enact ascribed sex and age roles." "Difficulties in enacting ascribed roles resulted from simultaneous stress occasioned by internal problems and demands made upon the client by those who stood in reciprocal role relationship to him." "The nature of the family configuration suggests that there was lack of consensus in the way role requirements and obligations were defined and some inability to meet the demands imposed by the obligations of familial roles."

TABLE 1. DISTRIBUTION OF RATINGS FOR EACH CASE

Rating Level	Cases		
	Larry	Sylvia	Mrs. L
7—Definitely superior	0	3	1
6—Excellent	8	4	5
5—Slightly above average	6	4	8
4—Average	2	5	2
3—Slightly below average	4	2	2
2—Poor	0	2	2
1—Definitely inadequate	0	0	0
Totals	20	20	20

nostic statement used with each of the three cases.

The mean rating for all three cases is almost identical—4.9 in the case of Larry, 4.75 for Sylvia, 4.75 for Mrs. L. A mean of 5 is the equivalent of a "slightly above average" rating. This implies that a student who had submitted this same diagnosis on any of the three cases, even before he saw the client, would have been given a rating close to "slightly above average" for his diagnostic ability.

In effect the supervisors were justified in their rating. The diagnostic summary is valid for each of these cases. Every statement in the summary is appropriate and applicable, and it would be equally valid for many other cases. But while it is correct as far as it goes, it does not go far enough. A diagnostic statement should have high discriminatory power; it should clearly differentiate and individualize. A universally valid diagnostic statement that has applicability to the majority of the population is meaningless because it tells us no more than we already knew before we met the client. The diagnostic process is a process of particularizing our generalizations so that we can differentiate this client from all other clients.

The diagnostic summary is only one of several kinds of statements made by social workers that, on occasion, contain much of the "Aunt Fanny" approach. Anyone who has frequent occasion to read supervisors' evaluations of students and workers recog-

nizes that it is often difficult to tell which one of a number of students the evaluation describes.

UNIVERSAL STUDENT EVALUATION

In appreciation for the supervisors' co-operation in the project (and perhaps in restitution for the momentary lapse in professional ethics in obtaining such co-operation under false pretenses), we offer the following universal student evaluation for supervisors' use. We estimate that the statement is applicable to about 70 percent of the students any supervisor is likely to be responsible for evaluating. The estimate is based on the percentage of cases lying within one standard deviation from the mean, given a normal distribution of students. The universal student evaluation best characterizes the average graduate student at the end of the first year of field work. The female pronoun is used throughout and the supervisor is cautioned to change the pronoun, if necessary, so that it is congruent with the sex of the student.

Miss M is, for the most part, sensitive to clients' feelings and seems to demonstrate in her relationships with people a basically warm and accepting attitude. She generally responds empathically to the client in his problem situation and demonstrates a desire to be helpful to the client. Miss M has shown some ability to establish a casework relationship and can, in most instances, use it effectively. While generally able to maintain the relationship on a professional basis, she initially showed some confusion regarding the differences between a social and professional relationship and tended to employ her skills in social relationships in her contact with the client. She is gradually developing a greater appreciation of the use of professional self. There are instances, however, when Miss M tends to overidentify with clients. The degree of overidentification is generally not so great as to considerably impair her potential helpfulness to the client.

Miss M tends to be more comfortable with clients who show an appreciation

74

of the services offered and reacts with some anxiety to hostile, resistive clients.

She hesitates, on occasion, to push into an area which may be painful to the client and has not yet developed her skills to the point where she can help him articulate with equanimity.

Miss M has some tendency to be impatient with the slow pace of client movement and there is some difficulty in accepting limited goals for some clients. However, she is making progress.

Miss M is using her knowledge of human behavior, gained in the methods courses and growth and development courses, to develop a more adequate understanding of the client. She is moving toward a greater integration of social work theory and diagnostic thinking with her field work practice. Though her diagnostic thinking does not, as yet, always go far enough and deep enough, it is, essentially, basically sound. She has, for her level of development, an adequate grasp of causative factors in behavior, although there is still some hesitancy to draw these together or to speculate as to their possible meanings.

Miss M is generally alert to significant clues in the interview, although there are occasions when she fails to perceive these. On the whole, Miss M continues to give indication of her interest in broadening and deepening her understanding of individual and family dynamics and she strives to make conscious efforts to apply such understanding to her case load.

Participation in the casework interviews has, for the most part, been appropriate. She has gained in her ability to focus the interview and in her ability to hear what the client is saying.

Miss M shows a good grasp of agency programs and policies and has established a relatively satisfactory relationship with the agency. She demonstrates capacity to work within the agency structure and function and generally applies agency policy appropriately.

Miss M operates more easily with situations that are structured and for which regular agency policies have been established, than in those situations requiring more creative use of self.

Miss M has shown some ability to plan, and use, her time effectively. She tends to resist recording and while she usually makes recordings available for supervisory conferences, there is considerable reluctance to record on a regular basis.

Miss M shows self-dependence and self-direction to an adequate degree, yet is able to depend on supervision for extending her learning and for help in functioning. She has a reasonably good understanding of the purpose of supervision and makes effective use of it. She is, at times, defensive when criticized and at such times needs reassurance and support.

In general I believe Miss M has demonstrated good capacity for professional development and is showing growth. It can be anticipated that, with growing confidence and developing skill, she will use herself more effectively with clients during the second year in training.

A critical evaluation of the above suggests that the recipe for developing a statement of this type includes the following: Take a liberal sprinkling of vague generalities, intersperse with a description of modal behavioral characteristics of the group, add a dash of universally valid adjectives, a soupçon of hedging clauses such as "generally," "on occasion," and "for the most part," a squirt of obvious trivialities, and a judicious use of balanced statements. Arrange logically according to topical outline.

This makes an acceptably palatable mixture, if not an entirely helpful one. The latter would require more preciseness as to the specific circumstances, the context under which a given behavior tends to be manifested, greater definition of the strength or level at which a given behavior occurs, a greater specificity as to the frequency with which a given behavior occurs, and a description of the behavior that differentiates this student from the generally expected behavior of students at this point in training —in short, an attempt to truly individualize the student.

And if somebody asks me if I am guilty of using the same recipe in teaching, I can only shamefacedly admit that, on occasion (hedge), I do—but shouldn't.

BY SCOTT BRIAR

Use of Theory in Studying Effects of Client Social Class on Students' Judgments

THE RELATIONSHIP between empirical research and theory is reciprocal. One criterion for the evaluation of theory is its capacity to generate empirical research. Conversely, a primary objective of empirical research is to test and extend theory. To be productive, therefore, the relationship between theory and research should be close and continuous.

The central purpose of this paper is to describe this relationship in a specific study, an investigation of social workers' judgments. Since in describing the study major emphasis will be given to the application of theory to a specific empirical problem, space will permit only an outline of the research methods used and no more than a brief sketch of some of the study findings. In connection with the findings it should be noted that, although this research is concerned with social work judgments, the data were obtained from social work students. Thus, in this and some other respects, the study is not definitive, but does suggest implications for further research and for social work practice.

SCOTT BRIAR, D.S.W., is assistant professor, School of Social Welfare, University of California, Berkeley, California. This paper was delivered at the National Conference on Social Welfare in Atlantic City, New Jersey, June 1960, and was based on research conducted as part of the writer's doctoral dissertation at the New York School of Social Work, Columbia University. It was selected for publication by the Social Work Research Section.

Reprinted with permission of the National Association of Social Workers, from SOCIAL WORK, Vol. 6, No. 3 (July 1961), pp. 91-97.

THE PROBLEM

The social work process can be viewed as a succession of judgments made by the social worker. First, the worker forms diagnostic judgments about the practice situation that confronts him. Next, he plans a course of action, and this step involves another set of judgments. The social caseworker, for example, repeats this sequence many times in the course of a single interview. That is, in a matter of seconds, the client makes a statement, the worker attributes meaning to the client's remarks, and then selects his response from a number of possible alternatives. Some clinical judgments are made slowly, consciously, and deliberately; many occur automatically without awareness. Further, some judgments may be relatively unimportant in their effect on the client; others, such as whether a child should be removed from his own home, will have long-range consequences of vital concern to the persons involved.

In view of the crucial importance of judgment in social work practice, surprisingly little is known about how these judgments are formed and about the factors that affect them. While it is true that judgment has been receiving increasing attention in social work research,[1] for the most part this

[1] For an overview of social work research on judgment and a discussion of some of the problems involved, see Use of Judgments as Data in Social Work Research (New York: National Association of Social Workers, 1959).

research has been concerned with the use of judgments as data for the purpose of studying other variables. One of the best known examples of this kind of judgment research is the work that has been done on the movement scale.[2] Relatively few studies, on the other hand, have focused on judgment as an object, rather than a means of research. Notable exceptions include the studies conducted by David Fanshel, Roger Miller, and Martin Wolins.[3] Further, these two types of judgment research are not unrelated. As Hunt emphasized at the 1958 conference on "The Use of Judgments as Data in Social Work Research," "if clinical judgments are to be depended upon to represent client behavior in life situations"[4] more research is needed on the judgment process and the factors that affect it.

Among the many obstacles that arise when one attempts research on judgment in social work, two problems seem especially difficult and perplexing. First is that of obtaining systematic measures for the variables involved without departing so far from the conditions of social work practice that the data obtained would be invalidated. A second problem is posed by the large number of variables that can be assumed to affect judgment, which makes it difficult to select and isolate the most important or most strategic variables for study. An added complication is the interrelation of these two problems. To control all other variables in order to isolate the effects of a few usually requires a research design approximating the laboratory experiment, a situation often far removed from the realities of social work practice. On the other hand, to approximate social work practice conditions leaves so many factors uncontrolled that the effects of a specific set of variables cannot be isolated from others. For these reasons, effective research on judgment in social work depends, in part, on the development of research methods that will yield reliable data and yet, at the same time, bear some plausible resemblance to the conditions of social work practice.

Consequently, one objective of the study on which this paper is based was to investigate the application of a particular theoretical framework and method of approach to research on the judgment process in social work practice. A second objective was to use this method of approach to test substantive hypotheses about selected variables presumed to affect the judgments social workers make about clients. The methodological objective will be discussed first, because the substantive hypotheses can be viewed in better perspective if the approach adopted in the study is clearly understood.

JUDGMENT THEORY

Although, as noted earlier, relatively little research on the judgment process per se has been done in social work, a large number of studies in this area have been conducted in other fields, principally those of personality and social psychology.[5] In psychological research, judgment has been

[2] J. McVicker Hunt and Leonard S. Kogan, *Measuring Results in Social Casework: A Manual on Judging Movement* (rev. ed.; New York: Family Service Association of America, 1952).

[3] David Fanshel, "A Study of Caseworkers' Perceptions of Their Clients," *Social Casework*, Vol. 39, No. 10 (December 1958), pp. 543–551; Roger Miller, "An Experimental Study of the Observational Process in Casework," *Social Work*, Vol. 3, No. 2 (April 1958), pp. 96–102; Martin Wolins, "Selection of Foster Parents: Early Stages in the Development of a Screen." Unpublished D.S.W. dissertation, New York School of Social Work, Columbia University, 1959.

[4] J. McVicker Hunt, "On the Judgment of Social Workers as a Source of Information in Social Work Research," in *Use of Judgments as Data in Social Work Research, op. cit.*, p. 52.

[5] For summaries of some of this research, *see* Jerome S. Bruner and Renato Tagiuri, "The Perception of People," *Handbook of Social Psychology*, Gardner Lindzey, ed. (Cambridge, Mass.: Addison-Wesley Publishing Co., 1954), Vol. 2, pp. 634–654; Theodore R. Sarbin, Ronald Taft, and Daniel E. Bailey, *Clinical Inference and Cognitive Theory* (New York: Holt, Rinehart, and Winston, 1960); Renato Tagiuri and Luigi Petrullo, eds., *Person Perception and Interpersonal Behavior* (Stanford, Calif.: Stanford Universtiy Press, 1958).

referred to by such terms as interpersonal perception, person perception, impression formation, and predictive behavior.

A number of investigators in these fields have made use of the concept of predictive behavior to study the perceptual and inferential processes in interpersonal judgment. Predictive behavior "represents an individual's attempts to perceive, understand and anticipate his own and other people's actions in the social environment."[6] This definition of predictive behavior serves to point out that a clinical judgment involves the following sequence of events: first, the perception of behavioral attributes in others; second, the meaningful organization of these attributes within the judge's personal cognitive system or frame of reference; and third, the use of these organized perceptions to anticipate or predict the behavior of others. Seen in this context, clinical judgment behavior is merely a special instance of the more general problem of how persons perceive each other and how these perceptions affect behavior.

The basic design in studies of predictive behavior can be described as follows: Each judge is asked to predict the responses which he thinks one or more other persons, designated by the investigator, would give to a series of items. Using this design, patterned differences in *predictive judgments* can be studied as a function of other variables selected by the investigator. With some elaboration, the design can yield measures for other variables. A number of investigators have been interested in studying *predictive accuracy*. In these studies, the prediction instruments are administered to the person whose behavior is being predicted, and his actual responses are used as the criterion for measuring the accuracy of the judge's predictions. When the judge also is asked to give his own response to the prediction instruments, measures can be obtained for the degree of *similarity* between the judge and the person whose behavior he is predicting. *Assumed similarity* is the degree of similarity the judge assumes to exist between himself and the person whose behavior he is predicting. *Actual similarity* is the extent to which the judge and the person being judged are in fact similar on the instruments used. It is only necessary to call attention to the possible relationships between these variables and such concepts as understanding, empathy, social distance, and countertransference to indicate the potential relevance this approach may have for studying important questions in social work practice.

HYPOTHESES

With this framework in mind some of the substantive hypotheses tested in this study and the theory from which they were derived can now be discussed. In this paper only hypotheses that have to do with social class theory will be presented.

On the basis of his studies of impression-formation, Asch concluded that "the views we establish of persons are, to a high degree, a function of their group-membership and group position."[7] This has a correlate in Gough's statement that "the position occupied by an individual in the social hierarchy is one of the most important variables determining his behavior."[8] These assumptions gain growing support from the increasing body of knowledge about behavioral differences between different class and cultural groups.[9] An ob-

[6] James Bieri, Edward Blacharsky, and J. William Reid, "Predictive Behavior and Personal Adjustment," *Journal of Consulting Psychology*, Vol. 19, No. 5 (October 1955), p. 351.

[7] Solomon E. Asch, *Social Psychology* (New York: Prentice-Hall, 1952), p. 219.

[8] Harrison G. Gough, "A New Dimension in Status: The Development of a Personality," *American Sociological Review*, Vol. 13, No. 4 (August 1948), p. 401.

[9] The literature on this subject is extensive. Two examples of works that attempt to survey major segments of this field are Reinhard Bendix and Seymour M. Lipset, eds., *Class, Status and Power*

vious implication of this body of knowledge for research on judgment is that, if interpersonal perception is to be accurate, the judge would need to make use of social class, status, and cultural information, because some group membership differences in behavior do seem to exist.

In recent years particularly, the social work literature has stressed the importance of group membership information for the practitioner.[10] However, questions have been raised about the extent to which social workers make use of, or even obtain, this kind of information about their clients.[11] It seems important, therefore, to know more about the effects of the client's group membership characteristics on the judgments the social worker makes about him. One important kind of group membership—social class status—was selected for investigation in this study.

An attempt to predict, from theory, the probable effect of client social class on social workers' judgments posed some difficult problems. Ideally, it would have been preferable if specific, directional hypotheses could have been formulated—hypotheses, for example, of the following kind: "Social workers will tend to judge lower-class clients as more overtly aggressive than middle-class clients." However, directional hypotheses of this type seemed premature for two reasons. One is the relative lack of reliable data about class-linked differences between individuals on the specific per-

sonality and attitudinal dimensions measured by the judgment instruments used in this study. A second, more basic reason, is that even less is known, in this precise sense, about differences in *judgment* in relation to social class status as a stimulus variable. The importance of this second point is illustrated by a study that attempted to replicate some of the findings reported by Hollingshead and Redlich in their research on social class and mental illness. One of the major findings of the Hollingshead and Redlich study was that the types of disorders mentally ill individuals present to psychiatrists vary significantly in relation to the social class of the patient.[12] They raised the question of whether this relationship reflected "the *kind* of disorders patients present to psychiatrists or the *way* psychiatrists diagnose the disorders of their patients."[13] By comparing data obtained from three different psychiatric hospitals, Robert Kahn found that upper-class patients tended, more often than lower-class patients, to be given the diagnosis that was preferred in the hospital culture.[14] If, for example, the staff in a specific hospital preferred to treat schizophrenics, then upper-class patients tended to be given this diagnosis more frequently than patients from lower-class groups.

It does not necessarily follow, however, that social class will have a similar effect on judgments made by social workers. It seemed, therefore, that the first step should be to determine whether social workers' judgments are affected by client social class. If they are, then the nature and direction of the differences found would, hopefully, provide leads for further research.

Consequently, one hypothesis in this

(Glencoe, Ill.: The Free Press, 1953); and Milton M. Gordon, *Social Class in American Sociology* (Durham, N. C.: Duke University Press, 1958).

[10] See, for example, John M. Martin, "Socio-Cultural Differences: Barriers in Casework with Delinquents," *Social Work*, Vol. 2, No. 3 (July 1957), pp. 22–31; Walter B. Miller, "Implications of Urban Lower-Class Culture for Social Work," *Social Service Review*, Vol. 33, No. 3 (September 1959), pp. 219–236; and Otto Pollak, *Integrating Sociological and Psychoanalytic Concepts* (New York: Russell Sage Foundation, 1956).

[11] See *Cultural Factors in Social Work Practice and Education* (New York: Council on Social Work Education, 1950); and Henry S. Maas *et al.*, "Socio-Cultural Factors in Psychiatric Clinic Services for Children," *Smith College Studies in Social Work*, Vol. 25, No. 2 (February 1955), pp. 1–90.

[12] August B. Hollingshead and Fredrick C. Redlich, *Social Class and Mental Illness* (New York: John Wiley & Sons, 1958), pp. 357–358.

[13] *Ibid.*, p. 223.

[14] Robert L. Kahn, Max Pollack, and Max Fink, "Sociopsychologic Aspects of Psychiatric Treatment in a Voluntary Mental Hospital," (Glen Oaks, N. Y.: Department of Experimental Psychiatry, Hillside Hospital, March 1959). (Mimeographed.)

study was that *the client's social class status will affect the judgments social work students make about him.* More specifically, when other characteristics of a client are held constant, it was predicted that students will make significantly different judgments when different social class status characteristics are ascribed to the client.

A variable closely related to client social class, with reference to predictive behavior, is the relative distance between the social class status of the client and that of the social worker. Otto Klineberg's assertion that social class distance between social workers and their clients can "create a definite barrier to mutual rapport and understanding"[15] is echoed in many quarters. Hollingshead and Redlich, in the study mentioned above, emphasize that the distance between the patient's social class status and the social class background of the psychiatrist constitutes a serious obstacle in treatment because it hampers the psychiatrist in his attempts to understand and communicate with the patient.[16] Studies of the relationship between several types of social distance variables and interpersonal perception tend to support the assumption that this distance variable has an important effect on the impressions persons form of others.[17]

[15] Otto Klineberg. Unpublished manuscript, 1957.
[16] Hollingshead and Redlich, *op. cit.*, p. 301.
[17] Fred E. Fiedler, "The Psychological Distance Dimension in Interpersonal Relations," *Journal of Personality*, Vol. 22, No. 1 (September 1953), pp. 142–150; Frances B. Newman, "The Adolescent in Social Groups: Studies in the Observation of Personality," *Applied Psychology Monographs*, No. 9 (Stanford, Calif.: Stanford University Press for the American Psychological Association, 1946), pp. 29–43; Margaret G. Powell, "Comparisons of Self-Ratings, Peer Ratings and Experts' Ratings of Personality Adjustment," *Educational and Psychological Measurement*, Vol. 8, No. 2 (Summer 1948), pp. 225–234; A. Scodel and Paul Mussen, "Social Perceptions of Authoritarians and Non-Authoritarians," *Journal of Abnormal and Social Psychology*, Vol. 48, No. 2 (April 1953), pp. 181–184; Ross Stagner, "Psychological Aspects of Industrial Conflict: I. Perception," *Personnel Psychology*, Vol. 1, No. 2 (Summer 1948), pp. 131–144; and Harry O. Triandis and Leigh M. Triandis, "Race, Social Class, Religion, and Nationality as Determinants of Social Distance," *Journal*

In the social work literature also, social distance, including social class distance specifically, has been recognized as a possible barrier between the social worker and the client.[18] Some writers have assumed that as the class distance between social worker and client increases, the social worker will find it more difficult to communicate and empathize with the client.[19] Empathy can be defined as the degree to which the social worker is able to establish similarities between what he perceives and senses in the client and the worker's own experiences, both personal and professional.[20] These similarities or parallels between what he sees and what he knows or has experienced provide the social worker with a frame of reference for attributing meaning to the client's communications and behavior. Consequently, it seems reasonable to infer that when a high degree of empathy exists between social worker and client, the social worker will tend to perceive greater similarity between himself and the client than when less empathy is present.

On the basis of this conception of empathy and the preceding discussion of the effects of social class distance on the social worker's ability to empathize with the client, a second hypothesis in this study was that *the degree of similarity that the social work student assumes to exist between himself and the client will be inversely related to the social class distance between the worker and the client.*

METHOD

The social worker sample in this study consisted of 130 first-year students enrolled at one school of social work. Consequently, the findings cannot be generalized to the

of Abnormal and Social Psychology, Vol. 61, No. 1 (July 1960), pp. 110–118.
[18] Berta Fantl, "Casework Practice in Lower-Class Districts," 1959 (mimeographed); and Miller, *op. cit.*
[19] Martin, *op. cit.*
[20] Charlotte Towle, *The Learner in Education for the Professions* (Chicago: University of Chicago Press, 1954), p. 290.

population of trained social workers, nor even to the population of social work students, since it is not known to what extent the students in this study may be representative of students in other schools of social work.

The clients about whom these social work students were asked to make judgments were obtained from the outpatient psychiatric clinic of a large city hospital. An attempt was made to select clients whose problems and behavior did not deviate markedly from that which social workers in a variety of settings might be expected to encounter. In an attempt to control for age, sex, race, religion, and family status, the selection was limited to white, Catholic mothers between the ages of 25 and 35. After screening a number of clients who met these criteria, two were selected for use in this study. Tape recorded interviews were conducted with each client. In addition, the client's actual responses to the judgment instruments were obtained.

For each client, a summary was prepared containing a description of the client, the problems she presented, her current life situation, and her past history. These summaries, plus verbatim excerpts transcribed from the recorded interviews, were given to the social work students as a basis for making their judgments about the clients. To study the effect of client social class, two summaries were prepared for each client. In one, middle-class occupational and educational characteristics were ascribed to the client, her husband, and her parents. The second summary was identical with the first in every respect except that lower-class occupational and educational characteristics were used.[21] The specific occupational

and educational designations ascribed were selected from Hollingshead's *Two Factor Index of Social Position*,[22] which was the social class index used consistently throughout the study.

Three instruments were used to measure the student's judgments about each client: (1) a self-concept check-list; (2) an attitude scale that included two dimensions, acceptance of authority and traditional family ideology; and (3) an inventory of clinical judgments that social workers are frequently asked to make about clients. This discussion will be confined to use of the first two instruments.

The data were collected in two stages. In the first stage, data were obtained about the students themselves, including their social class status and social class background. The students' own responses to the self-concept check-list and the attitude scales also were obtained at this time. In the second stage of data collection, four months later, the students were randomly assigned, without their knowledge at any point in the study, to one of two groups. Each student was given a summary for each of the two clients used in the study. Depending on the group to which he was assigned, the student received *either* the middle-class summary for the first client and the lower-class summary for the second, *or* vice versa. Thus, the only difference between the client material presented to the students in groups I and II was the

items of information according to how well each item would serve as an indicator of a client's social class position. More than 75 percent of the social workers in the pretest ranked either education or occupation first in importance as an indicator of the client's social class status. Further, all but one of the pretest subjects assigned at least a first or second rank to one of these two items. These findings suggest that social workers do perceive occupation and education as highly important indicators of the client's social class status.

[22] August B. Hollingshead, *Two Factor Index of Social Position* (New Haven: published by the author, 1957). Grateful acknowledgment is hereby given to Professor Hollingshead for his permission to use this index in this study.

---

[21] It will be noted that the method used to ascribe a specific social class status to the clients in this study involves an assumption that social workers are attuned to perceive a client's occupation and education as indicators of his social class position. Support for this assumption comes from several sources, but only one will be mentioned here. In a pretest for this research, 24 professionally trained and experienced social workers were asked to rank order

social class status attributed to the clients. After reading the summaries, the student was asked to predict the responses of each client to the self-concept instrument and the attitude scale and to rate each client on the clinical judgment inventory.

RESULTS

A major finding was that the social work students did make significantly different predictions about certain self-concepts and attitudes of both clients as a function of the client's social class status. According to their predictions, for example, both clients saw themselves as more self-confident, better liked, more independent, and more assertive when they were given middle-class status than when lower-class characteristics were ascribed to them. Further, when lower-class status was ascribed, both clients were judged to have more conforming and submissive attitudes to authority and less permissive and less democratic attitudes about family life than when these clients were given middle-class characteristics.

The second hypothesis discussed in this paper predicted that the degree of similarity between the student's own responses and his predictions of the client's responses (assumed similarity) would be inversely related to the social class distance between the worker and the client. Social class distance was measured in two ways: first, by the distance between the student's social class background and the current class status ascribed to the client; and second, by the distance between the current social class status of the student and that ascribed to the client. Actually, the latter measure was determined by the client's social class, since the Hollingshead Index defined all students in this study as belonging, currently, to the middle class.

No consistent relationship was found between assumed similarity and the distance between client social class and the student's social class background. However, the findings did reveal a tendency, which was not statistically significant, for the students to assume greater similarity between themselves and the client when middle- rather than lower-class status was attributed to the client.

SOME IMPLICATIONS

The cycle—from theory to data and back to theory again—can be completed by mentioning a few of the theoretical implications drawn from the findings of this study.

1. The findings suggest that social work students are attuned to perceive clients differently as a function of the client's social class status. However, these findings raise but do not answer this important question: Do the judgment differences that were found reflect an accurate or inaccurate use of information about the client's social class? Further research is needed to determine the validity of the differences perceived by the students.

2. Other findings from this study not presented here indicate that the effect of client social class on the student's judgment will vary with the personality characteristics of the client. This suggests the need for systematic study of the effect on judgment of the interaction between personality information and social class information.

3. With respect to the methodological objectives of this study, it should be noted that the predictive behavior approach passed two important tests. First, it led to findings that have relevance for social work practice. Second, most of the social work students were able to perform the judgment tasks with relative ease, and within the limits of their experience most of them seemed to feel that these tasks were not unlike the demands of social work practice.

BY MAX SIPORIN

Social Treatment: A New-Old Helping Method

■ As part of social work's response to the current social needs of individuals and families, there has been a reemergence and revitalization of social treatment as a helping method for the provision of direct services. The author describes the rediscoveries as well as innovative developments of operational concepts and procedures that express social work perspectives of the earlier and current social reform eras. ■

MAJOR CHANGES IN social work method have taken place in recent years as part of the social work profession's response to the crises and upheavals of our time. These changes have resulted in the emergence of professional modes of helping services that have important points of similarity with those of an earlier era of social reform.

From 1892 to 1917, and especially at the beginning of this century, the new profession of social work emphasized social legislative action, social institutional reform, and broad preventive programs as its preferred methods of practice. However, there was also a climate of opinion within certain social work circles that depreciated direct services to individuals and family groups. As Richmond later recalled, she was one of

the caseworkers who were "often waved aside as having outlived [their] usefulness" because "legislation and propaganda, between them, would render social work with and for individuals unnecessary." [1]

At this same time, though, there was a remarkable and common development, within both the Charity Organization Societies and the social settlements, of a social work helping method for use with individuals and families. It was variously called charity work, scientific philanthropy, friendly visiting, social casework, or social treatment. Of course the method that came to be known mostly as social casework had a long history. But it was during this social reform period that it gained a distinctive identity. It became a way of providing a wide range of individualized services in what today might be called a multifunctional set of procedures. The method evolved at a time when social workers were less fragmented and more unified in their helping approaches. They had a broad, idealistic yet realistic vision of serving the individual and society. They sought to aid the individual as a social being and the family as a social unit and thus help create

MAX SIPORIN, DSW, is Professor, School of Social Welfare, State University of New York at Albany, Albany, New York. A shortened version of this paper was presented at the Annual Meeting of the Maryland Chapter of the National Association of Social Workers, Baltimore, Maryland, June 12, 1969. The author expresses appreciation to his former casework students and faculty colleagues at the School of Social Work, University of Maryland, Baltimore, Maryland, who participated in an analysis of current and emerging social work practice with individuals and families on which this paper is partly based.

[1] Mary E. Richmond, *The Long View* (New York: Russell Sage Foundation, 1930), p. 586.

Reprinted with permission of the National Association of Social Workers, from SOCIAL WORK, Vol. 15, No. 3 (July 1970), pp. 13-25.

a new social order in which poverty and ill health could be prevented. The method they fashioned was highly conceptual and creative. It continued to have a great vitality in practice and in the development of practice theory during the 1920s and thereafter.

This methodological orientation suffered a decline in usefulness and popularity after 1917, when many social workers committed themselves to individual moral reform and psychoanalytic forms of therapy. It is indeed fortunate that in recent years the older, more traditional, larger conception of the social work helping method has been rediscovered and found relevant for current needs. There has been a rapid and exciting renewal of its development in social work practice and education. It is being referred to again as social treatment and also as comprehensive casework or clinical social work.

In this paper the concept and characteristics of social treatment will be examined both from a historical point of view and as they seem to be unfolding today. This discussion is based in large part on an analysis of current and emerging social work practice with individuals and families carried out by the author and his students. In examining practice and the relevant literature, there was a particular concern to determine how a problem-task focus is changing the patterns of helping procedures used by social workers in clinical practice, for example, in regard to the problems of alienated poverty, juvenile delinquency, child abuse and neglect, vocational maladjustment, psychosis, and marital conflict. What follows, then, is both a charting of current changes and a foreshadowing of new and needed developments in direct social work services to individuals and family groups.

THE CONCEPT

The term "social treatment" was used by many social workers prior to World War I and during the 1920s to mean social case treatment and social casework as well as to refer to its action-change aspect. Witmer observed that during the "social reform era of social work," social treatment was conceived largely in terms of the organization and coordination of community resources, so that social casework had a "community organization aspect." [2] It included family rehabilitation efforts as well as aid to individuals. This was the period when the procedures of what came to be called group work and community organization had not yet been separated out as specialized methods, but were part of a natural way by which one helped individuals and families. The social casework method as practiced before 1917 is described as having been family centered and as "group work with families." [3]

For Richmond, social treatment complemented social diagnosis as one of the two basic components of "social casework," a term she had resisted and did not care for. [4] She regarded social treatment as a "combination of services" through which "readjustments" were made within the individual and the social environment through "reeducation of habits," "the influence of mind upon mind," and changes in the network of social relationships among family members, friends, neighbors, religious congregations, schools, and so forth. Lee held that social treatment should incorporate financial relief programs; he later explicated this method as helping individuals and families through "executive" procedures (managing

---

[2] Helen L. Witmer, *Social Work* (New York: Farrar & Rinehart, 1942), pp. 161–180.

[3] Bertha C. Reynolds, "Rethinking Social Casework," *Social Work Today*, Vol. 5, No. 4 (April 1938), pp. 5–8; No. 5 (May 1938), pp. 5–7; No. 6 (June 1938), pp. 5–8.

[4] Mary E. Richmond, *What is Social Case Work?* (New York: Russell Sage Foundation, 1922), pp. 90, 108–112, and 122. On her preference for the term "friendly visiting" over that of "social casework," see *The Long View*, p. 97.

a service program) and "leadership" (relationship-motivational) procedures.[5]

This enlarged and wide-ranging conception of method was underlined by a number of social work leaders. Abbott, for example, spoke of social treatment (meaning social casework) as a "broad field [containing] the whole science of human relations," rather than limiting it to the specialized procedures of psychiatric social work.[6] In the Milford Conference report in 1929 social treatment was viewed as blending in a generic way the content of the social casework "specializations" that had arisen by that time.[7]

Despite the increasing dominance of the psychoanalytic point of view, there was a continued development of ideas about social treatment that amplified Richmond's conceptualization. Sheffield urged a "situational approach" in social casework in which "group adjustive" and "social learning" processes, involving changes in social perceptions and social relationships, could aid personal maturation and "family re-education." [8] Reynolds emphasized the sociopsychological bonds between client and community and the need for environmental change to meet clients' needs.[9]

Young presented social treatment as "a method of social therapy" for the juvenile delinquent that would achieve

. . . not only changes in his habits and

reactions but changes in the social relations which he maintains with his family, school and other groups, changes in the community and its institutions.[10]

She also considered treatment primarily a "reconditioning" and "re-education process," and, like Sheffield, gave prominence to "redefinition of the situation." This method included the "services of many professionals and resources," as well as the treatment of the family group and family life education about housekeeping and "child-training" practices.

In this perspective there was a remarkable interest in social processes and group dynamics, in emergent social values and purposes. Thus Richmond became enthusiastic about the new "small group psychology" that would provide a "stronger technique" for social treatment.[11] Reynolds sought to revive the direct social reformist intentions of the earlier period of practice. Lindeman conceived of "social therapeutics" as a form of social work practice in which "the forms of social organization" are adjusted "to produce cohesion among the constituent units, and the individuals . . . adjusted to the social forms without sacrificing their essential freedom."[12] This kind of procedural orientation was well expressed by Young, who sharply differentiated social treatment from psychotherapeutic casework:

Social therapy means linking the person to the structure and function of the social group which influences him, sustains him, and at the same time requires his support, cooperation, and the sharing of responsibilities for the common wealth . . . . It promotes the inherent social impulses

[5] Porter R. Lee, *Social Work as Cause and Function* (New York: Columbia University Press, 1937), pp. 39 and 191–199.

[6] Edith Abbott, *Social Welfare and Professional Education* (2d ed.; Chicago: University of Chicago Press, 1942), pp. 48–49.

[7] *Social Case Work: Generic and Specific* (New York: American Association of Social Workers, 1929).

[8] Ada E. Sheffield, *Social Insight in Case Situations* (New York: Appleton-Century Co., 1937).

[9] *See* Reynolds, op. cit.; and Reynolds, "Between Client and Community," *Smith College Studies in Social Work*, Vol. 5, No. 1 (September 1934), pp. 5–138.

[10] Pauline V. Young, *Social Treatment Probation and Delinquency* (New York: McGraw-Hill Book Co., 1937), p. 290.

[11] Richmond, *The Long View*, pp. 484–491.

[12] Eduard C. Lindeman, "From Social Work to Social Science," in Robert Gessner, ed., *The Democratic Man* (Boston: Beacon Press, 1956), p. 208.

of human beings and releases their energies for activity and service. Integration and participation in group life on a democratic basis creates that "wider social self" which tends to make life meaningful and useful. The socialized person tends to accept responsibility not only for himself but for others. . . . he tends to develop a social philosophy of life. . . . In short, mobilization of the latent powers of the family and group cooperating in full strength is one of the basic social techniques in aiding the person and the family to aid themselves and others.[13]

The social therapists were, however, out of tune with the prevailing Freudian ethic and the preoccupation with effecting personality change through psychological procedures. Virginia Robinson, Charlotte Towle, Gordon Hamilton, and others helped to redirect social caseworkers toward a psychotherapeutic ideology. The term social treatment fell into disuse and was replaced by references to the limited procedures of "environmental manipulation."[14]

Today the revived term social treatment is again an attempt to distinguish a pattern of direct service quite different from psychotherapeutic casework. There are certain negative connotations about alternative rubrics, such as comprehensive casework and clinical social work, that are avoided by the older term. In the social treatment approach the therapeutic objectives of personality growth and change remain of central importance, but they are regarded as inextricably bound up with and conditioned by social environmental structures and changes, particularly in family and community situations. The return to the concept of social treatment marks a major shift back to traditional perspectives, to a concern with person and situation, family

and community values, and socially progressive purposes and processes.

THE METHOD

Social treatment may be defined as a general method for helping individuals and family groups cope with their social problems and improve their social functioning. The scope and boundary of this method are determined by the focus of attention and effort on direct assistance to individuals and family groups, with their individualized problems and functioning.[15] This is in contrast to interventive programs aimed at helping to change neighborhood groups, social organizations, communities, or social welfare institutions to improve their corporate functioning. It has been fallacious to consider the casework method as being limited to one-to-one relationships between the social worker and client. This limitation forced therapeutic purposes to become narrow, fragmentary, and therefore inadequate for the attainment of needed objectives.

To help people with their social problems the systematic, skilled implementation of an extensive repertoire of specific, concrete procedures and resources, of powerful ways and means, is required. Traditionally these procedures consist of assessment, planning, implementation, evaluative feedback, corrective, and continued action activities. The intention is to assert influence through such procedures and processes so as to effect desired change in individuals, social environments, or, usually, in both systems and

[13] Pauline V. Young, *Social Case Work in National Defense* (New York: Prentice-Hall, 1941), p. 215.
[14] Gordon Hamilton, *Theory and Practice of Social Casework* (2d ed.; New York: Columbia University Press, 1951), pp. 246–249.

[15] Method as used here refers to purposeful, instrumental activity—an orderly use of means and procedures—including the application of knowledge, attitudes, and skills to accomplish tasks and achieve goals. As Buchler explains, it is "a power of purposive manipulation in a specific recognizable form and order of activity . . . a reproducible order of utterance . . . a tangled cluster of doings, makings and asserting." Justus Buchler, *The Concept of Method* (New York: Columbia University Press, 1961), pp. 135–144.

in the relationships between them.[16] The social treatment method thus consists of interventive procedures in which the social worker uses relationships with individuals, families, small groups, organizations, milieus, and communities and intervenes purposefully, adequately, and effectively in these systems to help individuals and families resolve their problems. Psychotherapy is but one set of procedures within the method of social treatment.

It is now recognized that many social workers in direct service use interventions that have been thought of as casework, group work, or community organization procedures.[17] But as Meyer has well asserted: "The traditional separation of casework, group work and community organization is no longer tenable."[18] Such an approach implies a rejection of ritualistic, methodical activism and a deemphasis on method in the sense of a "methodolatry" that lacks regard for aims and results.[19] Social treatment calls for a focus on the problems, goals, and tasks to which method is addressed.

PROBLEM-PERSON-SITUATION MODEL

Social treatment also represents a return to the problem-person-situation model that has been the basic, traditional model for casework.[20] It was Richmond who articulated this theoretical structure when she defined social diagnosis as the identification of the "social difficulty" (or "social need") of the human being and of his social situation.[21] What has also been referred to as the person-in-situation perspective was further developed by Cannon and Klein, Sheffield, Reynolds, Young, and Hamilton and was recently restated by Hollis.[22] It is a definite theoretical framework that was in large part abandoned when social work became preoccupied with psychodynamics and psychopathology.

This traditional model offers a more suitable alternative to the medical symptom-illness view of social problems. Furthermore, it clarifies and emphasizes the concepts of problem and situation (as distinguished from the concept of personality) more than does psychotherapeutic casework. The psychosocial problems of clients are now better understood as difficulties in social functioning and social relationships, as social disability and deviant behavior. They are therefore reactions to and outcomes of maladjustive transactional processes between person and situation, not properties of a person or situation.[23]

The traditional framework can now be understood as representing a systems model based on three interdependent, interacting elements: problem, person, and situation. Such a gestalt exhibits systemic, structural, functional, and change characteristics. Causality becomes a matter of a system's structure and part relationships, rather than of individual responsibility and blame.

[16] See Richmond, *The Long View*, p. 576; Hamilton, *op. cit.*, p. 239; and "Working Definition of Social Work Practice," in Harriett M. Bartlett, "Toward Clarification and Improvement of Social Work Practice," *Social Work*, Vol. 3, No. 2 (April 1958), pp. 3–9.

[17] Harriett M. Bartlett, "Characteristics of Social Work," *Building Social Work Knowledge* (New York: National Association of Social Workers, 1964), pp. 1–15.

[18] Carol H. Meyer, "The Changing Concept of Individualized Services," *Social Casework*, Vol. 47, No. 5 (May 1966), pp. 279–285.

[19] Buchler, op. cit., pp. 105–106.

[20] See Bernece K. Simon, "Borrowed Concepts: Problems and Issues for Curriculum Planning," *Health and Disability Concepts in Social Work Education* (Minneapolis: School of Social Work, University of Minnesota, 1964), pp. 31–41.

[21] Mary E. Richmond, *Social Diagnosis* (New York: Russell Sage Foundation, 1917), p. 62.

[22] M. Antoinette Cannon and Philip Klein, eds., *Social Casework: An Outline for Teaching* (New York: Columbia University Press, 1933); and Florence Hollis, *Casework: Psychosocial Therapy* (New York: Random House, 1964).

[23] A situation is a segment of the social environment that has meaning for the individual and refers to some social group in focused action at a certain time and place. Person-situation relationships become a focus for interventive effort, particularly for personality and identity change.

Behavior becomes problematic and deviant when defined as dysfunctional for the system's needs. Social workers are pulled away from a predilection for intrapsychic conflict issues, and resources become important elements for input-outcome relations.

From such a wide and holistic viewpoint, it is easier to see that interventive change in one variable of the system affects its other parts and thus affects the equilibrium and functioning of the whole. This means that strategic intervention has wide, amplifying consequences, as was noted by the pioneer social workers.[24] The systemic character of social treatment thus calls for a comprehensiveness in the helping approach and a concern with both dysfunctional personality and social system, with interactive personal and group objectives and tasks that will affect the parts and the whole of the case gestalt. Especially important is the need for feedback information loops and a self-monitoring kind of self-awareness to enable self-corrective, goal-directed interventive behavior.

The problem-person-situation model, because of its complex and multifactorial character, compels social workers to seek out and make use of a variety of theories and the interventive approaches, strategies, and programs derived from them. Thus we find ourselves applying relevant aspects of theories about social problems and deviant behavior; adapting personality change approaches based on psychoanalytic, behavioral learning, and humanistic-existentialist theories; and implementing social-situational change approaches based on theories about social situations and groups and marital, family, milieu, organizational, community, and welfare systems. Each of these

theories offers some mode of response to different aspects of therapeutic tasks. Practice "theory" needs to be eclectic and must evolve integrative links for the operational use of personality and social system theories, such as propositions about deviant behavior, role, identity, social situation, crisis, and conflict resolution. It would appear that during the past quarter of a century social workers have unknowingly evolved an integrative framework of personality and situational change procedures under the guise of "crisis therapy," whose principles seem to be applicable in both short-term and long-term interventive programs with individuals and family groups.

Within the context of social treatment the concepts of diagnosis and treatment take on different connotations and operational procedures. There is a greater tendency to apply phenomenological perspectives in understanding the social situation and the subjective world of the client as he experiences them. There is an explicit *assessment of the social situation,* including an appraisal of the structural adequacy and functional efficiency of the family and other groups, organizations, and communities in which the client is an active member. Social workers find that they are again more directly concerned with the assessment of work-employment situations and the vocational functioning of clients and that they actually do much vocational counseling without recognizing that it has remained a basic function for social workers in many settings.

Social workers are more interested now in *personality assessment* that emphasizes the sociopsychological, interactional aspects of personality. This requires them to evaluate and help individuals with their self-concepts and self-esteem, which are related to social, personal, and self-identities; social skills and interpersonal competence; and social learning and social reinforcement processes. There is a growing conviction about the validity of social work's charac-

---

[24] *See,* for example, Richmond, *What is Social Casework?* pp. 136–139. For a helpful discussion of systems theory, *see* Walter Buckley, *Sociology and Modern Systems Theory* (Englewood Cliffs, N.J.: Prentice-Hall, 1967), pp. 55–70; and Gordon Hearn, ed., *The General Systems Approach* (New York: Council on Social Work Education, 1969).

teristic way of helping clients with difficulties in social functioning and relationships so as to help resolve identity crises and social conflicts and to enable individuals and groups to achieve self-realization and development. Perlman has helped revitalize this orientation in her discussions of persona and identity.[25]

The therapeutic or *action-change process* is also understood in different terms. Such elements as skills, resources, and relationship are applied in a plan or program of action in which services and procedures are combined to realize specific tasks and goals. A basic element of treatment is a shared diagnostic experience between worker and client in which redefinitions of the client's situation and problems take place and mutual problem-solving plans are formulated. The task program is then carried out through the use of one or more strategies involving roles to be performed by the worker, client, and others, as well as specific resources and tactics to be used in some sequential order of process. The social worker's helping interventions are more than "techniques"; they are change-inducing units of behavior and are essentially interactional role performances responsive to heuristic task requirements.

Situational interventions are concerned with changing relationship and functioning patterns in a group and with altering the group's focus of attention and effort, its definition of experience, and its time-space characteristics. The family and extended family thus become a client, and intake is understood to involve inducting the family unit into the role of client. Change programs are geared to influence organizational and community networks. Marital, family, and milieu therapies as well as family life education programs are again reestablished as basic social work services. The provision of a situational support and reinforcement system for new behavior and interpersonal

relationship patterns is of critical importance in the rehabilitation and resocialization programs of social treatment. For example, in order for a woman to become a more effective mother, she may have to be helped to gain a new understanding of herself and resolve a negative self-image and transference reaction that confirm her to be rejecting and inadequate. In addition her home situation may be transformed into a learning experience. The mother, father, and child, individually and as a family unit, may be guided in learning new attitudes, self-expectations, and role performance skills. Also, family and neighborhood situations may be changed to create a positive environment that is socially reinforcing of more adaptive behavior and relationships.

PROBLEM-TASK FOCUS

Another aspect of the method of social treatment is its *problem-task focus*. The problems of social work clients can be understood as difficulties in completing crucial life tasks, especially the developmental tasks of identity formation and change and transition to new social roles and relationships that occur during the crises of life cycles and careers. Studt describes "task focus" as situational diagnosis and planning, an emphasis on interventive strategies, and a process of establishing and guiding task-oriented working relationships that center around the therapeutic organizational role of the client.[26] The social worker thus becomes a "strategy guide," implementing various kinds of resocializing strategies, with method being adapted creatively to task needs.

A problem-task focus operationally involves identifying and translating a problem into a task or set of tasks to be completed that will overcome obstacles, relieve

---

[25] Helen Harris Perlman, *Persona* (Chicago: University of Chicago Press, 1968).

[26] Elliot Studt, "Social Work Theory and Implications for the Practice of Methods," *Social Work Education Reporter*, Vol. 16, No. 2 (June 1968), pp. 22–24 and 42–46.

stress, and achieve desired and specific goals. The accomplishment of such tasks calls for certain essential elements—problem-solving attitudes, motivation, knowledge and skills, resources, consensual goals and strategies, and focused energy (elbow grease)—to be contributed by the client, social worker, social welfare aides, relatives, and other persons who may be available. Thus a depressive reaction on the part of a wife may be redefined as secondary to a marital conflict. Helping efforts would aim to resolve the conflicted role expectations and role performance difficulties between husband and wife, children, and in-laws, and would aim to help the couple learn the competencies needed for a satisfying marriage.

The problem-task orientation places responsibility on the client for conscious participation in decisions regarding goals, risks, costs, and resources to be used in achieving results. Rather than assuming the role of a dependent patient, the client becomes responsible for himself and the social worker acts as a task collaborator. This is a more democratic and efficient division of labor. The organizational role and treatment career of the client offer arrangements through which he can change deviant and discredited identities and learn new values and skills.[27]

The multiple, complicated, severe, and chronic problems often presented by clients also require many different kinds of helping persons—what Studt calls a "work group."[28] Such a helping system may consist of the social worker and client, his relatives and work colleagues, other social workers and helping professionals, as well as social work aides. The social worker often serves as a central member and "clini-

cal team leader." Tasks, rather than cases, may be referred when necessary to obtain external resources or expertise. There is much less dependence on psychiatric consultation or supervision. A premium is placed on role variety, the phasing and coordination of task effort, and team cohesion and morale.

Task structure becomes an important determinant of change strategies and roles as well as of group leadership. The structural elements may be identified, according to Fiedler, in terms of "decision verifiability," "goal clarity," "goal path multiplicity," and "solution specificity," so that tasks can be programmed in step-by-step fashion.[29] Fiedler also suggests certain characteristics of a task: the degree of the task's structure and stress, the interlocking of effort by group members, and the degree of chance or skill perceived as being involved in its completion. The effectiveness of group leadership in utilizing task-oriented or relationship-oriented styles and the productivity of the group are therefore determined by the task structure, the type of group involved, the nature of leader-member relationships, and the position and power of the leader.

One implication of these ideas about task focus and group leadership is that the group leadership role may alternate among worker, client, and others, depending on task needs. Also, it becomes a basic therapeutic objective to improve the leadership competence of the family and group members and the group's problem-solving skills. In addition the natural, unofficial helping system of mutual aid available to an individual and family needs to be strengthened to help them meet recurrent crises of the life cycle. Then the social worker can phase himself out of the client group and terminate treatment.

[27] Max Siporin, "Deviant Behavior Theory in Social Work: Diagnosis and Treatment," *Social Work* Vol. 10, No. 3 (July 1965), pp. 59–67.

[28] Studt, op. cit.; and Studt, "Fields of Social Work Practice," *Social Work*, Vol. 10, No. 4 (October 1965), pp. 156–165.

[29] Fred E. Fiedler, *A Theory of Leadership Effectiveness* (New York: McGraw-Hill Book Co., 1967), pp. 22–35 and 142–147.

TABLE 1. ROLE INTERVENTION MODEL FOR PERSONALITY AND SOCIAL SYSTEMS

System Function	Purpose and Outcome	Helping Process	Helping Roles
Pattern maintenance	Identity confirmation	Therapy and identity change	Therapist, healer, consoler, nurturer, confirmer, supporter
Integration	Inclusion, adjustment, unity	Friendship and communion	Friend, social parent, Big Brother, protector, custodian, controller
Adaptation	Growth and competence	Education and socialization	Teacher, guide, model, norm-sender, demonstrator
Goal attainment	Productivity, creativity, self-realization	Problem-solving and task performance	Counselor, expert, adviser, advocate, troubleshooter, mediator, resource person, expediter, referrer

ROLE INTERVENTION

Today the social worker is more helpful in group leadership and membership roles rather than limiting himself to being a confidante or "guru" in intimate encounters with individual clients. He needs to know and be skilled in both individual and group helping procedures and know how to be a group discussion leader. The helping stance is an activist one; he must be direct, self-assertive, and influential so that he can intervene and set in motion change processes that can alter severely pathological interaction patterns, particularly in family crisis situations. The activist, interventive posture has been well described in the case of the worker as family group therapist, but it needs to be extended to other helping situations.[30] Such an orientation encourages a more positive, autonomous kind of self-image for the worker, is self-confirming,

[30] Arthur L. Leader, "The Role of Intervention in Family Group Treatment," *Social Casework*, Vol. 45, No. 6 (June 1964), pp. 327–332; and Virginia Satir, *Conjoint Family Therapy* (Palo Alto, Calif.: Science and Behavior Books, 1967).

and encourages him to be more responsible and accountable for his practice.

The social worker also needs to learn to make a more conscious, direct, and therapeutic use of his authority so that he can alter power structures and communication patterns in a disorganized family, terminate vicious self-reinforcing habitual cycles of sadomasochistic relationships, or obtain scarce community resources. Not only in protective cases involving abused or neglected children, but in many other kinds of situations as well, therapeutic tasks demand a firm, limited, and directive influence based on important professional and personal forms of authority as well as on agency-delegated bureaucratic authority. The client views a therapeutic use of authority as real, powerful influence on his behalf. Such exercise of authority needs to be consistent with democratic ethics and forms—allowing freedom and choice for the client—within the collaborative contract and relationship between client and worker.

As a representative of the social work profession, the social worker takes on a multifunctional orientation as he seeks to help realize the profession's institutional and societal tasks. He does this by using helping processes that are problem solving, educational, therapeutic, and socially integrative. These processes articulate with the functional prerequisites of personality and social systems identified by Parsons as system "pattern variables" of pattern maintenance, integration, adaptation, and goal attainment.[31] The helping processes are also linked to outcomes of identity confirmation, social inclusion and adjustment, growth and competence, and productivity and self-realization for individuals and collectivities. In turn the helping processes are fulfilled through a wide repertoire of helping roles. These multidimensional relationships are listed in Table 1.

In social treatment the social worker serves as a system change agent for both personality and social systems. He seeks to be active and effective at several levels of intervention, choosing targets and entry points in individual, family, group, organizational, community, and institutional structures and domains of functioning. Geismar, Spergel, and others have illustrated this multilevel approach in the provision of individualized services.[32] There is, however, a growing awareness that it is through his role performances in situational interventions that the social worker gains entry and effects change for personality and social systems, including the social welfare system.

Role performances are extremely important in carrying out helping interventions. A social system consists of patterns of role relationships actualized by people in social situations. Meaningful action is role-patterned behavior oriented toward symbolic or overt situational interaction with others. One has to be a role-actor to participate socially and function as a human being. Role performances thus are ways of getting jobs done and of meeting reciprocal needs for identity and reality confirmation. They also dramatize and idealize a social situation so as to maximize one's influence on the behavior of others.[33] Therefore, it is through his role performances that the social worker acts in reciprocal and collaborative relationships with clients and carries out the jobs of giving information, changing attitudes and behavior, motivating, limiting, modeling, and so forth.

In order to have maximum therapeutic influence, the social worker needs to provide effective role performances in which he is genuine and committed. The roles may be culturally defined and should be geared to the client's expectations. But they will be interpreted personally by each worker and enacted in highly individualistic styles. Even when they are part of the social rituals of degradation or conversion ceremonies, the social worker may have to improvise the helping roles in response to the often unpredictable contingencies of situational events and the often unpredictable behavior of clients and others.

In social treatment processes, the social worker is active either within or outside a social agency office and intervenes directly or indirectly in the client's life situations. He accomplishes his therapeutic tasks through an extensive repertoire of general

[31] Talcott Parsons, "Pattern Variables Revisited," *American Sociological Review*, Vol. 25, No. 4 (August 1960), pp. 467–483. For an effort to relate these Parsonian pattern variables to helping roles in residential treatment, *see* Howard W. Polsky and Daniel S. Claster, "The Structure and Functions of Adult-Youth Systems," in Muzafer Sherif and Carolyn Sherif, eds., *Problems of Youth* (Chicago: Aldine Publishing Co., 1965), pp. 189–211.

[32] Ludwig L. Geismar, "Three Levels of Treatment for the Multiproblem Family," *Social Casework*, Vol. 42, No. 3 (March 1961), pp. 124–127; and Irving Spergel, "A Multi-Dimensional Model for Social Work Practice," *Social Service Review*, Vol. 36, No. 1 (March 1962), pp. 62–71.

[33] Erving Goffman, *The Presentation of Self in Everyday Life* (New York: Doubleday Anchor Books, 1969), pp. 17–76.

and specific situational roles.[34] The most highly valued role—therapist—is now often overshadowed by other diverse roles such as integrator and friend, problem-solving expert and innovator, mediator and negotiator, liaison person and coordinator of resources (broker), spokesman (advocate), and especially teacher.

The therapeutic work of consoling, nurturing, and confirming the self-worth and identity of a client needs to be done in conjunction with helping actions of the friend and social parent. The resolution of intrapsychic and interpersonal conflicts and the integration of new identities and social roles as well as the integration of individuals within collectivities are now seen as reciprocal aspects of a social inclusion process carried out with peers and parental surrogates.

The social worker is, as always, expected to be an expert troubleshooter who can intervene in severe crises, mediate violent disputes, negotiate and find innovative resolutions for impossible difficulties. But high value is accorded the provider and coordinator of social supports and community resources needed for the client's development and problem-solving adaptation. As resource person and procedural guide the worker actively uses intergroup community processes within the unofficial, natural helping system of the client's social network. Or he deals directly with the official social welfare community and bureaucracies to make available to the client varied social provisions and social utilities such as financial aid, day care, and homemaker and medical care services. The spokesman (advocate) role is one that does not relieve social workers of their obligations to the community and the social welfare institution they represent, but it does call for them to give priority again to the needs and interests of the clients and citizens the welfare community is intended to serve. It also demands that social workers be identified again as social reformers, encouraging changes in values and client participation in social action programs that have both therapeutic and social betterment objectives.

It is as a therapeutic teacher, guiding individual and group learning processes, that the social worker is meeting crucial needs in our society. The current conflicts and dislocations of the urban scene are in part due to processes of vast social migration and mobility; they require extensive social reforms and individualized resocialization-educational programs. Thus social workers help clients acquire the cognitive development, social competence, and the social adjustment or role satisfaction that is also called mental health. They teach clients the skills of deriving maximum benefits from the social security and welfare bureaucratic systems, about which knowledge and skill have become essential for socialization and rehabilitation programs.[35] Still further, they enable the client to learn meaningful personal and social philosophies, live by valid values and standards, and gain viable identities as individual and family members in human communities.

In these therapeutic, integrative, educational, and problem-solving processes, the dynamics of change depend heavily on potent group and situational forces.[36] These influences facilitate the emergence of creative individual and collective adjustment efforts and what Durkheim called a "collective consciousness." In social treatment programs, the social worker can direct

[35] Otto Pollak identifies these kinds of skills in "The Outlook for the American Family," *Journal of Marriage and the Family*, Vol. 29, No. 1 (February 1967), pp. 193–205.

[36] These situational change forces are well discussed by Alan F. Klein, "Individual Change Through Group Experience," *National Conference on Social Welfare, 1959* (New York: Columbia University Press, 1959), pp. 136–155.

[34] For a definition and discussion of situational roles, *see* Max Siporin, "Private Practice of Social Work: Functional Roles and Social Control," *Social Work*, Vol. 6, No. 2 (April 1961), pp. 52–60.

his role performances so that they are complementary and reinforcing for new and adaptive role identities and performances on the part of the client and other members of his natural groups. Expectations and mutual aid efforts that operate to effect behavioral and situational changes are activated.

Operationally this means that the social worker does not play Big Daddy to the Baby Boy or rescuer of the sinner, but he does encourage adult, friendly, altruistic relationships and corrective therapeutic experiences. He fosters dyadic and team task performances that move to accomplish concrete tasks and reward effort, learning, self-disclosure, and authenticity for the client and significant others. He enables the collective "interexperience," characterized by a common consciousness of meanings, values, and relationships and a mutual commitment to them.[37] It is through such an interexperience that problems get resolved and support is given to interdependence and individuality, to a sense of personal and social responsibility as well as to the inherent processes of individual and social growth.

SUMMARY AND CONCLUSIONS

Social treatment is a new-old mode of helping individuals and family groups. Social workers feel comfortable with it because of its old associations yet excited by the new aspects and rich potential for more relevant and effective service to clients.

In current practice social treatment is distinguished by patterns of service that may be said to constitute a new helping method. It is based on a traditional problem-person-situation model for diagnosis and interventive change (also found to be a systems model), for which a variety of theories are useful in an eclectic fashion.

[37] The concept and process of interexperience are presented by R. D. Laing, *The Politics of Experience* (New York: Pantheon, 1967), p. 19.

Assessment and treatment processes have new aspects in this approach, with a problem-task focus that has important consequences for a more democratic, collaborative relationship between client and worker. There is a renewed emphasis on social situational helping interventions and group leadership by the social worker through role performances that are activist, multifunctional, versatile, and directed toward the accomplishment of both personality and social system change. Situational interventions can use potent social interactional forces and enable the emergence of a collective consciousness and adaptive experience through which adjustment problems are resolved and individual and group growth are nourished.

Further development of the theory, principles, and procedures of social treatment need direct attention. There is need to determine, for example, how different kinds of problems shape different patterns of services and how differential tasks affect the choice of helping strategies and roles for client and social worker. There is also need to clarify the effectiveness of social treatment programs for specific change in individual behavior and social relationships. Hopefully research about social treatment will again provide, as it did in the past, the hard data about poverty, illness, pathology, and social conditions to support programs of social legislation.

The method of social treatment and the changes in practice associated with it have already stimulated much-needed change in social work education. The delivery of programmatic services and the social work manpower needed for such delivery systems have made for a vast increase in the training of different levels of personnel and for a renewed emphasis on preparation for administrative, program-planning, and evaluative functions. Because it is here that we have allowed unhelpful gaps and vacuums in leadership and service, there is also need to give greater priority to the training of doctorate-level practitioners for frontline service functions and team-leadership roles.

Social treatment appears eminently suitable for the needed structure of direct individualized social work services that can effect behavioral and situational change for clients. As developed during the earlier and the current social reform eras, social treatment gives prominence to the social purposes of the profession and helps social workers recapture the earlier utopian, yet pragmatic, social vision needed today.

Hopefully social workers may now be better able to halt the extreme oscillations and establish the balance between the individual rehabilitation and social reform orientations that Mary Richmond and Porter Lee wished for and that have yet to be achieved. With this new-old method of social treatment, social workers can better respond to today's social crises and aid people to achieve both the individual identity and community they so greatly desire.

The Prison of My Mind, by Barbara Field Benziger (Walker
                    and Company, 171 pages, $4.95).

Aftershock, by Ellen Wolfe (G. P. Putnam's Sons, 216 pages,
          $5.95).

                         Reviewed by
                         Morley Glicken

     To take the very private agony of mental illness and
then transform it into a book, requires the large talent
of a major writer. Hannah Green did it in, I Never
Promised You a Rose Garden, and few readers could say
that something very real inside of them had not been
touched. Theodore Issac Rubin did it in, Lisa and David,
and an entire generation began commiting itself to people.
     There is something in the experience of mental illness
so close to the madness of American life, that to lift it
beyond the common place requires the mind of a writer willing
to explore the edges of his own insanity.
     Barbara Benziger and Ellen Wolfe write of their
experiences with mental illness, but one isn't willing to
believe that they've sifted through the experience with
an eye for the unique. It's almost as if The Reader's
Digest had entered the psyche of each woman and then played
itself back in a lifeless, unmoving prose style. There
isn't a woman who hasn't seen the same stuff four-fold
over every afternoon on "Love of Life".
     If one can accept that we aren't dealing here with
books which dignify the human spirit or move the reader with
a larger vision of life, there are enough redeeming factors
to make each book worth reading.
     In The Prison of My Mind, Barbara Benziger describes
the despair of trying to find an understanding psychiatrist
to treat her long term depression. Page after page she
catalogues encounters with some of the most arrogant,
incompetent medical men one can imagine. And what is so
unusual in Mrs. Benziger's case is that she could easily
afford, and in fact sought, the best psychiatric help
available and yet received help not appreciably better than
that given in state hospitals.
     Dr. Robert Coles writes in his fine introduction to
Mrs. Benziger's book, "Barbara Benziger lets us know right
off that she is not poor. Her experiences are those of a
well-to-do woman who lives in a city too well supplied with
psychiatrists. She could afford the best, and she sought
it. Yet, she found out something I'm not sure many people
realize: not only do the rich suffer - hopefully, that is

ORIGINAL MANUSCRIPT, 1970.

obvious - but they can pay a lot and get cheated, pay
thousands of dollars and get no better care than a patient
brought into any city or state hospital. The rich can be
deceived and minipulated and lied to and cleverly, insis-
tently, outrageously stripped of all dignity. The rich can
be made to feel as vulnerable, defenseless, and worthless
as a pauper or a beggar - by the very people they pay so
much to be of help."

One could question Barbara Benziger's evaluation of
psychiatrists on grounds that she might have been too
disturbed to accurately judge the help she received. In
all fairness to her, the experiences she reports are so common,
so frequently reported by those who have lived with mental
illness that one feels justified in saying that as a group,
psychiatrists are a depressingly sorry lot - insensitive,
aloof and arrogant in their unwillingness to touch people's
soul on something near a human level.

In Aftershock, Ellen Wolfe gives a first hand tour of
the hell she experienced following extensive electro-shock
therapy. If Miss Wolfe's description of severe memory
loss, confusion, and fear of permanent brain damage fails
to frighten the many patients one sees who consider electro-
shock a quick, easy solution to their problems, then hopefully it should serve as some deterant to psychiatrists who
use it as freely as they use aspirins.

Shock therapy is one of those psychiatric hold overs
from the dark ages of treatment of the mentally ill which
works enough to be used when everything else has failed.
There are those who will use it under no circumstance,
feeling that it does no long range good and that it serves
to disorient and depress far too many patients. And then
there are others, depressingly too many others, who indiscriminately use shock therapy on everyone as if it were some
sort of medical panacea. One feels that its over use, when
perhaps a more human, personal approach such as psychotherapy
might work as well, is symptomatic of the unwillingness of
some psychiatrists to see people in light of the totally of
their existence. Admittedly it is easier to shock a patient
than spend time in therapy with him. It is also inhuman at
times, unfeeling, and simplistic, not to forget its questionable success as a treatment device.

Barbara Benziger and Ellen Wolfe have written books
which should help dispell the folk myth that psychiatrists
are warm, human people. Both women write of arrogance,
incompetence, and insensitivity.

It would be unfair not to assure the reader that some
psychiatrists are not like this. Fortunately, there are
those who somehow live through the soul deadening experience
of being stoned by their colleagues for caring too much

about people. One wishes they would rise above it all and declare their revulsion for the sorry state of treatment of the mentally ill before the public, in its disenchantment, return to faith-healers, witch-doctors, and medicine-men.... all of whom are infinitely less expensive, and if the mind will allow itself some fun, probably just as helpful.

BY HENRY MILLER

Value Dilemmas in Social Casework

■ *The value dilemmas of the title have their basis in the traditional social work belief in the inherent dignity of man: How can social workers minister to man without robbing him of his dignity? The paper is a plea for the profession to "get out of the business of dealing with involuntary clients," to return to its former role of advocate of its clients rather than forcing its services on them.* ■

THIS PAPER IS concerned with certain moral dimensions of the social casework enterprise. To the extent that it deals with what one should or should not do, it can hardly be buttressed with an empirical line of argument. Rather, the paper takes the form of an exhortation. The plea is for social caseworkers to maintain a constant focus on what has traditionally been the crucial value of their endeavor: the inherent dignity of man. This is a difficult focus to sustain, for it must inevitably clash with other professional moralities. This is especially so at the present time when the elaboration of technique has such high priority and when the cry for more knowledge, more predictability, and more control increases in modulation.

The central thesis of this paper is that social casework, as a therapeutic activity, is faced with a fundamental and perhaps insoluble value paradox. It poses for itself the ultimate end of a dignified and worthy human being; however, the methods it uses to accomplish that end are likely to be

HENRY MILLER, DSW, *is Associate Professor, School of Social Welfare, University of California, Berkeley, California. This paper was presented at the Annual Forum of the National Conference on Social Welfare, Dallas, Texas, May 1967.*

Reprinted with permission of the National Association of Social Workers, from SOCIAL WORK, Vol. 13, No. 1 (January 1968), pp. 27-33.

demeaning to the individual. The moral question for the caseworker, then, becomes one of deciding what he can legitimately *do* to his clients without giving offense to this intrinsic state of worth.

THE DIGNITY OF MAN

There are at least three elements to the paradox. The first bears on the end of the casework endeavor and embodies the aforementioned assumption about the value of an individual human being. It is the fundamental tenet not only of social casework but of all social welfare. It is a rather beautiful conception and an article of faith that brings credit to any social worker. It holds that man is a creature of dignity and that he is entitled to infinite respect—simply by virtue of the fact that he is a man. He may be, at times, a bad man or a mixed-up man or a stupid man—indeed, he may be so bad or mixed-up or stupid that society is forced to constrain or punish him—but, nonetheless, he remains proud in the face of his confusion and dignified in the isolation of his confinement. Society may incarcerate, commit, punish, or otherwise reap vengeance for his malice—but it cannot strip him of his nobility.

This conception of man runs persistently

throughout the thought of Western civilization. It is rooted in Homer, it reached a brilliant flowering during the Renaissance, and it is the foundation of the democratic ideal that was originally projected for the United States. It subsumes liberty and justice but, above all, equity, an equity that allows a person to say to any fellow human being: "You may be wiser, healthier, or richer than I; you may be more expert; you may be handsomer, classier, and luckier; but, where it really matters—in the innermost recesses of selfhood or soulhood, whatever and wherever that is—*you are no better than I.*"

At this point an empirically minded person may take exception and wonder about the availability of data to support the premise of a soul or a self. But this is not an argument for the existence of a soul—dignified or undignified. It is the postulation of a point of view toward mankind and it is a stance in which the writer and—it is hoped—the profession believe. It is a good belief. It may appear silly to the cynical, it may run in the face of man's long chronicle of abominable behavior, it may be contradicted by his irrefutable incumbency in the animal kingdom, but it is still a good and noble belief. And it is prerequisite for social welfare; without it the whole welfare edifice makes no sense at all.

LIFE IS SUFFERING

So man is dignified. But, alas, he lives in a sewer—a sewer of suffering. And this is the second element in the paradox: the human condition is one of suffering. Under the best of conditions life is cruel. It is not merely neutral—it is antagonistic. It may be unnecessary to pursue this line of argument in detail especially because it is so painfully self-evident in daily work with clients. Those who require additional documentation, however, may consult the written genius of the species: the Old and New Testaments, the scripture of Eastern theology, the incomparable poets, and, of course, the existentialists, who sometimes act as though they were the first to stumble on the fact of man's miraculous isolation.

Life is suffering because, in the first instance, we are ultimately betrayed by the mortality of our own bodies. We die and those we love die. We are ravaged by disease, we live with imminent and inevitable loss, we are harassed by the elements, we are oppressed by our institutions—in short, we suffer. Freud, the super-realist, summed up the human condition quite well when he wrote:

> Thus our possibilities of happiness are already restricted by our constitution. Unhappiness is much less difficult to experience. We are threatened with suffering from three directions: from our own body, which is doomed to decay and dissolution and which cannot even do without pain and anxiety as warning signals; from the external world, which may rage against us with overwhelming and merciless forces of destruction; and finally from our relations to other men. The suffering which comes from this last source is perhaps more painful to us than any other. We tend to regard it as a kind of gratuitous addition, although it cannot be any less fatefully inevitable than the suffering which comes from elsewhere.[1]

THE TERRIBLE DILEMMA

In any event, this premise of human suffering provides the second prerequisite for the institution of social welfare. Suffering argues that man needs attention, human dignity argues that he merits attention, and social welfare, the third element in the paradox, is there to do the job—along, it must be noted, with several other institutions in this civilization. But it is at this point that the terrible dilemma occurs: how is one to minister to man's suffering without robbing him of his dignity?

[1] Sigmund Freud, *Civilization and Its Discontents* (New York: W. W. Norton & Co., 1961), pp. 23–24.

Let us take as a starting point the traditional device that society has used to alleviate suffering—charity. It is obvious that the giving of alms is demeaning when it is accompanied by the implicit gratuity of "I, the donor, am better than you, the recipient." Such an implication can be communicated in various ways: in subtle vocalizations, in the physical bearing of the alms-giver as he drops his coin into the bowl, in the publicity given the act. Behind such a stance is always the notion: "I have given you something—be *grateful* to me!" And when the gratitude must be expressed by an obligation to listen to good counsel, the humiliation of the recipient is complete.

The current public assistance programs contain these implicit demeaning qualities. Indeed, most are all too explicit. That is why public welfare can never be a dignified source of assistance: the recipient is burdened with an expectation that he will be grateful to a more fortunate community and willing to take advice from it on how to manage his life. It is the means test, of course, that provides the sufficient condition for the degradation.

It is difficult to find an instance of a charitable institution that does not have this demeaning quality. Care must be taken here: to change the name of the device does not change its nature. Public assistance could be called "monthly reward" and the means test labeled "scholarship application," but the stigma would remain. As long as the recipient is subject to the conditional largess of another he is in a demeaning position.

But enough of charity. What about casework per se? Here the degradation may occur in a more insidious manner, but in a way that is no less real. Before proceeding further with this line of argument, however, it must be made clear what kind of casework is in question. This is casework that has been summarized under such rubrics as "aggressive casework," "reaching the unreached," "case-finding," "working with the involuntary client," and so forth. It is a casework that permits an unsolicited encounter with an initially unwilling client in the name of expertise. And it is a casework that occupies the preponderance of energies expended in the larger field of social welfare. If we consider, for example, the areas of public welfare, corrections, the services offered by the newer poverty programs, education, inpatient services, among others, we realize the enormous investment the profession has in offering a casework service to clients who make no request of it, who have little choice about their involvement and even less comprehension as to what the involvement entails.

In spite of some risk of overstatement, let us, for the sake of argument, put the case quite starkly: The social work profession presumes to confront a large number of people with the judgment that they are unhappy, confused, deviant, ill, maladapted —this list could be extended indefinitely— and, as such, require the benefits of our attentions. This judgment is based on either the conclusions of society in the form of legal adjudications or commitment procedures or the diagnostic acumen of our own expert knowledge. In the latter instance we look upon an individual and say that he suffers from an ailment, and we can say this because we are expert; he may not realize that he is afflicted—he may not even care that he is afflicted—but we know he is and it is our responsibility to minister to him. In the former instance we concur in the judgment of society that he is ailing and we accept the charge of that society to effect a remedy.

What is wrong with this stance and how does it impinge on the client's dignity? The wrong inheres in the assumption that we have a right to impose unsolicited advice upon another human being—*and he is not free either to withdraw himself from the situation or even to discount the advice.* If he is on welfare, his benefit is contingent on being counseled in the use of his money or more; if he is on probation or parole his physical freedom becomes a condition of his receptivity to counsel; if he hangs around on street corners he is assaulted by the insinuations of the street worker; if he is insane and hospitalized, the duration of his confinement becomes a function of a willingness to be counseled. He may not choose to be so advised—but if he is to eat or wander without constraint in the world he must submit himself to the good intentions of the expert.

By this position we deprive an individual of the one freedom that is primary to all others and that endows him with the core of his dignity: the freedom to make a shambles of his life. This may sound like a strange doctrine—that people should be free to err, to make mistakes, to fail, to be "ill." But, in a very basic sense, it is the mainspring of all other freedoms, especially in a culture premised on scientific determinism and reaching ever closer to an end wherein mankind *can* exercise control over his world and his brethren. The profession *does* have the expertise to diagnose maladaptive behavior. Our judgment is far from perfect in this regard, but it is improving and it will continue to improve. We are working in our research toward an end when we can control society and behavior, and, if we are not careful, we may succeed in that end. Then the awesome and terrible dilemma is immediately upon us: what happens to the humanity of man, to the rewards of failure, to the dignity of real choice when that day arrives? [2]

VOLUNTARY USE OF CASEWORK SERVICES

What is argued, then, is that man be offered the possibility of choice—and that

---

[2] It is in the creative imaginations of novelists that the terror of a controlled society becomes most evident. The writer does not have in mind here the political authoritarianism of *1984*, but rather the benign "scientific" worlds of *Walden II* [B. F. Skinner (New York: Macmillan Co., 1948)] or the society pictured in *A Clockwork Orange* [Anthony Burgess (New York: Ballantine Books, 1963)].

includes the choice of being maladaptive or deviant or even "ill." Society may—indeed, it must—demand a price for deviance; it cannot operate without a minimum degree of conformity and compliance. But the individual in question should be given the option of paying the price; the old convict notion of "serving one's time and paying a debt to society" has always been a most dignified formulation. The dignity inheres in a conception of responsibility. How humiliating to be told that one behaves in a particular manner because one cannot help it, that one is not responsible for one's actions, that X is a result of poor socialization and Y is a result of good socialization, that good deeds are as predetermined as are bad deeds, that narcissism and altruism are consequences rather than choices, and that man is nothing more than a wisp of straw caught in the winds of instinct and environment.

This moral stance should not be misunderstood: It is not an argument for bigger and better jails. It is not a testimony to a belief that poverty is ennobling. It does not advocate a doctrine of laissez-faire in terms of our social institutions. If people are poor let us either produce well-paying jobs or give them money; if people are ill, let us offer them hospitals and medicine and physicians; let us have schools and universities and houses and parks. We can be magnanimous in our construction of these resources and ingenious in making them available to all. But let us not wrap these goodies with strings that dangle so that if a man needs food he must suffer the insolence of well-intentioned advice or if he needs training he must submit to counsel about the legitimacy of his offspring. Alas, there will always be crime and criminals, and we will need prisons. By all means, let the prisons be infused with the spirit of humanism. But humanism does not mean group therapy as a precondition to parole.

If the poor want advice, let us advise them—but at *their* initiative and not ours.

If criminals wish their criminality treated, let us treat it—but after *they* request it. Let us have our clinics and our adjunctive services; indeed, let us advertise these remedies so that they are known—but let us not dare to act the parent with adult human beings and exclaim: "We know what's best for you, poor afflicted one, and —like it or not—take our medicine."

The plea, then, is for the voluntary use of casework services. But there are certain problematical situations that make such a dictum an oversimplification. The voluntary use of service presumes a clientele that is capable of making choices, and such a presumption does not hold in the case of children, the mentally deficient, and, probably, certain types of the mentally ill. With such classes of clients we have very little choice and society must impose its good intentions, but let us do this reluctantly and with parsimony and with the certainty that there is, in fact, no other viable alternative assumption.

Some would argue that there is another type of client who merits our attention but he has been so oppressed by a hostile society and so impoverished by deprivation that he has neither the knowledge nor the will to ask for our help. We must be careful, in this line of argument, that we are not merely substituting new pejoratives, in the guise of technical jargon, for old pejoratives. Of course Negroes are not racially inferior or lazy. But is it any less patronizing—or humiliating—to see them as culturally deprived, aspirationally stultified, lacking in a sense of basic integrity and identity because of a brittle family structure, or otherwise "not with it"? Let us beware the possibility of the more hideous colonialism that can stem from the white man's casework—a colonialism disguised by the language of science and an immaculate empiricism. It is not at all clear that if opportunities were available to the "deprived" they would use them. And, if they choose not to, it is nobody's business but their own.

So we deal, then, with the voluntary client. But even in this instance there are many value problems. Three of these stand out as being of primary importance.

INEVITABLE MORAL CONCERN OF CASEWORK

The first problem is perhaps the most difficult. It is premised on the notion that man's ailments are essentially disorders of moral style rather than disease entities per se. That is to say, clients come to us, not with mental illnesses of a classic medical order, but with problems of ethics—with confusions about values, with concerns of rightness and wrongness.[3] If this premise is true, the traditional therapeutic injunction of moral neutrality—which, by the way, is in itself a morality—becomes an absurdity. The caseworker cannot disengage himself from the moral concerns of his client when such happen to be the core of his difficulty and the very reason he asked for help in the first place. But if the caseworker must then enter into this once forbidden realm, he assumes the functions of a priest—but a priest without an explicit theology, a secular priest with an idiosyncratic dogma.

Again, we must be careful not to be seduced by our own language. As marriage counselors, for example, we cannot claim to be indifferent to divorce; if we try to salvage a marriage we are rather explicit in the positive value we put on the institution. If we claim to let the parties decide for themselves—a claim that, in most instances, is a self-deception—we still hold an implicit value toward marriage, namely, that marriages can legitimately be dissolved.

[3] Evidence for this assertion can be found in Thomas Szasz, *The Myth of Mental Illness* (New York: Harper & Row, 1961); O. Hobart Mowrer, *The Crisis in Psychiatry and Religion* (Princeton, N.J.: D. Van Nostrand Co., 1961); Mowrer, *The New Group Therapy* (Princeton, N.J.: D. Van Nostrand Co., 1964); and Perry London, *The Modes and Morals of Psychotherapy* (New York: Holt, Rinehart & Winston, 1964).

Either way we take a position and subscribe to a morality.

We take such positions all the time: we hold to dogmas about the worth of human relationships, about love, about fidelity, about honesty, about autonomy, about child rearing, about work and creativity—and these are the very concerns that torture the minds of our clients. They come to us for help with these agonizing issues and, if we are honest, we cannot help but admit our influence on them. In a very real sense we become proselytizers of our own morality. And that, it must be acknowledged, is a horrendous burden. God may be dead, but fifty thousand social workers have risen up to take his place!

DO CLIENTS SHARE SOCIAL WORK'S GOALS?

This is not our only problem with the voluntary client, however. Let us accept the premise that we are experts; surely, if we are not experts now, we will become so in the not-too-distant future. To the extent that we are experts we truly *do* know what is best for our clients—and for our voluntary clients at that. They come to us for help and we are then privileged to posit goals or outcomes to our endeavors. But would our clients share these goals or posit the same ones for themselves? Our client may want sexual restraint—we may offer a guiltless sexual license. He may want to forget—we may help him remember. He may want simplicity—we may offer complexity. He may want adaptation—we may offer autonomy. He may want a soft dream—we may confront him with a sharp reality. As experts we *do* posit goals: we study, we diagnose, we set a goal based on a diagnosis, and we work to that end in our treatment. We do, of course, consider what our client wants for himself, but that consideration is incorporated into the diagnosis; it is one more bit of data for us to take into account when we construct our own—usually private—objectives.

Physicians do the same thing. They know what is best and they know what a reasonable outcome may be. It would be a foolish physician who allowed his patient to make the prognosis and set the therapeutic regimen. It does not take many visits to the doctor to know that dignity is not a characteristic of the examining table; one's body is treated as an object. How much more undignified is it to have one's mind or thoughts or fantasies or dreams or hopes or needs treated as manipulable things? We may know what is best, but perhaps it is more in keeping with a tradition of decency to keep our knowledge and our prognoses to ourselves.

CAPITALIZING ON CLIENTS' HOPE

There is one final problem for social work, and this has to do with the nature of the therapeutic process itself. A great deal of evidence has accumulated by this time which suggests that the therapies stemming from a myriad different theoretical orientations have approximately the same efficacy.[4] These diverse orientations include the more traditional or primitive procedures of witchcraft, faith healing, magic, and other folk therapies. In many ways this accretion of evidence is quite remarkable; it concludes that in spite of some quite different technical procedures and rationales most patients get better and their improvement probably lies in what is common to all such procedures—the authority of the healer and the faith or expectation of the patient. What we do, then, is to capitalize on the gullibility of our clients: we are magicians who exploit their ignorance, their misery, their dependence, and their need. We do

---

[4] *See,* for example, Jerome Frank, *Persuasion and Healing* (New York: Schocken Books, 1961); and Ari Kiev, *Magic, Faith and Healing* (New York: Free Press of Glencoe, 1964). The classic paper on the disparate effects of therapy is by Hans J. Eysenck, "The Effects of Psychotherapy," *International Journal of Psychiatry,* Vol. 1, No. 1 (January 1965).

this, again, for their own good. Our intentions are honorable; we are not dabblers in black magic, but we are magicians nonetheless. Attention is called once more to the pitfall of self-deceptive language: a diagnosis in terms of libidinal energies, interaction patterns, and alienation may sound quite learned but is no more relevant to the outcome of treatment than is a diagnosis in terms of mana, possession, and juju. The shaman treats troubled souls much as we do—and quite as effectively. And he treats in the same way: he capitalizes on the desperate hope of his client.

If this assumption is correct we are again faced with an ethical dilemma: How far can we go in an exploitation of gullibility and desperate need? Shall we summon up our charismatic voice and lay hands on an ailing client if we have reason to believe it will help him? Do we deal in talismans and amulets? Some would say, "No, never—that is hypocrisy and fraud," but we are clever, so we support instead of charm; we modify defensive structures instead of burning candles; we offer interpretations instead of sacrificial goats.

All these considerations raise a basic question for the caseworker who must decide what things are permissible in the name of therapy. What means can be utilized to accomplish our ends—indeed, what ends are permissible for us to conjure? At this point professional integrity leads us to conclude: "I don't know"—but, surely, it is time to worry ourselves about these matters.

OUR BUSINESS IS WITH DIGNITY

But perhaps it is possible to offer a solution to our trouble or, at least, a direction in which we can move. It has been argued that any unsolicited treatment of clients is an affront. The consequence of this argument is clear: Social workers must get out of the business of dealing with involuntary clients, with people who do not want us. This is not out of sulk, but out of respect. It has also been argued that the treatment of even the voluntary client is shot through with ethical difficulties, but in these instances the client, in a sense, asks for it; he risks an intrusion into his ethical system. Social work's obligation with the voluntary client is to explicate these risks for him and to be careful and extremely critical of what we do.

But this was to be a paper on the dignity of man, and herein lies a wide and virgin domain for social work. There are in the world people who need us and want us. Confronting them is an array of frightful institutions and the inevitable tribulation that stems from human encounters. Let us join with these clients in a search for and reaffirmation of their dignity. Let us become their allies and champion their cause. Let us become mercenaries in their service —let us, in a word, become their advocates. There is no degradation in engaging the service of a mercenary; a mercenary is there to be used. Let our clients use us, then, use us to argue their cause, to maneuver, to obtain their rights and their justice, to move the immovable bureaucrats.[5] Social casework once had a marvelous tradition of advocacy. This writer would like to see us return to the best of that tradition, to see social caseworkers available to people who need an ally—an expert ally—who would advocate for them in this mad struggle of living. Our business is with people—not with organizations. And, above all, our business is with dignity.

---

5 There is no need here to discuss the role of advocate. This theme is covered elsewhere in this issue by Scott Briar, "Dodo or Phoenix? A View of the Current Crisis in Casework," *Social Work Practice 1967* (New York: Columbia University Press, 1967); and Irving Piliavin, "Restructuring the Provision of Social Services," pp. 34–41.

BY SAUL BERNSTEIN

Self-determination: King or Citizen in the Realm of Values?

PROBABLY SOME OF the most poignant inner searching among social workers has been and is around self-determination, which may be regarded as a technique, a fact, a cultural assumption, or a value. Many and apparently diverse meanings are attached to this concept. There is the deeply rooted sense on the part of social workers that building on the feelings and wishes of those served is essentially sound. On the other hand, many situations arise in which other considerations seem paramount. Just how determining should self-determination be? "Hard-to-reach" individuals, families, groups, and neighborhoods [1] throw up the question with force. They are not articulating requests for service. Under one concept of self-determination, we should leave them alone. The "hard-core family" on public assistance should receive the regular allowance to which it is legally entitled and nothing more, according to this position. The gang of teenagers creating aggressive mayhem should likewise be left to go its self-chosen way. Further illustrations could be multiplied, but it is more important to move on to the somewhat philosophic question rooted in and around the great idea of self-determination.

It seems helpful to proceed—evolutionary fashion—from the simple to the complex. I shall start with a kind of one-celled notion and develop the theme into a complex organism of values.

SELF-DETERMINATION NO. 1

The heart and extent of this concept is that we as social workers should help people to do what they want to do and not stimulate them to go beyond their wishes. Self-determination is the supreme value, and it maintains its top position in any hierarchy of values, including those in which there are conflicts. For the worker the situation is pure and clear: help the people served to do what they want to do. There is little or no conflict between the values of the client and the worker. The latter's function is entirely devoted to providing the means and opportunities for the fulfillment of the desires of the client.

This position is clear and internally consistent as long as self-determination is maintained as the king value, with all others subservient to it. The working and meditating

---

SAUL BERNSTEIN, M.S.W., is professor and head of the Group Work Department, Boston University School of Social Work, and on the staff of the Human Relations Center, Boston University, Boston, Massachusetts.

[1] Social work has no general term for the people it serves. Client, group, and community are commonly used. Clientele is perhaps an approach to generalization. In the "human relations field" there seems to be a growing use of the term client system. In this paper the term client will include individuals, families, groups, and communities.

Reprinted with permission of the National Association of Social Workers, from SOCIAL WORK, Vol. 5, No. 1 (January 1960), pp. 3-8.

hours of the worker are relieved of the tearing-apart kinds of conflict which beset devotees of other concepts of self-determination. But "Self-determination No. 1" is a simple soul who, if he ever existed, would not be helpfully related either to the practice of his profession or to the real world. There may be workers who sound as though they belong in this club, but usually one finds that questions bring forth many qualifications ("It depends," and so forth), so that the simple and pure notion of self-determination is soon lost. Essentially, however, this concept is basic and should not perish. Rather, it needs a special kind of company and context.

SELF-DETERMINATION NO. 2

Suppose we help a person do what he wants to do today, but tomorrow he wants the opposite. How do we know what he wants? By what he says? He may have been saying it for years without ever really acting on what he says. Ambivalence turns one straight path into at least two, going in different—sometimes opposite—directions. When a part of the client expresses a feeling and seems to reach a decision, the worker would be derelict if he moved quickly in this direction without devoting time, understanding, and skill to assessing whether this feeling and decision are in fact what the client wants, uncomplicated by other and even contrary wants.

Illustrations are common. A woman is so angry at her husband that she says she wants a divorce; as the situation unfolds, however, she shows much positive feeling and need for the husband, particularly if the worker is skillful in accepting her hostile feelings. A certain gang of girls made nasty remarks about a settlement house and everybody in it. They threw rocks at the windows, and unfortunately their aim was pretty good. Months later, after the worker had dealt with the girls and had come to know them well, she was convinced that the original hostile behavior was the method they used to ask for help from the agency,

without being able to put their need into words. Behavior was their language.

"Self-determination No. 2," then, recognizes ambivalence and nonverbal communication, and adds the dimensions of time and the worker's professional qualifications, so that the eventual decisions have increased stability, depth, and clarity resulting from some working through of conflicting feelings.

It is not always possible or even desirable to eliminate all conflict or ambivalence. Many situations have built-in and all-but-unresolvable conflicts. The client dealing with a chronically ill relative is doomed to mixed feelings. The unmarried mother is appropriately expected to be in conflict about the decision as to whether to keep or give up her baby. There is no satisfactory answer in the sense that it completely eliminates the appeal of the contrary decision or that no regrets will later be felt. People and life are not like that. But the contribution of the worker is around a new perspective on tense and mixed feelings. In assessing what the client wants and in helping him to achieve it, the aim is to take into full account the varieties of ambivalence and changes over time.

SELF-DETERMINATION NO. 3

Reality in its multitudinous forms enters the self-determination picture. It can be biological, as in principles of health. It can be economic, as related to a balanced budget (even installment buying requires that the payments be met). It can be legal, as in obeying laws. There are other forms of reality, but the essential point is the stubborn quality of it, which sets up rules and expectations not controlled by our clients, but which must be met by them. These factors narrow substantially the range of reasonable choices open to the client—and to us all. A man may want his public assistance allowance trebled and may be able to make a good case for the increase, but he is not the one who should or can make this decision. The same line of reasoning goes for bad health practices, illegal behavior, spending well beyond one's income, and the like. A frequent problem faced by social workers is that many of those we serve have so weak a grasp on reality that they become enmeshed in its retaliations, and the client thereby loses the opportunity to express his self-determination in matters appropriate for it.

Reality has a fixed and final sound which can distort social work diagnosis and functions. The assumption is too often made that the client meets role expectations, that he "adapts," "adjusts," to his physical and cultural setting. The latter is presumed to be right, or rigid, something that does not lend itself to planned change. This is a strange position in a world full of dramatic and large-scale social, economic, and political change. C. Wright Mills in *The Sociological Imagination* makes the effective point that "nowadays men often feel that their private lives are a series of traps." These are large-scale societal changes which individuals do not understand or control. The writer pleads for "sociological imagination," which grasps the connection between the inner life of the individual and the larger framework of society.

This orientation does not give the client of a public assistance agency the right to decide on the amount of his allowance, but it does suggest that various social aspects of his situation might be examined and changed. Perhaps the agency should offer larger amounts, perhaps he can be helped to become self-supporting; perhaps there is a need for new economic institutions which will employ him. A crucial criterion for social change is whether it will increase the opportunities for appropriate self-determination for many people.

Returning to the original point about reality: the kind of exercise of self-determination that disregards reality is full of fantasy—it is unhealthy and self-defeating. A good part of the function of the worker may be to help the client distinguish what is fixed and stubborn from what is open to his decision. Skill in diagnosis inevitably involves the sorting out of what is relatively fixed from what is relatively changeable. Wise strategy of helping people to change is based on concentrating on what is most flexible. The client may still decide to flout reality (as all of us do at times), but then at least he will be better prepared for the consequences. It may well be that we can do our best work at the stage when the wallop of reality has been felt. There are great learning opportunities in such crises.

SELF-DETERMINATION NO. 4

Almost always, other people are involved in the self-determination of the client. His sense of responsibility may encompass them in varying degrees. There are instances in which parents abandon their children, husbands desert their wives, the gang beats up an innocent victim just to express feelings. At the other extreme is the person who allows himself to be exploited by others so that he is not making for himself the kinds of decisions that are the right of every human being.

Self-determination is enmeshed in a complex network of social relationships which move the notion far from the simple level on which each client does what he wants to do, yields to his own impulses. Even Robinson Crusoe was not completely alone psychologically or culturally. The problem then is to find some principles that will offer guidelines out of this maze. One might be that the exercise of self-determination by one person should have minimum inconsistency with such exercise by others. This is a kind of equivalent to the golden rule and Kant's categorical imperative. It does not eliminate all conflicts—not necessarily a desirable goal—but it does provide a helpful framework and even rather specific guidance. As a homely illustration, it is not rare for a club of adolescent boys to plan an affair involving a girls' club without much consultation of the wishes of the latter. The group worker can easily make the suggestion to ask the girls about some idea that is being argued. A large area of potential contribution by social workers is embedded in this simple technique of consulting people who may be affected by a decision. How many times, in how many kinds of relationships, is this step omitted!

At the other extreme, with the person who is being exploited, the principle is rather different. The worker needs to diagnose carefully the areas in which legitimate self-determination is violated and then try to reinforce the client and influence the environment so that he may become able to enjoy the rights to which he is entitled.

With "Self-determination No. 4" we are in the midst of a question that has burned hot throughout much of human history. Egoism versus altruism is a kind of statement of it—a misleading one, I believe. Altruism asks for a kind of selfishness which seems unrealistic and unsound. Some of the worst acts of egoism have been perpetrated under the guise of altruism. The sense of selfhood is too deep, strong, pervasive, and instinctive to build on its elimination. More hopeful is the approach which recognizes and respects the drive toward selfhood in all of us, striving to help people understand how each can achieve identity only as he respects the same drive in others.

Many therapists have been so intrigued by the methods and orientation of their professions that they have overlooked the social dimension of self-determination. Individual dynamics are so intricate and fascinating that there is the temptation to regard them as all of significant reality. Perhaps subtly, the therapist is beguiled into an acceptance of what the client says about his social setting as being all that is important for the therapist to understand about it. The culture that has impregnated the client may be lost, as may be the impact of the client on the people he intimately affects. In just these areas social work has paid a price—the weakening of the "social" in its calling—for an otherwise fruitful dependence on psychiatry. It is a strange kind of ethic that elevates the desires of the client above those to whom he is socially related.

The "unseen audience" should not be victimized by therapy. Along with being an object of transference and other kinds of feelings, the therapist ought to be a kind of social conscience which helps the client relate his self-determination to all of those with whom he has relationships. To do anything else would contribute to social degeneration.

SELF-DETERMINATION NO. 5

Here we come close to the center of the human enterprise—to what, one may hope, distinguishes us from animals and from blind followers of instinct. A useful handle, much discussed in social work and elsewhere, is the process of decision-making. The infant when hungry "decides" to cry. It is a simple, instinctive reaction. A mature decision, at the other pole, is guided by rationality and intelligence. The learning of the ability to make the latter kind of decision is regarded by some as more important than the benefits which may accrue from any specific act of decision. Learning how to approach problems rationally is thereby elevated to the position of one of the most prized skills.

A whole flood of implications flows from "Self-determination No. 5." One is the growing concern about the probable consequences for oneself and for others from any given decision or action. Another is the need to attain sufficient perspective so that unconscious distortions and urges are kept at a minimum. Still another is the generation of a more or less conscious method for dealing with problems. In addition, there is the more thoughtful examination of previously assumed values. The list could be elaborated.

The content of intelligent decision-making has been given considerable attention by John Dewey and many others. The current human relations movement, with its ideologies and activities, is devoted to this end. In grand terms, it is the application of the scientific method to human affairs.

The social work client may be ready in

only modest and varying degrees to participate on these more rarified levels of human expression. Yet his self-determination takes on profundity only as he moves toward them. Each client needs our best diagnosis in terms of where he is and how far he can go, but the direction of change supported by the worker should be firmly derived from rationality. This may sound strange to those who strive so hard to understand all the perplexing irrationalities in people. But what is often overlooked is that the attempt to understand irrationality is essentially rational. Whatever concepts or constructs we may use to explain instinct-based behavior, they represent the struggles of intelligence to bring experience into some sort of order. The direction is clear.

The theme of freedom runs through this orchestration of the elements of self-determination. If one takes a pure and completely consistent deterministic position, self-determination is an illusion; it is simply acting in accord with controlling forces which may or may not be understood. In the Marxian context—*i.e.*, the idea that history is economically determined, especially in terms of class—the behavior of many of us would have to be considered a current and potent example of determinism; although that point of view leaves open the choice to join with the class that will presumably be victorious.

Social work is based on the assumption that people are free to make significant choices and that they can be helped to make better ones. But the attempt to use freedom to make decisions that are contrary to reality or largely irrational is self-defeating. Confusion rather than creativity flows from the disregard of facts and reason. Only as one takes account of the relevant factors does true freedom operate in decision making. Yielding to unexamined impulses is more a surrender to instinctive drives than the expression of mature self-determination.

This is not to claim that we are predominantly rational. Social work has dealt too much with raw ids to make this error. The orientation is rather to the effect that the forces within and outside of us should be recognized and scrutinized with whatever rational capabilities we have. To help in this process is a major function of the social worker. Insofar as this help is successful, the worker is enabling the client to reach toward "Self-determination No. 5"—a pretty high level of social functioning.

SELF-DETERMINATION NO. 6

The subtitle of this paper, "King or Citizen in the Realm of Values," raises the question of hierarchy or priority. It is hoped that what has been said makes clear that self-determination is *not* king, or a supreme value. The various qualifications and contexts are meant to show that the mere act or desire to act according to one's wishes is neither a final nor a complete basis for a professional point of view. Assuming this position, are we left in a kind of "it depends" vagueness as to which values rise above others in specific situations and in general? I think not. Value problems cannot be reduced to the simplicity or specificity of administrative charts which show clearly who is above whom, but there are meaningful patterns and points of reference.

Most basically, the supreme social work value is human worth, an enormous idea, probably the greatest discovery in human history. Perhaps it suffers from too frequent mention in social work without sufficient elaboration of its rich meanings. It is based only moderately on what people are; much more on what they can be. It applies not only to those immediately before the social worker, but also to every human being on this earth (we may yet need an interplanetary concept). The specific content of the human worth idea evolves with history. It has many facets: legal and civil rights, standard of living, freedom to develop potentialities, intellectual and artistic interests, and others.

With this supreme value, self-determination then becomes modified. If what the client wants will result in the exploitation of others or the degradation of himself, the worker should try to help him change his desires.

The steps suggested in this paper are meant to be criteria for judgments about self-determination which will help to place it appropriately in a hierarchy of values in any given situation. It seems more useful to approach the hierarchy question in this way (human worth at the top and self-determination subject to a set of criteria) than to attempt a rigid blueprint or chart. All this leads to the definite position that self-determination is *not* the king value, is not supreme in the realm of values.

CONCLUSION

While self-determination is not supreme, it is supremely important. Only through the rich utilization of this concept can we fully honor the human-worth value. This is in line with the best in democratic traditions. As we study and diagnose each situation, our concern should be for maximizing the choices for the people we serve, subject to the framework suggested above. Even with young children, there are appropriate matters about which they should be helped to make decisions. In an even more extreme example, the man in prison has many conditions imposed on him, but he might be helped to make his own decisions about jobs in the prison, recreation, what to do after he is released, and other matters. The point is that the value system of social work requires this maximization of self-determination.

In addition to its values, the methods of social work themselves require great stress on self-determination. People can be and are manipulated, but constructive changes which take root inside the person, group, or community usually need to be based on participation and consent. The Supreme Court decision on desegregation attempts to manipulate the environment—to eliminate by force the practice of discrimination in schools. It does not pretend to change the feelings of the prejudiced. Some have concluded that therefore this historic decision is useless or harmful. I do not agree, and think that over the long pull the lessening of discriminatory practices can and does lessen prejudice. In the legal and perhaps other power-packed arenas, it is often necessary to override the self-determination of some people for the sake of human worth. The alternative would be to wait for complete agreement, an impossible political goal on most issues.

In social action, then, social work adapts its concept of self-determination to the realities of the process of political change; but the great bulk of social work practice has internal change as its goal. Here we find that imposing, telling, or giving orders do not work well. Only as the client is thoroughly involved and comes to accept on deepening levels the process of change can our methods be effective in relation to our goals. We may not be able to produce research-based proof (although there is some) for this position, but it is supported by so much practice experience on the part of so many of us that we fully accept and act on it.

There is a deeper and weightier support for self-determination: its existence and potency is a fact. Social workers and other professionals may enable, stimulate, impose, and even use force, but what the client feels, thinks, and values is ultimately his private affair and more within his control than that of the professional. The delinquent can be forcibly placed in a training school, but he cannot be forced to change his notions of the kind of life he wants to lead. For this the inner boy must be involved, must decide to re-examine himself and to change. This is a very important reason for emphasizing so much the significance of the relationship with the worker. Through it our boy learns to trust and have confidence in the worker so that he is ready to share some of his precious inward self with a view toward changing it. Only the boy himself can make this decision. Without his consent we can probably modify his outward behavior; with it there is the opportunity for changes in inward values, an essential and basic purpose of social work.

BY JOHN J. STRETCH

Existentialism: A Proposed Philosophical Orientation for Social Work

■ Crisis or prevention—toward what should the orientation of social work as a profession be? To attempt to arrive at an answer, the author examines the tenets of the philosophy of existentialism. If one accepts existentialism, one accepts the existence of perennial crisis in our lives. And it is therefore in crisis management that prevention must be rooted. ■

ANTIGONE. I must go and bury my brother. Those men uncovered him.

CREON. What good will it do? You know that there are other men standing guard over Polynices. And even if you did cover him over with earth again, the earth would again be removed.

ANTIGONE. I know all that. I know it. But that much, at least, I can do. And what a person can do, a person ought to do.

—JEAN ANOUILH, *Antigone*
ACT 1, Sc. 1

THROUGHOUT HISTORY MAN has engaged in an endless search for a permanent and indisputable philosophy, one that will answer the fundamental questions: "What is the meaning of existence?" "What is life all about?" Contemporary man still asks these basic questions about his God, his world, and his self. Faced with the inadequacies of traditional religious answers, with the rapid changes in civilization that have made accustomed social institutions obsolete, and with the mounting realization of the awe-

JOHN J. STRETCH, Ph.D., is *Research Director, Social Welfare Planning Council, New Orleans, Louisiana, and Assistant Professor, Tulane University School of Social Work.*

some power he has over his world and the consequences for its survival inherent in relations among nations, man seeks a philosophy that will give relief to his growing anxiety and meaning to his life and to his world.

At the same time, the social work profession is experiencing serious internal doubts. No longer content just to do good, social work seeks assurance that what it does has meaning and significance beyond the confines of its own activities. Theories are being sought to give practice both justification and a reason for being.

Long accustomed to dealing with understanding and with feeling, social work now looks to rational science, which holds out the promise of knowledge. Experience, long the guide of the profession, must now give way to knowledge. The profession is uneasy, for although knowledge is revered and esteemed by modern man, to many social workers it calls forth a feeling of coldness, abstraction, and aloofness. Social workers seem much more at home with the term "understanding." Understanding is different from knowledge. The latter is an intellectual activity; the former, a feeling activity. Both seek a communion with reality but in different modes. Knowledge is

Reprinted with permission of the National Association of Social Workers, from SOCIAL WORK, Vol. 12, No. 4 (October 1967), pp. 97–102.

concerned with essential reality, with the abstract, universal, and ideal aspects of reality apart from particularities. Understanding is concerned with existential reality, with the concrete, particular, and imperfect aspects of reality in its contingencies.

Toward what should social work direct its energies? It has in the past dealt mainly with the handling of crisis, which demands understanding. But now, in these enlightened times, dealing with crisis must give way to concern with prevention. Guilt feelings are aroused over dealing solely with crisis. And prevention demands knowledge; it is easier to justify rationally. How can the everyday practice of social workers as they meet and deal with crisis be justified—as a "temporary" phase of social work?

This paper, through an explication of the philosophy of existentialism, will focus attention on crisis and its dimensions in an attempt to give philosophical substance to traditional and emerging social work practice and to offer justification for the profession to remain crisis oriented, at least in part.

FUNDAMENTAL TENETS

Existentialism has grown out of the conviction that what the future will bring cannot be known in advance. It cannot be computed in all of its multiple variations even with the aid of the most complex cybernetic device. It can only be faced in its totality instant by instant, individual by individual. Change is the only constant fact of existence. For the existentialist, reality assumes predominantly the character of becoming, of irregularity.[1]

In this unpredictable world in which nothing is preordained, man is faced with the necessity for constant decision-making. This fundamental characteristic of existentialism may be grasped in Kierkegaard's philosophical commitment to freedom and value as inherent in individual man: "Each individual is confronted with ethical choices which he alone can make and for which he assumes sole responsibility."[2] The act of choice does not terminate in that choice, since "every decision an individual makes is irrevocable and presents him with the necessity for subsequent decision."[3] Man alone realizes this intrinsic attribute of choice. He alone achieves freedom. He alone is faced fully with the consequences of freedom. For the existentialist, man is not only ultimately but totally responsible for his world. He shapes it by conscious design or by blind stumbling. Such is the awful power man has come to possess over his world that he finds to his horror that he now possesses the power to destroy it completely. In the end he may well destroy it, because he has lost the sense of his own human value.

Mass-mindedness is threatening to swallow up individual man and with him individual responsibility. The *I* and the *You* have become amalgamated into an impersonal *They* and in the process responsibility has altered. In our own times we have witnessed the state assume the moral sphere of the individual—Auschwitz and Buchenwald give testimony to the surrender of individual morality. As Jung states:

> The moral responsibility of the individual is . . . inevitably replaced by the policy of the State (*raison d'état*). Instead of moral and individual differentiation of the individual, you have public welfare and the raising of the living standard. The goal and meaning of individual life (which is the only *real* life) no longer lie in individual development but in the policy of the State, which is thrust upon the individual from outside and consists in the execution of an abstract idea which ultimately tends to attract all life to itself.

---

[1] Carl Jung, *The Undiscovered Self* (Boston: New American Library, 1958), p. 17.

[2] Frank Thilly and Ledger Wood, *A History of Philosophy* (New York: Henry Holt & Co., 1955), p. 579.

[3] *Ibid.*

The individual is increasingly deprived of the moral decision as to how he should live his own life, and instead is ruled, fed, clothed and educated as a social unit.[4]

Although his views of the welfare state are harsh, the lesson he is trying to put across does shine through. He senses a danger in reducing man to an abstraction, in this case what he terms the "social unit."

As a social unit [man] has lost his individuality and becomes a mere abstract number in the bureaus of statistics. He can only play the role of an interchangeable unit of infinitesimal importance. Looked at rationally and from the outside, this is exactly what he is, and from this point of view it seems positively absurd to go on talking about the value or meaning of the individual. Indeed, one can hardly imagine how one ever came to endow individual human life with so much dignity when the truth to the contrary is as plain as the palm of your hand.[5]

The real danger Jung would have us ponder is that individual man is being reduced to the level of a mass phenomenon. The bigger the crowd the more negligible the individual becomes. This realization seems more and more to be a fact of modern existence—a fact about which we are increasingly uncomfortable. Under these circumstances it is small wonder that individual judgment grows increasingly uncertain. Faced with seemingly irrational, uncontrolled fate, uncertain of his moral commitments (or if there are any such), modern man faces what has been described as the universal anxiety of our time.[6] This universal anxiety needs an explanation. Existentialism steps forth to offer one.

Heidegger, who posits that "the whole of human existence is permeated by a trag anxiety or anguish (*Angst*), induced by the sense of inevitability of death," emphasizes in his philosophy the element of risk in every decision and ultimately in all human action.[7] The interdependence of man on man followed to Heidegger's conclusion leads inevitably to pervasive uncertainty, since one cannot control the actions of others nor can one always exercise control over one's own actions. Fear associated with chance becomes dread.

Karl Jaspers, whose name is often associated with Heidegger's in the development of early existentialist thinking, likewise emphasizes in his philosophical writings the anxious, absolute responsibility inherent in man's unique freedom of choice. Jaspers is credited with having given existentialism its most lucid, articulate, and methodical formulation.[8] He considered that the basic philosophical explanations that man has evolved of his world were human responses of the individual faced with the inevitability of chance, evil, and death.

Summarizing, Thilly and Wood observe:

The significance of existentialism lies not in its contribution to technical philosophy, for as such it has little to say that has not been developed more lucidly, articulately and systematically by earlier philosophical systems, but rather, in its having given philosophical utterance to a pervasive mood of contemporary culture.

Existentialism is pre-eminently the philosophy of crisis; it has interpreted the whole of human, and likewise of cosmic existence, as a succession of critical situations . . . each fraught with danger and demanding for its resolution all the inner resources of the individual; each crisis gives rise to a new crisis requiring similar resolution. . . .[9]

Weiss has captured the existentialist ten-

---

[4] Jung, *op. cit.*, p. 24.
[5] *Ibid.*
[6] For a concise but insightful article on this subject *see* "The Anatomy of Angst," *Time*, March 31, 1961, pp. 44–51.

[7] Thilly and Wood, *op. cit.*, p. 581.
[8] *Ibid.*, p. 582.
[9] *Ibid.*, p. 584.

dency to juxtapose despair and hope:

> To be human is not only to live and grow, but to decline, to die or reach nonbeing. . . . How does man in his existence overcome this dread, this *"Sein zum Tode"* (Being unto death) of Heidegger's analysis? It is by affirmation of one's essential being in spite of desires and anxieties.[10]

Existentialism confronts the fundamental anxiety of everyday life and attempts to give it meaning by positing that man, precisely because he is free, is confronted with choices; the ultimate choice—plenary being—is unattainable because in the end man's being must give way to nonbeing. In this primary intuition of the possibility of man's eventual nonexistence despair is founded.

TWO MAINSTREAMS OF EXISTENTIALISM

How does man come to terms with the meaning of human existence? Whatever meaning it has is confirmed either through crisis or through communion. This distinguishes two mainstreams of existentialism: critical (crisis oriented) and social (communion or dialogue oriented).[11]

In order to follow these two lines of thought, attention must be shifted from existence as such to encountering existence. Attention to the meaning of existence must refocus on the human self in which existence is discovered, is intuitively known, and has its conceptual origin.

Critical existentialism examines the problem of ultimate nonvalue by means of the choice inherent in human freedom and concludes that peace and perfection are unattainable. Anxiety rules because reality is basically uncertain and under no lasting rational control. Without the certitude of knowledge or the sureness of ultimate value to guide man's actions, anxiety becomes overwhelming, penetrating every mode of human choice and palling man's existence.

> For if everything is possible nothing is determined and certain. And this experience of dread is at the same time man's awareness of his freedom—not the freedom to choose between good and evil but that more fundamental freedom which precedes and renders possible his commitment to a scale of values.[12]

This conception forms the basis for the crisis orientation of Kierkegaard and has been variously expanded and modified by other existentialist thinkers.[13] To explain man's quest for the ultimate fulfillment through and in life, existentialists must face the question of what the transcendent value is that makes experience meaningful and life worthwhile.[14] Existentialists who follow a critical bent, denying an answer to the question of ultimate meaning, see man as plunged into groping and despair. An exception is noted in Christian existentialism, which posits God as the synthesis of essence and existence (I am who am), and interprets man's anguish as a basic realization of his human imperfection and yearning for participation in the fullness of existence—his God.[15]

Atheistic existentialism starts from Neitzsche's premise that God is dead and man is god. The future is totally in man's fallible

---

[10] David Weiss, "The Ontological Dimension in Social Casework," *Social Worker* (Canada), Vol. 30, No. 1 (January 1962), p. 2.

[11] Helmut Kuhn, "Existentialism," in Vergilius Ferm, ed., *A History of Philosophical Systems* (New York: Philosophical Library, 1950), p. 407.

[12] *Ibid.*, p. 410.

[13] Walter Kaufman, ed., *Existentialism from Dostoevsky to Sartre: The Basic Writings of Existentialism* (Cleveland: Meridian Books, 1964).

[14] The rising tide of existential inquiry into the basic ethical issue of ultimate value has given birth to renewed interest in situational determinants of the moral act. *See,* for example, Joseph Fletcher, *Situation Ethics: The New Morality* (Philadelphia: Westminister Press, 1966).

[15] One of the most prominent of Christian existentialists is Gabriel Marcel. For an exposition of his branch of existentialism, *see* Eugene Fitzgerald, "Gabriel Marcel," in Frederick Patka, ed., *Existentialist Thinkers and Thought* (New York: Citadel Press, 1962), pp. 138–150.

and uncertain hands.[16] Jean Paul Sartre, the prototype of critical atheistic existentialism, boldly affirms that existence precedes essence.[17] Man exists but has no stable essence or nature.[18] His existence is defined by the act of the moment. Man can never predict his next act with certainty; he can never muster scientific conviction as to what he is becoming. Man is faced with built-in inequalities in existence yet he is and feels totally responsible for his actions. He must act, but he is never in full control of his total field of action. This lack of certainty finds expression in ontic anxiety.

Social existentialism focuses attention on the social genesis of the human person through an authentic communion of self with other. It draws attention to qualities that man acquires through social interaction instead of attending to what man is.

> The person, however, must not be understood as an isolated entity but as an ego in communication with an *alter ego*. As long as we deal with things which we measure, manipulate and subject to our dominion by use we are debarred from access to reality proper. The encounter with Being in its existential fullness takes place where, by an act which transcends the distinction between volition and cognition, we open ourselves in genuine communion to the import of another person.[19]

Social existentialism is concerned with man's potential for self-fulfillment through the social encounter in which the I and You blend into a communion of mutuality. Critical existentialism, on the other hand, emphasizes the crisis confrontation of the I with ultimate nothingness or nonbeing. In this intense confrontation man must either despair or find fulfillment—if not contentment—in a personal commitment, which may ultimately prove worthless. Social existentialism's concern is the resolution of social meaning for each man embodied in the collective search for fulfillment through life.

> Through the human encounter, each person who is "sent" or "thrown" into the world, fulfills his life in and through others with meaning and dignity. This is the way to achieve the courage to be, at the same time that the self is affirmed in and through the courage to be part of mankind.[20]

Inevitable exigencies, uncertainties, rapid social-structural changes, shifting values, and conflicting clamors for commitment force a recognition of life in which involvement cannot be put off. The meaning of life is to be unearthed in the social encounter.

APPLICATION TO SOCIAL WORK

There is common ground between existentialism and social work practice and belief. Social work has championed the right of each man to choose his own destiny and to assume responsibility for his choice. By social reform social work has sought to free man from inequality of opportunity and by using the "new psychology" from the 1920's to this day has worked to free man from the unconscious that influenced and restricted his freedom of choice.

Social work has taken a stand against those who would reduce man to a mere social unit in a totalitarian state. Social casework gives testimony to a professional position emphasizing the value of one person working with another to solve a problem that could not be solved as readily or possibly at all outside a relationship. The

[16] A renewed American theological interest in the implication of this position may be traced in Thomas J. Altizer and William Hamilton, *Radical Theology and the Death of God* (Indianapolis: Bobbs-Merrill Co., 1966).

[17] Kaufman, *op. cit.*, pp. 222–287.

[18] For a positive note on man's potential evolution *see* Pierre Teilhard de Chardin, *The Phenomenon of Man* (New York: Harper & Row, 1959).

[19] Kuhn, *op. cit.*, p. 414.

[20] Weiss, *op. cit.*, p. 5.

existentialist conviction that meaningful knowledge is found only in and through the encounter of person with person and by extension of person with group and group with group certainly finds sanction in social work. From social work's earliest efforts to bridge the gap between the rich and the poor through scientific philanthropy to the present emerging interest in international social work, the emphasis on the social encounter as a meaningful and more enduring method of social change can be traced.

The journal SOCIAL WORK has given evidence of the profession's perplexity regarding what stance it should assume with respect to what existentialists would term crisis. The racial issue in America has posed the problem of whether an intensive crisis situation (critical existentialism) or a more gradual social encounter (social existentialism) should be adopted to bring about social change.[21] The slower social encounter has not been productive of much interaction between Negro and white. However, since social work eschews violence and direct confrontation, it apparently cannot commit itself to a more direct—and drastic—social action philosophy. Consequently, social work may feel it has failed to evolve practical solutions to social problems. A critical appraisal of existential philosophy may offer a plausible rationale for action.

The concept that existence precedes essence affirms that there is no perfect world and there never will be one. If there can be no perfect world, it follows that there can be no perfect society or culture. Man will always seek but never achieve nirvana. It is the writer's conviction that social work has accepted this harsh reality, recognizing a perfectable world but not a perfect one.

Existentialism gives social work a system for viewing and ordering such a world. By its conception of man, existentialism affirms that social work should not abandon its emphasis on crisis intervention. If one accepts existentialism, one accepts perennial crisis. Prevention must be rooted in crisis management.[22]

The real problem of the meaning of existence for man cannot be resolved ideally. Each commitment of a person, a group, or a nation carries with it the ever present possibility of uselessness—it is a risk to commit oneself and it always will be. Social work as a profession must also face the danger inherent in risking itself through commitment to a system of values and programs of social change.

The real commitment of a person or a profession cannot be justified by trying to obtain a consensus that what one feels is right, good, and just is by everyone's standards right, good, and just. This ultimate validation must perforce come from within. Social work as a profession has been searching for other validators (usually in science) but has not found them.

Social work has been timid about its commitment to action and to using knowledge acquired through action. It has been overly concerned with whether it ought to impose its values and standards on the world through active social legislation. It has held back as a profession, hoping other professionals with more knowledge, or more theory, or more prestige—doctors, lawyers, sociologists, psychiatrists, legislators—would step forward and save the world. It has been reluctant to proclaim its values boldly as first principles of action. Existentialism would free the profession to do just that.

[21] See in Social Work Victoria Olds, "Freedom Rides: A Social Movement As an Aspect of Social Change," Vol. 8, No. 3 (July 1963), pp. 16–23; Leonard Simmons, " 'Crow Jim' ": Implications for Social Work," Vol. 8, No. 3 (July 1963), pp. 24–30; Joseph Golden, "Desegregation of Social Agencies in the South," Vol. 10, No. 1 (January 1965), pp. 58–67.

[22] Ego psychology is paying increased theoretical attention to the effects of successful crisis management in strengthening reality-adaptive ego-coping capacities. See Richard S. Lazarus, Psychological Stress and the Coping Process (New York: McGraw-Hill Book Co., 1966).

Robert B. Sinsheimer

The existential casework relationship

The therapeutic encounter is not
a special method of treatment but an attitudinal
framework within which the caseworker functions

Robert B. Sinsheimer is a social worker with
the Suffolk County Division of Children's
Services, Bay Shore, New York,
His article is based on a master's thesis submitted
to the Richmond School of Social Work,
Virginia Commonwealth University,
Richmond, Virginia, May 1968.

Social casework theorists and practitioners
appear to be largely oblivious of existential
philosophy and psychotherapy. It is my contention that selected existential concepts are
applicable to the client-worker relationship in
clinical practice. And in this article I shall
present a brief introduction to some of the
fundamental concepts of existential philosophy and therapy and set forth a construct
of the existential casework relationship. Although I am critical of the status quo in casework and plead that its theoretical position
be considered from a fresh point of view, I
am not advocating here the integration of
existential and traditional casework concepts
as the only possible basis of a valid theory for
casework.[1]

Existential philosophy

The term *existentialism* is derived from Soren
Kierkegaard's use of the term *existence* to

mean man's possibility of being himself by
realizing his potentialities to the full. Existentialism is a philosophy that has been described
as "an attempt to reach the inmost core of
human existence in a concrete and individual
fashion."[2] It is also a school of thought essentially concerned with the issues of human freedom, choice, and responsibility and with the
study of being.[3] Although it is not a new
philosophy, it has become popular in this
country only since World War II, largely
through the fictional works of Albert Camus,
Jean Paul Sartre, Eugene Ionesco, and Her-
mann Hesse, all strongly influenced by Fried-
rich Nietzsche, Martin Heidegger, Soren
Kierkegaard, and Martin Buber.

Blaise Pascal (1623–1662) was possibly the
first thinker to articulate the most basic and
problematic statement to which existentialists
have directed their investigations. "When I
consider the short extent of my life, swallowed
up in the eternity before and after, the small
space that I fill or even see, engulfed in the
infinite immensity of spaces unknown to me
and which know me not, I am terrified and
astounded to find myself here and not there."[4]

[1]The author acknowledges the advice and helpful
consultation of Professor Emanuel Tropp, who
supervised the thesis upon which this article
is based.

[2]K. Guru Dutt, *Existentialism and Indian Thought*
(Philosophical Library, New York, 1960), 2.

[3]Rollo May, The Origins and Significance of the
Existential Movement in Psychology, in Rollo May,
Ernest Angel, and Henri F. Ellenberger, eds.,
*Existence: A New Dimension in Psychiatry and
Psychology* (Basic Books, New York, 1958), 12.

[4]Blaise Pascal, *Pensées,* J. M. Cohen, trans. (Penguin
Books, Baltimore, 1961), 57.

SOCIAL CASEWORK, February 1969, Vol. 50, No. 2, pp. 67-73.

This statement poses questions involving the relation of man to the universe, the contingency of man's existence, and man's fearfulness when confronted not only with the fact of being but also with the possibility of ceasing to be. It has ramifications that concern the concepts of freedom and responsibility and the issue of choice and free will versus determinism.

Existential philosophy holds that man is a free agent who achieves his meaning through responsible choice and through the stance he takes toward life's pain and suffering. Although there are several major developments within this school of thought, all existentialist philosophers agree on the centrality of the concept of *Angst*—anguish, dread, or anxiety—as an emotion common to all mankind. Kierkegaard's monumental work deals with man's loss of freedom as he becomes deadened by absorption into the "universe of the immediate neighborhood" and experiences *Angst* through this egocentricity.[5]

Existential philosophy protests against the fragmentation of man, the search for underlying causal relationships in behavior, and a deterministic view of life. It protests against explanations, because in explaining, "the *man* disappears; we can no longer find *'the one'* to *whom* this or that experience has *happened*."[6] In essence existentialism seeks to restore man's sense of his wholeness.

Existential psychotherapy

Existential psychotherapy, which has been developed as a therapeutic method by psychiatrists and psychologists, is based on the use of both psychodynamic and existential concepts within the treatment relationship to effect change, restoration, or strengthening of personality functions. Existential psychotherapists operate on the following beliefs: (1) that man has the potential freedom to make choices in a responsible manner though this freedom may be impaired by inner conflicts or blockages in development; (2) that man can be helped to find meaning in life through

the liberation of his inner strengths; (3) that dignity is inherent in the human condition; (4) that man is a being in the process of becoming; and (5) that with help man may move to a higher level of authenticity.

In existential psychotherapy the therapist and the patient are obliged to regard each other with respect. The goal of therapy is the patient's achievement of a firm sense of wholeness and a fuller experiencing of freedom and autonomy with social awareness and social responsibility.

The therapist seeks not to grasp the whys and hows of the patient but to "grasp the patient in his reality."[7] The therapist sees the patient as a whole human being.

It is obvious, then, that existential therapists are opposed to society's and psychology's fragmentation of man. They are opposed to the adjustive psychologies seeking to force fragmented man into a harmonious relationship with a fragmented society. They are opposed to the modern objectivity that further fragments the patient through its assumption of the existence of mechanistic drives operating without regard to his essential humanity.

Existential therapists do not deny the insights of depth psychology. Rather they propose that one must understand man-as-being if any psychodynamic model is to have significance. One may know many things about a person and be able to fit him into one or more psychodynamic categories and yet fail to grasp the reality of this person as a human being.

Man is viewed as both *being* and *becoming*. Psychopathology is viewed as an arrest in man's ability to unfold his inner potentialities.

According to existential theory man's past is only a fragment of his being-in-the-world. Rather than attempt to explain the patient's history or its aberrations according to the teachings of any school of psychology,[8] the therapist tries to help the patient expe-

---

[5]Dutt, *Existentialism* ..., 12.

[6]Jean Paul Sartre, *Existential Psychoanalysis* (Philosophical Library, New York, 1953), 51.

[7]Rollo May, The Emergence of Existential Psychology, in Rollo May, ed., *Existential Psychology* (Random House, New York, 1961), 19.

[8]Ludwig Binswanger, Existential Analysis and Psychotherapy, in Frieda Fromm-Reichmann and Jacob Moreno, eds., *Progress in Psychotherapy* (Grune & Stratton, New York, 1956), 144.

rience his past as one part of his existence. This aim includes helping the patient take responsibility for what has happened to him in his past.[9] What is unconscious is viewed as an area of the patient's being-in-the-world of which he is not aware; it may constitute a limitation on the patient's ability to experience his complete being, but it is a psychic entity that *can* be experienced. Consequently, the fact of the patient's unconcious cannot be used to excuse him from his responsibility for doing, feeling, or thinking.

So-called intrapsychic conflicts are not explained by existential therapy as resulting from conflicts between the patient's id, ego, and superego. Rather pathology is viewed as a limitation in the patient's world-experiencing and world-disclosing possibilities.

The above paragraphs do not presume to offer a complete explication of existential therapy's concept of the patient; they serve only as brief statements of a few of the exceedingly complex formulations developed by numerous existential therapists. And the dynamic quality of existential therapy may arise from the fact that it does not have one central leader, but rather a large number of adherents who offer differing formulations.

Daseinsanalysis

Daseinsanalysis is a school of existential therapy closely allied to existential psychotherapy. Associated chiefly with Ludwig Binswanger and Medard Boss, it is a modified synthesis of classical psychoanalysis, phenomenology, and selected existential concepts.[10] Boss uses the term *Daseinsanalysis* to mean the "analysis of *Dasein.*" Translated literally, *Dasein* is "the being who is there." The characteristics of *Dasein* are being-in-the-world, primary comprehending, and luminating. Being-in-the-world is a concept inherent in many existential orientations. Primary comprehending is also termed *is-ness*; and this primary comprehending or awareness *is*

being. "Man . . . is a light which luminates whatever particular being comes into the realm of its rays."[11]

Daseinsanalysis seeks to analyze the being of the patient, to understand his limitations in world-relatedness and in world-disclosure, and to understand the totality of his inner and outer worlds. These worlds include the world of self-to-self, the world of self-to-other, and the world of self-to-things.

Phenomenology

Phenomenology is a system of philosophy, developed by Edmund Husserl, that emphasizes the direct experience of a phenomenon as it is given. Rollo May says of phenomenology that it is the "attitude of openness and readiness to hear."[12] A phenomenological orientation in psychology clears the mind of presuppositions and the tendency to project upon the patient the therapist's own theoretical framework. One who is attuned to phenomenology hears and sees the patient as the patient exists and attempts to plumb the depths of the experience with the patient to achieve an understanding of that patient as one who is implicated in being and becoming.[13]

With this brief summary of existential psychotherapy as a frame of reference, I shall now turn to a consideration of the therapeutic relationship in existential psychotherapy.

The existential therapeutic relationship

Rollo May has written that "any therapist is existential to the extent that . . . he is still able to relate to the patient as 'one existence communicating with another.'"[14] The existential communication between therapist and patient is known as an encounter, and in this discussion the existential therapeutic relationship and the encounter are considered to

[9]Erwin Straus, *Phenomenological Psychology* (Basic Books, New York, 1966), 65.

[10]Henri F. Ellenberger, A Clinical Introduction to Psychiatric Phenomenology and Existential Analysis, in May, Angel, and Ellenberger, eds., *Existence . . .* , 120.

[11]Medard Boss, *Psychoanalysis and Daseinsanalysis* (Basic Books, New York, 1963), 38 ff.

[12]May, The Emergence . . . , 26.

[13]Straus, *Phenomenological Psychology,* . . . 55.

[14]Rollo May, Contributions of Existential Psychotherapy, in May, Angel, and Ellenberger, eds., *Existence . . .* , 81.

be synonymous. The encounter is central to the conduct of existential therapy; it is the primary vehicle through which therapist and patient move together toward a higher level of authentic being.

Martin Buber's exposition of the concept of *I-Thou* and *I-It* relationships has formed the basis for many subsequent interpretations of the meaning of the encounter. Buber writes "The primary word *I-Thou* can only be spoken with the whole being. The primary word *I-It* can never be spoken with the whole being."[15] Richard Gotshalk has illuminated Buber's somewhat mystical statement in these words: "Whatever comes out of the world and into man's focus may come as *Thou* or as *It*, depending upon man's attitude. The *I* of the *I-Thou* is the whole being and the *I* of the *I-It* is the partial being. Within the *I-It* attitude, things in the world appear . . . as objects: something apart from man, not participated in by man and not participating in a present which is the filled moment of life. Within the *I-Thou* attitude, things appear as direct, and as immediate in their directedness, to the person in the present. They thus appear in a present, which insofar as the person gives himself to them wholeheartedly, is the real filled present of life. Things, then, appear within a relation of mutual giving and receiving, as over against one, yet affecting him and demanding of him a response."[16] Buber sums up his idea of therapy and of education in the succinct statement, "Healing, like educating, is only possible to the one who lives over against the other, and yet is detached."[17]

In the encounter an empathic exchange takes place whereby one not only looks at the other's world but also stands emotionally in the place of the other and subjectively feels the world as it is felt by the other without in the process losing one's own self. The subjective element of the encounter is of central importance. The transactions in an *I-Thou*

encounter occur between person and person rather than between role and role.[18] The participants in the encounter must detach themselves from their roles as doctor and patient; they must transcend these roles and communicate as one existent consulting with another existent.

Mark Stern describes two approaches toward psychotherapy: instrumental and sacramental. "The instrumental approach considers the patient's past as something to be overcome through emotional insight and regards his present as a problem to be resolved through learning how to adjust to reality. The sacramental approach considers the patient's past as worth respect, even though it may need to be transcended, and his present as an experience which can be transformed through concerned and appreciative confrontation.`. . . The therapist who reveres experience does not thus stand apart. He *accompanies* his patient to fulfillment. . . . The therapist stands witness to renewed emerging experience. . . . [The therapist] involve[s] himself in his patient's cry to be discovered." They journey together, and the therapist bears with "all that comes to be in the encounter."[19]

Paul Tillich considers acceptance within the therapeutic relationship to be the essence of healing. This acceptance must be between person and person; in it "the therapist comes alive to his patients as another significant person. . . ."[20] Moreover, the therapist, in effect, says to the patient: "Since I am still in process and my search is a continuing one, I invite you to join me in our common venture for meaning."[21]

Throughout the foregoing quotations there are some common threads that, taken together, form the essence of the encounter.

[15]Martin Buber, *I and Thou* (Charles Scribner's Sons, New York, 1958), 3.

[16]Richard Gotshalk, Buber's Conception of Responsibility, *Journal of Existentialism*, 6:1 (Fall 1965).

[17]Buber, *I and Thou*, . . . 133.

[18]Sidney Jourard, *The Transparent Self* (Van Nostrand Co., New York, 1964), 28.

[19]E. Mark Stern, Psychotherapy: Reverence for Experience, *Journal of Existentialism*, 6:279–86 *passim* (Spring 1966).

[20]Leif J. Braaten, Tillich and the Art of Healing: A Therapist's View, *Journal of Existential Psychiatry*, 4:9 ff. (Summer 1963).

[21]Hugh Mullan and Iris Sangiuliano, The Subjective Phenomenon in Existential Psychotherapy, *Journal of Existential Psychiatry*, 2:21 (Summer 1961).

The encounter is an active coming together of two participants. The therapist's subjective qualities are not denied or hidden behind a façade of inscrutability. He is *with* the patient on the common level of one existence responding to the existence of another human being. The encounter is characterized by love, the active caring and concern of one person for the other. It is an intersubjective phenomenon, a relationship of one subjective being to another subjective being. The two attempt to disclose themselves authentically and to merge with one another momentarily while simultaneously maintaining their own identities.

William Kloman writes: "The subject-object relationship which Sartre sees as the basic reality of human contact, and which describes most relationships grounded in the competitive ethic, is wholly inappropriate to the communicative mode of existing-with-the-other. Only in subjective relatedness with another can the personality be a person rather than a thing."[22] Acting as a bridge between reality and unreality, the existential therapist helps the patient identify concepts of self-to-self, self-to-other, and self-to-world that are not real, valid, or free from distortion. He helps the patient objectify that which exists only on the subjective level. However, both patient and therapist are subjective in that they attempt to share an involvement that is intensely human and personal. In short the therapeutic encounter is not a special method of treatment, but rather an attitudinal framework within which the therapist functions.

The existential casework relationship

Casework has experienced the hazards of embracing and adopting theory from another field in its wholesale commitment to psychoanalytic theory in past decades. There may be hazards of equal import in embracing existential concepts without acquiring a clear understanding of their meaning and relevance for casework practice. Today it is a sign of being modern to be "existential." Un-

fortunately adherence to a theoretical position tends to take on the emotional garb of commitment to a religion or cult, the members becoming committed to the "true" teaching of their school of thought and quite oblivious to questions of relevance and validity. Existential theory at the moment is in a state of flux and does not have an enshrined leader; it has not found its Freud. There are as many schools of thought as there are theoreticians. This leaves the practitioner who would like to take an existential position with the problem of choosing among many theories, with no assurance that his choice is best. To be truly existential, however, the practitioner must make a choice; he cannot deny his existential freedom.

Given this circumstance, it is pertinent that the existential caseworker does not view his client as a client. One of the definitions of client is *dependent,* or, perhaps, *follower.* And if there is a follower, there is necessarily a leader—one who can show the way. The relationship between follower and leader implies definite roles and expectations that the leader has superior knowledge or competence and that it is incumbent upon the follower to act as a believer and to be led. The existential caseworker sees his consultee as a fellow being; both worker and consultee must divest themselves of any masks that distort their true positions as two existents communicating with their whole beings. The relationship between the consultant and the consultee is between person and person, though each has a specific function. The consultant sees his consultee as a person engaged in the unending task of becoming, and the relationship is one of two persons moving together toward a higher level of authenticity and meaning for the benefit of the consultee.

The consultee is not viewed within the framework of any theoretical system that seeks to classify symptoms or illness or posits a system of behavior based on causality or determinism. To turn the consultee into an object by the application of a theoretical system is the antithesis of an existential approach. The reduction of the consultee to a mass of psychic mechanisms or drives serves to fragment his being and militates against any possible chance of restoring him to

---

[22]William Kloman, Aspects of Existential Communication, *Journal of Existentialism*, 6:64 (Fall 1965).

wholeness. The existential worker does not deny depth psychology, but rather insists that it has meaning only within the context of the consultee's total being-in-the-world.

The consultee's problems are considered to be the result of limitations in his ability to experience his self and his existence in their wholeness. Problems result from blockages in the consultee's world-disclosing potentialities—his capacity for opening himself to experiential and perceptual possibilities and for disclosing and making known his true self. His problems result in his not being able to unfold or open himself, and thus his world-view and self-view are distorted; his openness is limited and he cannot experience his existence as real.

The existential worker sees the consultee as living in three interlocking worlds: self-to-self, the inner world; self-to-other, the interpersonal world; and self-to-object, the world of things. The existential worker is interested in each of these worlds, and through the encounter he seeks to plumb their depths.

The concept of the inner world is somewhat analogous to the psychoanalytic concept of intrapsychic phenomena. But existentialists prefer to use the term inner world, or *Eigenwelt*, since it obviates the classical analytic model of physical energy. Blockages in the consultee's perception and experiencing of his inner world profoundly affect his concept of self and his ability to experience I-ness. To this extent the inner world affects the consultee's interpersonal world, or *Mitwelt*. The interpersonal world is the realm of social functioning, with which the caseworker has long been concerned and in which social work has carved its special niche. An existential worker sees distortions or blockages in either the inner or the interpersonal world of the consultee as barriers to his movement toward authenticity and is therefore deeply concerned with both. The world of objects, or *Umwelt,* concerns the relation of the consultee to the physical world. An interesting consideration is the extent to which the consultee becomes lost, entrapped, or swallowed up in the *Umwelt* to the exclusion or limitation of his ability to experience the *Mitwelt* or *Eigenwelt*. The consultee exists simultaneously in these three interlocking worlds,

and he may be afflicted by blockages or distortions in relation to any one or all of them. The removal of these blockages or the correction of distortion emanates from what transpires within the relationship between consultant and consultee. Problem-solving and true growth take place as a result of the dynamic interplay of forces within the consultation that serve to liberate the consultee's potential strengths.

It has been said that the consultant views the client, or consultee, as a fellow being with whom he is engaged in a mutual journey toward problem-solving, personality growth, and a higher level of being and meaning. Should one not ask, however, whether the professional training and competence, the expertise, of the worker is not a factor: Are consultant and consultee unequal by the very definition of their relationship? The answer to the question is implicit in the theory: By virtue of the consultant's experiencing of himself, his own tortuous movement toward self-understanding and authentic, spontaneous being, his own knowledge of the pain involved in the journey to selfhood and the resolution of his own emotional blockages and distortions, he is able very humbly to come together with the consultee as one human being existing with another. His professional training and his own struggles help him to help the consultee. He must have insight into his own inner self as well as into his professional self, and he must be engaged in a continuing effort toward liberation and self-expansion. Consultant and consultee are equal as human beings; they are similar but not equal in the professional encounter.

The professional consultation is an experience of communion, an intimate sharing of the consultee's experience. The consultant experiences the consultee "as if" he were the other; in other words, a high degree of empathy is involved. The consultee, on the other hand, does not experience the consultant as if he were the other. But to be effective, their relationship must not lose the "as if" quality; both must maintain their own identities.

The caseworker who has assumed the existential attitude seeks to know and experience the inner world of the consultee and to see and experience the consultee's world-view. The interpenetration and intersubjectivity of the experience of communion make the consultation a subjective, rather than an objective, phenomenon. It is a "we" experience. It is designed to help the consultee develop problem-solving ability that results from increased personality growth, an increased sense of self, that flows from and is a result of the dynamics of the consultation. The emphasis is on the immediacy of the present live moment because it is only the present moment that is available within the consultation—only the present moment from which the past can be viewed retrospectively and the future anticipated.

The consultation is an experience in authentic self-disclosure in which the consultee opens himself as a patient and the consultant opens himself as a person, in the hope that both will grow as self-disclosing, world-experiencing people. In the secure, intimate climate of the consultation, each is free to be himself. Each may shed the masks of daily life and experience the exhilaration and joy of being able safely to risk an open confrontation with another. From the confrontation comes greater strength with which to cope with the daily sorrows that beset every man.

In the immediacy of the consultation the consultant must maintain an open attitude, a sacramental approach. He must rid himself of preconceived dynamic formulations and ready-made diagnostic labels. To interpose abstract formulations reduces the consultee to an object. And the most important element of the consultation is the element of love. Love characterizes the consultation and sets it apart from other forms of therapeutic relationships. Love is the active caring and being concerned for the other. In love, two become one and yet remain apart. This is not erotic love nor is it the so-called transference and countertransference of psychoanalytic theory. The regard of each for the other is taken simply for what it is in reality. To the extent that the consultee is limited in his ability to experience his existence as real, so too may he be limited in his ability to experience love. The relationship does not necessarily begin with love on the part of the consultee; but the nurturing quality of the relationship, the ability of the consultant to give active care and concern, does encourage an enlargement of the consultee's ability to experience love.

In sum, the therapeutic consultation is composed of (but not limited to) a communion, an active coming together, an experience in continuing, authentic, self-disclosure and love.

Through the consultee's being himself and experiencing himself in the immediacy of the present moment within a safe relationship characterized by love, true growth in personality will take place. And he will gain increased strength with which to cope with the vicissitudes of life and will more deeply discover the wellsprings of his own existence. The existential caseworker focuses on those problems of a psychological or social nature appropriate to the field of social work. At the same time he does not neglect the understanding he must have of the consultee as a being who is uniquely human. With the growth and healing that come about and with his problem-solving ability enhanced, the consultee's ability to grapple with the myriad daily tribulations of contemporary human existence is strengthened. Most important, through the work done in the encounter, he moves toward the never attainable goal of existential authenticity and meaning.

Education for practice with minorities

by John B. Turner

During the past few years social welfare and social work have been increasingly faced with overt expressions of the racial and ethnic consciousness that presently grips America.[1] Therefore, two issues confront social work education: (1) how to equip social workers with the knowledge, skills, and attitudes that will enable them to improve the status of minorities and (2) how to attract more minority-group students into social work education. Schools of social work must bear the major responsibility for recruiting minority students and faculty and preparing all students to work competently in this area.

Given the sensitivity of many social workers to ethnic issues and the special activities of the Council on Social Work Education, especially with regard to accreditation standards, most schools of social work probably are already engaged in efforts to make their schools more responsive to ethnic concerns.[2] The range of responses is wide, however. Some schools limit their efforts to "handling" a local campus or community situation rather than adopting a broader educational approach to minority-majority power relations. Other schools limit their approach to a more abstract view of ethnic status and relations, ignoring the existence of pressing ethnic concerns within the agencies and communities in which their students are being educated.

TOOLING UP FOR CHANGE

To be responsive to the difficulties faced by racial and ethnic groups, an educational institution's efforts must be comprehensive, systematic, and sustained over time. Such

---

[1] John B. Turner, "Racial and Other Minority Groups," *Encyclopedia of Social Work*, Vol. II (New York: National Association of Social Workers, 1971), pp. 1068–1077.

[2] Among the Council on Social Work Education's activities are the Commission on Minority Groups, which sponsors several special task forces on the American Indian and Asian, Black, Chicano, and Puerto Rican Americans; publication of five bibliographies on minority groups; and the publication of a casebook for group relations practitioners (Jack Rothman, ed., *Promoting Social Justice in the Multigroup Society*, 1971).

Reprinted with permission of the National Association of Social Workers, from SOCIAL WORK, Vol. 17, No. 3 (May 1972), pp. 112-118.

a response should involve the school's mission, its curriculum, students, faculty and staff, and cooperating institutions. For some it may be a difficult and even painful step, but all schools must make the commitment to educate all students. They must be concerned, relevant, and more effective with regard to the differential socioeconomic status of minority groups. The importance of consistency in response throughout the educational enterprise cannot be overstated.

The policy implications of education for ethnic practice with regard to all aspects of the school's mission and educational programs should be examined and acted on by the faculty. If the school has an advisory committee or board or other related policy-setting groups within the school or university, they too should be involved in developing and sanctioning such policies. The composition and deliberations of these groups should reflect appropriate representation of minority concerns.

At a minimum the school's policies should seek to (1) clarify educational goals and programs, (2) make explicit professional and staff personnel and employment policies, and (3) specify student recruitment, admission, and support objectives.

Appropriate guidelines should be developed for use by faculty, staff, students, and cooperating agencies, and administrative procedures should be established to facilitate compliance and developmental feedback. The implications of policies for resource allocations should be made explicit.

It is difficult to single out any one component of a school as being more important than another. But the faculty's centrality in developing and operationalizing the school's mission is indisputable. By its composition, promotion patterns, choice of activities, and formal and informal behaviors, the faculty conveys to all the extent of the school's concern.

Employing minority faculty is an obvious first step. Both the Council on Social Work Education, in its accreditation standards, and government regulations, when federal funds are involved, require such action. A realistic problem has been the shortage of minority persons who are interested and have the formal educational qualifications to teach. Thus the following specific responses by the schools are necessary: (1) developmental recruitment, (2) willingness to pay a significant portion of the cost of teacher preparation, (3) willingness to employ minority group members at senior as well as junior levels, with appropriate supports for upgrading, (4) employment of more than token numbers of minority faculty, (5) reeducation of existing faculty about their roles in supporting employment of minority faculty, and (6) developing university administration support for employment of minority persons. These responses are not meant to define conditions that must be satisfied before employing minority faculty; they are responses that are necessary if the schools' efforts are to be sustained and reasonably successful.

RECRUITMENT PLANS

Developmental recruitment suggests that a school must have a recruitment plan that not only is aggressive and competitive with other recruitment efforts, but offers the recruit realistic opportunities to continue his preparation through advanced study, short-term seminars, participation in research projects, tutorial arrangements, and the like. Such a plan should allocate money to support faculty participation in such activities. It means recruiting people who have the potential for growth and upward career mobility through university hierarchies. Schools must also avoid concentrating their efforts on employing minority faculty at junior levels, especially if they clearly will remain frozen at these levels.

How many minority faculty should be employed? Using what criteria? Which minorities should be employed? It is difficult to find a universally accepted formula for answering these questions. One thing seems clear, however: the number of minority faculty employed must be above that defined as tokenism by interested parties. In most situations, except perhaps when the faculty is extremely small, one minority faculty member is simply insufficient.

For the time being, at least, two guides

> *"Tradition and history have made . . . ethnic and racial justice an inextricable part of the more general problem of social justice. The curriculum must make this connection clear to the student."*

appear to be relevant in determining which minorities should be hired: the composition and backgrounds of the student body and the composition of the population within the training community. The important thing for schools to remember is that the presence of able and promising minority educators at all levels is better than a thousand statements of intent.

WHO HAS THE RESPONSIBILITY?

The burden of operationalizing the school's commitment cannot be the exclusive responsibility of minority faculty. It must be shared by the entire faculty and the administration. To this end there must be agreed-on plans to pursue the definition, understanding, and instruction of relevant and useful solutions and remedies to problems created by America's treatment of minority groups. Experience indicates that most faculty members, even the more enlightened, need to reeducate themselves about their attitudes and behaviors. This is concomitant to tooling up the school to be more responsive. Administrative and faculty sanction is often necessary to provide adequate opportunities for this type of reeducation.

Few will dispute the desirability of having students from all minority groups. However, once again there are no universally accepted guidelines for establishing minimum enrollments. Frequently the goal is stated in terms of numbers that reflect the size of social service target populations in the geographic areas served by the school through its graduates, as well as the percentages of socioeconomically disadvantaged members of ethnic groups. Practically speaking, it appears that for most schools the number and makeup of minority students who apply for admission will be partly based on the ethnic makeup of the proximate geographic areas, since costs of education will be an important factor for many ethnic students in their choice of a school.

Among the several factors that must be taken into account in acquiring and maintaining adequate ethnic representation among students are (1) developmental recruitment, (2) adequate tuition and stipend support, (3) a climate of acceptance, and (4) educational programs perceived as relevant to ethnic concerns. In this context, developmental recruitment suggests a stronger reaching out, not merely to college seniors but to young adults who may be working in human service programs, college freshmen, and high school students. The latter group is particularly important with regard to ethnic groups whose college populations are still small.

For minority students who are ready for admission, the strongest attraction will be the school's ability to provide scholarships. A closely related factor will be the school's ability to help out-of-town students find decent housing in a nonhostile environment. In addition, students may need group and individual counseling or tutoring with regard to academic programs as well as cultural and class relations. The importance of the quality of relationships between students and faculty cannot be overstressed. Faculty must learn to be sensitive and responsive without being patronizing, to identify without losing their own identity, and to communicate in terms other than those that they alone have set.

It is quite likely that for a considerable time to come minority students will want to organize themselves. The school can view the existence of such groups or caucuses as a threat or as a potentially positive influence in the learning and teaching transac-

127

tion. It is also of utmost importance that the school be prepared to assist students who have no ethnic and racial identification to function comfortably in a multiethnic and racial context. A major part of this objective will be met in student-to-student interaction.

Minority students will be intensely interested in whether the curriculum is relevant to their concerns. They will want the opportunity to discuss and judge for themselves and have an input. The nature of their input may well change from year to year, from subgroup to subgroup, and from ethnic group to ethnic group. However, it is essential that the faculty accept its responsibility and initiative in designing and implementing curricular responses to ethnic concerns.

CURRICULUM

If the faculty is central to implementing the school's mission of educating students for work with racial and ethnic groups, the educational program—the curriculum and its format—is the medium through which that mission is accomplished. What content should be required for all students? What should students learn about all racial and ethnic groups? What special content should be taught to those students who are especially interested in working for racial and ethnic justice? Do learning objectives differ between students with and without ethnic and racial group identities? One way of identifying curriculum content is to specify worker performance—i.e., what should a worker be able to do in behavioral terms? It would be useful if practitioners, educators, and consumers as well could develop ongoing collaboration to devise such a statement on worker performance. The author suggests that in addition to the core expectations of social worker performance, all workers should be able to do the following:

1. Recognize racist policies and acts, individual or institutional, whenever they occur and know the facts about racial and ethnic injustice, its causes and consequences for human status, dignity, and society.

2. Bring racist practices to the attention of those who have the professional responsibility and the potential for stopping such practices.

3. Commit whatever resources they have at their administrative disposal to change or redesign policies, procedures, and services that are racist in orientation or consequences, intentionally or not.

4. Respond constructively and instrumentally to minority- or majority-group efforts that are intended to eliminate racism.

Social workers who specialize in minority-majority problems should be able to do the following:

1. Interpret and work constructively with norms, family patterns, leadership patterns, communal organization, and other cultural patterns of minority groups receiving major professional service. These factors include patterns of self-help among members of a specific minority group and how they respond to authority, stressful situations, and dependency.

2. Distinguish between behavior that is distinctly culture based and behavior that tends to be a function of class status.

3. Design and implement organizational activities that will help minority persons improve their status and help majority groups eliminate racist policies and practices. Workers should also be able to help both groups achieve racial, ethnic, and social justice.

4. Provide technical assistance in relevant areas such as economics, justice, education, health, family, and child development.

5. Provide technical assistance to bring about appropriate coalitions among minority groups and between minority and majority groups to achieve common objectives that neither can achieve effectively alone.

6. Translate minority groups' needs and problems into appropriate political and economic objectives.

7. Assist minority and majority groups to engage political structures and processes appropriately and effectively to achieve needed resources and policies.

8. Assist minority and majority groups to engage economic structures (public and

> *"The curriculum must not ignore or downgrade the importance of working with white majority groups."*

voluntary) appropriately and effectively to achieve needed resources for economic development and employment.

9. Provide technical assistance to minority groups to help them develop the political solidarity and discipline required to select and carry out political strategies and tactics.

10. Help political leaders use their political power to meet the legitimate social needs of their minority constituency.

11. Utilize administrative and legislative procedures to help minority group members obtain their rights and needed services.

Educators and students of various racial and ethnic groups generally agree that curriculum modifications are indeed necessary. However, they do not agree on the extent and nature of such modifications.

Van Til suggests that society's responses to complex social problems are characterized by five stages: missionary zeal, simple answers, practices that are promising, research, and the quest for desegregation and integration.[3] It may be that social work education is emerging from the simple-answer stage with regard to curriculum and is struggling to find some promising practices. The following is a brief discussion of some areas of curriculum content, issues, and questions that are related to worker performance.

SOCIAL JUSTICE

Tradition and history have made problems of ethnic and racial justice an inextricable part of the more general problem of social justice. The curriculum must make this connection clear to the student, for he who fights for one must be committed to fight for both.

The curriculum must also help students understand that the way various life-chance systems work in this country leads systematically and repeatedly to unjust consequences for the poor, uneducated or undereducated, and racial and ethnic minorities. For example, the curriculum must help students understand how institutions behave with regard to (1) hiring, upgrading, and firing practices, union apprentice procedures, lending and investment practices, and merchandising, franchising, and pricing practices, (2) pretrial and court practices in determining guilt and innocence, establishing punishment for violation of laws, and administering the laws differentially, (3) determining the distribution, costs, and administration of health care resources, facilities, and services, (4) educational practices with regard to selection, assignment, and performance expectations of teachers, curriculum content selection and administration, class and school size, and student performance expectations, and (5) determining who is eligible for social agency help and under what conditions, what help is to be given, how, for how long, and for what purpose.

Today there is much talk about an *open* society—a society of plural cultures. The struggle for satisfactory ethnic and racial minority-majority arrangements has caused some people to question or reject the concept of ethnic and racial integration at a time when many have just begun to support the idea. Others have become proponents of organized ethnic and racial solidarity as a necessary requisite for achieving and maintaining social justice. Still others seek a more complete separation of ethnic and racial groups into relatively independent socioeconomic-political units.

Forced segregation and voluntary separatism appear to have much in common and thus may be rejected by many. On the

---

[3] William Van Til, as described in Maxine Dunsee, *Ethnic Modification of the Curriculum* (Washington, D.C.: Association for Supervision and Curriculum Development and National Education Association, 1970), pp. 38–39.

other hand, the concept of integration has proved so impotent in its impact on racism that doubts are raised in the minds of the most ardent believers.

Given the multiethnic and racial composition of American society, what would ethnic and racial relations be like if racism could be eliminated? Perhaps an even more meaningful question is: What must such relations be like if we are to move more decisively toward eliminating racism? What must be learned about the impact of social class and other patterns of inclusion-exclusion and exploitation? Perhaps more important, what is to be taught about how to eliminate such practices?

Curriculum designers must decide what is to be taught about separate, integrated, and pluralistic structures, what conditions must be satisfied if an open society is to be created, what subgroup requisites, norms, and political and economic requirements must be satisfied, and how these conditions are to be brought about. Social work education must deal with the related functions of social work and the concomitant roles that social workers should be educated to perform.

Students should have an opportunity to become knowledgeable about the cultural symbols and patterns, community norms and organization, traditions, family patterns, decision-making behavior, and sex and age roles of their own as well as other ethnic or racial groups. Courses should deal with the ways in which minority groups have been politically and economically exploited and the consequences of this exploitation. In addition, they should cover individual and group coping behavior. Material should also be included about minority leaders and their social and intellectual ideas.

An important issue related to content concerns language and communication skills. As bilingualism increasingly becomes the norm, students should be encouraged to develop proficiency in a second language if it is relevant to their career goals. For some students, the goal may be to communicate across educational and class lines—rather than to speak a foreign language.

Thus the curriculum must deal with three distinct educational needs: (1) the need of the minority student to have a systematic and in-depth knowledge of his own group, (2) the need for all students to have basic information about the major ethnic and racial groups in America today, and

"It is unlikely that the more fundamental goals of ethnic and racial justice can be achieved without the white majority's collaboration and initiative."

(3) the need of the minority-majority problem specialist for more in-depth knowledge about any minority group he expects to work with.

Hopefully, students will increasingly have the opportunity to learn about their racial and ethnic heritage at the undergraduate level, if not earlier. At the present time, however, graduate schools must assume some responsibility in this area.

STRATEGIES FOR CHANGE

Whose responsibility is it to end ethnic and racial injustice? Who has a stake in bringing about racial and ethnic egalitarianism? The immense changes that have occurred in racial and ethnic relations over the past ten years seem attributable largely to the self-interested activities of minority groups. Nevertheless, it is unlikely that the more fundamental goals of ethnic and racial justice can be achieved without the white majority's collaboration and initiative.

This fact should not obscure the need for minorities to take action within and on behalf of their respective groups and work with each other and white majority groups. The curriculum must not ignore or downgrade the importance of working with white majority groups. All four arenas of action are required; thus the curriculum must include the social psychology of white persons' responses to racial and ethnic minorities' struggles as well as the social psychology of various minority groups. Not only is there a role for social work with minority groups, there is an equally important function and role with white majority groups.

Social work interventions must be incisive and sustained with respect to strategic objectives that improve the life chances of racial and ethnic group members in significant ways. Some of these goals are provision of stable and sufficient income over time; random distribution of minority persons throughout the social institutions that control and confer status, opportunity, and responsibility; and development of the capacity for instrumental action by minority groups in their own behalf.

What is suggested here is that social work interventions must deal not only with methods of working with people, but must exercise equal competence in substantive issues of economics, politics, education, justice, housing, health, and mobilization of group capacity. The approach cannot be a "welfare" orientation. Its objectives must be developmental systems change and social rehabilitation.

If curriculum reform is to occur, schools will need to prepare class and field teachers. First, faculties must learn new subject matter with regard to substantive as well as methodological areas. In addition, white middle-class interpretations of individual and group behavior must be revised. Schools must also help teachers to change their attitudes and behavior. For example, how can a teacher learn to think of ethnic and racial groups other than as problems? How can he learn to handle the transactional problems with students that will develop in a multiethnic and multiracial student population?

CONCLUSION

Graduate schools of social work must face squarely the need for major curricula, faculty, and student changes, rather than merely tinker with the educational enterprise. Those who are responsible for making these changes must be more flexible, encourage greater creativity, look for alternative ways of meeting standards, and discard requirements that are no longer relevant and only block access to learning by racial and ethnic minority students.

Preparation for practice that supports and reinforces in its totality a concept of a multiracial and ethnic society will initially be threatening to some faculty and students and perhaps the institution. Therefore, the school must be prepared to back up its intentions consciously by steadfast and aggressive policy implementation and resource allocation. The task is too large for any school to tackle alone. Thus it will be necessary for schools and agencies to share their successes and failures and their brainpower and other resources if they are quickly and successfully to prepare professionals who are committed and able to help bring about social justice.

The racial factor in the interview

by Alfred Kadushin

Ethnicity, broadly speaking, means membership in a group that is differentiated on the basis of some distinctive characteristic, which may be cultural, religious, linguistic, or racial. The nonwhite experience in America is sufficiently differentiated so that race can be regarded as a specific kind of ethnicity. Although the term nonwhite includes Mexican-Americans, American Indians, orientals, and blacks, this article on the racial factor in the interview is almost exclusively concerned with black-white differences, not only because blacks are the largest single nonwhite minority, but because most of the descriptive, clinical, and experimental literature concerned with this problem focuses on blacks.

The black client often presents the interviewer with the problem of socioeconomic background as well as differences in racial experience. Although the largest number of poor people are white, a disproportionate percentage of the black population is poor. Hence the racial barrier between the white worker and black client is frequently complicated further by the class barrier—white middle-class worker and black lower-class client. However, the exclusive concern here is with the racial factor, i.e., the differences that stem from the experiences in living white and living black.

THE PROBLEM

Racial difference between worker and client is an ethnic factor that creates problems in the relationship and the interview. Understanding and empathy are crucial ingredients for an effective interview. But how can the white worker imagine what it is like for the black client to live day after day in a society that grudgingly, halfheartedly, and belatedly accords him the self-respect, dignity, and acceptance that are his right as a person or, more often, refuses outright to grant them to him? How can the worker know what it is like to live on intimate terms with early rejection, discrimination, harassment, and exploitation?

A relaxed atmosphere and comfortable

Reprinted with permission of the National Association of Social Workers, from SOCIAL WORK, Vol. 17, No. 3 (May 1972), pp. 88-98.

interaction are required for a good interview. But how can this be achieved when the black client feels accusatory and hostile as the oppressed and the white worker feels anxious and guilty about his complicity with the oppressor? In such a situation the black client would tend to resort to concealment and disguise and respond with discretion or "accommodation" behavior.[1] Concealment and "putting the white man on" have been institutionalized as a way of life—they are necessary weapons for survival, but antithetical to the requirements of an effective interview. Often the black client openly refuses to share, as expressed in the following poem, "Impasse," by Langston Hughes:

I could tell you,
If I wanted to,
What makes me
What I am.

But I don't
Really want to—
And you don't
Give a damn.[2]

The attitude toward permeability of the racial barrier for the social work interview has changed over the last twenty years. In 1950 Brown attempted to assess the importance of the racial factor in the casework relationship by distributing questionnaires to social agencies in Seattle, Washington.[3] Eighty percent of the practitioners responded that the racial factor did intrude in the relationship, but it was not much of a problem for the experienced worker with some self-awareness.

By 1970 blacks' disillusionment with the integrationist stance and a greater accentuation on their special separate identity from the white culture and the unique effects of their historical experience resulted in frequently repeated assertions that no white could understand what it meant to be black. Consequently, it is said, an effective interview with a black client requires a black interviewer. Many who have studied this problem, although not ready to go this far, generally concede that currently the racial barrier in the interview makes rapport and understanding much more difficult than was previously imagined.[4]

Obviously people who share similar backgrounds, values, experiences, and problems are more likely to feel comfortable with and understand each other. In sociology the principles of homophyly (people who are alike like each other) and homogamy (like marries like) express these feelings. Synanon, Alcoholics Anonymous, and denominational agencies are organizational expressions of this idea.

Social workers tend to follow the same principles by selecting for continuing service those clients who are most like themselves and subtly discouraging or overtly rejecting those "who cannot effectively use the service." The rich research literature about differential access to mental health services by different class groups tends to

---

[1] Thelma Duvinage, "Accommodation Attitudes of Negroes to White Caseworkers and Their Influence on Casework," *Smith College Studies in Social Work*, Vol. 9. No, 3 (March 1939), p. 264.

[2] Copyright © 1967 by Arna Bontemps and George Huston Bass from/*The Panther and the Lash*. Reprinted by permission of Alfred A. Knopf, Inc.

[3] Luna B. Brown, "Race as a Factor in Establishing a Casework Relationship," *Social Casework*, Vol. 31, No. 3 (March 1950), pp. 91–97.

[4] *See*, for example, George P. Banks, "The Effects of Race on One-to-One Helping Interviews," *Social Science Review*, Vol. 45, No. 2 (June 1971), pp. 137–146; Dorcas Bowles, "Making Casework Relevant to Black People: Approaches, Techniques, Theoretical Implications," *Child Welfare*, Vol. 48, No. 8 (October 1969), pp. 468–475; Marylou Kincaid, "Identity and Therapy in the Black Community," *Personnel and Guidance Journal*, Vol. 47, No. 9 (May 1969), pp. 884–890; Jean Gochros, "Recognition and Use of Anger in Negro Clients," *Social Work*, Vol. 11, No. 1 (January 1966), pp. 28–38; Clemmont Vontross, "Counseling Blacks," *Personnel and Guidance Journal*, Vol. 48, No. 9 (May 1970), pp. 713–719; Vontross, "Cultural Barriers in Counseling Relationships," *Personnel and Guidance Journal*, Vol. 48, No. 1 (September 1969), pp. 11–16; and Vontross, "Racial Differences—Impediments to Rapport," *Journal of Counseling Psychology*, Vol. 18, No. 1 (January 1971), pp. 7–13.

> *"Social workers tend to . . . select for continuing service those clients who are most like themselves and subtly discourage or overtly reject those 'who cannot effectively use the service.' . . . This is a euphemism for people who are different from 'us.'"*

confirm that this is a euphemism for people who are different from "us."

There is similar research with regard to agency selectivity relating to race. For example, a study of patients seen for ten or more individual psychotherapy interviews at a metropolitan psychiatric outpatient clinic found that "Caucasian women were seen proportionally longest, followed by Caucasian men.[5] Racial minority group patients had proportionately fewer contacts—black males had the lowest number of interviews. Nonwhites not only had fewer contacts, but their attrition rate was higher. All therapists, including psychiatric social workers, were Caucasian. Therapist ethnocentricity was measured with the Bogardus Social Distance Scale. Those who scored low in ethnocentrism were more likely to see black patients for six or more interviews; those who scored high treated black patients for this length of time much less often. (Differences were statistically significant.) Worker ethnocentrism may help account for the higher attrition rate of black clients who apply for social services. It is certainly true for black clients in family service agencies and black applicants for adoption.[6]

But the following statement by a black mental health worker, retrospectively analyzing her own personal experience, indicates that a therapeutic relationship with a white person, although difficult, is possible:

> In answering the question of whether a white middle-class psychiatrist can treat a black family, I cannot help but think back over my own experiences. When I first came to New York and decided to go into psychotherapy I had two main thoughts: (1) that my problems were culturally determined, and (2) that they were related to my Catholic upbringing. I had grown up in an environment in which the Catholic Church had tremendous influence. With these factors in mind, I began to think in terms of the kind of therapist I could best relate to. In addition to being warm and sensitive, he had to be black and Catholic. Needless to say, that was like looking for a needle in a haystack. But after inquiring around, I was finally referred to a black Catholic psychiatrist.
>
> . . . he turned out to be not so sensitive and not so warm. I terminated my treatment with him and began to see another therapist who was warm, friendly, sensitive, understanding, and very much involved with me. Interestingly enough, he was neither black nor Catholic. As a result of that personal experience, I have come to believe that it is not so much a question of whether the therapist is black or white but whether he is competent, warm, and understanding. Feelings, after all, are neither black nor white.[7]

[5] Joe Yamamoto et al., "Factors in Patient Selection," *American Journal of Psychiatry*, Vol. 124, No. 5 (November 1967), pp. 630–636.

[6] *See* "Non-White Families Are Frequent Applicants for Family Service," *Family Service Highlights*, Vol. 25, No. 5 (May 1964), pp. 140–144; and Trudy Bradley, *An Exploration of Caseworkers' Perceptions of Adoptive Applicants* (New York: Child Welfare League of America, 1966).

[7] As quoted in Clifford J. Sager, Thomas L. Brayboy, and Barbara R. Waxenberg, *Black Ghetto Family in Therapy—A Laboratory Experience* (New York: Grove Press, 1970), pp. 210–211.

Thus the question of whether a white worker can establish contact with a black client is more correctly stated as "How can such contact be established?"

WHITE WORKER–BLACK CLIENT

What can be done to ease the real difficulties inherent in white worker–black client cross-racial integration? Because the white worker is initially regarded as a potential enemy, he should carefully observe all the formalities that are overt indications of respect—e.g., start the interview promptly, use Mr. and Mrs. rather than the client's surname or first name, shake hands and introduce himself, listen seriously and sincerely. Rituals and forms are not empty gestures to people who have consistently been denied the elementary symbols of civility and courtesy.

Discussions about racism have left every white with the uneasy suspicion that as a child of his culture he has imbibed prejudices in a thousand different subtle ways in repeated small doses and that the symptoms of his racism, although masked to himself, are readily apparent to a black person. These suspicions may be true. Thus a worker must frankly acknowledge to himself that he may have racist attitudes and make the effort to change. To paraphrase a Chinese maxim: The prospective white interviewer who says, "Other white interviewers are fools for being prejudiced, and when I am an interviewer I will not be such a fool," is already a fool.

To conduct a good interview, the worker must be relatively confident that he knows his subject matter. But how can he feel confident if he is aware that there is much about the black experience he does not and cannot know? Certainly he can dispel some of his ignorance by reading about and becoming familiar with black history, black culture, and black thinking and feeling. This is his professional responsibility. When a worker lacks knowledge about the client's situation, he appears "innocent." Thus he is less respected, more likely to be "conned," and less likely to be a source of influence.

The white worker may find it helpful to be explicitly aware of his reactions to racial differences. In making restitution for his felt or suspected racism, he may be overindulgent. He may oversimplify the client's problems and attribute certain behavior to racial differences that should be ascribed to personal malfunctioning. When color is exploited as a defensive rationalization, race is a weapon. Burns points out that black children

> . . . have learned how to manipulate the guilt feelings of their white workers for their own ends. They have also learned to exploit the conceptions most white workers have about the anger of black people.[8]

In interracial casework interviews the participants are keenly aware of the difference between them. Yet they rarely discuss the racial factor openly.[9] It is not clear whether this is because race is considered irrelevant to the work that needs to be done or because both participants agree to a conspiracy of silence about a potentially touchy issue. Nevertheless, race—like any other significant factor that contaminates interaction—must be at least tentatively discussed because to be "color-blind" is to deny real differences.[10]

The presumption of ignorance, necessary in all interviews, is more necessary when interviewing a black client because the worker is more likely to be ignorant of the client's situation. Therefore, he must listen more carefully, be less ready to come to conclusions, and be more open to having

---

[8] Crawford E. Burns, "White Staff, Black Children: Is There a Problem?" *Child Welfare*, Vol. 50, No. 2 (February 1971), p. 93.

[9] *See* Roger Miller, "Student Research Perspectives on Race," *Smith College Studies in Social Work*, Vol. 41, No. 1 (November 1970), pp. 1–23;

and Michele Seligman, "The Interracial Casework Relationship," *Smith College Studies in Social Work*, Vol. 39, No. 1 (November 1968), p. 84.

[10] Julia Bloch, "The White Worker and the Negro Client in Psychotherapy," *Social Work*, Vol. 13, No. 2 (April 1968), pp. 36–42.

> **"If the black client sees the white worker as . . . the enemy, he may see the black social worker as a traitor to his race."**

his presuppositions corrected by the client, i.e., he must want to know what the situation is and be receptive to being taught.

It is frequently asserted that lower-class black clients lack the fluency and facility with language that are required for a good interview. Yet studies of speech behavior in the ghetto suggest that blacks show great imaginativeness and skill with language.[11] Thus the worker has the obligation to learn the special language of the ghetto. The agency can help by hiring black clerical and professional staff. If the black client sees members of his own group working at the agency, he has a greater sense of assurance that he will be accepted and understood.

BLACK WORKER–BLACK CLIENT

If both worker and client are black, different problems may arise. The pervasiveness of the cultural definition of blackness does affect the black client. Thus he may feel that being assigned to a black worker is less desirable than being assigned to a white worker because the latter may have more influence and thus be in a better position to help him.

The fact that the black social worker has achieved middle-class professional status suggests that he has accepted some of the principal mores of the dominant culture—e.g., motivation to achieve, denial of gratification, the work ethic, punctuality. To get where he is, he probably was edu-cated in white schools, read the white literature, and associated with white classmates —as he now associates with white colleagues.

The black middle-class worker may feel estranged not only from whites but from his own blackness. The problem of establishing a clearly defined identification is more difficult for "oreos"—those who are black on the outside, but white on the inside because of their experiences while achieving middle-class status.

The black worker who returns to the ghetto after professional training may be viewed with suspicion.[12] An alien returning from the outside world, where he has been "worked over" by the educational enterprise to accept white assumptions, values, and language, he has supposedly lost contact with the fast-changing ghetto subculture in the interim.

If the black client sees the white worker as representing the enemy, he may see the black social worker as a traitor to his race, a collaborator with the establishment. Therefore, barriers to self-disclosure and openness may be as great between the black worker and black client as between the white worker and black client.

The black client is also a source of anxiety to the black worker in other ways. A black psychiatrist stated it as follows: "For the therapist who has fought his way out of the ghetto [the black patient] may awaken memories and fears he would prefer to leave undisturbed."[13] Thus Brown's findings that black workers were less sympathetic to black clients than to white clients is not surprising.[14] They were made anxious by black clients' failure to live up to the standards of the dominant culture and felt that such deviations reflected on the race as a whole—thus decreasing the acceptability of all blacks, including themselves.

Calnek aptly defines overidentification in

[11] See, for example, Thomas Kochman, "Rapping in the Black Ghetto," *Transaction*, Vol. 6, No. 4 (February 1969), pp. 26–34.

[12] Orville Townsend, "Vocational Rehabilitation and the Black Counselor: The Conventional Training Situation and the Battleground Across Town," *Journal of Rehabilitation*, Vol. 36, No. 6 (November–December 1970), pp. 26–31.

[13] As quoted in Sager, Brayboy, and Waxenberg, op. cit., p. 228.

[14] Brown, op. cit.

this context as a "felt bond with another black person who is seen as an extension of oneself because of a common racial experience." [15] A black AFDC client described it as follows:

> Sometimes the ones that have had hard times don't make you feel good. They're always telling you how hard *they* had to work—making you feel low and bad because you haven't done what they done. [16]

The black worker also may be the target of displacement, i.e., the black client's hostility toward whites is expressed toward the black worker because he is less dangerous.

One clear advantage in the black worker–black client situation, however, is that the black professional provides the client with a positive image he can identify with. Kincaid states that

> a Black counselor who has not rejected his own personal history may be most able to inspire a feeling of confidence and a sense of hope in his Black client. [17]

When the worker is black and the client is white, other problems may arise. The client may be reluctant to concede that the black worker is competent and may feel he has been assigned second best. If the client is from the South, he may be especially sensitive to the reversal in usual status positions. [18]

If the client sees himself as lacking prejudice, he may welcome being assigned to a black worker because it gives him a chance to parade his atypical feelings. He may be gratified to have a black worker since only an unusually accomplished black could, in his view, achieve professional standing. On the other hand, because the white who turns to a social agency for help often feels inadequate and inferior, he may more easily establish a positive identification with the "exploited" and "oppressed" black worker. [19]

MATCHING

Any discussion of the problems inherent in cross-cultural interviewing inevitably leads to the question of matching. On the whole, would it not be desirable to select a worker of the same race as the client? Would this not reduce social distance and the resistance and constraints in interactions that derive from differences in group affiliation, experiences, and life-style? If empathic under-

---

". . . the black client's hostility toward whites is often expressed toward the black worker because he is less dangerous."

---

standing is a necessary prerequisite for establishing a good relationship, would this not be enhanced by matching people who are culturally at home with each other?

Obviously, empathic understanding is most easily achieved if the worker shares the client's world. However, the difficulties of empathic understanding across subcultural barriers can be exaggerated and the disadvantages of matching worker and client can be underestimated.

The world's literature is a testimonial to the fact that people can understand and empathize with those whose backgrounds and living situations are different from their own. For example, an American

---

[15] Maynard Calnek, "Racial Factors in the Counter-Transference: The Black Therapist and the Black Client," *American Journal of Orthopsychiatry*, Vol. 40, No. 1 (January 1970), p. 42.

[16] As quoted in Hugh McIsaac and Harold Wilkinson, "Clients Talk About Their Caseworkers," *Public Welfare*, Vol. 23, No. 2 (July 1965), p. 153.

[17] Kincaid, op. cit., p. 888.

[18] Andrew D. Curry, "Negro Worker and White Client: A Commentary on the Treatment Relationship," *Social Casework*, Vol. 45, No. 3 (March 1964), pp. 131–136.

[19] William Grier. "When the Therapist is Negro: Some Effects on the Treatment Process," *American Journal of Psychiatry*, Vol. 123, No. 12 (June 1967), pp. 1587–1592.

Christian, John Hersey, demonstrated empathic understanding of a Polish Jew in *The Wall;* an American Jew, Elliot Liebow, demonstrated his ability to understand ghetto blacks in *Tally's Corner;* and a white South African psychiatrist, Wulf Sachs, showed his sensitive understanding of a Zulu in *Black Hamlet.*[20]

If the worker's professional training enhances his ability to empathize with and understand different groups and provides the knowledge base for such understanding, the social and psychological distance between worker and client can be reduced. If the gap is sufficiently reduced, the client perceives the worker as being capable of understanding him, even though he is a product of a different life experience.

Some of the relative merits and disadvantages of close matching and distant matching are succinctly summarized in the following statement by Carson and Heine:

> With very high similarity the therapist may be unable to maintain suitable distance and objectivity, whereas in the case of great dissimilarity he would not be able to empathize with, or understand, the patient's problems.[21]

Thus it is not surprising that relevant research suggests effective interviewing is not linearly related to rapport, i.e., it is not true that the more rapport, the better. The relationship appears to be curvilinear, i.e., little rapport is undesirable, but so is maximum rapport. The best combination is moderate closeness or moderate distance between participants. Weiss, in a study of the validity of responses of a group of welfare mothers, found that socially desirable rather than valid responses were more likely to result under conditions of high similarity and high rapport.[22]

Clinical evidence also suggests that racial matching is not always a crucial variable in the interview. A study that tested the degree of distortion in responses to black and white psychiatrists by patients in a county psychiatric ward concluded that "the factor of race did not significantly affect the behavior of the subjects in the interview situation." [23] The patients perceived and responded to black psychiatrists as psychiatrists rather than as members of a different race. In a California study AFDC recipients were asked to assess the help they received from their caseworkers. The study group was large enough so that black and white caseworkers were able to contact both black and white recipients. The general conclusion was that the "race of the worker, per se, did not make a significant contribution to the amount of 'help' recipients received from the social service." [24]

PARAPROFESSIONALS

The shortcomings of matching have become more apparent as a result of experience with indigenous paraprofessionals in the human services. In efforts to find new careers for the poor during the last few years, many social agencies have hired case aides from the area they serve. These indigenous

[20] New York: Alfred A. Knopf, 1950; and Boston: Little, Brown & Co., 1967 and 1947, respectively.

[21] R. C. Carson and R. W. Heine, "Similarity and Success in Therapeutic Dyads," *Journal of Consulting Psychology,* Vol. 26, No. 1 (February 1962), p. 38.

[22] Carol H. Weiss, *Validity of Interview Responses of Welfare Mothers—Final Report* (New York: Bureau of Applied Social Research, Columbia University, February 1968). *See also* Herbert H. Hyman, *Interviewing in Social Research* (Chicago, Ill.: University of Chicago Press, 1954); Barbara S. Dohrenwend, J. A. Williams, and Carol H. Weiss, "Interviewer Biasing Effects, Toward a Reconciliation of Findings," *Public Opinion Quarterly,* Vol. 33, No. 1 (Spring 1969), pp. 121–129; and Dohrenwend, John Colombotos, and B. P. Dohrenwend, "Social Distance and Interviewer Effects," *Public Opinion Quarterly,* Vol. 32, No. 3 (Fall 1968), pp. 410–422.

[23] William M. Womack, "Negro Interviewers and White Patients: The Question of Confidentiality and Trust," *Archives of General Psychiatry,* Vol. 16, No. 6 (June 1967), p. 690.

[24] *California Welfare: A Legislative Program for Reform* (Sacramento: Assembly Office of Research, California Legislature, February 1969), p. 10.

> *"The world's literature is a testimonial to the fact that people can understand and empathize with those whose backgrounds and living situations are different from their own."*

case aides live in the same neighborhood as the client group, generally have the same racial background, and often struggle with the same kinds of problems. Therefore, they are in an excellent position to empathize with and understand the problems of the poor, blacks, and poor blacks—and in fact they often do.

In a study of agency executives' and supervisors' evaluations of paraprofessional performance, it was found that these workers were rated high on their ability to establish rapport with clients. One agency administrator described this ability as follows:

> In intake interviewing, paraprofessionals are very good at picking up clues and cues from the clients. They have a good ear for false leads and "put-ons." Their maturity and accumulated life experience, combined with firsthand knowledge of the client population, assists the agency in establishing communication with clients rapidly. . . . The new client is more comfortable with a paraprofessional because he or she is someone like himself.[25]

Riessman, however, notes the following difficulties:

> Frequently professionals assume that NP's [nonprofessionals] identify with the poor and possess great warmth and feeling for the neighborhood of their origin. While many NP's exhibit some of these

characteristics, they simultaneously possess a number of other characteristics. Often, they see themselves as quite different from the other members of the poor community, whom they may view with pity, annoyance, or anger. Moreover, there are many different "types" of nonprofessionals; some are earthy, some are tough, some are angry, some are surprisingly articulate, some are slick, clever wheeler-dealers, and nearly all are greatly concerned about their new roles and their relationship to professionals.[26]

Much of the research on nonprofessionals confirms the fact that with close matching, the problems of overidentification and activation or reactivation of problems faced by the worker are similar to those that concern the client. The client, feeling a deep rapport with the worker and anxious to maintain his friendship, may give responses that he thinks will make him more acceptable. He has an investment in the relationship and does not want to risk it by saying or doing anything that would alienate the worker.

If the effects of matching are not invariably advantageous, the effects of difference in cultural background between worker and client are not always disadvantageous. The problem that is created when a worker is identified with one subculture (e.g., sex, race, age, color, or class) and the client is affiliated with another is one specific aspect

25 Karolyn Gould, *Where Do We Go From Here? —A Study of the Roads and Roadblocks to Career Mobility for Paraprofessionals Working in Human Service Agencies* (New York: National Committee on Employment of Youth, 1969), pp. 5–6.

26 Frank Riessman, "Strategies and Suggestions for Training Nonprofessionals," in Bernard Guerney, ed., *Psychotherapeutic Agents—New Roles for Nonprofessionals, Parents and Teachers* (New York:

Holt, Rinehart & Winston, 1969), p. 154. *See also* Charles Grosser, "Manpower Development Programs," and Gertrude Goldberg, "Nonprofessionals in the Human Services," in Grosser, William Henry, and James Kelly, eds., *Nonprofessionals in the Human Services* (San Francisco, Calif.: Jossey-Bass, 1969); and Francine Sobey, *The Nonprofessional Revolution in Mental Health* (New York: Columbia University Press, 1970).

> *"The prospective white interviewer who says, 'Other white interviewers are fools for being prejudiced, and when I am an interviewer I will not be such a fool,' is already a fool."*

of in-group–out-group relations generally. The worker, because of his higher status, may encourage communication from the client. In addition, because he is an outsider, he does not reflect in-group judgments. If the client has violated or disagrees with in-group values, this is an advantage. Currently, for instance, a middle-class white-oriented accommodative black client might find it more difficult to talk to a black worker than a white worker.

If the client with upwardly mobile aspirations is looking for sources of identification outside his own group, contact with a nonmatched worker is desirable. Thus the lower-class client, anxious to learn middle-class ways, would seek such a worker. The fact that the worker does not initially understand him may be helpful. In trying to make his situation clear, the client may be forced to look at it more explicitly than before—i.e., in explaining it to an outsider, he may explain it better to himself. Further, the client may feel that the white worker has more influence in the community. Thus he may feel more hopeful.

In contrast, however, numerous studies indicate that in most instances some disadvantages derive from racial difference between interviewer and interviewee.[27] With white interviewers blacks are more likely to make acceptable public responses; with black interviewers they give more private answers. For example, blacks are less ready to share their feelings about discrimination with white interviewers. Carkhuff, in a study in which black and white therapists from middle- and lower-class backgrounds interviewed white and black patients from various class backgrounds, found that both class background and race affected the readiness with which patients shared intimate material. They were most open to therapists of similar race and class.[28]

CLIENT PREFERENCE

Research on client preference does not uniformly support the contention that clients invariably select professionals from their own group. Dubey, for example, offers empirical support for the contention that blacks do not overwhelmingly prefer black workers.[29] Using black interviewers, he asked some five hundred ghetto residents questions such as "Would you rather talk with a Negro social worker or with a white social worker?" and "Would you rather go to an agency where the director is Negro or to one where the director is white?" About 78 percent of the respondents said they had no preference. Only 10–11 percent said they strongly preferred a black worker or agency director.

Backner encountered this problem over a three-year period as a counselor in the City College of New York's SEEK program, established to help high school graduates

---

[27] *See,* for example, Jerome A. Sattler, "Racial 'Experimenter Effects' in Experimentation, Testing, Interviewing and Psychotherapy," *Psychological Bulletin,* Vol. 73, No. 2 (February 1970), pp. 137–160.

[28] Robert R. Carkhuff and Richard Pierce, "Differential Effects of Therapist's Race and Social Class Upon Patient Depth of Self-Exploration in the Initial Clinical Interview," *Journal of Consulting Psychology,* Vol. 31, No. 6 (December 1967),

pp. 632–634. *See also* Eugene C. Bryant, Isaac Gardner, and Morton Goldman, "References on Racial Attitudes as Affected by Interviewers of Different Ethnic Groups," *Journal of Social Psychology,* Vol. 70, No. 1 (October 1966), pp. 95–100.

[29] Sumati Dubey, "Blacks' Preference for Black Professionals, Businessmen and Religious Leaders," *Public Opinion Quarterly,* Vol. 34, No. 1 (Spring 1970), pp. 113–116.

from poverty areas with problems encountered in college.[30] Eighty percent of the students in the program were black and 15 percent were Puerto Rican. Backner was constantly admonished by students that "a white counselor can never really undertand the black experience" and that "no black brother or black sister is really going to talk to whitey." However, the results of a questionnaire completed by about half of the 325 students in the program tended to substantiate the staff's impression that although the students responded negatively to white counselors in general, they reacted differently to their own white counselors. One item asked, "What quality in your counselor would make you feel most comfortable?" Only 12.7 percent of the respondents said that a counselor of the same racial background was the most important consideration. In response to the question, "Which SEEK teachers, counselors, and tutors are most effective and helpful to you?" 4.9 percent of the students checked "teacher, counselor, or student with the same ethnic and racial background," whereas 42 percent checked "those whose ability as teachers, counselors, tutors seems good."

In a subsequent survey of all SEEK students, using a mail questionnaire that was completed anonymously and returned by 45 percent of the students, the relevant question was, "Your own counselor's ethnic background (a) should be the same as yours, (b) doesn't matter." Although 25.3 percent of the respondents answered that their counselors should have the same background, 68.4 percent said it did not matter. Subsequent studies indicated that when a student felt ethnicity was important, he was often expressing his feelings about the counselor as a person rather than a white person. However, in another study in which respondents had the opportunity to view racially different counselors via video tapes in a standard interview based on a script, blacks selected black counselors and whites selected whites.[31]

Brieland showed that client preference was dependent on certain conditions.[32] Black and white social work students asked black ghetto residents the following question: "If both were equally good, would you prefer that the (doctor, caseworker, teacher, lawyer, parents' group leader) be Negro (Black, Colored) or White?" One interesting result demonstrated the important effects of similarity or dissimilarity between interviewer–interviewee pairs. The white interviewers had a significantly larger percentage of respondents who said they had no preference as compared with black interviewers to whom respondents confessed they preferred a black doctor, caseworker, teacher, and so forth. However, only 55 percent of the respondents interviewed by black interviewers said they preferred a black caseworker, and 45 percent had no preference or preferred a white caseworker. The basis for respondents' preference for a black caseworker, other factors being equal, was that a black interviewer was more likely to be interested in his problems, less likely to talk down to him or make him feel worthless, more likely to give him a feeling of hope, and more likely to know the meaning of poverty.

A second question, which introduced the factor of competence, asked the respondent to state his preference for a black or white worker if the white worker was better qualified. A large percentage of those who preferred "equally good" black caseworkers preferred a white caseworker if his qualifications were better. Competence, then, proved to be more important than race in determining black respondents' caseworker preferences.

Barrett's and Perlmutter's study of black clients' responses to black and white counselors at the Philadelphia Opportunities In-

[30] Burton L. Backner, "Counseling Black Students: Any Place for Whitey?" *Journal of Higher Education*, Vol. 41, No. 8 (November 1970), pp. 630–637.

[31] Richard J. Stranges and Anthony C. Riccio, "Counselee Preferences for Counselors: Some Implications for Counselor Education," *Counselor Education and Supervision*, Vol. 10, No. 3 (Fall 1970), pp. 39–45.

[32] Donald Brieland, "Black Identity and the Helping Person," *Children*, Vol. 16, No. 5 (September–October 1969), pp. 170–176.

dustrialization Center—which offers training, placement, and vocational guidance services—supports Brieland's findings.[33] Although black clients preferred black counselors in the abstract (the interviewers in the study were black), actual ongoing client-counselor contact indicated that competence was a more crucial and significant variable than race. However, Barrett and Perlmutter suggest that the importance of matching may be greater when the problems discussed focus on personal concerns rather than on concrete services and when the client initially contacts the agency.

CONCLUSION

After making the usual cautious provisos about the contradictory nature of the findings, the tentativeness of conclusions, the deficiencies in methodology, the dangers of extrapolation, and so forth, what do all these findings seem to say? They seem to say that although nonwhite workers may be necessary for nonwhite clients in some instances and therapeutically desirable in others, white workers can work and have worked effectively with nonwhite clients. They seem to say that although race is important, the nature of the interpersonal relationship established between two people is more important than skin color and that although there are disadvantages to racially mixed worker-client contacts, there are special advantages. Conversely, there are special advantages to racial similarity and there are countervailing disadvantages. In other words, the problem is not as clear cut as might be supposed.

Not only is the situation equivocal, it is complex. To talk in terms of white and nonwhite is to simplify dichotomously a variegated situation that includes many kinds of whites and nonwhites. For example, interview interaction with a lower-class black male militant is quite different from interview interaction with a middle-class female black integrationist.

Findings like the ones reviewed here are understandably resisted, resented, and likely to be rejected because of the political implications that can be drawn from them. Nonwhite community leaders, in fighting for control of social service institutions in their communities, point to the special advantages to community residents of nonwhite staff and administration. Some studies tend to suggest that the need for nonwhite staff and administration is not that urgent. However, this ignores the current underrepresentation in social agencies of nonwhite workers and administrators, the clear preference of some nonwhite clients for a worker of similar racial background, the fact that many clients need workers of similar racial background as sources of identification for change, and the fact that although white workers may be able to understand and empathize with the nonwhite experience, nonwhite workers achieve this sooner, more thoroughly, and at less cost to the relationship.

---

[33] Franklin T. Barrett and Felice Perlmutter, "Black Clients and White Workers: A Report from the Field," *Child Welfare*, Vol. 50, No. 1 (January 1972), pp. 19–24.

Initial contacts with Mexican-American families

by Ignacio Aguilar

Schools of social work have, for the most part, been oblivious to the need for adapting methods of practice to minority groups. Rather they teach practice derived from a generic method that is dictated primarily by the majority. Yet much social work practice is carried out in the United States with minority groups and, too often, social workers apply it by a blanket method supposedly effective with all people.

Each minority group has its own problems and personality—derived from long-existing cultural and moral values, language, patterns of behavior, socioeconomic conditions, ethnic background, and many other factors. Social work practice in a minority community shows that besides the variations that must be made in the generic method to suit individuals, certain adaptations should be made in applying social work methods to the specific minority group.

During ten years' experience in a California community made up mainly of Mexican-Americans, the author learned from the people in the community how to adapt some of the key concepts and techniques of social work to the needs and the life-style of Mexican-Americans and how to avoid some common obstacles to the development of goodwill.

This article briefly outlines different cultural values and patterns of behavior—and barriers to assimilation in an alien society—which the social worker should consider in making initial contacts with Mexican-American families. How social work method was adapted in this initial contact phase in order to provide effective counseling is illustrated by a case example of work with a family in the author's community.

INITIAL CONTACT

There is no doubt that one of the most important and difficult processes in social work is the beginning phase, that is, starting to work with a client. Green and Maloney describe this phase as one in which

. . . emotional interaction takes place. The worker focuses on an emotional en-

Reprinted with permission of the National Association of Social Workers, from SOCIAL WORK, Vol. 17, No. 3 (May 1972), pp. 66-70.

gagement with a purpose, explores the possibilities of person(s), agency and worker finding a realistic *common purpose*. On the other hand, the client(s) naturally and rightly questions moving into a relationship with the worker.[1]

Since the first encounter determines the dynamics of the relationship and the kind and quality of the interaction between worker and client, a correct start is vital.

Awareness of differences, an understanding of why the differences exist, and experience in dealing with people of the specific minority group—all these are important to the social worker in establishing feelings of friendliness and confidence from the outset. Without them, a worker can unknowingly arouse antagonism or cause the client to withdraw in fear or confusion.

PATTERNS OF LIVING

The social worker in a Mexican-American community finds that his ways of work are strongly influenced by the people's patterns of living, which differ in many respects from those of people having a Protestant Anglo-Saxon background. Consideration of concepts, attitudes, and patterns of behavior that are likely to have a marked effect on the beginning stages of social work method can help to assure that vital correct start.

The leisurely opening. When Mexican-Americans meet to negotiate or arrange affairs, the first step is to set the climate or *ambiente*. A preliminary period of warm, informal, personal conversation precedes the discussion of the concerns that brought them together. Jumping into the middle of serious and controversial affairs—as many persons in the United States are inclined to do—seems confusing and even discourteous to most Mexican-Americans.

Language. Language is of course one of the main problems in working with non-English-speaking people. How can a social worker help people if he cannot communicate with them? How can a common purpose be established if that purpose cannot be discussed? How can a worker start where his clients are and proceed at a pace comfortable to them when he cannot even start at all? Obviously, for any social worker in a Spanish-speaking community, fluency in the language is a tremendous asset and for those dealing directly with clients it is a necessity—both for communicating and establishing rapport.

Attitude toward the law. Having to deal with the law is considered shameful by the average Mexican-American family, and the family members are disinclined to accept it as a common practice. The social worker needs to reassure his clients that dealing with the law offers them an honorable way of protecting their interests and legal rights. He will also have to explain their relation to such persons as probation officers and the police and tell them about legal services available to them. Knowledge of the basic elements of the Mexican system of law, as well as the system in the United States, will enable him to interpret these subjects more intelligibly to his clients.

Influence of religion. Religion plays an important role in the Mexican-American home and shapes the lives of the entire family. As Heller notes:

Some observers have reported that the church continues to exercise a strong influence in the Mexican-American community. For example, Broom and Shevky contend that "the church is the principal agency of cultural conservatism for Mexicans in the United States and reinforces the separateness of the group." They specify that they have in mind not only the parish organization of the Catholic Church but also the Protestant Missions "with their functional sectarian attributes." There seems to be little doubt that the "religious factor" (to use Professor Lenski's phrase) plays an important role in the rate of acculturation of Mexican Americans.[2]

---

[1] Rose Green and Sara Maloney, "Characteristics of Movement in Phases of the Social Work Relationship." Unpublished paper, University of Southern California, Los Angeles, 1963. (Mimeographed.)

Role of the male. The concept of the male in society and in the family is important to the understanding of the person of Mexican ancestry. It is not only a concept of philosophy, it is a way of life, quite different from the "American way of life." Paz describes the *macho* concept as follows:

> The ideal manliness is never to "crack," never to back down. . . . Our masculine integrity is as much endangered by kindness as it is by hostility. Any opening in our defenses is a lessening of our manliness. . . . The Mexican macho—the male —is a hermetic being, closed up in himself, capable of guarding both himself and whatever has been confided to him.[3]

The traditional role of the husband and father in the Mexican-American family is explained by Heller, as follows:

> According to the traditional norms the husband is regarded as the authoritarian and patriarchal figure who is both the head and the master of the family, and the mother as the affectional figure in the family.[4]

The extended family. To Mexican-Americans the extended family is of great significance in their pattern of living; they take it for granted that in time of trouble they can always count on the family to help out. Again quoting Heller:

> Not only in size, but also in organization the Mexican American family displays an unusual persistence of traditional forms. It continues to be an extended type of family with strong ties spread through a number of generations in a large web of kinships. These ties impose obligations of mutual aid, respect and affection.[5]

BARRIERS TO COOPERATION

The social worker dealing with Mexican-Americans may well find that there are certain obstacles to be overcome before he can gain his clients' confidence and they can work together smoothly and effectively in endeavoring to solve problems. These obstacles may involve attitudes of other people with whom the Mexican-Americans associate or they may be related primarily to the clients' own attitudes.

Prejudice. Unfortunately, in many sections of the United States Mexican-Americans—especially the families of poor and unskilled workers—are likely to encounter prejudice. This can occur within the community at large, can reach out to the children in school, and can even be found among persons in the helping professions.

Unfriendly or antagonistic feelings conveyed by insensitive people in positions of authority hinder the progress of such families in becoming assimilated and assuming responsibility. These families with limited financial resources and limited knowledge of English are likely to become the target of prejudiced individuals reluctant to help those who do not fit readily into the mold of middle-class American society. Too often, help is not offered at all. Or it may be offered in such a way that acceptance requires departure from familiar behavioral patterns. Indeed, prejudice in its purest and ugliest manifestations becomes one of the most common problems the minorities face in their encounters with helping professionals. It can also be one of the social worker's greatest obstacles to building confidence.

The strange system. It is hard for the parents in a Mexican-American family to understand the "system" with which they have to deal as they endeavor to cope with their problems. It becomes in their minds a kind of hydra-headed creature, with authorities cropping up from all sides to make demands upon them and press in on their privacy. Yet these families have to learn how to deal with the system if they are to become active partners in the process of being helped. They have to learn how to ex-

2 Celia S. Heller, *Mexican American Youth: Forgotten Youth at the Crossroads* (New York: Random House, 1966), p. 19.

3 Octavio Paz, *The Labyrinth of Solitude,* Ly-sander Kamp, trans. (New York: Grove Press, 1962), pp. 29–31.

4 Heller, op. cit., p. 34.

5 Ibid., p. 34.

ercise their rights and to assert their self-worth and esteem as human beings in a society they do not understand. As Hollis notes:

> This emphasis upon the innate worth of the individual is an extremely important, fundamental characteristic of casework. It is the ingredient that makes it possible to establish the relationship of trust that is so essential to effective treatment. From it grow the two essential characteristics of the caseworker's attitude toward his client: acceptance and belief in self-determination.[6]

For truly effective social work practice with minority groups, the social worker must learn as well as the client. Much more needs to be done in the way of teaching the uniqueness of the cultures of these groups to social workers and others in the helping professions if they are to provide worthwhile assistance to those who need the most help.

The following case illustration presents only the beginning stages in working with a typical family in a Mexican-American community in California. With further involvement, all other orthodox social work methods had to be modified somewhat in order to help the family fully.

CASE ILLUSTRATION

Family X is made up of the parents and three children: a girl 6 years old and two boys, aged 7 and 16. Mr. and Mrs. X were legally married at one time, but because of serious marital problems and pressures from Mrs. X's family were divorced three years ago. However, they managed to resolve their problems and came together

---

[6] Florence Hollis, *Casework: Psychosocial Therapy* (New York: Random House, 1964), p. 12.

again; the church never considered them divorced. The family lives in a small house in the back of a large empty lot that has not been taken care of properly. Weeds have taken over the majority of the land, so that they conceal the house.

The probation department referred Family X to the community center because neither the father nor the mother were able to communicate in English. The probation officer explained that this family needed counseling and also "someone who could speak their language." The parents were unable to control their 16-year-old son, Freddy, who had been placed on probation for running away from home regularly.

Mrs. X had been told to call the center for an appointment. This might have been sufficient to start the helping process for an Anglo-Saxon Protestant family; for a Mexican-American family it was not. Not only was it difficult for the family to overcome the shame of having to deal with the law, but Mr. X—who made all the decisions—had been disregarded by the probation officer. It was decided that establishing contact was up to the center, on the assumption that this would be difficult or impossible for Mrs. X.

ESTABLISHING CONTACT

The director of the community center called Mrs. X, identifying himself in Spanish as a social worker who knew that her son had been in some trouble, and explained that the center was a voluntary not a governmental agency. It was suggested that Mrs. X ask her husband if he could come with her to the center. She agreed to do so and to call back later in the evening when her husband came home from work, adding,

"It is good to talk to someone who can speak Spanish." The fact that Mrs. X had been asked to consult her husband about a conference for the two of them put her in a situation in which she did not have to decide on her own. Her husband was now involved in the decision-making.

A few days later Mr. and Mrs. X came to the center for the interview. True to Latin custom, the first hour was leisurely, the talk mainly about familiar things that they could comfortably share with the worker. Conversation centered about Mexico, where they had lived until about two years before. They shared information about their respective families and mentioned how difficult it was for them to get used to the American way of life. Here they had no close relatives nearby to whom they could turn when problems arose. It was disconcerting for them to have to bother people outside the family.

ALIEN SURROUNDINGS

It was no wonder that Mr. and Mrs. X were having a hard time, not only with their son, but with the society surrounding them, which was completely alien to them and highly threatening to their way of life. In their own little house at the end of the big lot, hidden by the growing weeds, they had found an island isolated from the outside world—up to the time that their son had gotten into trouble. But then they had to face the world, and it was difficult to understand and more difficult to be understood.

They were not pressed to talk about their son's situation in detail. They decided to come back the following day to talk about this problem after the probation officer had come to see them.

The purposes in mind for this first interview were accomplished: to meet Mr. and Mrs. X personally and to establish a comfortable relationship that would lead to a partnership once they were able to share their problems with the social worker. The next step would be to share a common purpose, in this case, helping Freddy.

Mr. X was included in the helping process from the beginning. Had he been left out, it would have meant that Mrs. X was assuming an improper role, that Mr. X was being put down by her, and that his role as head of the household plus his *macho* role were being jeopardized.

The following day Mr. and Mrs. X came a little late to the meeting and were reluctant to talk about their conference with the probation officer. Mr. X just kept silent, looking down. Mrs. X, red-eyed, finally said, "I am very ashamed. You should have heard what the probation officer said about us. He blamed us for all the troubles with Freddy and said that if we were not able to speak English we should go back to Mexico. Perhaps worst of all, our daughter heard all of this because she had to translate for us."

It was suggested that they arrange to meet the probation officer the next time at the center; there the social worker could translate for them and make the necessary interpretations. Thus the harmful effect of the probation officer's prejudices against them would be minimized. Mr. and Mrs. X were assured that they had certain legal and moral rights that had to be respected—among them the right to be treated as human beings. Major differences between the systems of law in the United States and Mexico were explained, as were the functions of the probation department and the role of its officers.

Mr. and Mrs. X then seemed somewhat relieved and looked less tense and fearful. Mrs. X thanked the social worker and, looking at her husband, said: "We are not ignorant and dumb. We just did not understand anything about what was happening."

This family is not unusual. Nor are its problems. Many families in minority communities are facing problems like these every day. The situations can be far more critical when compounded by illness and poverty. Preparing the social worker in advance to serve such families effectively—rather than leaving it up to him to learn on the job from the community—offers a challenge to the schools of social work.

American Indian myths

by Herbert H. Locklear

Probably no other people in the United States is so misunderstood as the American Indian. Probably no other people has had so many myths woven about its way of life. Misinterpretations of Indian thinking, customs, and attitudes consistently and continually arise and spread. Myths about Indians are wide in range, from such prosaic subjects as everyday food preferences to philosophical and religious tenets. One or more of these myths about the first Americans has influenced the ideas of almost everyone, Indian and non-Indian alike.

To clear up some of the stereotyped misconceptions and thus illuminate the thinking about American Indians, a historical approach seems best. It has been said that the Indian wants essentially to go back to precolonial days, that he lives in the past, and that his constant looking backward impairs his potential for present and future development.

It is true that Indian people are oriented to the past. But this does not mean that they expect or even want a return to the ways of living three centuries ago. Nor does it mean that their usefulness and interest in the present and future are necessarily limited. Their orientation to the past is not surprising. With rare exceptions, the only achievements that Indian people in this country can point to with pride occurred long ago. It was in earlier centuries that the Indians' life-style provided a sense of heroism and adventure and brought them satisfaction and tranquility. As a people they have been able to make little or no contribution to the present. Therefore, their future seems vague and uncertain.

PRIORITIES

To have hope and plan effectively for the future, Indians must learn to reorder their priorities, and this is not an easy objective to attain. However, like people of other ethnic groups, American Indians are actively and diligently seeking ways to resolve the many problems that deter such a reordering. A change in priorities involves a

Reprinted with permission of the National Association of Social Workers, from SOCIAL WORK, Vol. 17, No. 3 (May 1972), pp. 72-80.

shift, in some degree at least, from past to present orientation. The greatest obstacles to this are tribalism and the lack of goals and purposes that are recognized and accepted by all Indians.

The patriarchal family system complicates the transition from a past to present focus. Under this system the older fathers and the grandfathers are to be shown respect at all times and their wishes strictly adhered to in most instances. These elders are of course traditionalists. They hold on to the ways of the past that have proved to be right and that have been gratifying for them and their people. This is natural. Why should a people disregard and abandon ways of life that have brought them satisfaction, just to try to be modern or to keep up with new ways of other people in this country? The wise course for the Indian would be to determine which are the best parts of the old and the best parts of the new, then integrate them into a workable present. While doing this, the Indian should also retain intact his image of himself as a member of his tribe and race and self-assurance in his relationships with people of other races and groups with whom he comes into contact.

Another factor complicates the Indians' move toward becoming more closely related to the present—and also complicates any efforts that Indians or non-Indians may make to relate the present more closely to the Indian. That factor is the stereotyped image of the Indian that certain communications media present, especially the movies and television. The media continue to present a distorted view of the conflicts during the past three centuries between the Indians and the white men, denigrating the Indians' role and glamorizing that of the settlers who were struggling to introduce new modes of living to forest and mountains, rivers and lakes, desert and plains. With the influence that television and the movies wield on public opinion, they have relegated the Indian to an unenviable position in American history. To the average American the Indian is a folk figure, historically playing the role of the villain, except for a few extraordinary heroic characters.

There are some anthropologists, sociologists, social workers, and historians who recognize that the Indian has contributed significantly to America's heritage and culture. The task is to help the majority of Americans see this and realize that the Indian is not a mere folk figure but a real person with needs, hopes, fears, and ambitions for his own future and that of his children.

The belief that Indians not only revere but want to return to the life of the past is a myth that is part of the folklore enveloping the first Americans. Actually most Indians want to participate actively in the life of the present. They will do so gladly and willingly if they are accepted and permitted to live in accord with at least some of the ideas they believe to be right and essential for man's well-being. It is the author's thesis that a person cannot truly be accepted unless what he stands for basically is also accepted.

INDIAN ECOLOGY

Many Indian ways should be accepted and preserved. They should be preserved not merely because the Indian wants to keep them but because time and experience have demonstrated that they are more likely to encourage man's survival than some ways of modern contemporary society. Consider, for example, the problems of pollution and preservation of natural resources, which have recently skyrocketed to global importance. Indian efforts in these areas are unsurpassed, even considering the upsurge of activities today to cope with current critical conditions. Although Indians were predominantly nomads for hundreds of years, they never polluted the territory in which they lived and moved. Instead they carefully disposed of their wastes so that the land and the water were not damaged or ruined for those who came after them. They never took more from nature than a man, a family, or a village needed or could consume. They did not kill for sport.

"Many Indian ways should be accepted and preserved . . . time and experience have demonstrated that they are more likely to encourage man's survival than some ways of modern contemporary society."

Can the Indians' customs related to conservation and pollution be applied today? Men are not going to eliminate the factories with deadly fumes billowing from their smokestacks—although they may perforce reduce the amount and the deadliness of the fumes. Nor will men discontinue hunting for sport. But cannot the Indian philosophy be applied to contemporary practices and development affecting natural resources?

For instance, when a corporation decides to build a multimillion dollar enterprise in a neighborhood, the planners' thinking should go beyond the financial returns on the investment, even beyond the working conditions of those they will employ. Plans should consider also how noise, appearance of the plant, physical or chemical residues, and other factors related to the enterprise's operation could affect the people of the neighborhood and the surrounding region. A commitment not to foul the area or create detrimental conditions for those who live and work there should be important in planning the enterprise—even though this means a reduction in short- or even long-term financial gain for investors.

The man who likes killing for sport should be involved in programs for conserving game animals. State and local authorities responsible for controlling shooting and hunting should encourage the killing of plentiful or overabundant species. If the species is scarce, the sportsmen and the authorities should cooperate in programs that prohibit or limit the kill and that promote conditions favorable to replenishment of the species. That is the Indian way: preserve and replenish. That is one of the Indian ways that should be maintained.

WORK HABITS

Myth has also been built up around the Indians' work habits. It has been said that Indians will not work, that all they do is laze around the reservations and wait for the government to support them. It is said that the Indians are happy doing nothing, that programs calling for their active participation are doomed to failure because of their lack of ambition, interest, and skill.

A first step in clarifying this myth is understanding why the Indians receive money from the government. The Indian people do not receive financial aid or assistance in kind from the state or federal government because they are destitute or merely because they are Indians. Most of the money paid to tribes or individual Indians comes from funds that already belong to the tribe but are being held in trust by the government. Some of the money may be from the proceeds of a 1971 land settlement of about forty-seven cents per acre, which had been pending for sixty or seventy years. Thus a young Indian who obtains partial support from government funds is quite comparable to the son of a well-to-do family, part of whose income is derived from land holdings of his father or his forefathers.

The Indians' innate initiative and ambition are too often stifled by the rigid work rules and regulations on the reservations. For example, if a young man wishes to do more productive work than herding goats and carrying water for long distances for individual and family use, then he may have to leave his home on the reservation to seek work elsewhere, because jobs are not available nearby. If he seeks work in an urban area, he is not likely to have more than physical strength and agility to offer

150

a potential employer, since he probably has little formal education or vocational or technical training.

According to 1968 statistics, the average Indian completes about five years of schooling, compared with 11.2 years for other Americans. Furthermore, the problem concerns the quality of education as well as the amount, for the longer an Indian child stays in a conventional Indian school, the farther behind is his achievement in comparison with white children.[1]

An Indian who leaves the reservation and is fortunate enough to find work upon his arrival in the city will probably land in a dead-end job. Then he discovers that his training has not prepared him adequately to handle the job's daily routines and the living problems involved.

The Indian aspires to reach a level of comfort comparable to that of other people. He has not attained this aspiration, but that does not mean that he lacks ability and ambition. His nonattainment is not due to neglect of opportunities but rather to lack of them. In many instances opportunities for the Indian are controlled and kept out of reach by complex governmental structures and paternalistic attitudes.

BUREAU OF INDIAN AFFAIRS

The Bureau of Indian Affairs, created by acts of Congress and supported by subsequent legislative and judicial actions, has the obligation to assist the Indian groups who fall under its jurisdiction. The bureau's primary functions are (1) holding in trust Indian lands and money, (2) helping to establish and maintain economic projects, (3) helping to develop self-sufficiency, (4) acting as an intermediary or referral source, (5) assisting Indian people with other governmental agencies, state and federal, and (6) providing educational, social, and health services.

Basically, the bureau's aims in carrying out these functions are to provide a higher standard of living for Indian people, develop Indians' responsibility for managing their own funds and other resources, and promote their political and social integration.

The following statistics are based upon the bureau's operations during 1968:

1. The bureau had an operating budget of $241 million. It employed about 16,000 persons, slightly more than half of them Indians.

2. The bureau held in trust 50 million acres of land for Indians, with an agricultural return of approximately $170 million or less than $3.50 per acre.

3. About 90 percent of the Indians on reservations were living in tin-roofed shacks, huts, brush shelters, or adobe huts—a few even in abandoned automobiles. A large percentage of these Indians still were hauling their drinking water more than a mile.

4. Indian unemployment ranged between 40 percent and 75 percent in comparison with about 4 percent for the nation as a whole.

5. The average weekly income for an Indian family was about $30 versus about $130 for a comparable non-Indian family.

6. The average life expectancy for an Indian was about 43 years; the percentage of deaths from infectious diseases was many times greater than the national average.[2]

Many programs designed by the bureau for the good of the American Indian are made less effective by the maze of red tape and bureaucracy that plague this agency. Few Indian persons hold high administrative positions in the bureau, probably less than 20. The programs are primarily administered by persons of the white middle-class majority, some of whom accept as fact the myth that Indians do not want to work. Seemingly, they assume that Indians do not want to take a part in the program or lack the necessary ability. They thus preclude the Indians' active participation in the pro-

---

[1] See Peter Farb, *Man's Rise to Civilization As Shown by the Indians of North America, from Primeval Times to the Coming of the Industrial State* (New York: E. P. Dutton & Co., 1968).

[2] See Bureau of Indian Affairs, *Answers to Your Questions about American Indians* (Washington, D.C.; U.S. Department of the Interior, May 1968); and Farb, op. cit.

gram's plans and operation and hinder his progress.

Experiencing such exclusion over a period of time generates in the Indians a "what's the use?" attitude and feelings of apathy, helplessness, and hopelessness. They ignore the programs. Then the program planners say "Indians won't work." The usual consequences of this perverse situation are that the young Indian, who for cultural reasons does not compete too well with non-Indians, starts believing that he is a failure in present-day America. So he withdraws into himself. His withdrawal creates a high degree of frustration, bewilderment, envy, and hostility. This helps to explain the extraordinarily high rate of suicide among Indian youths—ten times higher than the national average for non-Indians. Such withdrawal is also at the root of many other problems that are usually grouped under the term, "the plight of the Indian."

INDIAN LAND

Another myth in the folklore surrounding the Indian is the belief held by some people that Indians want to regain possession of the land they roamed over freely before the first white settlers came to this country. A few Indians today may claim that the land should be returned to them. The struggle of the overwhelming majority is not regaining the land their forefathers enjoyed but retaining the land that belongs to them by right of possession, title, and treaty. Most Indian dealings with the federal government about land involve hoping, praying, begging, or pressuring the authorities to honor at least the essence of treaties made years ago and trying to prevent a complete sellout of the remaining Indian lands to private interests.

Loss of present rights and properties would probably mean the annihilation of this country's Indians as a race. The wording of the treaties is clear and unequivocal in English as well as in the language of the specific tribes concerned. For example,

the treaty with Indians of the Northwest regarding fishing rights on the rivers gives these rights to the Indians "for as long as the rivers shall flow." The rivers in the Northwest are still flowing, and the Indians are still struggling with the state of Washington about the state's violations of the treaty's terms, even on the Indians' property.

There is a well-known saying, "Possession is nine-tenths of the law." The natives of Alaska might well question its validity. They possessed their land long before white men set foot upon this continent. Recently, however, oil was discovered there. What happened? The land suddenly became the property of the state of Alaska, to be leased or sold to private interests. Only a residue of the handsome profits trickled down to the natives, many of whom had to be relocated. One reason given for taking over the land was that the natives did not hold title to it. This was legally but not morally true. The crucial question is: Who gave the state of Alaska the legal title to the land?

ADJUSTMENT TO CITY LIFE

In becoming oriented to the present, many Indians daily face a major problem: adjustment to city life. Statistics show that one-half of the nation's Indians now live in urban areas.[3]

Unlike many other Americans who are drawn to the cities by exciting opportunities, most American Indians move to urban centers only because they are desperate. Instead of going to something, they are leaving something. They go to find work because there is nothing for them back home. They do not like the crowds, the heavy traffic, or the constant pressure of city life. Most of them would return home to the reservation if stable employment were available to them there.

Most people who move to American cities have the drive to get ahead and have accepted other prevalent values of the con-

[3] This data was supplied by the American Indian Information Center, New York City.

152

temporary industrial society. Therefore, urban adjustment is not so traumatic for them. But Indians do not esteem highly the intensive kind of competition and aggression around which the American society has developed. Traditionally, Indians do not place great value on aggressive and competitive behavior; instead, they favor economic equality and a fair sharing of material goods. They tend to be reticent about speaking up and demanding their rights. Thus they are not likely to exert the effort necessary to obtain agency support in time of need. Professional personnel who are administering programs for them may think that their reticence and social reserve indicate they do not intend to cooperate or are unwilling to do so.

EXTENDED FAMILY

Indians' strong family ties and feelings give total support and allegiance to the extended family group. They solve their problems within this group, which has its own vast maze of possible resources. When they move to a modern city and live in a small nuclear family, trying to be self-sufficient among other similar families, most Indians are completely lost. In the city they seldom have a host of relatives to rely on, and they are unwilling to go through the complicated formalities involved in asking a stranger for assistance or enduring the humiliation such action would mean to them. Indians' mystical view of being at one with the universe often leads them to accept unquestioningly the position in which they find themselves. They therefore may ask little of the agencies designed to serve them. They have tended to make better use of agency facilities when there has been a single multipurpose office in which someone they knew handled almost all their problems for them.

The differences in approaches by Indians and non-Indians have led to a rapid development of Indian centers in most major cities of the United States in which Indians have been relocating. Indians and non-

"The average Indian completes about 5 years of schooling compared with 11.2 years for other Americans."

Indians alike have felt that a consistent effort must be made to interpret each to the other, to build a bridge of appreciation and understanding between the two groups. The aim would be to enable Indians and non-Indians to share valid insights and special abilities that would enrich the lives of both.

From several years' experience in working with Indians, the St. Augustine Indian Center in Chicago assembled a list of specific attitudes and practices of Indian people that have persisted in an urban environment. Experience of other urban centers for Indians confirms the findings in Chicago. The list includes the following:

1. Generosity is still the paramount virtue among most Indians. Accumulation of wealth is not a major motivating factor. An Indian cares more about being able to work at a satisfying occupation and earn enough extra to share with relatives and friends than about putting money in the bank and purchasing a home in the city.

2. Many Indians continue to hold the old concepts of time. For them, time is circular rather than horizontal. Past, present, and future are all one. Living and working by the clock, as the white man does, are not considered important.

3. For most Indians work must be more than a steady job. It must be a vocation providing inner satisfaction as well as an income.

4. Family and interpersonal relationships have priority over all else. An Indian's first responsibility is to relatives, wherever they may be.

5. The extended family system continues to operate in many tribes, thus providing an enlarged sphere of family relationships

153

as well as family responsibilities. Keeping both tribal and Indian identification continues to be important for the majority of first Americans.

6. Many Indians are basically noncompetitive in their relationships to non-Indians. However, they continue to be intensely competitive with each other.

INDIANS IN BALTIMORE

Experience at the American Indian Study Center in Baltimore confirms the findings in Chicago. Those planning and setting up the program there found that organization was a key factor.

The concept of the Baltimore center originated with a group of parents whose children were attending a Head Start program. These parents realized that nowhere in the school system were any subjects dealing with the American Indians taught from an ethnocentric view. A meeting of interested parents and recognized community leaders was called, plans were formulated, and a schedule developed that would test community interest in an Indian study program. The responses indicated enthusiasm for the beginning of a center. With the start of the study program, other needs became evident. It was found that Indians who had not previously gone to public agencies for assistance were coming to the center for many types of help. Therefore, with much community input in planning, the program was expanded so that full-time assistance was available.

Indians began migrating to Baltimore in the early 1940s, primarily from the Lumbee tribe of Robeson County in North Carolina. However, the influx has been greater in numbers in the past ten to fifteen years than ever before. The city's Indian population is still increasing. The Lumbees are the largest tribal group, but there are families and individuals descended from other tribes who live in the Greater Baltimore metropolitan area.

Most of these Indians were originally hard-working tenant farmers from a racially segregated area. They are clannish and tend to cluster together for protection, security, and social activities. This clannishness—a trait they have brought to the city —has led to the development of the south-east section of Baltimore as an Indian settlement. In the main, these Indians have come from large families with a background of social, economic, educational, and cultural deprivation as well as a lack of other life experiences that most non-Indians consider to be societal norms.

Baltimore Indians have had a strict upbringing, with strong emphasis on religious beliefs, self-denial, and discipline. They come to the city totally unready to cope with even the everyday routines of living in a congested metropolitan center, much less to handle family crises adequately. These Indians have suffered a severe loss of self-identity and have become confused about personal values and goals. As a result of their unprepared-for exposure to different ways of living and their headlong projection into a competitive situation with non-Indians, most of them become skeptical of any contacts outside their own circle of family and friends. They are reluctant to become involved with governmental institutions and agencies and refuse to make use of established public services administered by non-Indians. The Indian who once considered himself equal to all in his old community now feels inferior to the strangers around him. He becomes alienated; he withdraws into himself as a defensive device, with resulting anomie.

The average adult in the Baltimore settlement is uneducated and has no motivation to educate his children. Those administrators responsible for curriculum-planning and policy-making in Baltimore's public school system have not acted to ameliorate these conditions. Indian history, arts, crafts, and culture have not been included in the schools' curricula. Nor have any adaptations been made in recognition of the special needs of American Indian children. Current conventional history of the United States is taught in the schools, presenting the Indian in a most unfavorable light. This adds to the Indian child's frustration and produces in him feelings of shame and embarrassment about his race. The outcome too often is low achievement, and many drop out of school at an early age. What the Indian child learns among his peers in the classroom about "his people" conflicts with his image of himself as an Indian.

Unemployment among the Baltimore Indians was about 25 percent in 1971, far higher than the city average of 7 percent. The Indian population is young, with about 70 percent of the people under 40 years old.

The Indian people in this city perhaps need most of all to be able to transcend the traditional unresisting acceptance of the status quo, expressed resignedly as "That's the way things are." They need to put their energies and talents into action to bring about change in their own behalf. Owing to sheer numbers, Baltimore Indians could have some voice in the development of the socioeconomic and political environment of the community in which they live.

Conditions among Indians in other cities basically echo those in Baltimore. Nor do statistics on urban Indians differ drastically from the national averages of comparable statistics of reservation Indians. On the reservations also the people's spirits are characterized by anomie and alienation. There too one hears the Indian say: "So what? The white man's rule will win."

STUDY CENTER

Out of the knowledge and recognition of the needs of the city's Indian people grew the Baltimore American Indian Study Center. It was established to assist the Indian community collectively and individually to overcome their social handicaps, which were partly related to urban living. The center's staff also works to develop greater political influence and economic self-sufficiency within the community and to further the Indians' drive toward self-determination.

Stated more specifically, the center's goals are as follows:

1. Establish and maintain an urban community center where Indian people, who traditionally have not used public services because of cultural factors, can obtain constructive suggestions regarding their next move and can ease their adjustment to urban living.

2. Make competent staff help available to counsel neighborhood residents in all problem areas, give them advice and direction, and refer them to community agencies that provide needed resources.

3. Stimulate social change through specific programs and direct action.

4. Stimulate the Indian community to act in its own behalf.

5. Identify community needs through research, then formulate projects and programs to meet those needs.

6. Promote understanding and harmony between the Indian and non-Indian communities through exchange activities, so that the various ethnic groups may work together and have greater power in the councilmanic and legislative districts.

7. Maintain programs that focus on reestablishing Indian self-identity and restoring the confidence of the Indian people so that they have the will and the stamina for positive sustained action.

CONCLUSION

Programs like this in all the major urban centers where there are significant numbers of Indians offer one means of refuting and counteracting the prevalent Indian myths that unfortunately are still being passed along from one person to another and, through such media as television and the movies, to many persons. It is a gross error to believe that all unfairness toward the Indians and all mistreatment of these first Americans is a thing of the past. Such unfairness and mistreatment are still happening right now—as the examples cited regarding treaty violations and land seizure indicate. And it seems quite possible that inequitable and oppressive treatment will continue as long as racism prevails.

The author believes that the pattern can be altered, that there are alternatives to continued prejudice and misunderstanding. He proposes that the following steps be taken to further the efforts of organizations such as the American Indian study centers to promote harmony and friendship: (1) Design programs for urban Indians that offer them the opportunity and stimulate their motivation to share in the control of their destiny—which every man, woman, and child has the right to do, at least in a collective sense, through community action. (2) Provide equal treatment where equality does not now exist, initiating programs to bring fairness and justice in education, work opportunities, housing, and other aspects of living to those who do not now have them. Fairness and justice are not only the right of those who now have unequal treatment and opportunity; seeing that unfairness and mistreatment do not exist is the responsibility of those who receive more favored treatment and have better opportunities. It has been said many times, but it is worth repeating, that as long as any of us is in bondage none of us is free.

THERE IS MONEY IN MISERY

HELP WITHOUT PSYCHOANALYSIS, by Dr. Herbert Fensterheim (Stein & Day, 239 pages, $6.95).

Reviewed by Morley Glicken

Let's have it out in the open from the start. "Help Without Psychoanalysis" is an O.K. book. Not great, not particularly good, just O.K. It doesn't leave the reader with a larger view of life. Probably it will not dramatically change even the most easily suggestible reader's mental health. In fact, given its large competition in the self-help field with the likes of "The Sensuous Man," "Woman" and "Old Man" trilogy, it will probably not make for the kind of voyeuristic, slightly seedy reading which seems to mark the taste of the literate in this the year of the poly-morphous-perverse.

As a positive, it does a nice job of explaining the techniques and virtues of be-havior therapy, although some of the virtues of this approach are less grounded in hard, well-supported research than one would like to see. Still and all, behavior therapy is an approach with much to say for it and the author does a valuable job of describing the how and why of the behavior approach with particular emphasis on techniques the reader might use in his own life. So much for the book.

After reading "Help Without Psychoanalysis" one cannot help but feel a process of saturation setting in as self-help books flood the market, and surprisingly, sell in large numbers. In fact, not a few poeple have made small fortunes out of the large core of misery which must exist to keep books like "Games People Play" on the best-seller list. I suppose, when all is said and done, the self-help book sells because most people have found it far easier to bury their anguish away inside themselves than to seek help from others, including the professional therapist, the reason being, unfortunately, that most help is less than helpful and far too many research projects show that, on the average, professional help is no more effective than no help at all. In fact, at least a third of all professional help causes the client psycho-logical damage.

Is it any wonder then that people seek help in whatever way they can even if some of the sources are enough to make one gag? Which is, sadly, a real shame because enough solid, reputable, effective therapists practice to truly help those in need, and to have experienced a successful therapeutic encounter is to know why one is less than happy with self-help books.

For the reader considering therapy the evidence would support the notion that the most effective therapist is one who is warm, genuine and empathic. Which is to say that one feels comfortable with him and can establish a degree of rapport rather quickly. If this isn't the case, then one is better off to seek a therapist with whom such a relationship is possible rather than continuing the agony of seeking help from someone with whom a meaningful therapeutic rela-tionship is difficult.

With the evidence showing that two-thirds of all professional help either does nothing or causes harm, one is afraid that self-help books will continue selling no matter how silly their message. Sad.

THE MINNEAPOLIS TRIBUNE, Book Section, September 1971.

BY ROBERT D. CARTER AND RICHARD B. STUART

Behavior Modification Theory and Practice: A Reply

■ In reply to a recent article in Social Work, the authors point out certain misconceptions contained in criticisms of behavior modification theory and practice. They argue that the behavioral approach has been empirically demonstrated to be effective in altering problem behavior and that, because of its close ties to experimental psychology and its insistence on operational specificity and conceptual parsimony, it offers decided advantages over more traditional psychodynamic approaches. Specific issues are discussed and the proposal is made that behavioral psychology can deal adequately with all important aspects of complex human behavior. ■

SOCIAL WORK HAS traditionally drawn on the theory and research of allied disciplines in an ongoing effort to enhance the effectiveness of its practice. While the need for caution in this borrowing has been cited,[1] the introduction of such material seems to have contributed to the development of a more comprehensive theory and an increase in the range of practice strategies available to social workers.[2]

The pattern for the introduction of new material is now familiar. First, zealots of a new approach introduce their doctrine. The field then closes ranks in an effort to preserve the familiar and reject the novel. Positions polarize and sharpen on both sides, each side (perhaps innocently) misrepresenting the viewpoint of the other. A period follows in which the field must choose between two alternative courses:

either the schism may widen and harden (as seems to have occurred in the functional-diagnostic controversy[3]) or a reconciliation may occur, shaping yesterday's novelty into tomorrow's orthodoxy.

The techniques of behavior modification have been introduced into social work literature and practice.[4] The field is now in the

ROBERT D. CARTER, Ph.D., is a Research Associate, and RICHARD B. STUART, DSW, is Associate Professor, School of Social Work, University of Michigan, Ann Arbor, Michigan. This paper is oriented around issues raised in Max Bruck, "Behavior Modification Theory and Practice: A Critical Review," Social Work, Vol. 13, No. 2 (April 1968), pp. 43–55.

[1] See Richard B. Stuart, "Promise and Paradox in Socioeconomic Status Conceptions," *Smith College Studies in Social Work*, Vol. 35, No. 2 (February 1965), pp. 110–124.

[2] See, for example, Leonard S. Kogan, ed., *Social Science Theory and Social Work Research* (New York: National Association of Social Workers, 1960); *Building Social Work Knowledge: Report of a Conference* (New York: National Association of Social Workers, 1964).

[3] Cora Kasius, ed., *A Comparison of Diagnostic and Functional Casework Concepts* (New York: Family Service Association of America, 1950).

[4] Derek Jehu, *Learning Theory and Social Work* (London, Eng.: Routledge & Kegan Paul, 1967); Edwin J. Thomas, ed., *The Socio-behavioral Approach and Applications to Social Work* (New York: Council on Social Work Education, 1967); Thomas, "Selected Sociobehavioral Techniques and Principles: An Approach to Interpersonal Helping," *Social Work*, Vol. 13, No. 1 (January 1968), pp. 12–26. A sample of Michigan agencies that have implemented behaviorally oriented so-

process of closing ranks through the publication of polemics. In a recent article, Bruck presented a provocative and, in the authors' opinion, invalid attack on the principles and techniques of behavior modification.[5] He has done this by (1) basing his commentary on what by now is a narrow sample of the relevant literature,[6] (2) treating even that sample both unfairly and inadequately, (3) relying too heavily on a critique written by Breger and McGaugh[7] (an article that has been given a status far in excess of its value as a source of accurate information[8]), and (4) attacking the proverbial straw man.[9] The authors' intention here is to correct certain misconceptions contained in the Bruck paper in an effort to forestall their proliferation in the social work literature.

In order to discuss what we regard as misconceptions, some specific issues have been abstracted from the Bruck article and will be dealt with one at a time. With the exception of the first ("the success issue"), all of these appear to be integral to Bruck's notion of "the whole person." This con-

cept seems to represent the crux of his discontent with behavior modification, and it provides a convenient focus of reply.

It should be clearly understood that we do not pretend to speak for all those who identify themselves with behavior modification. No one could do this adequately, because the referents of this label are so diverse and lacking in integration. The point of view expressed is our own, although we feel it is reasonably representative.

The terms behavioral and behaviorist will be used to indicate individuals, approaches, and products associated with the broader field of behavioral (stimulus-response, learning) theory and research.[10] Behavior modification (or behavioral therapy) refers to the application of the concepts and principles of the broader field in the treatment of people who show maladaptive behavior.[11] When we speak of psychodynamic or dynamic theory and therapy, we are referring to those approaches in psychotherapy that (1) place great theoretical emphasis on complex mental structures and processes and (2) rely mainly on the production of "insight," "awareness," "self-understanding," "self-acceptance," and the like, using the interview as the principal medium of treatment.

THE SUCCESS ISSUE

One point should be made regarding the standards of acceptable evidence implied in the Bruck article. Bruck appears to adopt more stringent criteria for the demonstra-

cial work programs includes Kent County Juvenile Court, Family Service of Ann Arbor, Fort Custer State Home, and Neighborhood Service Organization, among many others.

[5] Max Bruck, "Behavior Modification Theory and Practice: A Critical Review," *Social Work*, Vol. 13, No. 2 (April 1968), pp. 43–55.

[6] It is important to note that Dr. Bruck's review of the literature includes only one paper published after 1965. This is an especially serious omission when it is realized that over four hundred books and articles on the subject have appeared since that time.

[7] Louis Breger and James L. McGaugh, "Critique and Reformulation of 'Learning Theory' Approaches to Psychotherapy and Neurosis," *Psychological Bulletin*, Vol. 63, No. 5 (May 1965), pp. 338–358.

[8] *See* William M. Wiest, "Some Recent Criticisms of Behaviorism and Learning Theory," *Psychological Bulletin*, Vol. 67, No. 3 (March 1967), pp. 214–225.

[9] Bruck has constructed a caricature out of bits and pieces that, when taken together, fail to correspond to any existing theory or practice. Breger and McGaugh can be similarly accused, as indicated by Wiest, *ibid.*, pp. 215–218.

[10] *See* G. A. Kimble, *Hilgard and Marquis' Conditioning and Learning* (New York: Appleton-Century-Crofts, 1961); Werner K. Honig, ed., *Operant Behavior: Areas of Research and Application* (New York: Appleton-Century-Crofts, 1966).

[11] For descriptions of behavior modification or therapy, *see* Leonard P. Ullmann and Leonard Krasner, eds., *Case Studies in Behavior Modification* (New York: Holt, Rinehart & Winston, 1965), pp. 1–63; Frederick H. Kanfer and Jeanne S. Phillips, "Behavior Therapy," *Archives of General Psychiatry*, Vol. 15, No. 2 (August 1966), pp. 114–128; John M. Grossberg, "Behavior Therapy: A Review," *Psychological Bulletin*, Vol. 62, No. 2 (August 1964), pp. 73–88.

tion of effectiveness in behavioral therapy than he does for psychodynamic therapy. On the one hand, he seems to agree with Breger and McGaugh that controlled studies are necessary and that case studies are inadequate for this purpose. On the other hand, he seems to have no hesitancy in accepting as "evidence" the experiences of clinical practitioners (p. 47) and case material (p. 52) when he wishes to buttress his own claims as to what transpires in psychotherapy.

Research on the effectiveness of behavior modification offers several improvements on the psychotherapy outcome literature. The terms used in the planning and evaluation of treatment are usually operationally meaningful. They are generally cast at a low level of abstraction and describe objective and measurable events; therefore they permit high interjudge reliability. In contrast, the language of dynamic psychology has been demonstrated to have both notoriously low reliability (even among therapists who have shared the same training) and to bear little relationship to the ensuing treatment.[12]

Beyond this, it is generally agreed that studies that are based on good experimental design and utilize control groups are highly desirable in the demonstration of effectiveness. There are now a number of studies in behavior modification that have made use of control groups of both a no-treatment and a contrast-treatment type. However, we offer our references with the understanding that the question of therapeutic effectiveness is a complicated one indeed and that claims of success must always be evaluated with respect to the specifics of any particular investigation (e.g., what therapists, what methods, what clients, what problems, and what clinical setting).[13]

By far the greatest amount of research using control group designs has focused on the method of systematic desensitization.[14] This technique, used in the treatment of anxiety-based maladaptive behavior (e.g., phobias), has been examined and its effectiveness demonstrated in a number of different settings and in relation to a variety of treatment problems.[15] The reports of Gordon

---

[12] Herman O. Schmidt and Charles P. Fonda, "The Reliability of Psychiatric Diagnosis: A New Look," in Herbert C. Quay, ed., *Research in Psychopathology* (Princeton, N.J.: D. Van Nostrand Co., 1963); Frederick H. Kanfer and George Saslow, "Behavioral Diagnosis," in Cyril Franks, ed., *Assessment and Status of Behavior Therapies and Associated Developments* (New York: McGraw-Hill Book Co., in press); Richard B. Stuart, "Iatrogenic Illness: Causes, Illustrations and Cure," unpublished manuscript, 1968.

[13] *See* Donald J. Kiesler, "Some Myths of Psychotherapy Research and the Search for a Paradigm," *Psychological Bulletin*, Vol. 65, No. 2 (February 1966), pp. 110–136; and Gordon L. Paul, "Strategy of Outcome Research in Psychotherapy," *Journal of Consulting Psychology*, Vol. 31, No. 2 (April 1967), pp. 109–118.

[14] *See* Stanley Rachman, "Systematic Desensitization," *Psychological Bulletin*, Vol. 67, No. 2 (February 1967), pp. 93–103.

[15] *Ibid.*; Arnold A. Lazarus, "Group Therapy of Phobic Disorders by Systematic Desensitization," *Journal of Abnormal and Social Psychology*, Vol. 63, No. 3 (November 1961), pp. 504–510; Peter J. Lang, "Experimental Studies of Desensitization Psychotherapy," in Joseph Wolpe, Andrew Salter, and L. J. Reyna, eds., *The Conditioning Therapies* (New York: Holt, Rinehart & Winston, 1964), pp. 38–50; Gordon L. Paul, *Insight vs. Desensitization in Psychotherapy* (Stanford, Calif.: Stanford University Press, 1966); Gordon L. Paul and D. T. Shannon, "Treatment of Anxiety through Systematic Desensitization in Therapy Groups," *Journal of Abnormal Psychology*, Vol. 71, No. 2 (April 1966), pp. 124–135; James F. Lomont and James E. Edwards, "The Role of Relaxation in Systematic Desensitization," *Behaviour Research and Therapy*, Vol. 5, No. 1 (February 1967), pp. 11–25; Ray M. Zeisset, "Desensitization and Relaxation in the Modification of Psychiatric Patients' Interview Behavior," *Journal of Abnormal Psychology*, Vol. 73, No. 1 (February 1968), pp. 18–24; Gerald C. Davison, "Systematic Desensitization as a Counterconditioning Process," *Journal of Abnormal Psychology*, Vol. 73, No. 2 (April 1968), pp. 91–99; Stephen M. Johnson and Lee Sechrest, "Comparison of Desensitization and Progressive Relaxation in Treating Test Anxiety," *Journal of Consulting and Clinical Psychology*, Vol. 32, No. 3 (June 1968), pp. 280–286.

Paul are especially noteworthy. This investigator has not only carried out some of the most carefully designed treatment research (contrasting desensitization, insight, placebo, and no-treatment groups), he has also conducted what are probably two of the most scientifically respectable follow-up studies to be found anywhere.[16] Both of these studies reveal (1) maintenance of the improvement found earlier, (2) evidence of generalization of gain to related performance areas, and (3) no evidence of relapse or symptom substitution. Reference should also be made to some promising work by Bandura and his associates, combining modeling procedures with aspects of desensitization.[17]

Control group studies using operant techniques are also in evidence: Peters and Jenkins improved the problem-solving behavior of chronic schizophrenic patients using food as a reinforcer, King and associates used candy and cigarettes to move schizophrenic patients through a series of increasingly more complex tasks, Ullmann *et al.* used a standard verbal operant conditioning paradigm to increase the production of more common word associations in schizophrenic patients, and Clement and Milne conditioned greater social approach behavior in young boys using exchangeable tokens as reinforcers.[18]

The charge that most of the success claims of behavioral therapy rest on case studies is a less telling criticism than was true at one time, as this brief inventory indicates. But the criticism itself is faulty because it fails to take into account a peculiar property of many case studies in behavior modification, a property that makes these reports more valuable as evidence than is true in more traditional approaches. This property is the so-called single organism or own-control design that is characteristic of much of the experimental analysis of operant behavior. Paul describes this as an *A-B-A* design, characterized by the introduction of a therapeutic procedure (*A*), its temporary removal or alteration (*B*), and its reinstatement as before (*A*).[19] The idea is to apply a technique, produce a corresponding change in the target behavior, and then alter or discontinue the technique to see if the behavioral change just produced is dependent on it. The technique is then reapplied to see if the behavioral change can be recovered.[20]

---

[16] Paul, *op. cit.;* Paul and Shannon, *op. cit.;* Paul, "Insight versus Desensitization in Psychotherapy Two Years After Termination," *Journal of Consulting Psychology,* Vol. 31, No. 4 (August 1967), pp. 333–348; Paul, "Two-Year Follow-Up of Systematic Desensitization in Therapy Groups," *Journal of Abnormal Psychology,* Vol. 73, No. 2 (April 1968), pp. 119–130.

[17] Albert Bandura, Joan E. Grusec, and Frances L. Menlove, "Vicarious Extinction of Avoidance Behavior," *Journal of Personality and Social Psychology,* Vol. 5, No. 1 (January 1967), pp. 16–23; Bandura and Menlove, "Factors Determining Vicarious Extinction of Avoidance Behavior through Symbolic Modeling," *Journal of Personality and Social Psychology,* Vol. 8, No. 2 (February 1968), pp. 99–108. *See also* Brunhilde Ritter, "The Group Desensitization of Children's Snake Phobias Using Vicarious and Contact Desensitization Procedures," *Behaviour Research and Therapy,* Vol. 6, No. 1 (February 1968), pp. 1–6.

[18] Henry N. Peters and Richard L. Jenkins, "Improvement of Chronic Schizophrenic Patients with Guided Problem-Solving, Motivated by Hunger," *Psychiatric Quarterly Supplement,* Vol. 28 (1954), pp. 84–101; Gerald F. King, Stewart G. Armitage, and John R. Tilton, "A Therapeutic Approach to Schizophrenics of Extreme Pathology," in Ullmann and Krasner, *op. cit.,* pp. 99–112; Leonard P. Ullmann, Leonard Krasner, and Richard L. Edinger, "Verbal Conditioning of Common Associations in Long-Term Schizophrenic Patients," *Behaviour Research and Therapy,* Vol. 2, No. 1 (May 1964), pp. 15–18; Paul W. Clement and D. Courtney Milne, "Group Play Therapy and Tangible Reinforcers Used to Modify the Behavior of 8-Year-Old Boys," *Behaviour Research and Therapy,* Vol. 5, No. 4 (November 1967), pp. 301–312.

[19] Paul, "Strategy of Outcome Research in Psychotherapy," pp. 116–117.

[20] Donald M. Baer, Montrose M. Wolf, and Todd R. Risley, "Some Current Dimensions of Applied Behavior Analysis," *Journal of Applied Behavior Analysis,* Vol. 1, No. 1 (Spring 1968), p. 94.

As Gelfand and Hartmann state:

> Correlated changes in the observed response rate provide a convincing demonstration that the target behavior is unmistakably under the therapist's control and not due to adventitious, extratherapeutic factors.[21]

Numerous case studies have successfully utilized the *A-B-A* design or variations thereof. Five such reports recently appeared in the first issue of the new *Journal of Applied Behavior Analysis,* and many others could be cited.[22]

In the face of the evidence now available, it is difficult to avoid a conclusion that regardless of the problems associated with

outcome research wherever it is undertaken, the overall record for behavior modification represents the best there is in psychotherapy today. The authors agree with Bergin's seemingly impartial assessment:

> The cases presented and research studies reported provide more positive evidence of the usefulness of these methods than is the case in any form of traditional interview or dynamic psychotherapy.[23]

THE NATURE OF A RESPONSE

The assertion that behaviorists look to the "discrete response" as the fundamental unit of analysis represents a serious misunderstanding of behavioral theory. The experimental interest in studying quite circumscribed elements of animal (and human) behavior should not be confused with the fact that the actual Skinnerian unit of analysis is the *operant.* The operant is by definition a class of behaviors that is susceptible to reinforcement, and operants (or, simply, responses) can vary in size and complexity in accordance with the focus of any particular investigation or treatment effort.[24]

It is clearly belaboring the obvious to point out, as Bruck does (p. 48), that the behavioral repertoire of man is "infinitely more complex" than that of the rat. Of course man can perform relatively more complicated operants. The important point is that as long as a given behavior or set of behaviors conforms to the basic definition of an operant, it does not matter how complicated and intricate it is. It can then, in principle, become the object of behavioral analysis and perhaps modification. At the human level one can speak of knitting a sweater, walking to work, writing a book,

21 Donna M. Gelfand and Donald P. Hartmann, "Behavior Therapy with Children: A Review and Evaluation of Research Methodology," *Psychological Bulletin,* Vol. 69, No. 3 (March 1968), p. 211.

22 In *Journal of Applied Behavior Analysis,* Vol. 1, No. 1 (Spring 1968), *see* R. Vance Hall, Diane Lund, and Deloris Jackson, "Effects of Teacher Attention on Study Behavior," pp. 1–12; Todd R. Risley, "The Effects and Side Effects of Punishing the Autistic Behaviors of a Deviant Child," pp. 21–34; Don R. Thomas, Wesley C. Becker, and Marianne Armstrong, "Production and Elimination of Disruptive Classroom Behavior by Systematically Varying Teacher's Behavior," pp. 35–45; Don Bushell, Jr., Patricia Ann Wrobel, and Mary Louise Michaelis, "Applying 'Group' Contingencies to the Classroom Study Behavior of Preschool Children," pp. 55–61; and Betty M. Hart *et al.,* "Effect of Contingent and Non-Contingent Social Reinforcement on the Cooperative Play of a Preschool Child," pp. 73–76. *See also,* for example, Teodoro Ayllon and Nathan H. Azrin, "The Measurement and Reinforcement of Behavior of Psychotics," *Journal of Experimental Analysis of Behavior,* Vol. 8, No. 6 (November 1965, pp. 357–383; Florence R. Harris, Montrose M. Wolf, and Donald M. Baer, "Effects of Adult Social Reinforcement on Child Behavior," in Sidney W. Bijou and Donald M. Baer, eds., *Child Development: Readings in Experimental Analysis* (New York: Appleton-Century-Crofts, 1967), pp. 146–158; and John D. Burchard, "Systematic Socialization: A Programmed Environment for the Habilitation of Antisocial Retardates," *Psychological Record,* Vol. 17, No. 4 (October 1967), pp. 461–476.

23 Allen E. Bergin, "Some Implications of Psychotherapy Research for Therapeutic Practice," in Bernard G. Berenson and Robert R. Carkhuff, eds., *Sources of Gain in Counseling and Psychotherapy* (New York: Holt, Rinehart & Winston, 1967), p. 413.

24 J. R. Millenson, *Principles of Behavioral Analysis* (New York: Macmillan Co., 1967), p. 161.

conducting a symphony, telling a joke, running for office, or flying an airplane as operants that are subject to control by a reinforcing social environment.[25]

Some of the more complex operants that have been accepted as target responses in behavior modification are such things as maintaining a job, staying in school, budgeting money, buying and caring for clothes, doing chores, and studying.[26] The suggestion that behavior modification does not deal with complex behaviors is simply untenable.

Part of the misconception surrounding the units of analysis and change in behavioral therapy is probably attributable to the importance that is attached to response specification before treatment is undertaken. This is required by the very nature of the therapy. The problem of how detailed and circumscribed the specification should be is resolved on the basis of a consideration of such things as the makeup of the individual's current behavioral repertoire and the extent to which that repertoire is adaptive in the natural environment. In the case of severe behavioral deficits, one may have to try to accelerate as basic a social skill as engaging in eye contact with another human being or uttering simple sentences.[27] When

the individual already has a rich and reasonably adaptive repertoire, then more molar types of operants can become targets of change. Behavioral therapists do indeed start where the client or patient is.

In the broader arena of academic psychology, many types of complex human behavior have come under the purview of behavioral theorists and researchers in recent years. There appears to be literally no behavior that cannot be gainfully studied using behavioral methodology and concepts.[28]

Bruck gives his readers the impression that behavioral psychology is "rat psychology." This belief is unfortunately not uncommon. It overlooks the fact that early behavioral research was primarily concerned with the study of human responses and that this tradition has continued into the present day with the study of the changing of human behavior in both laboratory and natural environments.[29] On the other hand,

25 See C. B. Ferster, "Reinforcement and Punishment in the Control of Human Behavior by Social Agencies," in H. J. Eysenck, ed., *Experiments in Behaviour Therapy* (New York: Macmillan Co., 1964), pp. 189–206.

26 See, for example, Burchard, *op. cit.;* Gaylord L. Thorne, Roland G. Tharp, and Ralph J. Wetzel, "Behavioral Modification Techniques: New Tools for Probation Officers," *Federal Probation*, Vol. 31, No. 2 (June 1967), pp. 21–27; and Harold L. Cohen, "Educational Therapy: The Design of Learning Environments," in John M. Shlien, ed., *Research in Psychotherapy*, Vol. 3 (Washington, D.C.: American Psychological Association, 1968), pp. 21–53.

27 See Phillip Blake and Thelma Moss, "The Development of Socialization Skills in an Electively Mute Child," *Behaviour Research and Therapy*, Vol. 5, No. 4 (November 1967), pp. 349–356; and Wayne Isaacs, James Thomas, and Israel Goldiamond, "Application of Operant Conditioning to Reinstate Verbal Behavior in Psychotics," in Ullmann and Krasner, eds., *op. cit.*, pp. 69–73.

28 The interested reader can refer to work in the areas of (1) complex verbal behavior and concept formation, (2) attitude formation and change, (3) social interaction, and (4) social organization. *See* (1) Arthur W. Staats and Carolyn K. Staats, *Complex Human Behavior* (New York: Holt, Rinehart & Winston, 1963), esp. chaps. 4 & 5; Arthur W. Staats, ed., *Human Learning* (New York: Holt, Rinehart & Winston, 1964), chaps. 3 & 4; and Theodore R. Dixon and David L. Horton, eds., *Verbal Behavior and General Behavior Theory* (Englewood Cliffs, N.J.: Prentice Hall, 1968); (2) Daryl J. Bem, "Self-Perception: The Dependent Variable of Human Performance," *Organizational Behavior and Human Performance*, Vol. 2, No. 2 (May 1967), pp. 105–121; and Chester A. Insko, *Theories of Attitude Change* (New York: Appleton-Century-Crofts, 1967), chap. 2; (3) J. Stacy Adams and A. Kimball Romney, "A Functional Analysis of Authority," *Psychological Review*, Vol. 66, No. 4 (July 1959), pp. 234–251; and K. Weingarten and F. Mechner, "The Contingency as an Independent Variable of Social Interaction," in Thom Verhave, ed., *The Experimental Analysis of Behavior* (New York: Appleton-Century-Crofts, 1966), pp. 447–459; and (4) John H. Kunkel, "Some Behavioral Aspects of the Ecological Approach to Social Organization," *American Journal of Sociology*, Vol. 73, No. 1 (July 1967), pp. 12–29.

29 John B. Watson and Rosalie Rayner, "Conditioned Emotional Reactions," *Journal of Experimental Psychology*, Vol. 3, No. 1 (February 1920), pp. 1–14.

ne study of animal behavior as a source of hypotheses concerning human behavior has a long history. Infrahuman organisms are studied because experimental manipulations are permitted with animals that would be unethical with humans, such as long-term isolation, deprivation, or even continuous observation. The results of animal research may become the source of hypotheses concerning human behavior, but these hypotheses are acceptable only when they have been validated with humans. The same situation prevails in the study of the effects of drugs. If a drug is shown to cure cancer in rats, it is assumed that it may have comparable curative properties in men. However, this assumption is not accepted until it is tested. To naïvely deny behavioral parallels among pigeons, rats, guinea pigs, baboons, and men is not unlike disclaiming the common ancestry of man and the great apes, and its consequences may be even more costly.

INTERNAL RESPONDING

Few modern behaviorists adhere to so strict a doctrine of operationism that every response must be tied directly to an objectively measurable index of its occurrence. To adopt such a position would be to cut oneself off from an important domain of responding, the existence of which no one seriously disputes. However, the behaviorist insists that until contrary evidence warrants, internal responses are not to be assigned any properties not also attributable to observable responses.[30] (This is less true for much of so-called respondent behavior that is connected more directly with the autonomic nervous system. What is being referred to here is primarily behavior called "thinking," "imagining," and so on.) As yet, there seems to be no reason for consider-

ing these responses in terms of anything more than what Homme calls "coverants" (covert operants), which are subject to the same principles of learning and performance that apply to overt operants.[31]

It must of course be noted that behaviorists differ widely in the extent to which they make use of such mediating variables in their description and explanation of behavior. Skinnerians tend to make little if any use of them, whereas Hullians or Pavlovian theorists tend to use them liberally. As an example, Maltzman has suggested that the orienting reflex may account for much of verbal and semantic conditioning as well as for incidental learning phenomena.[32]

The authors' own position is that internal responses are a useful focus as long as one continues to treat them as intervening variables rather than as hypothetical constructs replete with surplus meaning.[33] One of the principal faults of much of dynamic theory is that concepts like ego, the unconscious, and libido have not only broken all bounds of operational specificity, they have also taken on a presumed reality status of their own. They have been stripped of their metaphorical heritage and treated as genuine mental entities.[34] The behaviorist seeks to avoid this critical error and gener-

[30] B. F. Skinner, "Behaviorism at Fifty," in T. W. Wann, ed., *Behaviorism and Phenomenology* (Chicago: University of Chicago Press, 1964), pp. 79–108; Lloyd E. Homme, "Control of Coverants, the Operants of the Mind," *Psychological Record*, Vol. 15, No. 4 (October 1965), pp. 501–511.

[31] *Op. cit.*

[32] Irving Maltzman, "Awareness: Cognitive Psychology vs. Behaviorism," *Journal of Experimental Research in Personality*, Vol. 1, No. 3 (May 1966), pp. 161–165; Maltzman and David C. Raskin, "Effects of Individual Differences in the Orienting Reflex on Conditioning and Complex Processes," *Journal of Experimental Research in Personality*, Vol. 1, No. 1 (March 1965), pp. 1–16.

[33] For a discussion of operationality, intervening variables, and hypothetical constructs, *see* Melvin H. Marx, "The Dimension of Operational Clarity," in Marx, ed., *Theories in Contemporary Psychology* (New York: Macmillan Co., 1963), pp. 187–202.

[34] *See* B. F. Skinner, "Critique of Psychoanalytic Concepts and Theories," in Staats, ed., *op. cit.*, pp. 387–395; and Theodore R. Sarbin, "On the Futility of the Proposition That Some People Be Labeled 'Mentally Ill,' " *Journal of Consulting Psychology*, Vol. 31, No. 5 (October 1967), pp. 447–453.

ally strives to minimize his dependence on terms that cannot be closely tied to observable events.

Behavioral therapists have made considerable use of implicit responses in their practice. Wolpe's systematic desensitization technique usually relies on the patient's construction of imagined scenes as a means of reducing anxiety responses to the actual physical counterparts of those scenes in the natural environment.[35] The same is true for the technique known as "covert sensitization," which is applicable to both maladaptive approach and avoidance tendencies.[36] Also, the use of self-management or instigation procedures often depends on the client's ability to engage in covert self-stimulation as well as his ability to manipulate variables in the external environment.[37]

INFLUENCES ON BEHAVIOR

The behavior of living organisms is highly complex and its attribution to a single cause can only be the product of naïve reductionism. Accordingly, the common accusation that behaviorists explain all behavior in terms of learning history is inaccurate. Behaviorists recognize as well the impact of physiology and contemporary events.[38] The relative contribution of each influence will vary as a function of the character of the organism, the nature of the response under study, and the conditions under which the study is being conducted.

Physiology influences both the selection of environmental events that function as stimuli for the organism and the nature of its response to these stimuli. While the change of a traffic light from green to red is an environmental event, it will have radically different stimulus value for the blind as contrasted to the sighted person. But physiology alone does not determine a response. Certain events that do have stimulus value may be interpreted differently by people who have had different learning histories. For example, research on the behavior of persons in the paths of tornados has shown that some failed to respond to the auditory cues available (a tornado is said to sound like an onrushing train).[39] Most of these individuals were neither deaf nor suicidal; they simply had not been trained to attend to the relevant cues with self-protective activity. When learning history is de-emphasized, one may erroneously attribute to physiology the failure of a response to occur. For example, it has been demonstrated that even vegetative idiots, who were presumed to be incapable of emitting social responses, can do so following careful shaping procedures.[40]

THE NATURE OF A STIMULUS

Just as an operant is defined by its relationship to events that can reinforce it, so too must the stimulus be characterized by a relational property. A stimulus is defined not by its content or composition but by its effect on behavior. Conceived in this way,

[35] See Joseph Wolpe and Arnold A. Lazarus, *Behavior Therapy Techniques* (New York: Pergamon Press, 1966), chap. 5.

[36] See Joseph R. Cautela, "Covert Sensitization," *Psychological Reports*, Vol. 20, No. 2 (April 1967), pp. 459–468.

[37] See Richard B. Stuart, "Behavioral Control of Overeating," *Behaviour Research and Therapy*, Vol. 5, No. 4 (November 1967), pp. 357–365; Homme, *op. cit.*; Israel Goldiamond, "Self-Control Procedures in Personal Behavior Problems," *Psychological Reports*, Vol. 17, No. 3 (December 1965), pp. 851–868.

[38] See B. F. Skinner, *The Behavior of Organisms* (New York: Appleton-Century-Crofts, 1938).

[39] Charles E. Fritz and Eli S. Marks, "The NORC Studies of Human Behavior in Disaster," *Journal of Social Issues*, Vol. 10, No. 3 (July 1954), pp. 26–41.

[40] Harold K. Rice and Martha W. McDaniel, "Operant Behavior in Vegetative Patients," *Psychological Record*, Vol. 16, No. 3 (July 1966), pp. 279–282; Rice *et al.*, "Operant Behavior in Vegetative Patients II," *Psychological Record*, Vol. 17, No. 4 (October 1967), pp. 449–460; Paul R. Fuller, "Operant Conditioning of a Vegetative Human Organism," *American Journal of Psychology*, Vol. 62, No. 4 (October 1949), pp. 587–590.

a stimulus can be as broad or as narrow as is useful in the analysis and control of behavior. Behaviorists do not hesitate to speak of an entire situation as a stimulus.[41] It is for this reason that Bruck's several suggestions that behaviorists do not take into account the context of any specific event (pp. 48–49) represent such a gross misconception. A stimulus can be as expansive as a festival or an argument or as minute as a pinprick, depending on what the analytical problem happens to be. Any specific component of a given stimulus situation should always be considered in relation to the other components with which it is combined, since no component stimulus has invariable effects across all stimulus situations.

The concept of the reinforcing stimulus, or simply the reinforcer, requires special attention. Again, it belabors the obvious to point out that man is frequently reinforced by stimuli different from those that influence the rat or pigeon. The same definition of a reinforcer is applicable up and down the phylogenetic scale, even though the concrete nature of any given reinforcer may have to be made species-specific (and often even individual-specific). Stated briefly, a positive reinforcer is one that strengthens behavior it follows and an aversive reinforcer is one that weakens behavior it follows or strengthens behavior it precedes.[42]

A useful manner in which to classify reinforcers is whether they are natural or synthetic consequences of a response. A natural consequence of combing one's hair is having it stay out of one's eyes, while a synthetic consequence might be receiving a penny or a sugar-frosted flake. Behaviorists can do little to manipulate natural consequences (a behaviorist cannot prevent a child from being burned when he touches

a hot stove) other than to increase or decrease the probability of the responses that produce them. Much of behavioral technology is therefore concerned with the manipulation of synthetic consequences.

The range of consequences available includes food, cigarettes, gum, and such generalized secondary reinforcers as attention, affection, money, and tokens. In addition, behaviors such as swimming, hiking, fishing, taking a walk, feeding animals, attending religious services, and interacting with a social worker have all been utilized as reinforcers in behavior modification.[43] The authors are sure that the activities of "dancing, laughing, or painting," mentioned by Bruck (p. 49) would also prove effective for many clients and patients. It is of utmost importance to note, however, that none of these events can be regarded as a universal reinforcer. At times a person's responses may be contingent on obtaining food, but this is less likely after a feast. Whether an event is to function as a reinforcer will depend on such factors as previous learning history, current physiological state, and other contiguous properties of the environment.

Contrary to the assertion made by Bruck, studies in latent learning, perceptual learning, and reversals in concept formation have not invalidated reinforcement as a necessary condition for learning to occur. The latent learning experiments (with animals) have been beset with the problem of ruling out sensory reinforcement (e.g., stimulus novelty and complexity) as contributing to the observed behavior. That this kind of reinforcement does occur has been fairly well demonstrated in other kinds of research,[44]

---

[41] See, for example, Millenson, op. cit., p. 121; and Charles C. Perkins, Jr., "An Analysis of the Concept of Reinforcement," Psychological Review, Vol. 75, No. 2 (March 1968), pp. 155–172.

[42] For a more complete discussion of reinforcers, see Millenson, op. cit., esp. chaps. 4, 5 & 17.

[43] See Burchard, op. cit.; John M. Atthowe, Jr., and Leonard Krasner, "Preliminary Report on the Application of Contingent Reinforcement Procedures (Token Economy) on a 'Chronic' Psychiatric Ward," Journal of Abnormal Psychology, Vol. 73, No. 1 (February 1968), pp. 37–43; and Ayllon and Azrin, op. cit.

[44] See G. B. Kish, "Studies of Sensory Reinforcement," in Honig, ed., op. cit., pp. 109–159.

and one recent report suggests that even for the rat, stimulus novelty may be as strong a reinforcer as food.[45]

As for perceptual and concept learning studies, it must be kept in mind that these are usually problem-solving situations in which the human subject is required to try to match his performance to some criterion of correctness. Being right is probably a high-priority positive reinforcer and being wrong a negative one among most subjects, as evidenced by research in verbal operant conditioning and other performance feedback research.[46] That problem-solving behavior is subject to a behavioral analysis is demonstrated by Millenson's treatment of this and related topics.[47]

However, we do not wish to commit ourselves to a prematurely adamant stand on the question of whether reinforcement is necessary to all learning. We tend to agree with Tolman and Bandura that one can frequently make a distinction between the learning or *acquisition* of some responses and their *performance*.[48] The principle of reinforcement seems to be most strategic to the performance of a behavior. This distinction is especially useful in the study of modeling or imitation behavior,[49] and the use of models appears to hold considerable promise for psychotherapy.[50]

MEANING

The study of meaning has traditionally been the province of cognitively oriented psychologists, and the effort to approach the topic in learning theory terms is relatively recent. Again, there is a distinction to be made between those who rely on some mediational concepts in their theory (e.g., Staats and Staats) and those who maintain a peripheral, "outside-the-skin" stance (e.g., Millenson).[51] Depending on the problem under investigation, either one or the other point of view may be more appropriate. In either case, the rigor provided by behavioral terminology may help tighten up an area of inquiry in which the temptation to be vague is great.

Following Millenson, we conceive of meaning as a more complex form of discrimination or concept behavior. How does one conclude that a person has developed a concept of some object? The answer is, by the behavior (including verbal behavior) he displays in relation to that object. A concept is a fact of behavior, a response or set of responses that has come under the control of a class of discriminative stimuli. For example, one might say that a child has developed the concept of "yellowness" if he demonstrates the ability to select from among a multiplicity of items those that bear this color.

The analysis of meaning (or, preferably, meaning behavior) can be regarded as the

---

[45] Bruce T. Leckart and Kay S. Bennett, "Reinforcement Effects of Food and Stimulus Novelty," *Psychological Record*, Vol. 18, No. 2 (April 1968), pp. 253–260.

[46] *See* Leonard Krasner, "Studies of the Conditioning of Verbal Behavior," *Psychological Bulletin*, Vol. 55, No. 3 (May 1958), pp. 121–148; Edwin A. Locke, "Relationship of Success and Expectation to Affect on Goal-Seeking Tasks," *Journal of Personality and Social Psychology*, Vol. 7, No. 2 (October 1967), pp. 125–134; and N. T. Feather, "Change in Confidence Following Success or Failure as a Predictor of Subsequent Performance," *Journal of Personality and Social Psychology*, Vol. 9, No. 1 (May 1968), pp. 38–46.

[47] *Op. cit.*, chaps. 13 & 14.

[48] E. C. Tolman, *Purposive Behavior in Animals* (New York: Century Co., 1932); Albert Bandura, "Vicarious Processes: A Case of No-Trial Learning," in Leonard Berkowitz, ed., *Advances in Experimental Social Psychology*, Vol. 2 (New York: Academic Press, 1965), pp. 6–7.

[49] Bandura, *op. cit.*; James P. Flanders, "A Review of Research on Imitative Behavior," *Psychological Bulletin*, Vol. 69, No. 5 (May 1968), pp. 316–337.

[50] *See* Albert Bandura and Richard H. Walters, *Social Learning and Personality Development* (New York: Holt, Rinehart & Winston, 1963), pp. 242–246; O. Ivar Lovaas *et al.*, "The Establishment of Imitation and Its Use for the Development of Complex Behavior in Schizophrenic Children," *Behaviour Research and Therapy*, Vol. 5, No. 3 (August 1967), pp. 171–181; and Bandura and Menlove, *op. cit.*

[51] *See* Staats and Staats, *op. cit.*, esp. pp. 91–94 and 140–153; and Millenson, *op. cit.*, chap. 13.

study of the interrelations among concept behaviors. In effect, such behavior represents a process of abstraction whereby relatively concrete stimuli are brought together into more comprehensive units (as, for example, when usage of the term "parents" reflects a combining of the stimuli designated as "mother" and "father"). The therapist who places the label "character disorder" on a given patient has very likely interrelated a variety of more specific concepts that pertain to observable features of that patient's behavior (such as the repetitive occurrence of certain antisocial operants, the failure to verbalize a sense of "guilt," and a lack of behavioral control by delayed reinforcers). These more concrete stimuli become incorporated within the same meaning behavior through the use of relational concepts such as "acting out" and "ego-syntonic." [52] While this doubtless does involve "thought" processes on the part of the therapist, a productive analysis of his meaning behavior can nonetheless be conducted without the need for concern with such internal events. Attention is instead given to the discriminative concepts he uses to denote a specific stimuli and to the way he pulls these terms together through the use of relational concepts into more abstract units.

Probably the greater part of human meaning behavior takes the form of verbal responses. However, behaviorists generally agree that although verbal behavior is important, there has been a tendency on the part of psychodynamic theorists to exaggerate the value of verbal responses as (1) valid indexes of underlying feelings and thoughts and (2) variables controlling nonverbal behavior. That verbal reports produced by introspection and efforts to create insight and self-awareness are subject to operant conditioning has been amply demonstrated.[53] And in the absence of conclusive evidence to the contrary, the causal chain of verbal——>nonverbal should not be emphasized to the neglect of the alternative possibilities of no relationship or a reverse relationship obtaining between these two classes of variables.[54]

AFFECT AND ITS COMMUNICATION

It is difficult to understand Bruck's contention that feelings are overlooked by the behaviorist. Much of the myth surrounding terms like this can be reduced if we but ask the question of what it is that controls one's use of such labels. We are all conditioned by our social environment to attach labels to that which we observe, and one of the most prevalent kinds of labeling processes involved in the perception of people has to do with the presumed emotional quality of their observed behavior. We say a man is "angry," is "in love," or is "sad," basing such inferences on observed behavior, verbal and otherwise. Viewed in this way, it is absurd to suggest that behavioral therapists ignore feelings. They deal with any kind of behavior, regardless of its label, if that behavior happens to be problematic in the life of the client or patient.

Social Reinforcement Machine," in H. H. Strupp and L. Luborsky, eds., *Research in Psychotherapy,* Vol. 2 (Washington, D.C.: American Psychological Association, 1962), pp. 61–94; and Charles D. Noblin, Edwin O. Timmons, and Marian C. Reynard, "Psychoanalytic Interpretations as Verbal Reinforcers: Importance of Interpretation Content," in Goldstein and Dean, eds., *op. cit.,* pp. 416–418. *See also* Marvin Karno, "Communication, Reinforcement and 'Insight': The Problem of Psychotherapeutic Effect," *American Journal of Psychotherapy,* Vol. 19, No. 3 (July 1965), pp. 467–479.
[54] *See* Joseph H. Cautela, "Desensitization and Insight," *Behaviour Research and Therapy,* Vol. 3, No. 3 (August 1965), pp. 59–64; Maltzman, *op. cit.;* Bem, *op. cit.;* Gerry Brodsky, "The Relation between Verbal and Non-Verbal Behavior Change," *Behaviour Research and Therapy,* Vol. 5, No. 3 (August 1967), pp. 183–191; and Robert C. Wahler and Howard R. Pollio, "Behavior and Insight: A Case Study in Behavior Therapy," *Journal of Experimental Research in Personality,* Vol. 3, No. 1 (June 1968), pp. 45–56.

---

[52] *See* Merl M. Jackel, "Clients with Character Disorders," *Social Casework,* Vol. 44, No. 6 (June 1963), pp. 315–322.
[53] *See* Leonard Krasner, "The Therapist as a

None of this in any way represents a denial or a neglect of the internal components of emotional response. However, the internal dynamics of emotion and their relation to overt behavior represent one of the most controversial and confused areas in psychology.[55] The casualness with which some theorists assume an understanding of such phenomena reveals a naïveté that only serves to obscure the extent of our ignorance. Some value can be attached to experimental evidence pointing to an important self-labeling component in much of emotional and attitudinal response.[56] If this is so, then manipulation of the variables controlling self-labeling (e.g., observation of one's own overt behavior, observation of the behavior of others, the labeling of an individual's behavior by others) may result in appropriate changes in both the physiological and subjective experiential aspects of emotion, as well as in its overt motor aspects. The techniques of role-playing, model presentation, assertive training, and self-management may be of use in this regard. It should also be mentioned that the important affect of anxiety, which has probably received more investigative and therapeutic attention than has any other emotional state, is the specific focus of a number of behavioral therapy techniques (especially systematic densitization).[57]

Besides the suggestion that behavioral therapists ignore feelings as such, we are puzzled by the further implication that they may be unmindful of what Bruck refers to as "emotional transactions" between people (p. 49). The use of florid terms like this and like "total emotional relationship" illustrates the very kind of conceptual ambiguity that most behaviorists struggle to overcome. What is meant by an emotional transaction? Is this not once again a label placed on observed behavior, this time of a social interactional sort? And if this is so, is there not once again a need to specify the behaviors involved so that they can be better understood and controlled?

Experimental psychology has made some headway in the specification of behaviors that communicate interpersonal affect, especially that implied by dimensions such as "liking-disliking" and "pleasant-unpleasant." Much of this appears to transpire through paralinguistic (e.g., tone and pitch of voice, rate of speech) and nonverbal (e.g., smiling, gazing, body orientation, and physical distance) channels.[58] Social workers might do well to acquaint themselves with this research, since it has important implications for both worker-client interaction and that which takes place among members of client groups.

---

55 See Henry N. Peters, "Affect and Emotion," in Marx, ed., *Theories in Contemporary Psychology*, pp. 435–454; and Melvin L. Goldstein, "Physiological Theories of Emotion: A Critical Historical Review from the Standpoint of Behavior Theory," *Psychological Bulletin*, Vol. 69, No. 1 (January 1968), pp. 23–40.

56 See Stanley Schachter, "The Interaction of Cognitive and Physiological Determinants of Emotional States," in Leonard Berkowitz, ed., *Advances in Experimental Social Psychology*, Vol. 1 (New York: Academic Press, 1964), pp. 49–80; and Bem, *op. cit.*

57 See Charles D. Speilberger, ed., *Anxiety and Behavior* (New York: Academic Press, 1966); and Eileen Gambrill, "Modification of Anxiety by Behavioral Methods," unpublished manuscript, 1967.

58 See Joel R. Davitz, ed., *The Communication of Emotional Meaning* (New York: McGraw-Hill Book Co., 1964); Michael Argyle and Adam Kendon, "The Experimental Analysis of Social Performance," in Leonard Berkowitz, ed., *Advances in Experimental Social Psychology*, Vol. 3 (New York: Academic Press, 1967), esp. pp. 62–80; Howard M. Rosenfeld, "Nonverbal Reciprocation of Approval: An Experimental Analysis," *Journal of Experimental Social Psychology*, Vol. 3, No. 1 (January 1967), pp. 102–111; Robert Sommer, "Small Group Ecology," *Psychological Bulletin*, Vol. 67, No. 2 (February 1967), pp. 145–152; Albert Mehrabian, "The Inference of Attitudes from the Posture, Orientation, and Distance of a Communicator," *Journal of Consulting and Clinical Psychology*, Vol. 32, No. 3 (June 1968), pp. 296–308; Mehrabian, "Communication without Words," *Psychology Today*, Vol. 2, No. 4 (September 1968), pp. 53–55.

MOTIVATION

Many theories of motivation have been developed and many disputes still exist, but one of the most troublesome controversies has to do with the extent to which it is necessary to posit causal forces within the individual. Some of the difficulties inherent in the intra-individual view may be summarized as follows: (1) a tendency toward reification of terms (descriptive adjectives such as "unconscious" are transformed into explanatory nouns such as "the unconscious"), (2) the study of the individual is taken out of the context of the conditions surrounding his behavior,[59] (3) issues of causality are resolved through debate rather than research because the terms of the theory are not operational,[60] and (4) circular reasoning is invoked. For example, Bruck uses the term need repeatedly, the implication being that behaviorists do not adequately handle whatever psychological phenomena are implied by this term. The question that arises is: What are the referents of a term like need? The typical reply usually reduces to a recitation of specific behaviors. It is at this point that a basic error in logic becomes manifest: the presumed cause becomes indistinguishable from that which is caused. How do we know a person has a dependency need? Because he behaves in a dependent manner. This is circular thinking, and it turns out that what is being presented as explanation is really simply disguised description, a mere labeling of behavior. When operationally defined, descriptive terms like dependency and aggression are useful; as explanatory terms, they are inadequate.[61]

In the interest of parsimony as well as operational specificity and the desire to avoid circular logic, behaviorists tend to rely on factors external to the organism in drawing causal inferences about behavior. Bolles has recently presented a cogent argument to the effect that the traditional concept of motivation is largely translatable into the behavioral concept of reinforcer.[62] Note that this reverses the usual imagery; external stimuli are seen as acting *on* individuals rather than being acted on *by* individuals. It seems, as Bolles suggests, that a list of so-called needs (such as Murray's) can just as easily be viewed as a list of reinforcers and does not require elaborate and unparsimonious assumptions about internal states. Hence a "need for affection," for example, is better described simply as approach behavior in relation to certain reinforcers (e.g., smiles, hugs, praise, attention) that not only control that behavior but also an observer's use of the label "affection." And the problem of motivation itself can be reduced to an analysis of the several variables that establish and maintain reinforcers.[63]

SELF-CONTROL

It is simply not true that behaviorists regard individuals as devoid of self-control.[64] To be sure, much of current therapy of whatever description does render the client or patient more of a passive than an active agent in the treatment program, but this is not by any means something that blankets all of behavior modification. The reader is urged to examine a recent article by Kanfer and Phillips, giving special atten-

[59] Julian B. Rotter, *Social Learning and Clinical Psychology* (Englewood Cliffs, N.J.: Prentice-Hall, 1954), chaps. 1–3.

[60] *See* Marx, "The Dimensions of Operational Clarity."

[61] For a discussion of description versus explanation in theories of motivation, *see* Staats and Staats, *op. cit.*, chap. 7.

[62] Robert C. Bolles, *Theory of Motivation* (New York: Harper & Row, 1967), chap. 15. *See also* the excellent behavioral treatment given the topic of motivation by Millenson, *op. cit.*, chaps. 15 & 16.

[63] For an excellent treatment of motivation in these terms, *see* Millenson, *op. cit.*, chaps. 15 & 16.

[64] For behavioral discussions of "self-control," *see* B. F. Skinner, *Science and Human Behavior* (New York: Free Press of Glencoe, 1953), chap. 15; and Bandura and Walters, *op. cit.*, chap. 4.

tion to their discussion of "instigation therapy." In this behavioral approach:

> The patient is taught to modify his extra-therapeutic environment and to apply learning techniques to his own behavior. This approach is best characterized as one in which the patient learns to become his own therapist. Self-regulating and self-evaluative behaviors are often directly reinforced during psychotherapy but the actual execution of new behaviors is practiced outside the therapy session.[65]

In addition, Wolpe's assertive training relies heavily on the client's ability to exercise considerable self-control.[66]

CONCLUSION

The article by Bruck raises many other issues that could be addressed were it not for the inevitable limitations of space. In addition, the ones that have been touched on really deserve more attention in depth than can possibly be provided here. However, perhaps enough has been presented to indicate the extent to which behavioral psychology does take into account what Bruck calls the "whole person," and in language that goes a long way toward eliminating much of the ambiguity and surplus

meaning that characterize most current personality theories.

The richness of psychodynamic language has traditionally given considerable reward to those who use it. To speak in terms of complex inner states is to gain a sense of understanding of the mysterious while at the same time preserving the dignity of the mystery. From a behavioral science point of view, however, it is possible to argue that this richness not only goes well beyond any data presently available, it also tends to get in the way of the practitioner's task of giving effective and efficient service to people with problems. In the last analysis, this is the testing ground of any theoretical scheme and it is the primary reason why the present writers, in spite of our own largely psychodynamic backgrounds, have elected to move in the direction of behavioral psychology within the context of social work.

In coming months, social workers can expect to have available more and more literature that attempts to relate behavior modification theory and practice to their own field. It is hoped that this material will not only be read and considered, but that it will be approached without prejudgment. The gravity of social workers' responsibility to present and future clients is such that we can ill afford to dismiss out of hand that which may materially expand and enrich existing levels of therapeutic competence.

---

[65] Kanfer and Phillips, "Behavior Therapy,"
[66] *See* Wolpe and Lazarus, *op. cit.*, chap. 4.
p. 116.

Rational Counseling:

A Dynamic Approach to Children

MORLEY D. GLICKEN

As a by-product of psychoanalytic thought, few treatment groups have quite the mystique of the latency-aged child. One has only to read any number of famous studies by Freud, Ericson, Anna Freud and other psychoanalytic thinkers to be somewhat awed by their often brilliant "detective" work. The unfortunate result of this complex, difficult approach has been a great deal of illogical, unsupported thinking concerning the latency-aged child with emotional difficulties and an effective treatment for the resolution of his problems.

The Psychoanalytic Approach to the Latency-Aged Child

Psychoanalytic theory suggests that children are often unable to discuss their problems because they tend to repress important material. It further assumes that one can often uncover relevant motives, events, and traumas by providing an atmosphere in which the child can relate freely. We call this atmosphere or approach "Play Therapy." It is assumed that, either in play or in his random dialogue with the therapist, the child will often unconsciously bring to the surface important material. As the child forms a close, healthy relationship with the therapist, he begins to develop insight into his feelings. This insight, when properly developed, frees the child of his difficulties and allows changes in behavior to develop gradually.

JOURNAL OF ELEMENTARY COUNSELING AND GUIDANCE, May 1968, Vol. 2, No. 4, pp. 261-267.

While few therapists in the school setting rely completely on the analytic approach, many remnants of it remain which tend to decrease the effectiveness of the therapist in his treatment of children.

To begin with, it is, in the author's opinion, fallacious to assume that most children cannot readily and quickly discuss their problems in regard to either school or home. Most children in the author's elementary school social work caseload can and do discuss their difficulties without being coaxed by saccharine words or play therapy.

Too often we overtly or covertly convey to the child the same ego-deflating attitudes of the parent when we assume that, because of his age, the child is incapable of involving himself in a treatment-oriented verbal dialogue. By assuming that we need play objects or other gimmicks with most children, we effectively undermine the child's ability to discuss problems and resolve conflicts and we may often avoid facing important issues by turning the therapy session into a fun-and-games time for clay throwing and paint splashing.

This avoidance of issues seems grounded in our illogical premise that disturbed children are too brittle to face their problems actively. This is just not true. Many disturbed children have undergone years of the most violent psychologically damaging conditioning one can imagine and still function beyond our expectations.

Another psychoanalytic remnant too often inculcated in our treatment of children is the notion that once a child understands his feelings more accurately change will take place. Understanding feelings seldom precipitates change since disturbed feelings are end products of pathological decision making and are in themselves only symptoms. What occurs too often is that the therapist is a "nice" person and the child consciously improves to please the therapist or to gain the therapist's love. Such improvement sometimes is long term, but more often than not it disappears when treatment ends. When treatment fails we often wooden-leggedly assert that the child has only intellectual understanding and lacks the emotional

173

understanding necessary for change, or that the child lacks motivation and doesn't really want to change because he fears losing the attention of his mother, with whom he is still involved.

The need for a new approach

What should be obvious to most child therapists is that we are woefully inefficient, ineffectual, and inaccurate in our treatment of children. We have neither a very good theory nor a very useful treatment approach in psychoanalytically oriented therapy, counseling or casework—all of which mean the same. We, particularly those of us who work within the reality confines of a school setting, should be thinking more in terms of an effective, short term, truly depth-oriented approach.

Rational-Emotive Psychotherapy

If the author's experiences are at all transferable to other school counselors, it is suggested that Rational-Emotive Psychotherapy might be just such an approach. The rational approach holds that disturbed emotions, the outward sign of malfunctioning, develop because the child acquires irrational thoughts, beliefs, attitudes, or philosophies about himself and his environment (Ellis, 1962). When a child bases a decision upon an illogical idea the outcome is often a self-defeating emotion or act. It is held that if the counselor can, by aggressively challenging him, help the child see the illogic of his thinking then the child can often significantly improve his functioning. This means that the therapist must be able to isolate the illogical idea, prove to the child why it might be illogical and what harm it does to him, and then help the child accept a saner view of himself and his world by actively encouraging and supporting the child in his attempt to live more logically.

It might sound at this point as if the rational therapist is a walking logician without feelings or emotions. Not so. He challenges only disturbed ideas, not all ideas. People will always emote and feel no matter how logical or bright. But the healthier the internal logic and self-spoken sentences, the healthier their outward manifestations. This assumes, of course, that people think before they act even if the thought is spontaneous or illogical. If we see a dog at the door we might react a number of ways, usually not violently. However, if the dog is foaming at the mouth, our reaction often indicates fear or panic. We then consciously make choices based upon past experiences before we act.

Therapists Need Understanding of Irrational Ideas Probably most helpful to the rational therapist is a good working understanding of common irrational ideas. Most of the children seen by the author use one or more of the following irrational ideas in making self-defeating decisions (Ellis, 1962).

1. It is a dire necessity to be loved or approved by virtually every significant person in our environment.
2. One must be thoroughly competent, adequate, and achieving in all possible respects if one is to consider oneself worthwhile.
3. It is catastrophic when things are not the way one would very much like them to be.
4. It is easier to avoid than to face life difficulties and self-responsibilities.
5. One's past history is an all important determiner of one's present behavior; because something once affected strongly one's life, it will indefinitely have a similar effect.

The Counselor Must Convey Belief in the Child Along with isolation of illogical ideas must come the counselor's belief, conveyed directly to the child, that the child is capable of resolving his problems with minimal intervention from the therapist. The therapist functions essentially as an educator by teaching the child a new way of looking at himself and his world. In no way does he, as is so common in many forms of therapy, subtly encourage the child to improve by offering the child his love. The child is encouraged to improve for his *own* benefit, *not* the benefit of parents or therapist. Too many children who function well in the school setting mainly to win the approval of their parents face extreme frustration when the parent's interest wanes. The rational approach attempts to help the child learn that achieving to win the acceptance or love of others is often self-defeating. Not everyone can possibly like or accept us. If one attempts to win the approval of virtually everyone, the few who refuse to accept us, particularly if they are parents or other significant persons in our environment, tend to negate the other 98 percent who like us. More important than demanding total acceptance of others is the child's ability to relate more positively toward difficult objects in his life, be they disagreeable parents or a rejecting teacher. The concept of forming healthy working relationships rather than unhealthy "love" relationships should be stressed by the therapist.

Once the child has a fairly good understanding of the rational approach and has been able to isolate his irrational thoughts, the therapist begins assigning homework in the form of practical experiences geared to help the child overcome his school or home difficulty.

The Underachiever

A most common type of difficulty in the worker's case load is the underachiever. Very often the underachiever is a relatively bright child so brainwashed into perfectionistic thinking by his demanding parents that school becomes a nightmare of continual defeat. The underachiever often is convinced that unless he can do virtually everything well, he is really a terribly worthless person. If he fails to achieve competence in a subject quickly, he gives up. Effort, he irrationally maintains, might indicate that he really isn't a very competent person. After all, he might really try to master a subject and only get a B or a C, and that, he equally illogically declares, would be catastrophic, indicative of the fact that he really *is* the worthless, inadequate person he believes himself to be. Consequently, the defeatist attitude or belligerent facade is often an excellent coverup for his own fears (Glicken, 1967). Not trying but still passing at least gives him the excuse that had he *tried* harder, he would have done better. He easily lapses into lethargy, continues avoiding the issue, and is, to all practical outward appearances, poorly motivated. On the contrary, the underachiever in almost all instances is a terribly ambitious, power hungry, perfectionistic child.

How the therapist can encourage the underachiever

Once the therapist isolates the underlying illogical ideas of the underachiever, he begins to encourage attempts at new behavior by assigning homework. The child might be encouraged to complete his classroom paper no matter how poor a job he does just to prove that part of a job is better than none at all and that improved competence in anything requires practice. The child might also be assigned the task of trying to point out to the parent that the more he (the child) attempts to do all things well, the more difficult it might become, because of his increased internal stress, to do *anything* well. The child attempts to show the parent that he can't become the perfect student overnight and possibly that he never will. He might, however, by continued practice significantly improve with time. The therapist at no time lectures the child on the need to get good grades. Instead, he helps the child see that if he wants good grades for the right reasons (his own feeling of accomplishment, *not* just to please his parents), practice and effort rather than Jehovian thinking are the most realistic means to achieve his goal.

Of course, no child lives in the therapist's perfect world and he sometimes makes mistakes in his attempts to change. The therapist non-judgmentally helps the child break through these blocks. In most cases children do follow through on assignments, and over the past two years the author has noted significant improvement in about 90 per cent of all cases referred using such measurements as pre- and post-therapy personality testing, improvement in grades, teacher reports, and evaluation of parents. (The author's caseload is unscreened and consists of a good number of underachievers, acter-outers, pre-delinquents, neurotics, and even some borderline psychotics.)

Teachers Join the Picture . . . To serve the children in the author's caseload more effectively, teachers are seen in group consultation sessions and an attempt is made to help them gain insight not only into the child's problems, but also into ways in which the teacher can cope more effectively with the troubled child in the classroom (Glicken, 1968). This often means that teachers must begin questioning their own ideas and attitudes toward teaching, particularly as it relates to the troubled child. The group acts as a stimulating force to educate, to motivate, and often to change the way teachers teach. Many school mental health workers facing the awesome number of troubled children in the school as compared to static treatment resources, are beginning to see the importance of preparing teachers to cope with children, not necessarily as therapists, but as knowledgeable, helpful adults who are in contact with the child a good part of his day. No thinking therapist should ever underestimate the treatment impact of a good teacher on a child.

And Parents Follow Suit — Parents too are seen by the worker and an attempt is made to help them cope with their troubled child more rationally. The author has been impressed with the similarities between the Rational and Adlerian approaches and has been active in developing, for the referral of parents in his school district, a family education facility which uses the Adlerian concept of counseling families before groups of other parents. Such a facility helps parents resolve their child management difficulties by questioning their internal logic as it relates to the child and his behavior and role in the home.

In Summary — It should be clear to the reader that the rational approach is not effective for all therapists. Its effectiveness is highly dependent upon the therapist's ability to aggressively intervene in the therapeutic dialogue by challenging the child's illogical thinking and then by encouraging new thinking so that improved behavior may result. What must also be stressed is the therapist's acceptance of the *person*, though not necessarily his *behavior*. If properly done it is possible to be therapeutically critical of the child's behavior and thinking and yet convey to him your acceptance of his worthiness as a person.

The rational approach also challenges the premise that one's past behavior is the all-important determiner of one's present and future behavior. It stresses instead changing "here and now" thinking. As such, it has been found to be a highly effective treatment approach for use in the school setting with all varieties of pathology.

References — Ellis, A. *Reason and emotion in psychotherapy.* N.Y.: Lyle Stuart, 1962.

Glicken, M. Counseling children: two methods. *Rational Living*, 1967, *1, 2,* p. 36.

Glicken, M. The training of teachers: a mental health issue. *Illinois School Journal*, 1968, 47(1), 259-261.

BY L. D. HANKOFF AND JOHN W. GALVIN

Psychopharmacological Treatment and Its Implications for Social Work

■ The universality of psychopharmacological treatment in the care of the mentally ill requires that the social worker have a knowledge of the specific drugs used and their main areas of action, the side effects of medication, and the important nondrug factors affecting treatment outcome. The aim of this paper is to provide the basis for an orientation of the social worker to this treatment method. Drugs in common usage are categorized together with their target symptoms and possible side effects. ■

IN CURRENT CLINICAL practice, most patients with psychiatric disorders receive medication at some point in their treatment. Psychopharmacological treatment, i.e., the use of medication in the treatment of psychiatric disorders and symptoms, is applied so extensively today that every form and aspect of psychiatric patients' care is in some way affected by it. As background for psychopharmacological treatment in relation to social work, a few specific points on the origins of contemporary somatic treatments may be pertinent.

The modern roots may be traced to the first half of the nineteenth century when there was a great elaboration of somatic treatment methods and volumes were written describing the use of purgatives, emetics, skin irritants, bloodletting, hot baths, cold baths, and numerous mechanical devices in the treatment of mental disorders.[1] Following the introduction of bromides, these became the basic drug treatment for mental disorders in the second half of the nineteenth century.[2] The next great wave of somatic treatment innovations took place in the five years between 1933 and 1938 when insulin coma therapy, convulsive (electroshock) therapy, and psychosurgery (e.g., prefrontal lobotomy) were all introduced.[3] In the 1950's a series of advances heralded the present psychopharmacological development. In 1952, chlorpromazine was introduced for its tranquilizing effects and iproniazid for its stimulating effects on psychiatric patients.[4] The subsequent proliferation of psychopharmacological medications has been accompanied by a basic change in the orientation toward organic techniques by psychiatrists, and the use of medication by psychiatrists is almost universal. For example, a recent survey of more than one thousand psychiatrists found that 98 percent prescribed drugs and that

L. D. HANKOFF, MD, is Director, and JOHN W. GALVIN, MSW, is Assistant Chief Social Worker, Department of Psychiatry, Queens Hospital Center, Jamaica, New York.

[1] Emil Kraepelin, One Hundred Years of Psychiatry (New York: Philosophical Library, 1962).

[2] Louis S. Goodman and Alfred Gilman, The Pharmacological Basis of Therapeutics (New York: Macmillan Co., 1965).

[3] Lothar B. Kalinowsky and Paul H. Hoch, Somatic Treatments in Psychiatry (New York: Grune & Stratton, 1961).

[4] Ibid.

Reprinted with permission of the National Association of Social Workers, from SOCIAL WORK, Vol. 13, No. 3 (July 1968), pp. 40-47.

the psychiatrist's training and orientation made little difference in this respect.[5]

While the value of psychopharmacological treatment is to a considerable degree a matter for further research, there is fair agreement on its valuable contribution to the care of the psychotic patient and to the currently noted reduction in size of state hospital patient rolls. The use of drugs has contributed significantly to both prevention of hospitalization and shortening of hospital stay for the psychotic patient.[6]

It is evident that social workers in many different settings encounter patients receiving psychopharmacological treatment and thus require adequate knowledge in this area. The greatly extended treatment of the seriously ill patient in the community setting has increased the need for social workers to integrate knowledge about the psychopharmacological agents and to aid the patient's family in this phase of the treatment process. A system of collaborative functioning between the social worker and psychiatrist must exist so that each profession adds its utmost to the therapeutic approach. The aim of this paper is to provide the basis for an orientation of the social worker to psychopharmacological treatment and to make suggestions for continued assimilation of knowledge in this area.

METHODS AND GOALS OF TREATMENT

The basis for the selection and prescription of psychopharmacological medication in clinical practice is essentially an empirical one. The rationale of the treatment process is derived primarily from two ingredients: the manifest symptomatology of the patient and the known therapeutic activity of the

medication. Psychopharmacological agents may be classified according to a "target symptoms" approach.[7] The target symptoms are the major symptoms for which the specific psychopharmacological agents are selected and are usually the most urgent symptoms requiring attention. (Although the practicing physician may not explicitly adhere to the target symptom concept as here presented, it is believed that some similar focus is basic to psychopharmacological practice.)

In Table 1 are shown the main categories of psychopharmacological agents, examples of target symptoms, and some of the most common side effects of the drugs. As seen in the table, the commonly used agents may be divided into two large categories, psychoinhibitors and psychoactivators, according to whether they decrease or increase energy levels. The psychoinhibitors are, in general, used in treatment of excitation or excess in activity, energy, tension, or mood, the psychoactivators, in treatment of depression or deficiency in activity, energy, tension, or mood.

Within the psychoinhibitor category, the subgroup of tranquilizers (also called minor tranquilizers) is used principally for the relief of anxiety and related symptoms. The second subgroup, antipsychotics (also called major tranquilizers), is considered of most specific value in relation to the secondary symptoms of psychosis. The third subgroup, the hypnotic drugs, includes the conventional sedatives commonly used for insomnia and daytime sedation.

Within the psychoactivator category, the antidepressant drugs are used for significant depression. They are divided into two subgroups with the non-MAO inhibitors being faster acting than the MAO inhibitors. The remaining psychoactivator subgroup, the psychomotor stimulants, is of use in increasing energy levels in patients whose depressions are not severe.

Drugs are ordinarily administered to the

[5] Helen H. Avnet, *Psychiatric Insurance* (New York: Group Health Insurance, 1962).

[6] Francis E. Kelley, "Research in Schizophrenia: Implications for Social Workers," *Social Work*, Vol. 10, No. 1 (January 1965), pp. 32–44; Carroll M. Brodsky, Ames Fischer, and Morton R. Weinstein, "Modern Treatment of Psychosis: New Tasks for Social Therapies," *Social Work*, Vol. 9, No. 3 (July 1964), pp. 71–78.

[7] Kalinowsky and Hoch, *op. cit.*

TABLE 1. CLASSIFICATION OF PSYCHOPHARMACOLOGICAL AGENTS

Drug Category	Target Symptoms	Drug Example	Side Effects
Psychoinhibitor (psycholeptic, tranquilizer, ataraxic)			
Tranquilizer (minor tranquilizer, sedative)	Anxiety, mild agitation	Meprobamate (Miltown, Equanil), chlordiazepoxide (Librium)	Drowsiness, ataxia, tremors
Antipsychotic (major tranquilizer, neuroleptic)	Delusions, hallucinations, hyperactivity	Chlorpromazine (Thorazine), promazine (Sparine), thioridazine (Mellaril), trifluperazine (Stelazine), perphenazine (Trilafon), reserpine	Extrapyramidal reactions, hypotension, photosensitivity, liver dysfunction, constipation
Hypnotic	Insomnia, mild anxiety	Barbiturates, chloral hydrate, glutethimide (Doriden)	Drowsiness
Psychoactivator (psychoanaleptic)			
Antidepressant	Depression, apathy		
Monoamine oxidase (MAO) inhibitor (psychic energizer)		Isocarboxazide (Marplan), tranylcy-promine (Parnate)	Hypotension, insomnia, tremor, liver dysfunction
Non-MAO inhibitor (thymoleptic, psychostimulant)		Imipramine (Tofranil), amitryptyline (Elavil)	Hypotension, tremor, sweating, constipation
Psychomotor stimulant	Mild depression	Amphetamine (Dexedrine, Benzedrine), methylphenidate (Ritalin)	Insomnia, tremor, tension

point at which the symptoms are controlled and the clinical condition of the patient is stabilized. The starting dose is based on the predicted need of the patient for medication and is revised with time according to (1) the developing response of the patient to the medication, (2) side effects of the medication, and (3) the evolving total clinical picture.

In addition to the psychopathology, a most important consideration in prescribing medication is the total context of psychiatric treatment and management. Obviously, medication should be given to the patient in conjunction and co-ordination with all other appropriate measures of care.

The target symptom concept is merely a guide in the selection of a specific drug.

A major use of the tranquilizers not readily subsumed under the target symptom approach lies in maintenance management of the chronic patient.[8] Growing experience points to the value of and need for long-term drug treatment of chronic patients of many types. A typical example is the schizophrenic patient discharged from the state hospital who fares much better if maintained on small daily doses of tranquilizers long after he is free of any signifi-

[8] *Ibid.;* Kelley, *op. cit.;* and Brodsky, Fischer, and Weinstein, *op. cit.*

181

cant symptoms. Premature termination of medication (either at the patient's or the physician's initiative) may often be followed by a resurgence of schizophrenic symptomatology.

Other important areas of psychopharmacological treatment are being explored in current research; these should be mentioned briefly: (1) metabolic replacement therapy for chronic brain syndrome, such as the use of ribonucleic acid for senile brain damage,[9] (2) the psychotomimetics as adjuncts to the psychotherapeutic process, such as the use of LSD-25 in the treatment of alcoholics,[10] (3) motor stimulants used for behavior disorders, such as the use of amphetamines in the treatment of disturbed children,[11] and (4) preventives in addiction, such as the use of methadone maintenance in the treatment of former heroin addicts [12] or metronidazole for alcoholics.

SIDE EFFECTS

Drug treatment invariably carries a risk in terms of undesirable side effects, which may range from the trivial to the fatal, are ordinarily well known and categorized for the established individual drug, and at times merge with the therapeutic effects of the drug. Understanding and interpretation of side effects must include the facts that use of placebos is associated with a regular incidence of side effects and that the somatic concomitants of psychiatric disorders are sometimes indistinguishable from drugs' side effects. In depressed patients, for ex-

ample, the somatic symptoms of constipation, dry mouth, and insomnia may be symptoms of the original disorder, side effects associated with use of antidepressant medication, or both. The social worker must be aware of somatic complaints occurring during treatment in order to relate his course of management to them.

The problem of side effects is complicated especially by the wide variety of untoward central nervous system effects that psychopharmacological agents may produce, and the diagnostic and treatment situation may become a most difficult one for both social worker and psychiatrist. Central nervous system side effects may appear as behavioral side effects in the form of an excessive therapeutic action, i.e., overstimulation as a side effect of antidepressant treatment or lethargy as a result of tranquilizer therapy. Neurological side effects may occur with the antipsychotics in the form of one of three distinctive syndromes: (1) parkinsonian (drug-induced) symptoms, e.g., cogwheel rigidity and masklike facies, (2) dystonic or dyskinetic symptoms, e.g., involuntary muscular twitching or torsion spasms, or (3) akathisia, a restless, quivering state.[13] It is the diagnostician's problem to distinguish between symptoms of the original mental disorder and symptoms of the superimposed side effects.

Additional medication is sometimes necessary with psychopharmacological agents for the control of side effects, e.g., antiparkinsonian agents as adjuncts to phenothiazine antipsychotics. Similarly, other side effects such as constipation, insomnia, or drowsiness may be managed by various adjunctive medications.

Of some consequence is the effect that the major tranquilizers have when they are taken in combination with alcohol or barbiturates. The result is an augmentation of the sedative effects of alcohol or barbiturates as much as tenfold. A similar effect may occur when the patient receiving major tranquilizers is given a general anesthetic.

[9] Joseph Wortis, "Psychopharmacology and Physiological Treatment," *American Journal of Psychiatry*, Vol. 21, No. 7 (January 1965), pp. 648–652.

[10] Richard A. Crocket, R. A. Sandison, and Alexander Walk, *Hallucinogenic Drugs and Their Psychotherapeutic Use* (Springfield, Ill.: Charles C Thomas, 1963).

[11] Harry Bakwin and Ruth M. Bakwin, *Clinical Management of Behavior Disorders in Children* (Philadelphia: W. B. Saunders Co., 1953).

[12] Vincent P. Dole and Marie Nyswander, "A Medical Treatment for Diacetylmorphine (Heroin) Addiction," *Journal of the American Medical Association*, Vol. 193, No. 8 (August 23, 1965), pp. 646–650.

[13] Kalinowsky and Hoch, *op. cit.*

PHYSIOLOGICAL CONSIDERATIONS

Psychopharmacological agents produce various disturbances in the physiology of the patient. These effects are often difficult to evaluate fully and the social worker collaborating in the care of patients receiving medication can be of considerable help. He can obtain from the family of the patient the important environmental and psychological facts needed in the interpretation and management of side effects. For example, in relation to the behavioral and neurological side effects mentioned, the social worker might obtain information from the family about the patient's mental state immediately prior to development of any new symptoms to help ascertain possible nondrug causes. Was any new stress placed on the patient prior to the onset of the new behavioral or neurological symptoms? Was the patient taking his medication regularly prior to onset of the symptoms? Were there any previous similar episodes? The social worker's or a relative's observations of the patient's new symptoms may provide the psychiatrist with the information needed to diagnose the side effect.

Many side effects are minor and reversible but, nevertheless, are a concern to the patient or his family. Constipation, dryness of the mouth, a fine tremor, dizziness, nausea, and disturbance of the menstrual cycle may occur. Mellaril, a major tranquilizer, may temporarily inhibit ejaculation. Some patients receiving major tranquilizers experience a decrease in their sex drive, while an increase sometimes occurs with psychoactivators. Many patients taking phenothiazines experience drowsiness and depletion of energy and have difficulty responding to family needs. The phenothiazines often increase appetite and this, coupled with the decrease in activity, may cause a weight gain of as much as forty pounds.[14] Although drug related, such changes are susceptible to environmental influences to which the social worker may address himself.

The questions of addiction and the possible harmful effects from long-term use of psychopharmacological agents have often been raised. Psychological dependency (as opposed to physiological dependency or addiction) is a definite danger in any long-term drug use. Physiological dependency may also occur but is limited to specific drug subgroups. Fortunately, the majority of psychopharmacological agents do not produce physiological dependency. Only the minor tranquilizers, the psychoinhibitors of the hypnotic type, and the psychomotor stimulant subgroup of psychoactivators produce such dependency. Among these drugs cases of true addiction may result from prolonged high-dosage use. The social worker can instruct the families of patients about these dangers and can greatly reduce addictive problems. Abrupt discontinuance of the addictive drug may result in a withdrawal syndrome similar to that seen with narcotics or alcohol addiction. The most valued agents, the antipsychotics and antidepressants, do not have true addictive properties. For example, a depressed patient treated with an antidepressant has no physiological need for the medication when the depressive symptomatology has been relieved. Similarly, in the case of the antipsychotics, addiction does not develop with use, and when the clinical condition of the patient allows discontinuance of the medication there is no withdrawal syndrome.

THE FAMILY AND DRUG TREATMENT

The complicated reaction of a family to its mentally ill member is altered in significant ways by the introduction of psychopharmacological treatment. When an antipsychotic medication (major tranquilizer) is taken, a calming effect is often noted after a few doses. This change in observable behavior is often encouraging to the family, the pa-

---

14 N. S. Apter, "Our Growing Restlessness with Problems of Chronic Schizophrenia," in Lawrence Appleby, J. M. Scher, and John Cumming, eds., *Chronic Schizophrenia* (Glencoe, Ill.: Free Press, 1960), pp. 1–35.

tient perceives this as a greater degree of acceptance, and an improvement in family interaction is attained.[15] However, another family may view this initial improvement as an indication that the crisis is over, encourage the patient to discontinue the medication, and in other ways minimize the value of the treatment. When there is a sudden cessation of antipsychotic medication there is often an increase in the energy level of a patient, hyperactivity, and the return of the initial picture of illness.

A converse situation may occur with a psychoactivator (psychoanaleptic) given to a depressed patient. These medications need as much as six weeks to take effective action and the family may become discouraged when immediate improvement is not seen. The patient often feels more isolated and may view his lack of response to the medication as evidence that he is useless and impotent. The social worker with access to the family members is in a strategic position for direct intervention and can handle the family's psychological interaction with the patient and enable continuation of psychopharmacological treatment. The worker can support the family and, by knowing the expected drug reaction, can encourage them to await treatment benefits.

The widespread use of psychopharmacological medication has as one of its consequences the accumulation of large drug supplies in a household. This availability of medication is of serious concern because the patient or another family member may accidentally or intentionally take an overdose. The psychopharmacological medications are not usually lethal, even in large doses, but may cause major physiological disturbances. As with other medications there is always the danger that children will mistake them for candy and appropriate precautions should be urged. It has been noted that medications prescribed for a patient are often taken by other members of a family. The social worker should discourage other family members from indiscriminate use of medication while recog-

15 *Ibid.*

nizing that the person in question may also be in need of help.

INTAKE AND REFERRAL

The social worker who can recognize the symptoms that can possibly be relieved by psychopharmacological treatment can initiate the process by making an appropriate referral. A careful study of the target symptom approach can greatly aid the social worker in definitively selecting the most appropriate treatment resource available. The need to develop an efficient and yet economical transition from one treatment modality to another requires skillful management. A patient who receives casework treatment or who applies to a social agency for help may require psychopharmacological treatment as an adjunct to casework or as the exclusive treatment. Too often, however, patients are frightened by the referral even when made by the best-intentioned worker, and view the referring agency as being disinterested and shifting the problem-solving to another source.

A referral for psychopharmacological treatment may introduce some special factors that both the social worker and psychiatrist need to consider. With patients who feel that their problems stem from family, friend, or employer, prescription of a medication may mean to the patient that the problem is ascribed to him alone and no account is being taken of the other parties. Such patients may terminate their treatment contacts. Other patients welcome receipt of medication rather than a verbal discourse for which they may see no particular value. For these patients the transition usually is completed smoothly. However, the medication must prove effective quickly, or those patients may terminate their treatment. It is essential with these patients that medication response time be discussed fully, especially in the case of the psychic energizers, which require three to five weeks to have an appreciable effect.

The social worker must painstakingly outline for each referred patient the process

184

of psychopharmacological treatment. The medication alone is often less important than the setting and the attitudes of the care-giving professionals. He must be aware of the specific clinic to which his patient is being referred and be prepared to follow through until maximum benefits are obtained.

To facilitate the referral, sufficient and yet not burdensome material must be transmitted from one agency to another. The referral for psychopharmacological treatment should include an appraisal of the patient's current mental condition. Specific complaints should be gathered with their duration and intensity documented by collateral family information. The patient's past use of medication—with dosage and known side effects—should be given. If a previous medication was discontinued, the circumstances leading to such a decision must be explored. Too often a patient discontinues a medication after a few doses and will not reconsider taking it again. In other cases a medication continued over a long period becomes a psychological crutch and may not be indicated for the present target symptoms. Such a patient may resist a change of medication.

Sometimes the patient's family will decide which medication is acceptable or encourage a patient to experiment when immediate beneficial results do not occur. With a stockpile of medications at home, especially for the chronic patient who has received treatment from different sources, family members, rather than the doctor, may choose the medication they believe is the most helpful. The worker should handle this by instructing the family members to dispose of old medications and to rely on the current physician's appraisal of the patient's need for medication. If a specific positive or negative response occurred with a certain medication, the family should be encouraged to discuss this with the physician.

As in any other referral situation, the process does not end with the sending of material or making of the initial appointment. There should be follow-up contacts to insure that the patient has been able to utilize the services of the other agency.

COLLABORATIVE TREATMENT APPROACH

Some patients require medication and social casework so closely co-ordinated that simultaneous management should be undertaken within one agency, with the psychiatrist and social worker as a team focusing on many aspects of the patient's problem. With medication alleviating specific symptoms, the social worker can make early plans for social and vocational rehabilitation. Furthermore, the family members can be drawn into the treatment program and urged to co-operate more fully.

This collaboration of both disciplines in one agency can be quite timesaving. The burdensome interagency communication process can be eliminated and a smooth flow of treatment plans can be expedited. There is also less delay in initiating a specific action. The social worker can focus his interviews on his areas of competence, while the problems encountered with medications, side effects, and so on can be channeled to the psychiatrist. In much the same way, the psychiatrist may more effectively deal with the problem of medication usage and direct the patient to the social worker for problems in coping with family or employment. If a medication is producing side effects, some patients may withhold this information from the physician while freely informing the social worker. The family members can also perceive the collaboration of both psychiatrist and social worker and feel assured that the contacts with the social worker are clearly related to the psychopharmacological treatment. Psychopharmacological clinics with collaborative approaches have been established and appear to be serving a valuable community function.[16]

[16] L. D. Hankoff and Leon Rudorfer, "A Psychopharmacological Clinic: An Approach to a Community Need," *Medical Times*, Vol. 92, No. 12 (December 1964), pp. 1248–1252.

CONCLUSIONS

The universality of psychopharmacological treatment in the care of the mentally ill requires that the social worker have an understanding of this area and be prepared to collaborate in its use. The social worker needs to have a knowledge of the specific drugs used and their main areas of action, the side effects of medication, and the important nondrug factors affecting treatment outcome.

The social worker must be competent and knowledgeable in a number of areas pertaining to psychopharmacological treatment: making the referral for treatment, introducing the patient and family to this type of treatment, dealing with changes in patient and family as the patient responds to medication, explaining side effects and symptom changes to the patient and family, and collaborating with the prescribing psychiatrist in total care of the patient.

TOWARD A STRATEGY OF GROUP WORK PRACTICE

WILLIAM SCHWARTZ

The author is a member of the faculty of the New York School of Social Work of Columbia University. This article is based on a paper read at the Problem-finding Conference, Research Institute for Group Work in Jewish Agencies, Arden House, New York, April 28, 1961.

IN THE long history of the helping professions, it has been only recently that the working processes of the practitioner have been accepted as an appropriate field for scientific study. Once it has defined its body of knowledge, its social aspirations, and its goal-commitments, a profession must say something equally precise about the ways in which these entities are put to use in the working relationship between the practitioner and his clients.

In the group work segment of the social work profession the methodological problem had not yet become apparent when, in 1948, a committee of the American Association of Group Workers issued the now classical "Definition of the Function of the Group Worker."[1] This statement, used as a basis for teaching and interpreting group work practice during the past decade, has until recently served as an excellent model of the state of professional thinking. In its time, it served to formulate social goals, define the field of operations, stake a claim to certain kinds of expertness, and reveal some basic assumptions about people and groups in a democratic society.

What it did not do was to make the necessary distinctions between means and ends which could have helped to dissipate the strong teleological emphasis and to challenge the intrenched assumption that professional skill was somehow inherent in the worker's goals, his knowledge, his feeling for the client, his value-commitments, and certain of his personal attributes. The gap between the worker's intent and his effect was bridged with terms like "enables," "provides for," "functions in such a way that," "aims to," and other phrases that produced closure without coming to grips with the theoretical problems involved in designing a strategy of professional practice.[2] The difficulty was aptly summed up by Louis Towley, who pointed out in 1957 that "this specialized field is rich in democratic concepts; it has a wealth of examples; but in professionally unique concepts, 'method theory,' it has been curiously poor."[3]

The newer interest in the systematic study of professional practice is part of a similar impetus in social work as a whole. Although there are those who see

[1] Dorothea F. Sullivan (ed.), *Readings in Group Work* (New York: Association Press, 1952), pp. 421–22.

[2] For a more extended historical treatment of the means-ends relationship in group work, see William Schwartz, "Group Work and the Social Scene," *Issues in American Social Work*, ed. Alfred J. Kahn (New York: Columbia University Press, 1959), pp. 110–37.

[3] Frank J. Bruno (with chapters by Louis Towley), *Trends in Social Work, 1874–1956* (New York: Columbia University Press, 1957), p. 422.

SOCIAL SERVICE REVIEW, 1962, Vol. 36, No. 3, pp. 268-279.

this development as a "retreat into technique" and as a distraction from the "real" purposes of the profession, practitioners and teachers are gradually becoming excited by the possibility of finding out, after many years, what the exact nature of group work skill is, what it looks like in action, and how it can be conceptualized and taught.

How does a profession proceed to develop and systematize its concepts of practice? To say that it needs to build a more intimate working relationship with science is only the beginning of an answer. Certainly the liaison of science and practice is a historic one; professions that do not keep pace with new knowledge soon cease to be professions. But it is also true that an orientation to scientific inquiry does not provide a simple method of converting facts into acts, scientific findings into appropriate professional behavior. The transition from knowing to doing is more complex.

The complexity arises from two major problems faced by all the human-relations professions as they survey their appropriate fields of knowledge. One is that the body of potentially useful information is encyclopedic, encompassing every conceivable aspect of human development and organization; the other is that action cannot be deduced directly from knowledge, no matter how vast that knowledge may be.

In relation to the first problem—the overwhelming array of pertinent information—Max Millikan has pointed out that the Bavelas-Perlmutter experiments at the Center for International Studies suggest that "an individual's capacity for making sound judgment about a complex situation may be seriously impaired by supplying him with

a lot of information which he believes should be relevant but whose influence on the situation is not clear to him."[4] Harold Lasswell comments that "the idea of strategy does not depend upon omniscience."[5] The dilemma Millikan describes, a familiar one to group workers, seems to stem directly from the fact that the worker finds himself burdened with a great many answers for which he has no questions. He can make little use of such information until he has ordered his experience into some coherent frame of reference from which he can develop his questions and focus his inquiry into the undifferentiated mass of scientific data. Thus the search for significant problems—for the questions that will draw forth the kinds of information most needed to throw light on the practical tasks of the group worker—calls for a theoretical effort designed to develop a system of interconnected concepts drawn from the experience of practice.[6]

It is when we question what these concepts shall be about that we come to the second difficulty mentioned above —that action is not deducible from knowledge. Those who assume that scientific evidence carries within it its own implications for behavior make the same mistake made by those in an earlier time who believed that action flowed inevitably and appropriately

[4] Max F. Millikan, "Inquiry and Policy: The Relation of Knowledge to Action," *The Human Meaning of the Social Sciences*, ed. Daniel Lerner (New York: Meridian Books, 1959), p. 160.

[5] Harold D. Lasswell, "Strategies of Inquiry: The Rational Use of Observation," *The Human Meaning of the Social Sciences*, p. 89.

[6] For a discussion of theory-building and empiricism, see James B. Conant, *Modern Science and Modern Man* (New York: Doubleday Anchor Books, 1953).

from one's convictions about values and goals. It is what Millikan refers to as the "inductive fallacy—the assumption that the solution of any problem will be advanced by the simple collection of fact."[7] The fact is that the gap between what is known and what should be done is invariably bridged by value-goal orientations, often implicit and unformulated. When knowledge is converted into action on the basis of subtle and unstated values, the principle is unverifiable, except by those who unconsciously share the same assumptions. When creeds and valued outcomes are made explicit, practice principles are verifiable by all, on the basis of whether, given the first two variables—a fact and a valued outcome—the third will provide the implementing force. Practice cannot be "testable" in any other sense.

It is, therefore, suggested that practice theory, or method theory, can be defined as a system of concepts integrating three conceptual subsystems: one which organizes the appropriate aspects of social reality, as drawn from the findings of science; one which defines and conceptualizes specific values and goals, which we might call the problems of policy; and one which deals with the formulation of interrelated principles of action. Each of these constitutes a major area of investigation, each has its own conceptual problems, and each is related to the others within a total scheme. The purpose of this paper is to point up some of the major conceptual problems in each of these areas and to show how each area depends upon the others for its own clarity and coherence.

[7] *Op. cit.,* p. 163.

As we turn to the social sciences for information about human behavior and social organization, our task is to establish those lines of inquiry which emerge most directly from our experiences with people. Gordon Hearn has suggested some proposals to focus the study of social work practice in general[8] and Robert Vinter has discussed some lines of work within the context of his frame of reference for group work.[9] From my own orientation to the tasks of the group work practitioner,[10] the following are suggested as some of the central themes around which the struggles of practice have taken place.

The individual and the social.—Probably the most enduring and pervasive methodological problems have stemmed from an inability to develop an integrative conception of the relationship between individual need and social demand. This is the difficulty that gives birth to the issue of "content versus process"—the dilemma wherein the practitioner is forced to make impossible choices between the functional necessities of individual growth and the social requirements of the culture in which he operates. The early efforts of

[8] Gordon Hearn, *Theory Building in Social Work* (Toronto: University of Toronto Press, 1958), p. 25.

[9] Robert D. Vinter, "Group Work with Children and Youth: Research Problems and Possibilities," *Social Service Review,* XXX (September, 1956), 310–21. See also his "Small-Group Theory and Research: Implications for Group Work Practice Theory and Research," *Social Science Theory and Social Work Research,* ed. Leonard S. Kogan (New York: National Association of Social Workers, 1960), pp. 123–34.

[10] William Schwartz, "The Social Worker in the Group," *Social Welfare Forum, 1961* (New York: Columbia University Press, 1961), pp. 146–71.

Sherif,[11] Mead,[12] Kropotkin,[13] and others to effect a workable synthesis were significant, but group workers were not yet in a position to formulate their problems so that these concepts could be used. In recent years, social scientists have come alive to the issue. Alex Inkeles' attempt to analyze this work without regard to internal professional boundaries has been helpful.[14] For practitioners, the present problem is that much scientific work is pegged either at a very high level of abstraction or at empirical laboratory efforts with artificial groupings that are difficult to translate into terms relevant to group work experience. As in so many other problem areas, the need is to break down the general question into some middle-range propositions that can be tested in our own situational field. Lippitt, Watson, and Westley have suggested work on the "forces toward innovation" through which people attempt to use, control, and change the people and things around them.[15] Another more specific line of inquiry might consist in the effort to develop motivational typologies with which to ascertain elements of consensus among group members and agency personnel.

[11] Muzafer Sherif, *The Psychology of Social Norms* (New York: Harper, 1936).

[12] George Herbert Mead, *Mind, Self, and Society* (Chicago: University of Chicago Press, 1934).

[13] Peter Alekseevich Kropotkin, *Mutual Aid: A Factor of Evolution* (New York: Alfred A. Knopf, 1917).

[14] Alex Inkeles, "Personality and Social Structure," *Sociology Today: Problems and Prospects,* ed. Robert K. Merton, Leonard Broom, and Leonard S. Cottrell, Jr. (New York: Basic Books, 1959), pp. 249–75.

[15] Ronald Lippitt, Jeanne Watson, and Bruce Westley, *The Dynamics of Planned Change* (New York: Harcourt, Brace, 1958), pp. 4–5.

From my own frame of reference, which assumes a symbiotic interdependence between the individual and his culture and which conceives the agency as a special case of the individual-social engagement, my prediction would be that mutually perceived "success" would take place primarily in these areas of motivational consensus.

The group work setting—as a living laboratory of the individual-social encounter—has failed conspicuously to produce its own research and add to the systematic study of this relationship in action. The field was so completely captured, early in its development, by the character-building, social-conformity pressures of the group work "movement" that the need to change people far outweighed the need to understand them and to examine carefully the ways in which their natural tendencies carry them into the society in which they develop. Thus, the move was made from socialization as a process—which needed to be analyzed and understood—to socialization as a demand. From that point, the road was a short one to the dilemma of "content versus process" and, ultimately, to the individual versus the group.

The structural and the dynamic.— Our historic tendency has been to rely heavily on structural descriptions— "diagnostic" typologies—to describe the people with whom we work. The study-diagnosis-treatment model— based partly on the physician's detection and cure of disease and partly on the methods of research—is built from the assumption that these structural characteristics are stable enough for workers to base predictions, referrals, and "treatment" decisions upon them. However, it has been difficult to show that this model bears any practical relation to the moment-to-moment, situationally fluid realities of the helping process in action. Hubert Bonner reports that "research has shown that it is difficult to predict the behavior of persons in a group from pre-measures of personality variables,"[16] and Gordon Allport has scored the "faddism" involved in the "overemphasis on diagnosis." "It is simply not true," he states, "that successful treatment invariably presupposes accurate diagnosis."[17]

Interest is mounting in elaborations of a newer approach, which has particular implications for the situational field in which the group worker operates. This approach points up the "circular, reciprocal relations . . . through which the component members of the field participate in and thereby create the field of the whole, which field in turn regulates and patterns their individual activities."[18] This model calls attention to the interdependent transactions within a functional system—an organic whole "within which the relations determine the properties of its parts."[19] The emphasis on relational determinants of behavior, while at the same time subjecting structural determinants to more critical scrutiny, has a strong potential impact on all group work practice conceptions. It may provide the stimulus for closer analysis of the differential forms of stress, social demand, and social opportunity offered by the various settings of group work practice.[20] It may also stimulate the development of terminology—and perhaps new typologies—that will help us to express relations as well as structure and to distinguish more clearly between the two.

The group as "it" and as "they."— We have not yet developed a working conception of the group as a whole which might help the group worker to implement his traditional claim that group work skills are directed to the group as well as to the individuals within it. If the small group is a system which—like society itself—both integrates and differentiates its parts,[21] group workers remain far more perceptive about the attributes of individuals than they are about the activity of the group as a whole. Familiar evidence is found in recorded anthropomorphisms like "the group laughed," in references to the group as "they," and in models of confusion, like "the group looked at each other." This failure to distinguish between the attributes of members and those of the collective has made it difficult to isolate and describe those professional skills which are designed to affect the system itself rather than any of its component parts.[22] Efforts have been made to use the wealth of em-

[16] Hubert Bonner, *Group Dynamics: Principles and Applications* (New York: Ronald Press Co., 1959), p. 20.

[17] Gordon W. Allport, *Personality and Social Encounter* (Boston: Beacon Press, 1960), p. 283. Discussed in chapter entitled "Social Service in Perspective."

[18] Lawrence K. Frank, "Research for What?" *Journal of Social Issues,* Supplement Series, X (1957), 12.

[19] Talcott Parsons, *The Structure of Social Action* (Glencoe, Ill.: Free Press, 1949), p. 32.

[20] For a limited attempt of this type, see William Schwartz, "Characteristics of the Group Experience in Resident Camping," *Social Work,* V (April, 1960), 91–96.

[21] See A. Paul Hare, Edgar F. Borgatta, and Robert F. Bales, *Small Groups: Studies in Social Interaction* (New York: Alfred A. Knopf, 1955), pp. 345–47.

[22] Robert D. Vinter's conception of "indirect means of influence" is an effort in this direction. See his "Small-Group Theory and Research . . . ," *op. cit.,* p. 128.

pirical research on group dimensions, but again the lack of theoretical models has been a barrier. Much energy has been devoted to building longer inventories of group traits, but there is little knowledge of how these traits may be related to each other in the life of the group.

The recent work of the organizational theorists,[23] the developing insight into the interdisciplinary implications of the system construct,[24] and other integrative attempts now offer group workers the opportunity to analyze the group work experience in a new way. In the process they may begin to make their own unique contribution to this field of inquiry. The growing diversity of small-group systems in which they operate gives group workers the chance to observe both similarities and differences in the ways in which different kinds of groups integrate and differentiate their human components and relate themselves to the larger systems in which they operate.

Internal and external determinants of change.—Much of the discussion on "self-determination versus manipulation" has been carried on in a high moral tone, while a great deal of work needs to be done in studying the specific conditions under which people enlist the aid of others in their attempts to solve problems. The group worker is in a unique position to study the uses of help and the nature of influence, since he works within a system the essence of which is that people create many helping relationships in addition to, and

concurrent with, the one formed with the worker. The problems of the group members in using each other are co-existent with their problems in using the worker. The group worker has an opportunity to examine in microcosm a very old idea, long since forgotten in a highly specialized civilization. This is the idea that the client-worker relationship is simply a special case of what Kropotkin described as the evolutionary theme of mutual aid[25]—that is, the social devices through which human beings establish conditions of mutual support in the struggle for survival. More specifically, the group work situation offers the conditions for studying peer help and professional help within the same dynamic system, guided by the strong possibility that these two sets of movements have much in common and that, in fact, the latter may be a stylized, intensified version of the former.[26]

PROBLEMS OF POLICY

The relationship between science and policy is reciprocal. Science takes its cues from human problems and yields its best answers to those who are disciplined and urgent in their search for solutions. The contribution of science to policy is to define boundaries, limit expectations, and clarify the range of alternatives.[27] This idea of knowledge as a disciplining, limiting force is important in each of the problems to be discussed briefly below. It should be remembered that we are still in the

[23] See, for example, Mason Haire (ed.), *Modern Organization Theory* (New York: John Wiley & Sons, 1959).

[24] See Roy R. Grinker, M.D., *Toward a Unified Theory of Human Behavior* (New York: Basic Books, 1956).

[25] Kropotkin, *op. cit.*

[26] Bertha Capen Reynolds' *Social Work and Social Living* (New York: Citadel Press, 1951) explores this basic proposition in detail.

[27] For a detailed discussion of the science-policy relationship, see Millikan, *loc. cit.*, and Lasswell, *loc. cit.*

context of the study of practice, and these problems are viewed from that perspective.

Functional definition.—Much of the difficulty in understanding the nature of group work skill stems from the lack of a clear and limited statement about the unique, operative function of the worker in his group. Such a statement, made in terms of action rather than intent, of function rather than purpose,[28] would provide a focal point for a general strategy of practice. The strategic lines of action would be appropriate to the worker's ascribed function, would be directed to certain tasks and not to others, would be related to the functional performance of the members, and would be directed to the specific and limited factors over which the worker exercises some influence.[29]

The components of the functional statement would be drawn from three main areas of investigation: the specific problems faced by group members as they move to relate their own sense of need to the social demands implicit in the collective tasks of the group; the functional assignment of the agency within its own dynamic system of neighborhood and community; and the social function of the profession itself as it lends itself to the agencies in which it works.[30] This general orientation to the operational problem offers many questions for study: In what precise ways does the practice of group workers reflect the degree of conflict—and consensus—about the proper function of the worker within the group, as viewed by group members, agency administrators, and the worker himself? What are the conditions under which certain kinds of group behavior may be functional to the members and dysfunctional to the requirements of the agency, or vice versa? Under what conditions is it desirable to convert latent functions into manifest ones?

Structural ordering.—The task here is to study the circumstances under which the group establishes and maintains its position within the agency, for these circumstances create the framework within which the worker interprets and performs his tasks. If the structure is unclear and ambiguous—as in situations in which the agency secretly aspires to build character while it teaches clay-modeling—the worker's function becomes diffuse and unmanageable.

Several aspects of the relationship between the client group and its host system seem profitable for study. One is the process through which the stage of group formation or group intake establishes conditions of consensus or conflict about the nature of the "contract" between the group and its agency —what each may expect from the other, the normative requirements to which each may be held, and other factors which bind them together. Another important structural aspect lies in the complex of prepared events, activities, and ethical commitments which agency

[28] The distinction between purpose and function is helpfully discussed in Robert K. Merton, *Social Theory and Social Structure* (Glencoe, Ill.: Free Press, 1957), chap. i.

[29] These criteria are elaborated in Schwartz, "Group Work and the Social Scene," *op. cit.*, pp. 130–32.

[30] Cf. Everett Cherrington Hughes, "The Study of Occupations," *Sociology Today: Problems and Prospects*, pp. 442–58: "The composition of an occupation can be understood only in the frame of the pertinent social and institutional complex (which must in turn be discovered, not merely assumed). The allocating and grouping of activities is itself a fundamental social process" (p. 455).

administrations perceive as integral to their function and as substantial elements in their contributions to group life. Under what conditions do these prepared events and prestructured experiences become functional or dysfunctional for the groups for which they are intended?

Much of this problem of structural ordering lies in the relationship between what George C. Homans calls the "external" and the "internal" systems of the group—between "group behavior that enables the group to survive in its environment" and "group behavior that is an expression of the sentiments towards one another developed by the members of the group in the course of their life together."[31] The tension between these two systems of group behavior sets up some of the central methodological problems of the group worker.

Value orientation.—A great deal has been said and written about the worker's obligation to acknowledge values and to profess them openly. But these injunctions are hard to obey, because they suffer from the same shortcomings as do the value formulations themselves—that is, they are too global, internally inconsistent, and unrelated to the specific conditions of group life. The professional commandments to stand for absolute and overgeneralized themes like "Jewish belongingness" or "social maturity," to "bear" values but not to "impose" them, to uphold both religious and secular-humanistic values at the same time,[32] to extol modesty and thrift to children whose family modes are prevailingly those of conspicuous consumption—these are very complex materials from which to compose a ra-

tionale for the position of values in the strategy of practice. At this stage what is needed is more exact information about the value themes which merge or conflict within the lives of different groups and about the conditions under which these circumstances vary from group to group and from setting to setting—the religious and the secular, the sectarian and the non-sectarian, the therapeutic and the recreational. Content analyses of group work recording may help uncover some of the conflicts and inconsistencies which have made it difficult to break up the problem of value orientation without seeming to attack value systems themselves. Most important would be an attempt to isolate and formulate value items of limited scope which apply directly to the life of the group itself, which are drawn from its own history, and which represent normative guides without which the worker actually could not function.

Goal setting.—What kinds of knowledge would be best designed to help "place limits on the range of possible outcomes"?[33] Here, as in the value question, the first requirement is that we begin with a willingness to drop exorbitant claims.[34] Caught up early in the social promise of the small-group experience, it has been hard for group workers to give up the claim that the

[31] George C. Homans, *The Human Group* (New York: Harcourt, Brace, 1950), p. 110.

[32] For a thorough discussion of this point, see Alfred J. Kutzik, *Social Work and Jewish Values* (Washington, D.C.: Public Affairs Press, 1959). Also see Herbert Bisno, *The Philosophy of Social Work* (Washington, D.C.: Public Affairs Press, 1952).

[33] Millikan, *op. cit.*, p. 166.

[34] Barbara Wooton, *Social Science and Social Pathology* (London: George Allen & Unwin, 1959). Chapter ix, entitled "Contemporary Attitudes in Social Work," makes particular reference to the American scene. Here the author characterizes some claims of American group workers as "arrogant" and "self-deceptive."

club group in the leisure-time agency alters personality, creates new value systems, and effects other profound changes in people's lives. This abstract and totalistic way of framing its objectives has prevented the field from examining the real, if limited, influence that skilful group work practice probably has, and the kinds of specific help that people in groups are actually able to use.

There are several lines of study that may help to bring practice goals closer to reality. There is, for example, the problem of separating worker goals from member goals, so that one can distinguish between the process of teaching and the process of learning— or, in social work terms, the dynamics of giving help and those of taking help. Study of the moment-to-moment interaction of these two processes should help clarify the means-ends structures of each and relate the desired outcomes more closely to possible ones.

A second line of inquiry may be directed toward the definition of outcomes that may reasonably be expected. If, for example, a worker aspires to help a group develop a wider variety of problem-solving devices, he may then create instruments to measure his degree of success. This is what Martin Wolins calls "a single, readily ascertainable development."[35] By contrast, a change-objective like "achieving socially desirable goals" is both unmeasurable and unachievable since the behavioral indexes are undefined and, even if they were defined, they would

[35] Martin Wolins, "Measuring the Effect of Social Work Intervention," *Social Work Research*, ed. Norman A. Polansky (Chicago: University of Chicago Press, 1960), p. 263.

still remain far beyond any conceivable range of influence to be expected of a single worker operating in a small sector of people's lives.

PROBLEMS OF ACTION

Given a body of knowledge about the social realities of group experience, and given a use of this knowledge to work out a realistic function and achievable value-goal objectives, one must next lay out a plan of action. Such a plan is essentially a way of breaking down a broad functional assignment into its component classes of activity.

At this point an organizing construct is needed from which to create the categories in which to gather up the various acts that the worker performs as he goes about his job. This is the point at which there might be advantages in using the "role" construct, an action-oriented idea designed to relate the worker's movements to those of others in a dynamic system. However, the term is so overladen with ambiguities and special uses that one experiences difficulty in using it without developing a specialized rationale for its meaning in this context. For the present, the term "task" may serve. Any function can be divided into a number of tasks necessary to perform it, and any specific act may be understood as related to one or another of these task headings.

Once having determined what these implementing tasks are, one must define and describe the skills necessary to carry them out. In this framework, then, the problems of action which climax the methodological study are those of task definition and skill definition.

Task definition.—The problems of task analysis revolve around three main points. Each task (a) must emerge from the theoretical scheme to which it is related, (b) must be directed to the tasks of the group members themselves, and (c) must be broad enough to encompass a number of helping activities, which should be specifiable in concrete terms.

For example, if "the general functional assignment of the social work profession is to mediate the process through which the individual and his society reach out for each other through a mutual need for self-fulfilment,"[36] we may then conceive of five implementing tasks: (1) to search out the common ground between the client's need-perception and the social demands with which he is faced; (2) to detect and challenge the obstacles that obscure this common ground; (3) to contribute otherwise unavailable and potentially useful data; (4) to reveal and project the worker's own feeling for the client and his problem; and (5) to define the limits and requirements of the situation in which the client-worker relationship is set.[37] The analytic process in examining the second of these tasks, for example, would proceed as follows. It would begin by describing the ways in which this task is designed to implement the functional statement. It would then proceed to describe and document some of the specific social realities involved—the origin of obstacles, what they look like in action, and the forms in which they are perceived by the members. Finally, it would describe the worker's activities—revealing impediments to action, supporting the members as they enter the area of taboo, and protecting the focus of work, lest it be lost in the preoccupation with obstacles. This is of course a highly condensed account but it may serve to give some inkling of the possibilities offered in carving out limited areas for intensive study.

Skill definition.—The difficulty in defining skill in human relations is the problem of describing an act in its own terms, rather than in terms of its results. One may jibe at the notion that "the operation was a success, but the patient died," but the fact remains that it is impossible to develop a communicable art of surgery until we are willing to admit that it is possible for an operation to be well performed and for the patient to die. All this means is that the human material has a dynamic of its own and that the process of helping consists of two interdependent processes—the offer of help (the worker's act) and the use of it (the client's response). To say that the skill of an act is to be measured by its effect is to equate skill with predictive certainty and to leave out the client entirely. Social work cannot use a model borrowed from those who work with completely controllable materials—that is, inanimate objects.

It is true, of course, that the concern with skill is designed to help us narrow the range of uncertainty—that is, to find those acts which go most directly toward their purpose. Such acts must reflect "the greatest degree of consideration for and utilization of the quality and capacity of the material,"[38]

---

[36] Schwartz, "The Social Worker in the Group," *op. cit.*, pp. 154–55.

[37] *Ibid.*, pp. 157–58.

[38] Virginia P. Robinson, "The Meaning of Skill," *Training for Skill in Social Casework* (Philadelphia: University of Pennsylvania Press, 1942), p. 12.

but unless we can develop some descriptions of skilful activity, independent of effect, we cannot judge skill or order its "levels," or teach it; we certainly cannot, as we have often complained, interpret it to the general public.

This is a difficult job, but there are some indications that it is not an impossible one. We know, for example, that skill is an action concept. Skill is observable behavior of an actor-with-a-purpose toward others in a relational system. There are, of course, a number of mental acts—expressed mainly in the concept of "diagnosis"—but these have no value until they are translated into overt behavior guided by purpose. We know, too, that the factor of immediacy is important—that is, the further we move from the idea of present purpose, the "next step," the more difficult it is to define an act in its own terms. Thus, the ability to read a hidden message and to show the client his problem in a new form is a response to an immediate problem in helping. As such, it is definable, teachable, perhaps even measurable. By contrast, the attempt to formulate skills designed to "make the client more self-sufficient" is an impossible task.

A major contribution can be made in this area by those whose responsibility it is to educate for professional skill— social work teachers, agency supervisors, administrators of in-training programs. In this connection, an interesting attempt has been made by a group of field instructors to develop some models of group work skill, to make some determinations about levels of practice, and to describe the specific teaching and learning problems associated with the various models.

Despite the impatience of those who would like to move as quickly as possible into studies of outcome and effectiveness, our main progress for a time will probably be in studies of process and of limited effects.[39] In the course of what Bartlett has called "learning to ask better questions,"[40] our important devices are still descriptive, exploratory, and theory-developing; our major tools are still the group record, the life-history, the critical incident, and other techniques for codifying and conceptualizing the experience of practice. Perhaps our most critical problem is that so much of this experience is unavailable to us, since so little systematic and analytic work has been emerging from our potentially richest sources of information—the leisure-time agencies and their practitioners.

This is a period in which the social scientists are increasingly aware that the study of social systems—small and large—presents new challenges to the partnership of science and practice. Lawrence Frank put it this way to an assemblage of psychologists:

Perhaps we can devise new and appropriate methods if we will focus on the situation or difficulty, as in operations research, instead of relying so much on the assumptions and formulations of our discipline, especially since these offer little help in approaching organized complexities.

What the practitioner seeks is not merely a presentation of what exists or is occurring, or what trends may be revealed, no matter how

[39] See Wolins, op. cit., for his distinction between "effectiveness" and "effect."

[40] Harriet M. Bartlett, "Ways of Analyzing Social Work Practice," Social Welfare Forum, 1960 (New York: Columbia University Press, 1960), p. 205.

precisely these are measured or correlated. Rather, he needs a plan of action, a strategy for dealing with situations so that desired ends may be attained through a kind of action research which will help people to change their ideas, expectations, and behavior.[41]

It is this development of a "plan of action"—a strategy of helping people in groups—that represents the next major task of the group worker in social work.

[41] Frank, "Research for What?" *op. cit.*, p. 19.

Family Treatment Concepts

FRANCES H. SCHERZ

FAMILY TREATMENT is in a stage of development similar to that of the young child who is struggling to establish his identity by asking: Who am I? Who am I in relation to my parents? How am I different from them? In this developmental stage, which is a normal part of his growth, the child is in a state of productive and exciting confusion. Family treatment is also in a state of exciting confusion. It is good that this is so because it serves to prevent a premature crystallization of concepts and theories of family treatment that are now emerging. Even so our practice must continue while theoretical speculations continue to be put forward, formulated, altered, and reformulated.

At this point there are almost as many definitions of family treatment as there are practitioners in the field and writers on the subject. The one used in this article is the working definition developed by the Committee on Family Diagnosis and Treatment of the Midwestern Regional Committee of the Family Service Association of America: "Family treatment is the process of planned intervention in an area of family dysfunctioning. Family treatment is centered upon the dynamic functioning of the family as a unit, and some form of multiple interviewing is the primary treatment technique. Shifts to other treatment techniques (individual, joint, and total-family interviews) are related to the emergence of new diagnostic data or treatment developments, and are undertaken in the context of the total-family treatment goal. Since the goal of treatment requires focus on the family, some form of multiple interviewing remains the major treatment technique." [1]

According to this definition family treatment is a new therapeutic model. It focuses on the system of interpersonal relationships of the total family; each family system is made up of a unique blend of biological, social, psychological, and cultural components that are expressed through the patterns of relationships among family members. Theories of personality are, of course, relevant to all forms of treatment. But when the family system is the unit of attention, the worker must also apply knowledge derived from theories of group interaction and group communication. The conceptual framework for family diagnosis must incorporate these theories. Moreover, in practice, in the course of exploration and treatment, the family must be viewed as a network of forces and of roles discharged through interactional and transactional processes.

In this article I shall discuss some of the assumptions and concepts that underlie the working definition given above. The essential assumption is that the family is the most important shaper and influencer of human destiny, the matrix in which human development takes place. How the individual matures, how he learns to manage himself in the family and the outside world, how he conducts himself in relation to stress—in other words, his identity as an individual—is largely determined by intrafamilial patterns of conflict and integration.

These patterns are the family's accustomed ways of behaving and the rhythms it develops in the course of the continuous process of resolving differences as it faces new developmental tasks in each successive phase of family life. Eric Berne describes these patterns as "games" a family fashions and plays

SOCIAL CASEWORK, 1966, Vol. 47, No. 4, pp. 234-240.

according to complex rules it develops both consciously and unconsciously.[2] The rules are designed to help the family perform its life tasks: ensure the security and physical survival of its members; provide a context for emotional and social functioning, sexual differentiation, and the training of children; and support the growth of individual family members. Each newly formed family develops a unique set of rules that are based on the meshing of the individual members' needs and responsive to the family's changing tasks. The rules shape the family network. The games, or the forms of conflict and integration, are played out through explicit roles—parent, husband, wife, son, daughter, breadwinner, and so forth—and through implicit emotional roles.

The Concept of Family Equilibrium

Recognition of the dynamic interplay between these complex sets of rules and patterns of conflict and integration has led to the concept of family equilibrium, viewed as the family's design to provide avenues of stability and change in the interest of performing life tasks and fulfilling growth needs as economically as possible. Economy of operation is achieved by agreements, compacts, alliances, and collusions that are shaped by the rules and, in turn, shape the patterns of conflict and integration. At any given time, or even throughout the course of a family's life, the equilibrium may be either predominantly adaptive or predominantly maladaptive. Often it is adaptive in some respects and maladaptive in others. In any event it is always designed to meet the family's operational needs.

The significance of family equilibrium and marital equilibrium is readily apparent in the phenomena of scapegoating and projective identification. Additional evidence is to be seen in the familiar treatment situation in which one family member becomes sicker as another becomes healthier. A ten-year-old boy (the less competent of two brothers) put this very well in a family interview when he said: "If my grades go up, Steve's grades will go down." What caseworkers have observed in their practice points to the fact that the more fixed the maladaptive family

equilibrium is and, therefore, the less adequate for coping with new tasks, the more the family needs to cling to established ways as if it would be totally destroyed if the equilibrium were shifted.

Inherent in the concept of family equilibrium is the idea that each family member has a stake in stability and in change; when an individual is in trouble, the family is in trouble, and vice versa. Each family member is a beneficiary of family well-being and a victim of family maladaptation; he is also a producer of, and participant and collaborator in, the family system network for good and ill. He has his own problems, wishes, and goals that must be understood, but they can be understood only in the context of his family. Also inherent in the concept of family equilibrium is the idea that the nature of a family's equilibrium is closely related to its stage of development and the tasks characteristic of that stage. For example, family maturational tasks requiring a shift in family equilibrium may precipitate crises at certain transitional stages in the family's life—from the early years of marriage to the child-rearing years, from those years to the middle years, and so on.

Marital equilibrium is basic to family equilibrium. Therefore, the concept of marital complementarity—that marital interaction is based on intermeshing needs, hopes, and wishes—is an integral component of the theory of family treatment. An important current idea is that most persons choose as a marital partner a person whose personality structure is basically identical with their own and that the conflicts and defensive patterns of the partners dovetail. The nature and depth of psychopathology in each partner in a disturbed marriage are identical; basic conflicts, points of fixation and regression, and general ego integration are the same, despite differences in behavioral expression. The new family unit created by marriage develops its own rules and operational dynamics and has its own unique modes of adaptation and maladaptation.

One of the caseworker's major therapeutic endeavors in family treatment is to understand the nature of the family's equilibrium through learning to know the sets of rules and the patterns of conflict and integration that govern that equilibrium. Such knowledge is gained through direct observation of the processes of family interaction. The worker must also know at what stage the family is in its development and the specific forces or incidents that have upset its equilibrium, causing family dysfunctioning that requires treatment intervention. Having this knowledge, the worker can assess the nature and degree of change in equilibrium that is necessary, desirable, and possible. To use Berne's theory, one might say that a major goal of family treatment is to interrupt the destructive games, change or modify the overt and covert rules, and set in motion more constructive games with new or modified rules. Family treatment, then, attempts to influence the family system network for the purpose of reducing or altering dysfunctional stress on all members of the family. When treatment is effective, individual and family symptoms and problems disappear or are reduced.

In emphasizing the concept of family equilibrium, I wish to convey the idea that neither individual pathology nor particular presenting problems are, in and of themselves, overriding determinants in choosing the treatment method. Individual neuroses, character disorders, or psychoses may need to be explored, but they do not necessarily require individual treatment. Similarly, such presenting problem constellations as marital conflict, parent-child conflict, and problems of aging may suggest the use of different kinds of interviews during the exploratory period, but they do not necessarily determine the treatment method to be employed. More significant than individual pathology or presenting problems in determining treatment methodology are such factors as the degree of alienation and of intimacy in the family; the identity needs of each individual; the ability of each family member to perceive and respond to the feelings, actions, beliefs, values, and aspirations of other family members; and problems of self-esteem. Assessment of these factors should help the worker decide when various forms of family treatment are appropriate. The intent of the family approach is to discover in what ways

the individual symptoms or presenting problem constellations represent family dysfunction. If there is an indication that the family's current problem—no matter how it is described—should concern the total family, family interviews should be used to shift the focus from the individual so that the entire family can be involved in working on the problem.

Communication

Communication is the index of family operations, and so the family system network is influenced through working with family interaction as it is expressed in communication. Communication is the means whereby the family transacts the business of life. It is carried on at all levels—conscious, preconscious, and unconscious. It takes many forms—verbal, nonverbal, attitudinal, and behavioral. It is revealed through the explicit and implicit use of roles and the expression of emotion, which may be bland or highly charged. The family's characteristic modes of communication reveal the cultural forces impinging on it; the social and personal values it embraces; its view of itself in relation to the outside world; its fears, permissions, taboos, and secrets; its defenses and adaptations; and the affective needs and responses of its members: in short, they reveal the family's life style. The messages family members communicate to each other may be congruent or incongruent. They may reflect the double-bind communication found in neurotic and psychotic family dysfunctioning. They may be clear, direct, and constructive in some areas of family communication, but clouded, confused, and confusing in others. It is through understanding the family's communication at all levels and its content, form, and affect that the worker gains knowledge of the family's life style, its adaptive and maladaptive equilibrium, and the immediate area of crucial dysfunction. Communication, then, is the channel for diagnosis.

Communication is also both the medium for treatment and a treatment goal. In the broadest sense, in family treatment the worker moves from observing the patterns of family communication to identifying the patterns that are crucial in family dysfunctioning, and then to working on better ways of communicating. A variety of techniques may be used: teaching family members how to communicate verbally; developing understandable connections between behavior, feeling, and verbalization; reducing or correcting misperceptions; clarifying the nature of double-bind messages; and trying to understand the roots of the difficulty in communicating. In using these techniques, the worker provides an example of clear, direct communication. A major treatment goal is to enable the family to open lines of communication by focusing on the development of a constructive fusion of verbalization, meaning, feeling, and behavior.

Communication between the family and the worker is the basic ingredient in the therapeutic relationship. The worker's activity is conditioned by such factors as whether he is functioning, for example, as a model parental ego and superego figure with the psychologically chaotic family, or as a moderator or catalyst with the relatively healthy family, or as an auxiliary ego with the family that is caught in neurotic double-bind communication. Families seem to establish modes of communication with the worker that are characteristic of them in such matters as trust, incorporation, identification, and the like and to express these modes through family defenses of projection, denial, displacement, and so on. In other words, there appear to be identifiable features in a family's communication with the worker that reflect its adaptive and maladaptive operations.

On the whole there appear to be fewer interfering transference phenomena in family treatment than in individual treatment because the emphasis is on family interpersonal communication rather than on individual intrapsychic problems. Intensity of feeling is more likely to be expressed to other family members than to the worker. Moreover, the family members are often engaged in seeking satisfaction of their affectional needs from each other rather than from the worker. Complicating transference reactions seem more likely to develop when exploration begins with individuals—which points to the value of holding family interviews very early in the contact in a new case. Experience shows that it is more difficult to shift from individual to family treatment than from family to individual treatment because of the likelihood that strong transference phenomena will appear during individual treatment.

Despite the fact that individual transference is limited in family treatment, it is not easy to develop appropriate treatment communication. The worker may encounter massive family defenses or resistance displayed through the beclouding of issues by excessive verbalizing, fighting, withdrawing, and the like. When this happens, the form that resistance takes, whether behavioral or verbal, should be explored as a family phenomenon because of the possibility that the resistance expressed by the one member is also felt by the others. It is not uncommon for one family member to use himself and be used by the others to express resistance for all of them. In one family interview a worker questioned this, the parents reinforced her behavior, saying that the office child refused to take off her coat. When the was cold. In this way the family was questioning the purpose of coming for treatment. Resistance may, however, be expressed in different ways by each family member, which may tempt the worker to shift to individual treatment. The worker should pay attention to the form resistance takes rather than the specific verbal content. One family engaged in bitter fighting during a number of interviews, each member turning to the worker at points to enlist him as the judge of who was right or wrong. The worker struggled to keep himself removed but could not always succeed and found himself lost in the minutiae of the content. When it became clear to him that the family not only obtained great gratification from the battles but also used fighting as a way of excluding him and denying the need for treatment, he told them this repeatedly until the fighting abated and the family became involved.

Whether dealing with family resistance or family defenses—and whether one or another family member takes the center of the stage in a particular interview or withdraws—the worker should keep in mind that the behavior is serving a purpose for all family members and that his communications must be addressed to all of them.

Other difficulties in communication—such as explosive hostility, excessive passivity or withdrawal, or nonverbalization—may also be encountered, and they may propel the worker away from family treatment. The purpose and meaning of these kinds of behavior should be understood, however, before the worker makes a shift in treatment. It is not uncommon, for example, for a family member to sit passively for many interviews, seemingly unobservant and nonparticipating, only to become suddenly active in interviews or to reveal that productive changes in his behavior have been taking place in the home, at school, or on the job. Perhaps the most difficult aspect of communication in family treatment is the worker's having to enter actively into the family system, in the sense that he is often forced to expose and express his personal and professional values. Although workers have always influenced people through their own values, the family interactional process creates a climate in which the worker must often intervene directly, with the result that he is uncomfortable and, at times, confused and self-doubting.

Family Constellations

I should like now to present a few ideas about family constellations that may offer broad guidelines to the use of family treatment. I shall describe briefly four typical constellations in relation to the nature of family equilibrium, the family tasks, the areas of dysfunction, the broad treatment methodology to be employed, and the treatment goals. I should like to emphasize, however, that these are not to be interpreted as distinct classifications or typologies of families. No family unit will exactly fit any one of the broad descriptions outlined.

1. One family constellation presents a socially and psychologically unstable equilibrium. This type of family can be described as chaotic. There is a lack of individuation among family members, and they fuse their identities and rely indiscriminately on one another. They function as a family of sib-

lings; there is little explicit or implicit role differentiation between the spouses or between them and their children. This family often comes to the agency because the members' action orientation to life has created problems for them in the social environment, because they have failed in role performance in marriage and child rearing, because their primitive behavior makes it difficult for them to know how to manage themselves in the outside world, or because active or latent psychosis creates special problems of communication in the family. Frequently the members of this family behave in rigid, stereotyped ways and have ineffective patterns of control. They have little capacity for abstract thought. Life is lived in the present for immediate gratification and release of tension. The pervasive life style of the family is characterized by a lack of structure or stability and frequently by low self-esteem, fear of close relations, and overpowering affectional needs.

When such a constellation emerges, family treatment is frequently the treatment of choice; the action orientation of the members of such families and their lack of individuation may make one-to-one treatment intolerable or incomprehensible, and sibling competitiveness may not permit focus on one person. They are more likely to perceive the nature and implications of dysfunctional behavior and communication when they are worked with transactionally. Sometimes rivalry over having narcissistic affectional needs met is so intense that concurrent, supplementary nurturing of an individual or the marital pair is indicated. In some cases initiated at a particular point of stress the narcissistic affectional needs and hurt self-esteem of a family member are so great that individual treatment may need to be the forerunner of some form of family treatment.

Appropriate treatment techniques for such a family include demonstration of the nature of the dysfunctional behavior to increase perception of its consequences, education in the use of language and communication, demonstration and teaching of role performance, and exposition of connections between behavior and affect. For some time emphasis may have to be placed on the content and form of the behavior rather than on its meaning and sources.

The immediate goal is to establish some structure and stability in explicit role performance through suggesting a series of tasks that the family can perform successfully. With some families, the long-range goal may be the achievement of an equilibrium of adequate role performances that will permit some individual identity. If the latter is possible, treatment may move, for example, to conjoint treatment of parents for the purpose of reinforcing parental development and concurrent individual treatment of a child to reinforce individual identity.

2. The second family constellation presents a flexible, adaptive equilibrium that has been equal to most of the maturational tasks but is temporarily dysfunctional or regressive because of an acute crisis brought about by disabling illness, death, employment changes, or the like. Family-unit treatment is often effective in quickly mobilizing and solidifying the family so that a new equilibrium can be established, perhaps through calling upon existing strengths or through bringing to the fore latent strengths and supports. Experience shows that this kind of family can often find a new equilibrium more quickly when family members work on a problem together. For example, when the family unit works with common feelings of loss, grief, and rage over the death of a family member—giving each other permission to mourn—the children may be helped to give up their anxiety-provoking fantasies about their responsibility for the death. Similarly when residual conflicts between aged parents and adult children are aroused by the need for a new living plan for the aged member, family-unit interviews may aid in reducing the conflicts enough for effective plans to be worked out.

The main technique is the furtherance of open communication among family members. The worker functions as a catalyst in helping the family identify feelings, clarify misperceptions, and develop new perceptions about each other and the family's life situation.

3. Between the two kinds of family constellation already described, there is a grouping that includes a variety of family constellations in which the equilibrium can be broadly described as neurotic. The over-all equilibrium presents, side by side, adaptation, maladaptation, and ambivalence in explicit and implicit role performance. Internalized conflicts and high ambivalence in family relationships are characteristic. The over-all treatment plan depends on whether the crucial area of dysfunction is fixed, regressive, or representative of minor maturational delay. Also significant is the level and stage of personal and family development and the degree of flexibility in ego adaptation. The broad treatment goals may involve loosening fixed alliances, shifting the family members to new alignments, or changing the nature of family equilibrium. All combinations of family treatment techniques may be employed.

One family constellation within this broad category presents a disturbed equilibrium because of an inability to master certain maturational tasks, in spite of a history of marital complementarity and reasonable child-rearing practices. The equilibrium can be described as temporarily regressive in the area of dysfunction. The problem may occur because the specific maturational task comes at a time when there are other crucial tasks for the family—for example, employment difficulties on the part of the father at the same time his adolescent son is moving into competition with him. Or the disequilibrium may be caused by structural changes in the family, such as the birth of a child, the departure of a child for college or marriage, retirement from work, and so forth. In other words, when maturational tasks prompt a resurgence of partially resolved conflicts in such areas as identity formation, separation, and the like, or when the task is accompanied by special social stresses, some form of family treatment may be effective. Treatment techniques are used that enable the family to analyze misperceptions in communication; that enable them to work on such problems as identity, separateness, and interdependence; and that show links between past experiences and present tasks.

Another family constellation in this grouping presents a neurotic equilibrium in which characteristic adaptive modes are based on highly ambivalent, regressive, or fixated interaction that prevent the accomplishment of maturational tasks. One of the main diagnostic clues for the identification of this constellation is the family's use of double-bind or ambivalent communication in a specific or encapsulated area. With such a family it frequently appears that the marital equilibrium is stable, though a child manifests specific problems; closer scrutiny reveals the ambivalent marital equilibrium, which is held steady by the parents' using the child as a tool. Family-unit treatment may be the preferred initial technique for the purpose of clarifying and later reducing or resolving double-bind communication. The child's presence seems to further exposure of the neurotic binds.

Some of these families show neurotic dysfunction that is in a fluid, uncrystallized state, with evidence of a high degree of available, appropriate affect and a quality of flexible, perceptive communication that makes some form of continuing family treatment a good choice. They can use the worker as an auxiliary ego to work on the meaning and sources of double-bind, incongruent communications. When the dysfunction indicates a mild maturational delay with regressive features—which is often the case with the young married partners who have not yet mastered the developmental tasks of adolescence—the most effective treatment technique is the joint interview.

4. The family constellation that has a psychotic equilibrium is often characterized by pervasive double-bind communication. The literature is replete with evidence that families described as schizophrenic use pervasive double-bind communication in the total family unit or express it through one member. Our experience supports the evidence that family-unit treatment is the treatment of choice in such cases and that such a family can be worked with in a noninstitutional setting.

Conclusion

In an over-all sense, some form of family treatment appears to be effective when the family's therapeutic assets include the following: freedom to interact, some verbal communication, recognition of a family problem, shifting equilibrium as expressed in flexible family alliances, ability to use group diagnostic sessions, and acceptance of the principle of family treatment.

It may well be that experience will show that some form of family treatment is suitable for all families. Moreover, it may eventuate that the main therapeutic problems will be technical in nature, that is, problems of knowing when and how to alter family equilibrium, when and how to work with the family unit or with various combinations of family members, how shifts in diagnosis and treatment objectives affect the use of specific techniques, and how to use a growing body of knowledge about specific relationship and communication techniques. The goal of family treatment is to influence the family system by loosening, shifting, or changing maladaptive family equilibrium and by strengthening adaptive equilibrium so that family energy can be released to meet its tasks and the individual freed to grow.

REFERENCES

[1] *Casebook on Family Diagnosis and Treatment,* Family Service Association of America, New York, 1965, p. viii.

[2] Eric Berne, *Transactional Analysis in Psychotherapy,* Grove Press, New York, 1961, pp. 98–115.

BY OLIVE T. WERTZ

Social Workers and the Therapeutic Community

■ A discussion of some of the implicit and explicit assumptions on which most therapeutic communities are based. Questions are raised regarding the contribution of the therapeutic milieu to the rehabilitation of the mental patient. Implications for the social worker in the psychiatric setting are examined. ■

THE THERAPEUTIC COMMUNITY or milieu, accepted enthusiastically by workers in the mental health field as another treatment approach to the continually baffling problem of mental illness, has become a *sine qua non* of any mental hospital setting that purports to be progressive and in tune with the latest developments in social psychiatry. Psychiatrists and social scientists, separately and together, have become increasingly concerned with the patient's day-to-day living arrangements and patterns of relationships and how these impede or retard his recovery.[1] Among others, Stanton and Schwartz and Greenblatt operated on the assumption that the sociocultural environment may be of greater critical importance than more specific treatments; out of their work and that of Jones and other psychiatrists and social scientists working in England emerged the concept of the therapeutic community.[2]

The social worker in the psychiatric setting has been caught up in this enthusiasm along with other professional and subprofessional hospital staff. He has been involved in breaking down some of the rigid hierarchical barriers in psychiatric hospitals and setting up more egalitarian structures that have permitted less formalized patterns of communication, broader participation in decision-making, and the conscious use of the setting per se in treatment. Now that we have had several years of experience with therapeutic communities even some of its most ardent proponents are taking a second look at some of the implications and effects of this new approach.

The concept of a therapeutic milieu has been used in so many ways that it has be-

---

[1] *See*, for example, William A. Caudill, *The Psychiatric Hospital as a Small Society* (Cambridge, Mass.: Harvard University Press, 1958); John Cumming and Elaine Cumming, *Ego and Milieu* (New York: Atherton Press, 1962); Milton Greenblatt, Daniel Levinson, and R. H. Williams, eds., *The Patient and the Mental Hospital* (Glencoe, Ill.: Free Press, 1957); Greenblatt, Richard H. York, and Esther L. Brown, *From Custodial to Therapeutic Patient Care in Mental Hospitals* (New York: Russell Sage Foundation, 1955); Fritz Redl, "The Concept of a Therapeutic Milieu," *American Journal of Orthopsychiatry*, Vol. 29, No. 4 (October 1959); Alfred Stanton and Morris S. Schwartz, *The Mental Hospital* (New York: Basic Books, 1954).

[2] Stanton and Schwartz, *op. cit.*; Greenblatt, Levinson, and Williams, eds., *op. cit.*; Maxwell Jones, *The Therapeutic Community* (New York: Basic Books, 1953).

OLIVE T. WERTZ, MSSA, is Lecturer, School of Applied Social Sciences, Western Reserve University, Cleveland, Ohio.

Reprinted with permission of the National Association of Social Workers, from SOCIAL WORK, Vol. 11, No. 4 (October 1966), pp. 43-49.

come vague and confusing.[3] It has covered all extremes, from the paternalistic ward where patients are treated benignly and staff are devoted to their welfare to the highly structured community described by Jones where all relationships are carefully managed and patients and staff alike are involved in both the clinical administration of the hospital and in therapy.[4] It has been described as democratic as opposed to authoritarian, treatment rather than custodial oriented, humanitarian instead of oppressive, and flexible as opposed to rigid. In further breaking down the concept, Schwartz suggests that it should provide the patient with experiences that will minimize his distortions of reality, facilitate his realistic and meaningful communication with others so that he will derive greater satisfaction and security, reduce his anxiety, increase his comfort and self-esteem, provide him with insight into the causes and manifestations of his illness, mobilize his initiative, and motivate him to realize more fully his potential for creativity and productiveness.[5]

There is no general agreement as to how all these goals can be achieved most effectively. The way different settings have chosen to structure themselves in order to become "therapeutic" varies considerably. However, certain assumptions emerge from a study of the literature, some of which are more problematic than valid.

The writer will examine the therapeutic community in terms of some of these implicit and explicit assumptions and raise questions as to whether the "democratic" structure is the most effective way to meet the needs of both patients and staff. Its implications for the social worker in particular will be discussed.

UNVALIDATED ASSUMPTIONS

Either explicitly or implicitly the idea exists that the more patients are involved in decisions regarding their own treatment, the more all staff are involved in decision-making, the more interaction there is between patients and between staff and patients, and the less status differential there is, the more therapeutic the milieu will be. This represents an oversocialized and too psychologically simple conception of the mental patient and the kind of environment that can answer his needs.

Oversocialized, oversimplified view of the patient. An approach which accepts the idea that psychotic patients are susceptible to exactly the same influences that determine the behavior of adjusted persons is based on an unvalidated assumption. Hartmann states that sociologists may make valid predictions with no consideration of the total personality of the individual, but that these predictions will most likely be correct when

the social action is predominantly determined by the conscious or preconscious ego as in rational action involving such ego interests as we plausibly may assume are present in the *average member of a group.* [Author's italics.] There are other social actions and functions where one cannot rely on such a simple psychological model if one wishes to make valid predictions . . . these models will prove a source of failure for the sociologist in matters where functions of the personality other than rational or ego interest

[3] *See,* for example, in addition to the works cited in n. 1, G. W. Brooks, *Chronic Schizophrenia: Exploration in Theory and Treatment* (Glencoe, Ill.: Free Press, 1960); M. Cohen, "The Therapeutic Community and Therapy," *Psychiatry,* Vol. 20, No. 2 (May 1957); LaVerne F. Irvine and S. Joel Derry, "An Investigation of Problem Areas Relating to the Therapeutic Community Concept," *Mental Hygiene,* Vol. 45, No. 3 (July 1961); Richard F. Salisbury, *Structure of Custodial Care* (Berkeley: University of California Press, 1962); Eugene Talbot, Stuart C. Miller, and Robert B. White, "Some Aspects of Self-Concepts and Role Demands in a Therapeutic Community," *Journal of Abnormal and Social Psychology,* Vol. 63, No. 2 (September 1961).

[4] Jones, *op. cit.*

[5] Morris Schwartz, "What is a Therapeutic Milieu?" in Greenblatt, Levinson, and Williams, eds., *op. cit.,* p. 131.

come into play in a way which is dynamically relevant. These are likely to differ from individual to individual.[6]

The mental patient is far from being an average member of a group—the need for socialization and group activities, for status, for conforming to group norms, and the like may be the least important of his needs in certain illnesses or in a particular stage of his illness. Yet the milieu that stresses those aspects is considered by many to be the most therapeutic regardless of the kinds of patients it is trying to treat.

Trap of the "democratic" structure. Another assumption that appears in so many therapeutic communities is that the more "democratic" the structure and the less traditional hierarchical role differentiation there is, the more the therapeutic potential of each staff member with whom the patient comes in contact will be utilized, with increased job satisfaction as a concomitant. Lefton *et al.* have discussed this idea with particular attention to the social worker:

> Leaders of this school seem already to have translated "potentiality" into a somewhat dubious form of "actuality"— i.e., they have so heavily stressed the importance of interpersonal relationships between patients and staff that they have literally blurred, and in many instances, virtually eliminated the valuation of any real functional distinctions among them.[7]

The same group found that the discrepancy between perceived and ideal decision-making was related to position in the hierarchy of the professional groups studied and that the lower the group in the hierarchy, the greater the discrepancy.[8]

The therapeutic orientation of the ward to which they were assigned modified or accentuated the magnitude of the discrepancy; i.e., bureaucratic rigidities were viewed more negatively by precisely those personnel assigned to wards on which the orientation was specifically designed to minimize the presumed inadequacies of formal organization!

Schwartz brings in another facet to be considered, namely, expertise. He says that the optimal relationship between democratic participation and expertise has yet to be found: "Variations in expertness mean that some kind of stratification is necessary in the mental hospital."[9] To find a balance between the modes and content of stratification on the one hand and efficiency, expertise, democratic participation, and leadership on the other poses a difficult and complex problem.

In discussing authority, limit-setting, and social control, Galione *et al.* decided that the issue was problematical and should by no means be settled on the simple assumption that anything savoring of authority and control was undemocratic and automatically bad.[10] Polansky stated: "Hell hath no fury like the democratic process," and Elaine Cumming said that it takes a tough ego to survive it.[11] Mental patients are not notable for the toughness of their egos—this is also the case with many staff members!

It would thus appear that changes which involve more democratic participation have not necessarily or automatically resulted in a more therapeutic milieu and greater job

---

[6] Heinz Hartmann, "The Application of Psychoanalytic Concepts to Social Science," in Hendrik M. Ruitenbeek, ed., *Psychoanalysis and Social Science* (New York: E. P. Dutton & Co., 1962), pp. 63–64.

[7] Mark Lefton, Salomon Rettig, Simon Dinitz, and Benjamin Pasamanick, "Status Perceptions of Psychiatric Social Workers and Their Implications for Work Satisfaction," *American Journal of Orthopsychiatry*, Vol. 31, No. 1 (January 1961), p. 103.

[8] Mark Lefton, Simon Dinitz, and Benjamin Pasamanick, "Decision-Making in a Mental Hospital: Real, Perceived and Ideal," *American Sociological Review*, Vol. 26, No. 6 (December 1959), pp. 828–829.

[9] Schwartz, *op. cit.*, p. 135.

[10] E. F. Galione, Ralph R. Notman, Alfred H. Stanton, and Richard H. Williams, "The Nature and Purpose of Mental Hospital Wards," in Greenblatt, Levinson, and Williams, eds., *op. cit.*, p. 342.

[11] *Ibid.*, p. 342.

satisfaction, and that there is no simple correlation between the two.

The faith factor. Different models of the therapeutic community appear to work even though their divergencies are so wide and deep as to imply fundamentally different conceptual frames of reference. Some base their approach on a belief in the patient's need for greater responsibility—this may be offered to or urged or forced on the patient. In others, the patient's need to regress is given the greatest weight when a respectful acceptance of the infantile and deeper unconscious drives is seen as the atmosphere that will foster an emerging ability to deal with reality and assume responsibility. Both allowing the patient to regress or forcing him to take on responsibility can be equally nontherapeutic.

According to Cohen, the factor that seems to stand out is that of belief or "faith":

> In the successes there is consistently a dedicated leader who sparks the whole community hierarchy with hope, expectation of improvement, a sense of knowing what to do and how to do it.[12]

He has the impression that when the leader dies or moves away the community settles down to something humdrum. Was the therapeutic value of the milieu only an apparent value—that is, was what was actually being observed "the magic of the transference"?

GOALS OF TREATMENT AND REHABILITATION

A further complication arises when the relationship of the therapeutic milieu to what happens to the patient after he leaves the hospital is examined. If the goals of treatment are met, are those of rehabilitation also being achieved?

Salisbury advocates a "rehabilitation milieu" where the professional therapeutic role would be minimized and a "rehabilitation worker" role would include both attendants and therapists.

> The gradualness and the lack of pushing would militate against active patients' reverting to fantasy as occurs sometimes under present programs of intensive therapy.[13]

Brooks states in relation to chronic schizophrenics that their overt behavior and secondary symptoms have been changed after intensification of treatment but the primary symptoms of schizophrenia were not affected.

Discharge rates of schizophrenics appear to be influenced by therapeutic enthusiasm but this is not a reliable index of improvement or of ability to remain in the community. On the other hand, rehabilitative efforts directed toward utilizing the schizophrenic's remaining capacities rather than toward changing him show some promise. These efforts are *not* within the usual definition of the therapeutic community, although their social importance is obvious. [Author's italics.] [14]

Despite attempts to make conditions in the treatment unit more like those in the outside world, it was seen by Rapoport, in his study of the Social Rehabilitation Unit at Belmont Hospital in England, as an atypical environment with norms different from those of the outside environment.[15] He argues that if the values and attitudes were applied to the outside world they might produce serious conflicts when patients return to the wider community. Follow-up data showed less satisfactory adjustment on the part of those who tended to change their values in the direction of the unit's. This suggests the need to distinguish conceptually between treatment and rehabilitation goals, which may in some circumstances work at cross-purposes. Maxwell Jones, in his introduction to Rapoport's study, says:

---

[12] Cohen, *op. cit.*, p. 173.

[13] Salisbury, *op. cit.*, p. 174.
[14] Brooks, *op. cit.*, p. 178.
[15] Robert Rapoport, *Community as Doctor* (Springfield, Ill.: Charles C Thomas, 1960).

We know little about how to apply group and community methods most efficiently to the problem of rehabilitation in the outside world. Presumably the same argument applies to any type of psychiatric patient exposed to hospital treatment.[16]

Jones and Sidebotham raise the question —in relation to current shorter stays and increasing patient turnover—of how it is possible for the short-term patient to have very much responsibility in the hospital setting and to identify with the hospital. They felt it was valuable for long-term patients who were sufficiently articulate or in touch with events around them to participate in this kind of verbal expression, but thought that for most patients activity groups provided a better means of socialization.

Assuming that a proportion of short-stay patients are in hospitals long enough to make the system worth while, we may further question whether they should be encouraged to identify with the hospital group or whether attempts should not be made to turn their interests outward to the community. For them, hospital life is only a passing phase.[17]

SOCIAL WORKERS AND THE STATUS TRAP

It is obvious from the foregoing that there are many problems—for both patients and staff—inherent in the nature of the therapeutic milieu. Only further study and the perspective of time will make clear what its contribution to the treatment of the mentally ill can be.

In the meantime, however, what has been happening to the social worker in the psychiatric setting under the impact of this new treatment approach? Previously, he had been struggling to find his place in the psychiatric hospital. He had adopted the

clinical treatment model and fought for a place on the treatment team, doing direct therapy with patients. He wanted to be involved in critical decisions regarding planning for individual patients and for the setting in which he worked. He welcomed the breaking down of some of the hierarchical barriers and the opportunity for more democratic participation brought about by the concept of the therapeutic community.

Now his efforts were focused on becoming involved in the various facets of the restructured environment with its emphasis on greater staff and patient participation in all aspects of treatment. But now not only he but other staff members who had been lower in the status hierarchy were "in on the act." While he no longer had to prove his competence to become involved in some of the aspects of the treatment program to which he had formerly aspired, neither did anyone else! Everyone was involved in treatment and in decision-making, and he was now functioning in a much more fluid and less structured situation. Some of the old status differentials were not nearly so apparent, and yet his status needs were not fulfilled. He had been led to believe that his desire for greater status and influence was legitimate, yet he frequently lacked the technical competence (or its equivalent, the MD or Ph.D.) to challenge successfully the prerogatives of those above him in the status hierarchy.[18] And he was now competing with other professionals and subprofessionals whose status desires had also been increased and whose position had formerly been below his.

How can he extricate himself from this status trap? Lefton et al. suggest that when functions are made specific, there is less opportunity for aggrandizement of specific duties, and thus the stress and concern for status become minimized.[19] This leaves us with the question of who makes the func-

---

[16] Ibid., p. 4.
[17] Kathleen Jones and Roy Sidebotham, Mental Hospitals at Work (New York: Humanities Press, 1962), p. 181.

[18] Lefton, Rettig, Dinitz, and Pasamanick, op. cit.
[19] Ibid., p. 109.

tions specific—who defines the social worker's role in this new community?

The time has come for the worker to define his own role. Instead of becoming involved in what amounts to internecine warfare in some therapeutic communities and struggling for status vis-à-vis other professionals, he should be concentrating on what his unique contribution can be to the patient's welfare and to the rest of the clinical team.

WORKER AS LIAISON

This unique contribution can be as a liaison between the clinical setting and the family and community. The worker should turn from the therapeutic community toward the larger community of which the patient is a part and to which he must return. It has been demonstrated that the therapeutic milieu has not been successful in preparing the patient for the community. The social worker's knowledge of the family and of the patient's former milieu could be a vital factor in bridging this gap. Or, if the gap cannot be bridged successfully, he can concentrate his efforts on rehabilitative goals. He must remember that he is an applied social scientist as well as a clinician and should not confine himself to forms of treatment that have not been demonstrated empirically to be effective. To make a meaningful contribution he must keep in mind the uniqueness of each patient and that no one model, milieu, or therapist can adequately answer the patient's needs. He must be able to bring to bear all the resources within and especially outside the hospital that are essential to each patient *and his family* and do this in the differential ways each case demands.

The writer disputes Wootton's statement that the social worker's main focus of activity should be "mobilizing the various forms of practical assistance that are now available for dealing with certain problems of situation or behavior, her relation with her client being merely incidental to this

task."[20] Wootton seems to see the social worker as a sort of middleman whose major professional function is to steer the less privileged to those resources and services that the well-to-do are able to provide for themselves. This implies that they will then make use of these services—which is not necessarily the case. It also minimizes, if not denies, the importance of relationship and unconscious motivations that are often crucial in enabling the patient or client to make productive use of what is available. The writer does agree, however, with her statement that with the strong influence of psychiatry in social work we have tended to "emphasize certain aspects of social work out of all proportion to their real significance while playing down others that are potentially at least as valuable."[21]

Comprehensive community mental health planning will bring about further changes in the role of the social worker as well as in that of other mental health professionals. It opens up a new realm outside the clinical setting. If the goals of this program are to be met, the social worker, along with others, will become involved less and less in direct work and more and more in consultation, in-service training, community education, and interpretation. In preparation for this he badly needs to become reacquainted with the community he has temporarily neglected in his enthusiasm for clinical and milieu treatment.

CONCLUSIONS

As happens so often when new treatment approaches are introduced, we seem inclined to "throw the baby out with the bath water." Because we have become aware of the dysfunctional aspects of the highly bureaucratic structure does not mean that an absence of structure is necessarily the best solution. Hierarchical rigidities can be

---

[20] Barbara Wootton, *Social Science and Social Pathology* (New York: Humanities Press, 1959), p. 275.

[21] *Ibid.,* p. 271.

modified without giving up role differentiation and specialization. Patients and staff at all levels can be involved meaningfully in decision-making without eliminating lines of authority and responsibility. Stein states:

It is true that non-bureaucratic systems can provide greater latitude for innovation, individualization, professional self-fulfillment and ready adaptability to change than can more complex organizations. They also provide for conditions that can make for instability, role confusion and interpersonal tensions which, if they become severe, can militate against the interests of clientele.[22]

He suggests that drastic debureaucratization is not the answer, but rather "developing a balance between those elements of structure and process conducive to rational management of the organization and those elements essential for optimum client service." [23]

The lack of agreement as to how to achieve improvement or recovery in the mental patient is nowhere more apparent than in the literature on the therapeutic community. This points to a crying need for further research and additional clinical experience. The value of the therapeutic milieu as another weapon in the pathetically small armamentarium of effective treatment modalities cannot be gainsaid, but, like other widely heralded discoveries in the mental health field, it requires time and further study before its real contribution can be assessed. In the meantime, it might behoove the social worker in the psychiatric setting to concentrate his energies in those areas in which his knowledge and skill can be utilized most effectively.

---

[22] Herman D. Stein, "Administrative Leadership in Complex Service Organizations," p. 4. Paper presented at the Annual Forum of the National Conference on Social Welfare, Atlantic City, N.J., May 1965.

[23] *Ibid.*, pp. 4–5.

Crisis intervention: theory in search of a program

by Richard A. Pasewark
and Dale A. Albers

Tremendous strides have been made in the field of public health in recent decades. Many former scourges, threatening young or old or both, have been drastically cut down or even practically eliminated—such as tuberculosis, polio, malaria, and typhoid fever. The mental health field cannot point proudly to similar dramatic advances.

Can some of the same concepts and basic techniques that have proved successful in public health be applied effectively on a wide scale to the field of mental health? The authors believe that this can be done through crisis intervention.

Crisis intervention has been developing over a number of years. Workers using the crisis approach have reported many instances of success in dealing with problems arising from specific situations and events such as illegitimacy, pregnancy and birth, suicide and other deaths, and poverty.[1] However, there is a notable absence of programs either totally or primarily oriented to this approach.

To substantiate the viewpoint that general application of crisis intervention can revitalize the mental health field and offer hope for successful primary prevention of mental disorders, an explanation is presented of what crisis theory is, how it developed, and how it might be applied broadly to mental health and the helping services.

The development of crisis intervention theory owes much to Erikson, Lindemann, and Caplan—all associated with Harvard University or the Harvard Medical School. They evolved three cornerstones of the theory: the concept of developmental crises, redefinition of transient personality disorders as life crises having a predictable pattern, and application of the public health model to mental health.

Erikson contributed the idea that in nor-

[1] See Karen A. Signell, "The Crisis of Unwed Motherhood: A Consultation Approach," *Community Mental Health Journal*, Vol. 5, No. 4 (August 1969), pp. 304-313; Gerald Caplan, "Mental Hygiene Work with Expectant Mothers," *Mental Hygiene*, Vol. 35, No. 1 (January 1951), pp. 41-50; Gerald Caplan, Edward A. Mason, and David M. Kaplan, "Four Studies of Crisis in Parents of Prematures," *Community Mental Health Journal*, Vol.

Reprinted with permission of the National Association of Social Workers, from SOCIAL WORK, Vol. 17, No. 2 (March 1972), pp. 70-77.

mal growth the individual experiences several specific developmental crises that he must surmount if he is to become a mature, integrated adult. He defined crisis as "a necessary turning point, a crucial moment, when development must move one way or another, marshaling resources of growth, recovery, and further differentiation."[2] He identified eight such types of developmental crises occurring during the normal span of life from infancy through childhood, adolescence, and maturity, to old age and senescence.

Lindemann's interest focused on transient personality disorders—precipitated by unusual environmental stress. The assumption is that removing stress will ameliorate or eliminate the observed behavioral symptoms. Lindemann was especially concerned with grief reactions following a loved one's death and concluded that an individual had to make an adjustment to the crisis such a death precipitated. His investigations contributed to crisis theory the idea that reactions to crisis follow a predictable pattern and have specific, identifiable stages.[3]

Caplan was a forceful advocate of crisis intervention theory. A major thrust of his work was toward applying public health principles to community mental health problems. Specifically, Caplan was concerned with primary, secondary, and tertiary prevention and ways to apply these public health concepts to mental health activities.[4]

Primary prevention aims to reduce the incidence of a disorder by altering the environment so that it restrains the disease process or by making the individual less susceptible. Secondary prevention tries to keep a mild disorder from becoming a severe one. Early case-finding and treatment are stressed. Tertiary prevention aims to keep a serious disorder from producing permanent disability. All three endeavor to prevent any individual from being a source of contagion.

In essence, a crisis might be considered analogous to a learning dilemma. In both the person experiences a new situation or event for which he has no adequate coping behaviors. The strategy in crisis intervention is to provide the individual with appropriate behavioral patterns that will enable him to deal effectively with the specific crisis. Crisis theorists have not delineated the mode of intervention; one assumes that the techniques to be used remain the prerogative of the intervenor.

A number of overt or tacit assumptions are made in crisis theory, such as:

Crisis is not a pathological experience. Acute symptoms manifested in crisis do not necessarily indicate previous personality disturbance or reflect current pathology. Instead they mirror first a dearth of available mechanisms for dealing with the situation, then groping behavior that seeks to resolve it effectively, and eventually the behavior adopted for coping with the crisis. The basic optimism of the theory is seen in the point of view that a person's troubled behavior in a crisis may reflect struggle with a current problem rather than past or present deviation from the normal. In some ways, this assumption is reminiscent of Jung's view of psychiatric disturbance as symptomatic of the organism's dissatisfaction with a current developmental state and of the flux in personality as it attempts to deal with the situation.[5]

1, No. 2 (Summer 1965), pp. 149–161; Edwin S. Shneidman and Norman L. Farberow, "The Los Angeles Suicide Prevention Center: A Demonstration of Public Health Feasibilities," *American Journal of Public Health*, Vol. 55, No. 1 (January 1965), pp. 21–26; Erich Lindemann, "Symptomatology and Management of Acute Grief," *American Journal of Psychiatry*, Vol. 101, No. 2 (September 1944), pp. 141–148; Erich Lindemann, Warren Vaughn, and Manon McGinnis, "Preventive Intervention in a Four Year Old Child Whose Father Committed Suicide," in Caplan, ed., *Emotional Problems of Early Childhood* (New York: Basic Books, 1955), pp. 5–30; and Harris B. Peck, Seymour R. Kaplan, and Melvin Roman, "Prevention, Treatment, and Social Action: A Strategy of Intervention in a Disadvantaged Urban Area," *American Journal of Orthopsychiatry*, Vol. 36, No. 1 (January 1966), pp. 57–69.

2 Erik H. Erikson, *Identity: Youth and Crisis* (New York: W. W. Norton & Co., 1968), p. 16.

3 Op. cit.

4 Gerald Caplan, *Principles of Preventive Psychiatry* (New York: Basic Books, 1964), pp. 35–127.

Crises are temporary and therefore self-limiting. All crises must come to an end; none continues indefinitely. Some adjustment is made to the event be it adequate or inadequate. It is assumed that different categories of crises have different temporal histories. For example, the crisis precipitated by the death of a loved one differs in length from that caused by the incarceration of a spouse or son.

Each type of crisis pursues a course made up of typical, identifiable stages. Crisis behaviors and reaction patterns can be anticipated. Further, each crisis category has an individualized progression that is theoretically discrete from that of all others. For example, Lindemann distinguished the following successive stages in grief and bereavement: (1) disbelief, (2) denial, (3) symptoms of grief or bereavement that include (a) somatic distress, (b) preoccupation with images of the deceased, (c) guilt, (d) hostility toward the deceased and others such as physicians, nurses, and friends, and (e) loss of typical patterns of conduct and emergence of such behaviors as withdrawal, lack of initiative, and dependence, (4) emancipation from bondage to the deceased, (5) readjustment to an environment in which the deceased is missing, and (6) formation of new interpersonal relationships and behavior patterns.[6] It is normal for a person to experience each stage of crisis. In fact, omission of any stage in the progression suggests that he may not be coping adequately with the crisis.

The individual in crisis is especially amenable to help. Crisis is a critical period during which the individual actively seeks new resources and activities. He is therefore prone to accept help and to learn and incorporate new behaviors.

A small amount of assistance makes it possible for a person to surmount a crisis. This assumption holds that only limited resources and assistance must be expended in the intervention process. Old defenses are weakened and resistance to the development of new behaviors is diminished.

Weathering a current crisis permits the individual to cope more effectively with future crises. This is probably the most important assumption made in crisis theory. Problem-solving behaviors learned in the immediate situation can be applied effectively to subsequently encountered crises. It may be presumed that inadequate reactions can make future adjustments to new crises less effective.

Various workers in crisis theory have categorized the different types of crises that can be experienced. Caplan, Hill, and Eliot have probably evolved the most meaningful classification systems.

Caplan identifies two categories.[7] The first group includes crises precipitated by changes in the everyday course of living—such as entry into school, birth of a sibling, emergence of heterosexual interests, marriage, birth of a child, retirement, and death. The second category includes crises occasioned by unusually hazardous events—such as acute or chronic illness, accidents, or family dislocations—which might occur to an individual, a member of his immediate or extended family, or a close associate.

Hill also names two categories, but places greater stress on the family as the focus of crisis.[8] His first group includes crises precipitated by extrafamilial events, such as war, flood, economic depression, or religious persecution. Crises in his second

---

[5] Carl G. Jung, "Two Essays on Analytical Psychology," in Herbert Read, Michael Fordham, and Gerhard Adler, eds., *The Collected Works of C. G. Jung*, Vol. 7 (New York: Pantheon Books, 1966), p. 10.

[6] Lindemann, op. cit.

[7] *Principles of Preventive Psychiatry*, pp. 34–55.

[8] Reuben Hill, "Generic Features of Families Under Stress," *Social Casework*, Vol. 39, Nos. 2–3 (February–March 1958), pp. 139–150.

category are precipitated by intrafamilial events or situations, such as desertion, alcoholism, or infidelity. Hill believes that extrafamilial crises tend to solidify the family and enhance its crisis-meeting resources but that intrafamilial crises typically lead to its demoralization.

Eliot lists four categories also built around the family unit.[9] In the first, crises of "dismemberment," loss of a family member is experienced either through death or from extended separation because of war, imprisonment, employment dislocation, or hospitalization for physical or mental disorders.

His second category, crises of "ascension," involves an unplanned addition to the family unit. Examples are an unwanted pregnancy, an illegitimate birth, the return of a deserting father, or the unwanted addition of a stepsibling, a stepparent, or an aged parent.

In Eliot's third category, crises of demoralization, the family unit remains the same size, but one of its members experiences an undesirable event or condition. These crises include a husband's or father's nonsupport, infidelity, alcoholism, drug addiction, delinquency, unemployment, vocational demotion, or mental disorder. Eliot's fourth class embraces crises of demoralization accompanied by either dismemberment or ascension (loss or addition of a family member). Examples are a runaway adolescent, a father's desertion, divorce, imprisonment, suicide, homicide, or institutionalization for a mental disorder.

STAGES OF CRISIS

In the sequence of interactions leading up to the state of perceived crisis, an objective event first takes place, such as the death of a loved one, unemployment of the breadwinner, or birth of a child.[10] The event then interacts with the individual's or group's crisis-meeting resources, which may

be excellent, adequate, poor, or nonexistent. From this interaction, a definition of the event is made. The same event might be defined similarly or quite differently by different individuals or families. For instance, because of varying crisis-meeting resources and extenuating circumstances, a breadwinner's sudden unemployment might be defined as a severe, moderate, or mild crisis or even as no crisis at all.

If defining the event leads to a perception of crisis, then a period of disorganization inevitably follows. This is characterized by various maladaptive behaviors or psychiatric syndromes such as grief, withdrawal, inactivity, or heightened anxiety. There is exaggerated use of currently available defense systems and behaviors that are not suited to the crisis situation. Because the individual is experiencing difficulty in his groping and problem-solving behavior, he tends to be more receptive to outside assistance and resources during this period.

The period of disorganization is followed by a period of reorganization, which has clearly identifiable phases. In the initial phase of correct cognitive perception, the problem is maintained at a conscious level. For example, in the case of death the individual recognizes that feelings of dependency and support can no longer be anchored to the deceased. During the next phase, management of affect through awareness of feelings, there is an appropriate acceptance and release of feelings associated with the crisis. After the death of a loved one, emotions such as remorse, guilt, and hostility are accepted and find suitable expression.

The last phase is the development of patterns for seeking and using help. The individual begins to adopt constructive means for dealing with the problem and uses other persons and organizations to help him in this task. For example, the widow may use the state employment agency to find a job or, encouraged by a friend, she may

[9] T. D. Eliot, "Handling Family Strains and Shocks," in Howard Becker and Reuben Hill, eds., *Family, Marriage, and Parenthood* (Boston: D. C. Heath & Co., 1955), pp. 616–641.

[10] The following description of the stages of crisis is derived from the work of Hill, op. cit.; and Lydia Rapoport, "The State of Crisis: Some Theoretical Considerations," *Social Service Review*, Vol. 36, No. 2 (June 1962), pp. 212–213.

become active in volunteer associations to fill the void created by her husband's death. At the end of this phase, habitual behavioral patterns have developed that allow flexible use of persons and external resources not only in crisis but in ordinary situations. Essentially, the individual's horizons and resources have expanded. In other words, the level of reorganization achieved after crisis is higher than the precrisis behavior level. However, this does not always occur. The reorganization level can be the same as, lower, or higher than the precrisis level.

Various writers have cataloged the following characteristics that seem to be associated with an individual's or a family's ability to cope successfully with crisis-producing events: [11] (1) behavioral adaptability and flexibility within the family, (2) affection among family members, (3) good marital adjustment between husband and wife, (4) companionable parent-child relations, (5) family members' participation in decision-making, (6) wife's participation in husband's social activities, (7) nonmarginal economic status, (8) individual's or family's direct or vicarious experience with the type of crisis encountered, (9) objective knowledge of facets of a specific crisis before it occurs—which presupposes the individual's or group's capacity to discuss openly feelings about events that might precipitate crisis, such as drug abuse or impending birth, marriage, or death—(10) established patterns of interaction with the extended family, neighbors, and friends.[12]

Two conclusions emerge from a study of this list. First, an individual needs and may even require other persons to surmount a crisis. These persons may be members of the immediate or extended family, friends, or social workers. Second, facilitating communication between the individual and these persons mitigates the severity of the crisis.

PRIMARY PREVENTION

The principles of crisis intervention, practically applied, have profound implications for mental health and the helping services. Crisis concepts seem particularly applicable to primary and secondary prevention efforts.

In primary prevention, the intervenor may direct his efforts chiefly toward eliminating or minimizing events capable of inducing crisis. Distinction should be made between different classes of events. There are some events that, with present knowledge, can be eliminated or minimized by appropriate social action. Unemployment and marginal economic circumstances might be practically abolished by vast social and economic reforms. The possibility of war might be greatly reduced by forming an international government invested with viable responsibility. Birth injuries, some forms of mental retardation, and certain types of illness leading to death might be prevented through expanded medical services. Birth of children can be prevented through contraception or abortion. Accident control might reduce accidental deaths. Premarital counseling might prevent certain divorces. Increased use of community facilities and homebound programs for the mentally ill could minimize family separations occurring from hospitalization.

Knowledge is currently lacking about ways to prevent or minimize certain events. Among these would be death resulting from

---

[11] See Caplan, *Principles of Preventive Psychiatry*, pp. 44–48; Hill, op. cit., p. 148; Rapoport, op. cit., p. 216; Jay L. Rooney, "Special Stress on Low-Income Families," *Social Casework*, Vol. 39, Nos. 2–3 (February–March, 1958), pp. 150–158.

[12] Individuals and families best able to surmount the crisis of separation in Great Britain during World War II frequently mentioned friends, neighbors, and relatives who provided assistance. Much to the chagrin of the helping professions, these families rarely mentioned that the church, physicians, or social agencies played a significant role in their adjustment. See Hill, op. cit., p. 148.

certain disease processes and aging, hospitalization for various forms of physical and mental illness, and many divorces. Optimistically, increased knowledge should extend life and promote health and marital well-being so that most of these events should eventually be classified in the first category.

There are also events that cannot be prevented, including those that people would not wish to prevent even if they could. Among these are the broad developmental crises experienced in life, such as birth, adolescence, marriage, and retirement.

Effective primary prevention measures, besides influencing events, may strengthen the individual's or group's crisis-meeting resources. The intervenor's efforts would be directed toward developing patterns of interpersonal relations that aim to increase family members' communication, individual and group experience with crises, and accessibility to social resources at appropriate crisis points.

Increasing communication within family units might prove to be essentially educational. Procedures used could include premarital, marital, and ongoing educative group counseling and discussions emphasizing the necessity of familial communication, ways to maintain it, and ways to avoid communication breakdown.

Increasing the experience with crises might also be an educational task. Efforts would be directed toward permitting individuals to experience "sham" crises. To a greater degree than at present, the helping professions would be concerned with preparing premarital groups, groups of expectant parents, and drug groups to handle experiences likely to be encountered. These programs would focus not only on presenting factual information about the event but also on dealing with the resultant crisis. Thus the focus of a drug group would not be limited to incidence rates, laws, and physiological effects related to drugs. The group would also discuss anticipated personal and familial crises, such as that which might occur when a mother discovers a "joint" in her son's jacket pocket. They would "experience" these crises also through such techniques as role-playing, psychodrama, and sensitivity sessions. Similar programs might be developed on mental disorders, retirement, death, and many other topics. These mock experiences would be somewhat comparable to the childhood fantasies that Erikson regards as valuable preparation for future roles.[13]

To make social resources more readily accessible to individuals in crisis, two approaches seem feasible. First, currently available personnel and services might be brought closer. To accomplish this, the helping professions would have to assume a more active stance than at present. Rather than passively waiting for the client experiencing crisis to be referred or voluntarily come to the social work agency, manpower resources would be deployed to locales in which crises were most likely to occur. For example, rather than establishing a network of mental health centers, mental health personnel would be located in potential crisis sites, such as day care centers, schools, obstetrical wards, and community centers in slum areas. A second complementary approach would be to identify crisis-prone individuals and then mobilize resources to provide them with readily accessible services. In this area, development of "risk registers" might be fruitful. Thus a crisis-prone pregnant woman would, on reporting to her physician, find a group of persons ready to assist her in pregnancy—the alerted physician himself, the pediatrician who would eventually care for her newborn child, the public health nurse who could provide pre- and postnatal care, perhaps even a mental health worker to involve her in group discussions, and a housekeeper aide to assist her during the difficult early postnatal months. If the intervenor can affect either the event or the individual's crisis resources, the event's defini-

---

[13] Erik H. Erikson, *Insight and Responsibility* (New York: W. W. Norton & Co., 1964), pp. 120–121.

tion and the nature of the perceived crisis will be altered considerably.

SECONDARY PREVENTION

Applying crisis theory to secondary prevention is basically dealing with the intervenor's role when an event is already experienced as a crisis. The efforts that might be taken roughly parallel the phases in the period of reorganization.

Establishing or facilitating communication. In crisis situations communication between family members is often lacking or blocked. For example, a family's discovery that a son or daughter is to be the parent of an illegitimate child or is a drug-user frequently causes abrupt cessation of communication between family members and the offender. In such cases, professional skills and resources might well be most efficaciously used to try to restore disrupted family communication and initiate contacts with community agencies potentially able to assist in the crisis.

Individuals experiencing crisis often have no previous knowledge of, let alone contacts with, agencies providing assistance. A case in point is that of parents who give birth to a retarded child. They may be unaware of the immediate help available through the National Association for Retarded Children and the crippled children's division of the local health department. Nor are such parents necessarily aware of help obtainable later from state vocational rehabilitation agencies for training activities. Similarly, a woman of 40, suddenly widowed, may not know about such community resources as state unemployment or child welfare services. A paramount role of helping persons in time of crisis, and probably one of the more meaningful ones, would be to help the individual identify and get in touch with community social agencies most able to provide assistance.

Assisting the individual or family to perceive the event correctly and to understand it. Cases in point would be the parents of a youth apprehended for possession of marijuana and the parents whose unmarried daughter tells them she is pregnant. In the former instance, the intervenor might help the parents recognize the conflict between law and reality in drug use and understand other "reality-myth" distinctions concerning drug use and abuse. In the latter instance, the intervenor could explain the effects of the birth on the daughter and the family and present various alternatives for dealing with the situation.

Assisting the individual or family to manage emotions and feelings, keep affects conscious, and deal with them openly. In the cases of the drug offender and the unmarried mother, the intervenor might best serve by helping those involved to recognize and express feelings of shame and to realize how this emotion is related to their hostile reactions. The intervenor might also provide appropriate means for releasing these sentiments in discussion.

CONCLUSIONS

At the time when mental health workers are critically reexamining modes of service delivery, the application of crisis theory principles to mental health seems especially worthy of attention. More than most approaches and models, it offers a consistent view of mental health problems and suggests guidelines for the direction and thrust of mental health efforts. Essentially, it advocates an active and preventive stance—eliminating specific events associated with crisis, enhancing crisis-meeting resources before crisis is experienced, and intervening actively in crisis before maladaptive problem-solving patterns develop.

There are a number of reasons, however, why the crisis approach has not been widely adopted in the mental health field. First, it seems reasonable to suppose that a much greater commitment in finances and personnel would be required to implement crisis theory principles than is now made in mental health efforts. Current efforts, lip service to the contrary, focus primarily on tertiary prevention endeavors.

Second, widespread adoption of the crisis

approach is risky. Despite reported successes in various limited endeavors, there is no conclusive evidence that such promising results will in fact be realized if the crisis model is generally adopted and resources are directed to the primary prevention efforts it involves.

Third, implementing crisis principles would demand a rather abrupt adjustment by mental health workers. They would have to become much more aggressive. They would have to make active efforts to eliminate or minimize crisis-producing events by altering social situations. They would have to intervene in the social scene to increase the crisis-resistance resources of normal individuals before society or these individuals themselves realized the need of such assistance. They would have to seek out actively individuals at an early stage of personal disorganization. In many ways the mental health worker's role would become that of social architect. Considerable question exists within the field itself about whether such intervention is an appropriate function of the mental health technician and professional.[14] The lay public is as yet unaware of this potential role.

Fourth, adoption of crisis principles would also raise considerable question concerning the wisdom of the field's present investment in the community mental health center model. Crisis theory principles at least create doubt concerning the efficacy of the community mental health center model for deploying services, in fact create doubt about whether these centers offer the most appropriate and effective means of dealing with mental health problems. Thus crisis intervention, although it has much to offer, is still a theory in search of a program.

---

14 See Dale Albers and Richard A. Pasewark, "How New are the New Comprehensive Mental Health Centers," in Willard F. Richan, ed., *Human Services and Social Work Responsibility* (New York: National Association of Social Workers, 1969), pp. 148–155; H. Warren Dunham, "Community Psychiatry: The Newest Therapeutic Bandwagon," *Archives of General Psychiatry*, Vol. 12, No. 3 (March 1965), pp. 303–313; David M. Mechanic, "Community Psychiatry: Some Sociological Perspectives and Implications," in Leigh M. Roberts, Seymour L. Halleck, and Martin B. Loeb, eds., *Community Psychiatry* (Madison: University of Wisconsin Press, 1966), pp. 201–222; Richard A. Pasewark and Max W. Rardin, "Theoretical Models in Community Mental Health," *Mental Hygiene*, Vol. 55, No. 3 (July 1971), pp. 358–364.

INDICTMENT OF WELFARE SYSTEMS

THE BLACK BADGE, by Frank Gell (Harper and Row, 226 pages, $5.95).

Reviewed by Morley Glicken

Reading Frank Gell's book on welfare in New York City had a profoundly depressing effect on this reviewer. More than once I had to throttle an impulse to give up and just not read any more.

Because Gell has in a more objective and articulate way than any recent writer been able to show the flaws and unbelievable ineffectiveness of welfare. At the same time, writing of his experiences as a social worker, he directly links the sorry state of welfare programs to social work's inability to touch people.

And as a social worker, I found it a totally upsetting experience.

There is something in the makeup of social workers which breeds a sort of universal contempt. We tell people how we want to help them and yet we work within the structure of organizations so devoid of feeling for people, under policies so potently inhumane, that we seem ludicrous and god-awful insincere. What Gell has to say makes this all the more obvious.

The welfare system of any large city is, at best, a sort of jungle. The client who knows how to manipulate the laws, his social worker and political influence is the person who gets near the services guaranteed him by law.

The remainder, and that means most welfare recipients, receive a quality of help often so low, and grants so out of keeping with the needs of people in today's world, that the effect is a gradual killing of one's will to exist.

What Gell says in his book about the cumulative effect of his job is perhaps as accurate a statement of social work's role in society as one has ever seen. (See the accompanying italic quotation.)

Perhaps as relevant a point in face of social work's unwillingness to change the system is what Gell describes in his book as the profession's perpetuation of large welfare departments encouraged to expand in size and decrease in effectiveness.

Several years ago the social work union of New York went on strike against the welfare department. To fill in until the strike was settled, a small number of social workers with graduate degrees did intensive treatment, with all paper work and investigative functions held to a minimum. What was found was that clients applying for welfare did not in any appreciable way cheat, that the level of help was high, and that recipients seemed to respond.

In light of this, the union made it clear that it would not allow jobs to be eliminated. And so the old system with over 8,000 workers was reinstated for the primary purpose not of helping, but to see that cheating not occur, to maintain adequate statistics and to make sure that the bureaucratic maze might ensure jobs for a worker's lifetime.

THE MINNEAPOLIS TRIBUNE, Book Section, January 11, 1970.

Gell's book does one additional service — it graphically shows what social workers in welfare departments do. It shows how an effective worker must have a real grasp of dynamics of behavior and of how social institutions move in cities. How he must understand the law and the politics of corruption.

It shows how welfare departments tend to hire people with minimal backgrounds and poor motivation for helping rather than concentrating on social workers trained in graduate schools with higher levels of competence.

Most of all, it shows the essential hopelessness of the work, how one rushes from crisis to crisis without much of a feel for any basic change having taken place in the people one serves or in the society one feels increasing concern for.

Frank Gell's "The Black Badge" is a moving indictment of welfare systems and social work. It effectively shows how our national concern for people has become diluted, strained and is now nearly nonexistent. It is hopefully a plea for the elimination of a system which perpetuates suffering on such a monumental level that it constitutes a national tragedy.

And more, it is a calling out to America to feel something in its collective heart for a growing number of people who, down to the core of their existence, hurt.

"You are paying me to muffle the shouts of the million recipients of public welfare in New York City. From birth to death I keep your eye on them. When they plead for a piece of that sweet American pie, I turn your deaf ear. When they scream, I gag them with your dollar bills. When they grope for the levers of social and economic justice, I entangle their hands in red tape. And when they die, I get their remains shipped to an island off the shores of the Bronx, so that even in death they will be out of sight and out of mind. When they are buried, I cross their names off my caseload to make room for the names of their grand-children."

— Frank Gell in THE BLACK BADGE

Student attitudes toward the poor

by James W. Grimm
and James D. Orten

One of the dogmas of social work is that both worker and client will recognize each other's attitudes. And the worker's attitudes are a crucial factor in the way he will deliver services to the poor and how clients, in turn, will react to the services they receive. Yet surprisingly little is known about how social workers' attitudes toward their clients are formed.

During the past few years, several articles about the factors that determine workers' attitudes have appeared in social work journals. Some deal with differences in workers' feelings about the life-styles and social characteristics of the indigent.[1] Others focus on differences in attitudes toward various action strategies that can be used when advocating on behalf of poor clients' rights or grievances.[2] In evaluating the reasons for attitudinal differences among workers, the authors usually focus on the settings in which social workers practice, the degree to which they identify with their profession, and the administrative level of their agency positions.

The results of much previous research support the hypothesis that the higher the worker is in the organization, the less likely he is to identify with the poor or support radical action on their behalf.[3] Workers who identify strongly with their profession are less likely to have positive attitudes toward poor clients; they are also less likely to support noninstitutionalized action strategies (demonstrations, rent strikes, and so forth) as a means of solving clients' problems. In addition, occupational specialization appears to be related to divergence in attitudes: administrators and casework or group work practitioners (especially those with extended experience in public welfare departments) have less-positive attitudes toward the poor than those who practice other types of social work.

SHIFT OF FOCUS

In this study the focus of concern was shifted from work settings and profession-based determinants to factors that may account for differences in orientation toward

Reprinted with permission of the National Association of Social Workers, from SOCIAL WORK, Vol. 18, No. 1 (January 1973), pp. 94-100.

"The authors' findings demonstrate that differences in orientation observed among social workers practicing in various work settings have their antecedents (and perhaps their explanations) in the backgrounds of those who enter the profession."

the indigent before the student enters graduate training. This perspective has merit for several reasons. First, sociodemographic background and prior work experience may be important determinants of attitudes toward the poor. Second, students' attitudes may not be neutralized by the relatively short period of professional socialization. Third, if the evidence supports this view, it may be possible to find ways of rectifying the situation during professional training.

As recent critics of the traditional approach to studying the impact of professional education point out:

If a major objective (if not *the* objective) of the study of professional socialization is to understand the processes of developing a professional identity and commitment to a field, then what the trainees were like when they began must be part of the analysis. Clearly, trainees do not come in as . . . tabula[e] rasa[e], even though many researchers appear to tacitly make this assumption. It is not enough to focus solely upon the events of the training period because these events are experienced by persons who already have a perspective toward the situation, naïve though it may be. . . .[4]

When considering the field of social work from this vantage point, several major reasons for divergent socialization are apparent: (1) the socioeconomic backgrounds of social work students are more diverse than those of students entering a number of other professions, (2) although beginning students vary as to whether they have had actual experience in social service agencies, public welfare departments are a major source of financial support for persons seriously interested in obtaining a graduate

degree in social work. This particular pattern of pre-graduate-school work experience partially explains the fact that the decision to make social work one's career often occurs somewhat later than in other fields such as nursing, in which formal training starts in the first post-high-school year.[5] Social work students vary in age and marital status as a consequence of the delay in obtaining the professional degree.

Two paths to a graduate school of social work are thus distinguishable. The *short route* leads directly from the undergraduate degree to the professional school with little or no training or job experience intervening. The *long route* includes experience in social service agencies or other occupations as well as marriage before professional training. This article stresses that the length of the route of entry into graduate training is associated with the differential impact of work experience, marital status, aging, and other factors on a social work student's attitudes in general and toward the poor in particular. In addition, of course, the student's socioeconomic background affects his attitudes toward future clients and other issues, no matter when he enters a school of social work.

THE STUDY

Data for this study were gathered from 117 first-year, full-time students at the University of Tennessee School of Social Work. (This number represents 94 percent of the total first-year enrollment.)

The school offers an accredited program leading to the MSSW degree. In accordance with the university's policy of offering educational opportunities in each of the state's three major geographic regions (eastern, central, and western), the school maintains branches in Knoxville, Nashville, and Memphis. Forty-seven respondents were enrolled in the Nashville branch, forty attended the Knoxville branch, and thirty attended the Memphis branch. Approximately half the students were residents of Tennessee, 25 percent came from the southeastern region of the United States, and the remainder came from other regions of the country, primarily the Atlantic coast and Midwest.

Because the research objectives required that data be collected before the students were significantly exposed to the school environment, questionnaires and attitude measurement scales were administered to them during the week following registration for the 1971–72 academic year. The testing instruments were administered during the same required course on each campus, and written instructions and explanatory comments were read by those who distributed the materials to minimize the proctors' influence on the project. The questionnaire was pretested for clarity and substantive content with several second-year students and was revised appropriately before administering it to the first-year class.

The students' response rate was excellent. Unanswered questions did not amount to more than 3 percent in any of the three samples. The questionnaire elicited standard sociodemographic information and additional important data, such as length of time between undergraduate and graduate school and types of prior full-time employment.

Attitudes toward the poor were measured by Peterson's disguised-structured attitude scale, which is similar to the instrument developed by Hovland and Sherif for measuring attitudes toward blacks.[7] Peterson's attitude scale consists of forty selected statements about the poor. Subjects are asked to judge each statement by indicating on an eleven-point scale whether they view it as favorable or unfavorable toward the indigent. The list contains anchor items for the favorable and unfavorable ends of the scale; the majority of items are neutral and thus easily displaceable.

Peterson's studies of attitudes toward the poor corroborate Sherif's and Hovland's findings that subjects tend to displace more statements, especially neutral ones, on to the opposite end of the scale from their own position.[8] The scale yields a quantifiable measure of the subject's attitudes and the intensity with which he holds his position. The latter value is thought to be a measure of the respondent's affective, as opposed to cognitive involvement with the subject matter and thus may be viewed as a measure of the emotional component of his identification with the poor.[9] This article presents findings based on an analysis of position scores only.[10] Position scores on attitudes toward the indigent were divided at the median, with positive scores falling above the median and negative scores falling below.

SOCIODEMOGRAPHIC DATA

Table 1 presents the percentage of students who scored above the median on the attitude scale on the basis of selected sociodemographic characteristics. The attributes associated with negative attitudes are age, marriage, parenthood, and low socioeconomic origin.

Age. The sample population ranged in age from 21 to 48 years (with a median age of 25). The wide age range of the students was strongly associated with disparity in attitudes toward the poor. The effect of age is noteworthy since it mirrors important differences in family life-styles and work experiences.

Sex. In this study, the sex of the student was not associated with major differences in attitudes toward the indigent. Given the widespread belief that society encourages women, rather than men, to enter helping occupations, greater differences in attitudes based on sex were expected. However, the findings suggest that both men and women who are attracted to social work have already acquired a service orientation and display a marked desire to relate to clients in holistic ways before they enter graduate school.[11]

Marriage and parenthood. Perhaps the most important differences in attitudes reflected by the diverse ages of social work students are those resulting from marriage and parenthood. Fifty-six percent of the never married students scored above the median on attitudes toward the poor, as compared to 47 percent of those who were married, widowed, or divorced. This relationship was further refined by dividing the students into the following categories: unmarried, married with no children, and married with children. It was found that as family responsibilities increased, students were less likely to have positive attitudes toward poor people. These data supplement those of Fox, who found a relationship between marital status per se and attitudes toward the poor.[12] If the present sample had been larger, it might have been possible to establish a relationship between the number of children a respondent had and his attitudes toward the poor.

Socioeconomic background. The lower the student's socioeconomic background, the less sympathetic were his attitudes toward the poor. The students whose fathers had obtained at least a high school education or were employed in high-status occupations when the students were growing up displayed noticeably more positive attitudes toward the indigent.[13] This suggests that even moderate increments in educational achievement and occupational status among the students' families of origin were associated with more sympathetic interpretations of poor people's problems.[14]

EDUCATION AND EXPERIENCE

Table 2 shows the percentage of students who had positive attitudes toward the poor on the basis of their education and previous work experience. The pre-graduate-school experiences associated with positive identification with the poor were (1) an undergraduate major in social work or sociology, (2) an undergraduate degree from a public university or a school not in the South, and (3) little or no previous work experience in fields other than social work.

Undergraduate major. The authors' interest in the students' undergraduate majors was stimulated by Heisler, who suggested that sociologists and social workers are more liberal politically than persons in many other academic fields.[15] Thus an objective of the present research was to determine how early these liberal perspectives developed and whether they included liberal attitudes toward the poor. The results suggest that students who have an undergraduate background in sociology or social work do have more positive attitudes toward the poor than their counterparts who major in other areas.

Undergraduate institution attended. Although few studies of professional socialization have focused on the type of undergraduate institution students attend, the

TABLE 1. SOCIODEMOGRAPHIC CHARACTERISTICS AND STUDENTS', ATTITUDES TOWARD THE POOR
(N=117)

Characteristics	Number of Students[a]	Percentage of Students Scoring Above the Median
Age		
25 or below	59	56
26 or above	58	44
Sex		
Male	48	48
Female	69	52
Marital status		
Never married	45	56
Married	72	47
Children		
No children	42	52
Children	31	37
Father's education		
Grade school or less	26	35
High school	43	58
Some college	48	52
Family's socioeconomic status		
Low	41	46
Middle	44	50
High	31	58

[a] Variations in the number of respondents occur because some questionnaire items were inadvertently left unanswered.

present study indicates that graduates of public universities or private colleges outside the South have more-liberal attitudes toward the poor than those who attend private colleges in the South. Therefore, one can speculate that the nature of the recruitment base of a school of social work may be related in important ways to the likelihood that its curriculum can shape students' attitudes toward the indigent.

Prior work experience. Wasserman has argued that professional social workers who have not had preprofessional welfare experience find that working in a public welfare department early in their professional career is disillusioning, primarily because of bureaucratic conflicts with professional decision-making.[16] He collected his data from twelve beginning social workers in the first two years of their employment in a department of public welfare.

The present study dramatically supplements Wasserman's observations. Fifty-nine percent of the first-year students who had no previous public welfare experience scored above the median on attitudes toward the poor, as compared to only 26 percent of those with three or more years of such experience. Wasserman concluded that employment in public welfare departments after graduate training may undermine professionalism, but the present study indicates that it may undermine the objectives of professional education as well, since it often intervenes before students receive formal training. Therefore, the question social work educators must consider is: What are the facilitating conditions under which professional social work may be *learned* as well as practiced?

If it is true that the field of social work attracts many students who hold sympathetic attitudes toward social problems and the poor, then it should also hold true that trainees who have never wavered in their choice of career are sympathetic toward the poor. As seen in Table 2, those students who had no previous full-time job experience in fields other than social work were much more likely to have positive attitudes toward the poor, and those students with

employment experience in two or more other fields had the least positive attitudes toward the poor. Again, important differences in attitudes exist among first-year social work students because many of them do not enter the profession directly from an undergraduate institution.

PROFESSIONAL SPECIALIZATION

A number of studies have suggested that a social worker's area of specialization and his organizational position affect his attitudes and ideologies.[17] Although detailed findings on this subject are not presented here, a major goal of this study was to determine whether the area of specialization in which the beginning student was interested was related to his attitudes toward the poor.

The data indicated that this is indeed the case. Among the twenty-four students who were primarily interested in administrative positions, only 42 percent had positive at-

TABLE 2. EDUCATIONAL AND OCCUPATIONAL CHARACTERISTICS AND STUDENTS' ATTITUDES TOWARD THE POOR
(*N*=117)

Characteristics	Number of Students[a]	Percentage of Students Scoring Above the Median
Undergraduate major		
Social work/sociology	58	55
Other	59	46
Undergraduate school		
Private	47	43
Public	69	56
Location of school		
Southern state	94	48
Other regions	22	59
Experience in public welfare agency		
None	67	59
Two years or less	38	56
Three years or more	22	26
Non-social work job held six-months or more		
None	60	58
One	35	43
Two or more	22	41

[a] Variations in the number of respondents occur because some questionnaire items were inadvertently left unanswered.

titudes toward the indigent. However, those interested in casework or group work (seventy-four) or community organization (fifteen) were more likely to score within the positive range (51 and 60 percent, respectively). This supports the prevalent assumption that community organization is the radical wing of the profession. Moreover, this radicalism is already well developed by the time the student enters graduate school.

These results suggest that divergent attitudes among social workers may not be simply the result of practice within a specific setting or area of specialization, but may be among those factors that lead students into different careers within the profession. A similar assumption is appropriate when explaining the types of students that particular schools of social work attract. The mean scores on the attitude scale varied little between the Nashville and Memphis branches of the School of Social Work. Those of the Knoxville branch were five points higher. This disparity may be explained by the fact that the school's community organization curriculum, which attracts the most liberal recruits, is taught at Knoxville.

CONCLUSION

First-year graduate students in social work have varying attitudes toward the poor. These differences are associated with differences in socioeconomic background, undergraduate training, work experience between undergraduate and graduate school, age, and marital status. The most noteworthy variation in pre-graduate-school experience that is related to differences in attitudes is whether the student entered graduate school relatively soon after graduation from college or waited a considerable length of time. The later the student's entry into the school of social work, the more important are the intervening effects of his job experience and family life.

The major implication of this study is that the importance of the pre-graduate-school environment as a socializing milieu

for future professionals has been underemphasized. Given the fact that graduate training in social work is relatively short, it seems imperative that additional research be devoted to the pretraining period of occupational socialization.

The authors' findings demonstrate that the differences in orientation observed among social workers practicing in various work settings have their antecedents (and perhaps their explanations) in the backgrounds of those who enter the profession. The current emphasis on organizational analysis in social work, although by no means irrelevant, might be supplemented significantly by a sociodemographic approach to studying attitudes toward the poor. Because this study has established some of the pre-social work school orientations that relate to positive and negative attitudes toward clients, future researchers should be able to assess the continuity of these orientations beyond the presumed liberalizing influence of professional training.

NOTES AND REFERENCES

1. *See*, for example, Lois Pratt, "Optimism–Pessimism About Helping the Poor with Health Problems." *Social Work*, 15 (April 1970), pp. 29–33.
2. *See*, for example, Irwin Epstein, "Organizational Careers, Professionalization, and Social Worker Radicalism," *Social Service Review*, 44 (June 1970), pp. 123–131.
3. *See*, for example, Joseph W. Heffernan, "Political Activity and Social Work Executives," *Social Work*, 9 (April 1964), pp. 18–23; and Irwin Epstein, "Social Work and Social Action: Attitudes Toward Social Action Strategies," *Social Work*, 13 (April 1968), pp. 101–108.
4. Rue Bucher, Joan Stelling, and Paul Dommermuth, "Differential Prior Socialization: A Comparison of Four Professional Training Programs," *Social Forces*, 48 (December 1969), p. 220.
5. Richard L. Simpson and Ida Harper Simpson, "Women and Bureaucracy in the Semi-Professions," in Amitai Etzioni, ed., *The Semi-Professions and Their Organization* (New York: Free Press, 1969), pp. 201–202.
6. The remaining students attended school part time and were judged to be too peripherally involved for the purpose of this analysis.
7. J. H. Peterson, "A Disguised Structured Instrument for the Assessment of Attitudes Toward the Poor," unpublished Ph.D. dissertation, University of Oklahoma, Norman, Oklahoma, 1967;

C. I. Hovland and Musafer Sherif, "Judgmental Phenomena and Scales of Attitude Measurement: Item Displacement in Thurstone Scales," *Journal of Abnormal and Social Psychology*, 47 (October 1952), pp. 822–832; and Sherif and Hovland, "Judgmental Phenomena and Scales of Attitude Measurement: Placement of Items with Individual Choice of Number Categories," *Journal of Abnormal and Social Psychology*, 48 (January 1953), pp. 135–141.

8. This displacement tendency may be illustrated by the observation that politically liberal persons tend to see even middle-of-the-roaders as politically conservative. Similarly, a person with a strong position in favor of the poor perceives neutral statements about the poor as representing an antipoor attitude.

9. *See* P. E. Fox III, "Demographic Characteristics Related to Populational Attitudes Toward the Poor." Unpublished master's thesis, University of Oklahoma, Norman, Oklahoma, 1968.

10. The theoretical range of scores in Peterson's attitude scale is 40 to 440. Scores in the present sample ranged from 243 to 381. The frequency distribution of score values was almost perfectly normal, with a median of 301 and a mean of 302. Since the study sample consisted of the entire relevant study population, tests of statistical significance that serve as a basis for inductive inferences were not considered appropriate or necessary. Percentage distributions are the basis for conclusions drawn in this article.

11. *See* Jane Prather, "Why Can't Women Be More Like Men?" *American Behavioral Scientist*, 15 (November-December 1971), pp. 172–182. For a review of the service orientation in social work, *see* Simpson and Simpson, op. cit., pp. 234–240.

12. Op. cit., p. 25.

13. The fathers' occupations were categorized according to U.S. Census Bureau classifications. *See* U.S. Bureau of the Census, *1960 Census of the Population*, Final Report, PC(1)-1D, Table 201. The status of each respondent's family of origin was also measured by the Hollingshead Two-Factor Index, which yielded findings similar to those reported here. *See* A. B. Hollingshead, R. D. Ellis, and E. C. Kirby, "Social Mobility and Mental Illness," in S. Kirson Weinberg, ed., *The Sociology of Mental Illness* (Chicago: Aldine Publishing Co., 1967), pp. 48–54.

14. Forty-eight respondents reported that their fathers had attended college, but half had not received their degrees.

15. Martin O. Heisler, "The Academic Marketplace in Political Science for the Next Decade: A Preliminary Report on a Survey," *Political Science*, 3 (Summer 1970), pp. 372–386.

16. *See* Harry Wasserman, "Early Careers of Professional Social Workers in a Public Child Welfare Agency," *Social Work*, 15 (July 1970), pp. 93–101.

17. *See*, for example, Epstein, "Organizational Careers, Professionalization, and Social Worker Radicalism."

BY JOAN ALDOUS AND REUBEN HILL

Breaking the Poverty Cycle: Strategic Points for Intervention

■ *Analysis of the changing balance of needs and resources over the family life span highlights two periods when poverty-prone families would benefit most from an income maintenance program: (1) the childbearing stage (most vulnerable to stress owing to insufficiencies of instrumental resources) and (2) the period of adolescence when families face most acutely the social placement of their offspring. Income supplements at these two points would tend to keep families intact in the early years and later in the social placement period would break the current cycle of transmitting poverty patterns from generation to generation.* ■

THE DAY OF taking families for granted is drawing to a close in America. For too long, families have been called upon to take up the slack in a poorly integrated social order. We have drifted along as a nation, assuming that families could and would cope with the changes of industrialization and urbanization without attention and support. Now the evidence of tension and insecurity among millions of families that have not been able to adapt cannot be denied. Research teams and national statistics document the critical situation for those who will listen. Under contemporary conditions of affluence, millions of families of the underclass are not only not finding exits from poverty but are experiencing even greater deprivation because it is relative deprivation. As a consequence, after more than two centuries of neglect by state and federal legislatures and government agencies, families have become the focus of concern and discussion.

Today America's Gross National Product is such that government programs can go beyond keeping families from starvation and seek to improve the general quality of family life. By supplying resources at critical junctures in the family's existence, such programs can increase the family's control over its own destiny. The nation has long left it to the individual to decide how best he can develop his capacities from the range of social opportunities available to him. As with the individual, the authors believe each family is best qualified to determine what choices are optimal. But to insure that families do not experience a foreclosure of choices for financial reasons, some kind of governmental income maintenance program is necessary.

This paper attempts to examine changes in family needs and resources over the family life span. Its purpose is to indicate periods when some sort of governmental income maintenance program would be most effective in giving families greater control over their own destinies.

JOAN ALDOUS, Ph.D., *is Associate Professor, Family Studies and Sociology, and* REUBEN HILL, Ph.D., *is Professor of Sociology, and Director, Minnesota Family Study Center, University of Minnesota, Minneapolis, Minnesota. This paper is a revised version of one presented to the U. S. Department of Health, Education, and Welfare's Task Force on Exits from Poverty, April 1967.*

Reprinted with permission of the National Association of Social Workers, from SOCIAL WORK, Vol. 14, No. 3 (July 1969), pp. 3-12.

The stages of family development begin with the establishment phase and end with the aging period.[1] They are defined as follows:

Establishment stage. The period from marriage to the birth of the first child. The husband and wife comprise the family.
Childbearing stage. The oldest child is not yet in school.
School-age children. The oldest child is in primary school.
Family with adolescents. The oldest child has reached adolescence.
Launching stage. The family is beginning to lose some of its members as they leave home for occupational, educational, or family reasons.
Postparental stage. All children have left home. The conjugal couple again constitute the family.
Aging. The final period from the husband's retirement to the death of one of the spouses.

Families are especially vulnerable to a loss of control over their future at certain stages of their development, for example, the childbearing phase and when their children become adolescents. The needs and demands of individual family members peak at points when the resources to meet the increased responsibilities are not yet at a maximum. To provide a crude balance sheet of the family's assets and liabilities at various periods in its history, a number of research findings have been summarized in Tables 1, 2, and 3. Among the poor, this lack of fit between responsibilities and resources to finance them is especially exacerbated. As a result, too many families face too many decisions without options in matters that determine the course of their members' lives—e.g., how long to continue in school, when to marry, and what occupation to enter.

WHEN MARRIAGE IS NOT A MATTER OF CHOICE

It can be argued that by the time many lower-class couples marry, they have already lost control of their destiny as a family. Their entry into marriage, as into the occupational world, has been premature—less a matter of conscious decision than of drift or circumstances not of their choosing. Their parental families lacked the resources to prepare their children for good jobs and marriages and were even less able to assist these young couples in averting the difficulties that lay ahead. Thus, marriage for the new generation began under the very conditions that held their parents in perpetual poverty.

Marriages involving persons who are under 19 years old are disproportionately found in groups with lower levels of education and among persons holding unskilled and semiskilled jobs.[2] It is within the group of adolescents who leave school early and who have the associated occupational handicaps that one finds large numbers who are faced with adult family responsibilities. One in five boys aged 18 or 19 who dropped out of high school before receiving a diploma is a family head by this time, but only one in nine high school graduates

---

[1] For the present analysis, the family life cycle has been divided into stages based on the family's size, the age of its oldest child, and the husband's occupational status. Because of the high proportion of low-income families in which the father is absent, the discussion will also necessarily take into account one-parent families.

[2] Thus, among 18 and 19 year olds in 1950, 32.7 percent of the single men had completed high school, which was true for only 22.5 percent of the married men. The difference was even more marked for women: 45.2 percent of the unmarried women had completed high school compared to 28.7 percent of those who were married. (Data from the 1950's were used because data from the 1960's are not categorized according to such age breaks.) *See* Lee Burchinal, "Trends and Prospects for Young Marriages in the United States," *Journal of Marriage and the Family*, Vol. 27, No. 2 (May 1965), Table 2, p. 248. In Iowa during the years 1953–1957, 39.2 percent of men marrying at 18 years old or younger held low-status occupations as compared with 27.3 percent of those marrying at 19 years or older. *Ibid.*, p. 249 (reworking of data in Table 3).

and only one in one hundred college students have taken on this family responsibility.

A comparable situation exists among girls. At 18 years of age, three-fifths of school dropouts are married and only one-third of the single girls are still living with their parents. In contrast, three-fifths of this age group who have graduated from high school are still unmarried and living at home even if they are not in school.[3] Yet marriage largely prevents school dropouts from completing the education necessary to obtain the higher paying jobs necessary to support a family. Indeed, they may be fortunate to obtain any job, since unemployment rates are especially high in the 16–21-year-old age group.[4] As a result, their income potentials are meager and are likely to remain so in the future.[5]

Just as the premature taking on of an occupational role restricts a youth to low-paying, unstable jobs of which he has little option, so, too, premature marriage is often an outcome that he has had little choice in making. This is particularly true when premarital pregnancy—a factor in one-third to over one-half of all young marriages—presses a couple to legitimize the child's status regardless of personal feelings

or readiness to accept family responsibilities. By getting married and dropping out of school, the young couple has drastically narrowed the range of occupational choice. Moreover, a child born too early according to cultural norms further unsettles the economic outlook.

A Detroit survey shows a positive relationship between a couple's current income and economic asset accumulation and the time interval from marriage to the first child's birth. This relationship is particularly marked for the premaritally pregnant who never seem to catch up with couples who have waited two years or longer to have their first child. Furthermore, the premaritally pregnant have subsequent children more quickly than others.[6]

Even among young low-income couples who have not faced the pressure of premarital conception, marriage often does not represent a positive choice. It may be the result of a feeling of fatalism about taking on an inevitable commitment or a desire to escape unpleasant home conditions. In any case, these young couples have shorter child-spacing intervals so that they are soon faced by mounting family responsibilities and insufficient earnings.[7]

Moreover, sharing a residence with relatives is more apt to occur among those marrying at earlier ages.[8] Instead of marriage serving as an escape from the parental family, it can mean even more intensive

[3] Mollie Orshansky, "Recounting the Poor: A Five-Year Review," *Social Security Bulletin*, Vol. 29, No. 4 (April 1966), p. 35.

[4] *Employment and Earnings and Monthly Report on the Labor Force*, U. S. Bureau of Labor Statistics, Vol. 13, No. 4 (April 1967), Table A-3, p. 8.

[5] Burchinal reports two studies showing the yearly mean income of young couples to be under $4,000. *Op. cit.*, p. 249. Of men 16–21 years old in 1964 who were family heads and were neither attending school nor high school graduates, 34 percent were poor, according to the 1964 poverty index of the Social Security Administration. The comparable figure for family heads with high school diplomas in the same age range was 15 percent. The same situation exists for women. One-third of married 16–17-year-old girls and one-fourth of married 18–19-year-old girls without high school diplomas are living in poverty. This was true for one in seven 18–19-year-old wives who had a high school diploma. Orshansky, *op. cit.*, p. 35.

[6] Ronald Freedman and Lolagene Coombs, "Childspacing and Family Economic Position," *American Sociological Review*, Vol. 31, No. 5 (October 1966), p. 648.

[7] *Ibid.*, p. 638.

[8] Of the total number of couples living with other families, the highest proportions are in the establishment phase of their family. Thus, 29.5 percent of the husbands in husband-wife white subfamilies —the census term for families living with other families—are 14–24 years old. Almost one-third (32.3 percent) of the husbands in the nonwhite husband-wife subfamilies were in the same category. U. S. Bureau of the Census, "Household and Family Characteristics, March 1966," *Current Population Reports*, Series P-20, No. 164 (Washington, D.C.: U. S. Government Printing Office, April 1967), pp. 20–24.

involvement, with the attendant problems of cramped quarters and intergenerational conflict. Because of our society's emphasis on neolocal residence, this involvement is often viewed by at least one marital partner as interference and can endanger the new couple's cohesiveness. Even when the extended family's aid is other than sharing a residence, there is evidence that the assistance constitutes a divisive factor. The spouses, in order to ensure some economic assistance, cultivate kinship ties at the expense of the marital relationship. Thus, through a series of cumulative events, beginning with too little education before marriage and ending with a too precipitous increase in family responsibilities afterward, the precociously married often find themselves unable to ameliorate a steadily deteriorating marital situation.[9]

For couples who marry from choice and are ready to accept family responsibilities, the period before the arrival of the first child can be an economic and interpersonal accumulation of assets. The couple can then draw on these resources during the succeeding deficit stages when family demands are high but income is not yet at a peak and marital relations are weakened by the competing parent-child system. Table 1 shows how relatively satisfactory this beginning stage is in the expressive resources that integrate the marriage. Marital communication is high—both husband and wife confide their problems to each other.[10]

Husbands are more active in household tasks. There is less role segregation with a greater willingness to share duties and fewer set assignments.[11] Decision-making power in family affairs centers in the husband, but love and marital satisfaction are at high enough levels to soften possible inequities.[12]

Even external affairs (see Tables 2 and 3) are more positive. The husband's job satisfaction is high [13] while the wife's high level of employment provides a supplement to her husband's low starting salary and makes for high rates of satisfaction with the economic level of living.[14] In Tables 2 and 3, in which the resources and responsibilities of the family at various stages are compared, one can see how the establishment phase creates a momentum that can carry the couple over ensuing peaks of vulnerability. It is true that divorce and separation are also at a peak during the first year of marriage but, because they occur so soon after marriage, this screening eliminates bad marital risks before children are born.[15]

When couples do not have the breathing period of the establishment phase to gather their resources for the demanding childbearing years, they can quickly reach a point of no return. The Detroit survey cited earlier shows that "the lower the current income level, the more likely the marriage occurred at an early age and that the children were born early in the marriage." [16]

[9] Divorce rates were twice as high for men who married at 18 as for those who married at ages 23–24 during the five–fifteen years prior to the 1960 census. Robert Parke, Jr., and Paul C. Glick, "Prospective Changes in Marriage and the Family," *Journal of Marriage and the Family*, Vol. 29, No. 2 (May 1967), p. 251.

[10] Robert O. Blood, Jr., and Donald M. Wolfe, *Husbands and Wives: The Dynamics of Married Living* (Glencoe, Ill.: Free Press, 1960), p. 189. Unpublished data from a sample of employed, urban blue-collar men (46 Negroes and 122 whites) showed problems in communication to be highest among the Negroes. For a detailed description of the sample, *see* Joan Aldous, "Lower Class Males' Integration into Community and Family,"

p. 11. Paper presented at the Sixth World Congress of Sociology, Auvergne, France, August 1966.

[11] Blood and Wolfe, *op cit.*, pp. 7–71.

[12] *Ibid.*, pp. 42, 232, and 265.

[13] Harold L. Wilensky, "Life Cycle, Work Situation and Participation in Formal Associations," in Robert W. Kleemeier, ed., *Aging and Leisure: Research Perspectives on Meaningful Use of Time* (New York: Oxford University Press, 1961), p. 229.

[14] Blood and Wolfe, *op. cit.*, p. 112.

[15] Thomas P. Monahan, "When Married Couples Part: Statistical Trends and Relationships in American Divorce," *American Sociological Review*, Vol. 27, No. 5 (October 1962), Table 1, p. 630.

[16] Freedman and Coombs, *op. cit.*, p. 636.

Deficit	Establish-ment	Child-bearing	School-age Children	Adolescents	Launch-ing	Postparental	Aging
Incidence of divorce and separation [b]	5	3	2	2	1	1	1
Degree of marital dissatisfaction [c]	1	1	2	3	5	4	5
Dissatisfaction with love [d]	1	1	2	3	5	3	4
Dissatisfaction with companionship [e]	1	2	3	4	5	3	4
Lack of marital communication [f]	1	2	5	4	3	2	2
Segregation of marital roles [g]	1	2	2	3	5	4	5
Husband's alienation from home tasks [h]	1	2	5	5	5	3	3
Wife's failure to share problems with husband [i]	1	3	4	5	5	4	5
Total vulnerability score	12	16	25	29	34	22	29
Duration of marriage (in years)	0–1	2–7	8–14	15–21	22–29	30–43	44–50
Husband's age	22	24–30	31–37	38–44	45–52	53–65	66–72

[a] The scores range from least vulnerable (1) to most vulnerable (5).

[b] Thomas P. Monahan, "When Couples Part," *American Sociological Review*, Vol. 27, No. 5 (October 1962), Table 1, p. 630.

[c] Robert O. Blood, Jr., and Donald M. Wolfe, *Husbands and Wives: The Dynamics of Married Living* (Glencoe, Ill.: Free Press, 1960), p. 265.

[d] *Ibid.*, p. 232.

[e] *Ibid.*, p. 156.

[f] Harold Feldman, *Development of the Husband-Wife Relationship* (Ithaca, N.Y.: Department of Child Development and Family Relationships, Cornell University, 1964), p. 126. (Mimeographed.)

[g] *Ibid.*, p. 70.

[h] *Ibid.*, p. 71.

[i] *Ibid.*, p. 188.

HAZARDS OF THE CHILDBEARING PHASE

There is evidence that a reduction in the interval between children for young couples in the United States results in a pileup of the financial, health, and physical maintenance problems associated with the childbearing years. The problems present in all families are exacerbated among the poor and near poor. As the financial pressure increases with more and more children, the husband begins withdrawing from family responsibilities. In a sample of regularly employed blue-collar Negro males in Minneapolis, fathers with three or fewer children tended to be more active in taking care of their children than those with four or more children.[17]

There is at least indirect evidence that nonwhite men faced with an increasingly deteriorating family situation compounded of unemployment and too many mouths to feed desert their families. One-fourth of all nonwhite families with five or more chil-

[17] Joan Aldous, "Wives' Employe Status and Men as Husband-Fathers: Support for the Moynihan Thesis." To be published in a forthcoming issue of *Journal of Marriage and the Family*.

TABLE 2. THE FAMILY'S VULNERABILITY TO STRESS OWING TO THE INSUFFICIENCY OF INSTRUMENTAL RESOURCES [a]

Deficit	Family Stage						
	Establishment	Child-bearing	School-age Children	Adolescents	Launching	Postparental	Aging
Income per member [b]	5	4	4	3	3	1	5
Size of family [c]	1	4	5	5	3	1	1
Adequacy of housing [d]	4	5	4	3	3	2	2
Medical expenses [e]	1	4	5	3	2	2	5
Family debts [f]	2	5	5	4	3	1	1
Job changes [g]	5	5	3	3	2	2	1
Wife in labor force supplementing income [h]	1	5	4	3	2	3	5
Total vulnerability score	19	32	30	24	18	12	20
Duration of marriage (in years)	0–1	2–7	8–14	15–21	22–29	30–43	44–50
Husband's age	22	24–30	31–37	38–44	45–52	53–65	66–72

[a] The scores range from least vulnerable (1) to most vulnerable (5).

[b] Paul C. Glick and Robert Parke, Jr., "New Approaches in Studying the Life Cycle of the Family," *Demography* (1965), pp. 187–202.

[c] Reuben Hill and Nelson Foote, *Household Inventory Changes Among Three Generations of Minneapolis Families* (New York: General Electric Co., 1962), Chart 2.

[d] Nelson Foote *et al.*, *Housing Choices and Housing Constraints* (New York: McGraw-Hill Book Co., 1960), Table 19, p. 99.

[e] John B. Lansing and James N. Morgan, "Consumer Finances Over the Life Cycle," in Lincoln Clark, ed., *The Life Cycle and Consumer Behavior* (New York: New York University Press, 1955), p. 49.

[f] *Ibid.*, p. 44.

[g] Hill and Foote, *op. cit.*, Chart 4.

[h] Robert O. Blood, Jr., and Donald M. Wolfe, *Husbands and Wives: The Dynamics of Married Living* (Glencoe, Ill.: Free Press, 1960), p. 98.

TABLE 3. THE FAMILY'S VULNERABILITY TO STRESS OWING TO DISSATISFACTION WITH INSTRUMENTAL RESOURCES [a]

Evaluation	Family Stage						
	Establishment	Child-bearing	School-age Children	Adolescents	Launching	Postparental	Aging
Satisfaction with level of living [b]	1	3	4	4	3	5	2
Satisfaction with job [c]	1	3	5	5	3	1	1
Disagreements over money [d]	1	5	4	4	4	4	3
Worries about financial cost of children [e]	1	3	5	2	4	2	1
Total vulnerability score	4	14	18	15	14	12	7
Duration of marriage (in years)	0–1	2–7	8–14	15–21	22–29	30–43	44–50
Husband's age	22	24–30	31–37	38–44	45–52	53–65	66–72

[a] The scores range from least vulnerable (1) to most vulnerable (5).

[b] Robert O. Blood, Jr., and Donald M. Wolfe, *Husbands and Wives: The Dynamics of Married Living* (Glencoe, Ill.: Free Press, 1960), p. 112.

[c] Harold L. Wilensky, "Life Cycle, Work Situation and Participation in Formal Associations," in Robert W. Kleemeier, ed., *Aging and Leisure* (New York: Oxford University Press, 1961), pp. 228–229.

[d] Blood and Wolfe, *op. cit.*, p. 247.

[e] *Ibid.*, p. 143.

dren are headed by women, as compared with 8 percent of equally large white families.[18] Moreover, in the states of Iowa, Tennessee, Wisconsin, and Hawaii—four states for which there are fairly complete divorce data—age-specific divorce rates are highest among nonwhite males, 25 to 29 years old, when their families are presumably at the stage when children are present. In contrast, the highest divorce rates for white males and females occur among persons under 20 years old, when there is less probability of children being present.[19] Certainly, there is much evidence that low-income men have higher divorce rates than the more affluent. Of men 45 to 54 years old in 1960, 29 percent of those with incomes less than $3,000 but only 16 percent of those having $10,000 or more a year were no longer living with their first wives.[20] Thus, for couples who find their family responsibilities overwhelming, the only viable escape appears to be desertion and family dissolution.

PREPARING ADOLESCENTS FOR ADULT ROLES

The poverty-prone family is found most wanting in the stage in which adolescents are present—when the family faces the awesome responsibility of social placement for the younger generation. Even when the family's composition is overbalanced with the weight of dependents during the school-

age period, the consequences for children are less serious.

The young adult is often trapped into disastrous adult roles through contingencies over which he and his family have little control. His plight is due to inept scheduling in taking on these roles. There appear to be two possible scheduling patterns whereby the young adult can achieve control over his destiny. In one, entry into adult family and occupational roles is staggered so that the individual does not have to take on both sets of responsibilities at one time. In the second, the young adult begins his family and occupational careers at the same time but only under conditions that enable him to master the tasks involved in both. These conditions would include advanced education to assure a choice of occupations with adequate income or adequate economic assistance from some source to permit him to continue his education even after marriage.

Parents can assist their children to meet either of these timetables, but only if they themselves have had the resources to be able to shape the course of their lives. With sufficient economic resources, parents can encourage children to stay in school while exercising supervision over their peer relationships to discourage premature marriage. Yet it is during this period when there are adolescents in the family that economic demands are heaviest and the income per family member has still not reached its peak.[21]

The discrepancy between the burgeoning needs and demands of young people and the family's capacity to fulfill them exists to some extent among all families but is particularly marked in poor families. Habitually living as they do under circumstances in which demands are greater than resources, they experience adolescence as a period not of temporary discrepancy, but of ever increasing deficits. It is probably at this point in the family cycle that parental poverty patterns are most likely to be trans-

---

[18] Orshansky, *op. cit.*, p. 27.

[19] National Center for Health Statistics, U.S. Public Health Service, "Divorce Statistics Analysis, United States—1962," *Vital and Health Statistics Reports*, Series 21, No. 7 (Washington, D.C.: U. S. Government Printing Office, 1965), Fig. 3, p. 6. The highest rate for Negro women occurs among 20–24 year olds. The interpretation is complicated by the older age at which nonwhite men marry. Thus, at ages 20–24, just 39.1 percent of nonwhite males are married as compared with 48.7 percent of white males. U. S. Bureau of the Census, "Marital Status and Family Status, March 1966," *Current Population Reports*, Series P-20, No. 159 (Washington, D.C.: U. S. Government Printing Office, January 1967), Table 3, pp. 9–10.

[20] Parke and Glick, *op. cit.*, p. 254.

[21] Wilensky, *op. cit.*, pp. 228–229.

mitted to the next generation. The period of entry into adult responsibilities brings into critical juxtaposition the timetables of the old and the new generations. The launching period of the parental family coincides with the establishment phase of the newly married. And the disadvantaged are tragically ill prepared to function as social placement agents for their children. These parents have long since lost control of their family's destiny and must now see their children enter adult life less on their terms than on those of society.

The very words used to identify the family function whereby children are given adult responsibilities are inappropriate for the poor. These families neither launch their children nor engage in social placement. More frequently, children leave or are pushed out to fend for themselves because the deficit in family resources associated with their presence becomes intolerable. Thus, school dropouts are often family castoffs who take on occupational and marital roles prematurely.

It can be shown that poor families do not serve as preparation centers for entering society for as long a period as do more prosperous families. Orshansky reports that relatively few adolescents are still living with their parents in families that were defined as poor by the Social Security Administration's 1964 basic poverty index. Moreover, even among those aged 16 to 21 who still live at home, more than one-third are not high school graduates and yet are not in school. This situation is true of only one person in seven of those in the same age range who are not poor.[22]

Three categories of families are especially likely to experience the hopelessness that results from being unable to prevent their children from repeating the poverty cycle of premature school-leaving, inadequate jobs, and early family responsibilities. They are the one-parent family, the family with many children, and the nonwhite family.

One-parent families. The overwhelming number of these families are headed by women. Such families are disproportionately found among Negroes—24.9 percent of all Negro families are headed by women, as compared with 8.9 percent of white families.[23] Of female-headed households, 44 percent were at the poverty level in 1964.[24] And while 38.3 percent of all persons in the country aged 18 to 24 years had not graduated from high school, this was true of 69.7 percent of youths from families receiving Aid to Families with Dependent Children in 1960.[25] Moreover, marriage and pregnancy accounted for a large portion of the female dropouts among these families. Nearly 25 percent of the white girls and 16 percent of the Negro girls who left school before 18 did so to marry. There is no information on the number who were pregnant when married, but an additional 5 percent of the white girls and 36 percent of the Negro girls left school not because of marriage but because of pregnancy.

Large families also have more than their share of poverty and are consequently less able to assure that their children will follow an optimal schedule for meeting adult role responsibilities. Almost one-half (45 percent) of all children under 18 years old who are poor are in families with as many as five children.[26] The association of large families and poverty is particularly marked among nonwhites, the majority of whom are Negroes. In 1964, seventy-six out of one hundred nonwhite families with five or more children were poor.[27]

[23] U.S. Bureau of the Census, "Negro Population: March 1966," *Current Population Reports,* Series P-20, No. 168 (Washington, D.C.: U. S. Government Printing Office, December 1967), Table 11, p. 28.
[24] Orshansky, *op. cit.,* p. 27.
[25] M. Elaine Burgess and Daniel O. Price, *An American Dependency Challenge* (Chicago: American Public Welfare Association, 1963), pp. 108, 110.
[26] Orshansky, *op. cit.,* p. 30.
[27] *Ibid.,* p. 26. High birthrates among Negroes are associated with large family size. In March 1964, the average size of white families was 3.6 persons as compared with 4.3 persons for Negro fam-

[22] Orshansky, *op. cit.,* p. 34.

Nonwhites constitute the third large group of families that are more often economically unable to assist their children to take on adult roles. Over four out of ten families with a nonwhite head are poor and, as noted earlier, Negro families are also disproportionately found among the poverty-prone categories of the one-parent and large family types.[28] Nonwhite males lack access to rewarding occupational careers that pay enough to support a wife and family; nonwhite females often face maternal responsibilities before they are married, and the general society considers marriage to be an essential precondition to childbearing. Thus, 18.4 percent of nonwhite males aged 16 to 21 years were in the labor force but not gainfully employed and 13.8 percent of nonwhite female household heads who had children under 18 in 1960 were single.[29] The comparable unemployment percentage for white youths was 6.8 and the illegitimacy rate for white women was 3.0 percent.[30]

IMPLICATIONS FOR AN INCOME MAINTENANCE PROGRAM

What has this examination of the relative vulnerability of families in certain stages of the life cycle suggested for an income

maintenance program that might break the poverty cycle? Two stages—the family-with-adolescents stage and the childbearing stage—appear especially strategic for income supplementation for quite different reasons.

The primary legacy that poor families pass on to adolescents is poverty. When families are unable to meet their needs, children are more apt to telescope the schedule for taking on adult roles without going through the concentrated preparation period that would enable them to cope with the attendant problems. The discrepancy between family needs and resources would appear to be greatest in the family-with-adolescents stage. Increased economic resources at this period, through some sort of governmental income maintenance program, would enable the family to fulfill its social placement function and maintain some control over the destiny of its children.

The disastrous sequence of foreshortening this period in the family life cycle, followed by an early establishment period of a new conjugal unit in the next generation, would become less common. It is not that families lack aspirations for their children. Even the most hopeless want to be able to give their children a better start. They are also aware of the necessary means—more education, better jobs, and postponed marriages and children. They need the means for holding their children at home for a longer period of preparation so that aspirations may become reality. In this way, a benign cycle of intergenerational social inheritance can be started. The next generation, instead of being handicapped from the beginning, will be prepared to play its adult roles more effectively and, in time, to give its children a heritage from which they can build a still better life.[31]

ilies. U. S. Bureau of the Census, "Negro Population," *Current Population Reports*, Series P-20, No. 142 (Washington, D.C.: U. S. Government Printing Office, March 1964), Table F, p. 5. While the number of fifth or higher order births per thousand women aged 15–44 was 15 for whites in 1964, it was 42.3 for nonwhites. National Center for Health Statistics, *Natality Statistics Analysis: United States, 1964*, Series 21, No. 11 (Washington, D.C.: U. S. Government Printing Office, February 1967), p. 13.

[28] Orshansky, *op. cit.*, p. 27.

[29] *Employment and Earnings and Monthly Report on the Labor Force*, Table A-3, p. 8; and Jessie Bernard, *Marriage and Family Among Negroes* (Englewood Cliffs, N.J.: Prentice-Hall, 1966), p. 17.

[30] *Employment and Earnings and Monthly Report on the Labor Force*, Table A-3, p. 8; and U. S. Bureau of the Census, *1960 Census of Population: Subject Reports—Families*, Final Report (Washington, D.C.: U. S. Government Printing Office, 1963), Table 3, p. 18.

[31] Even among the disadvantaged AFDC heads of families studied in 1960, there was some indication that the more advantaged were able to give their children better preparation for adult roles. "The

The childbearing stage is also a strategic point for the operation of a governmental income maintenance program. It would reduce the economic pressures on the low-income father that lead him to desert his family. Such families more often than not are moving on dead-end occupational tracks, their only future being assistance from public welfare. Supplementary income would give the hard-pressed father the option of entering a special training program, even if it resulted in a temporarily reduced income, or moving his family from a depressed area to one with more opportunity. Such options would give families increased elbowroom for determining their own development while the family is still intact.

ASSISTANCE AT OTHER STAGES

An income maintenance program, as the authors have envisioned it, is justified primarily because it would improve the quality of family life and prevent the transmission of poverty from one generation to the next.[32] Thus, this paper has focused less on the establishment phase, in which marital satisfaction and financial resources are relatively high, and more on the stages of the family with adolescents and the childbearing family as the periods of maximum payoff for governmental economic intervention.

The authors have not considered the family with school-age children a particularly strategic period for economic intervention. To be sure, health and housing

demands continue to be high relative to resources, and conjugal interaction is less satisfactory during this period than during the establishment phase. There does not appear to be, however, the same susceptibility to family dissolution than one finds during the desertion-prone period of heavy childbearing responsibilities nor the dangers of premature family leave-taking by children characteristic of the later adolescent stage.

An income maintenance program when the family cycle is drawing to a close is, of course, essential. For couples fortunate enough to remain intact as family units after the retirement of the breadwinner, some sort of income supplement is often necessary. This is especially the case for the widowed—the existing remnants of previously functioning families. But this assistance, necessary as it is for giving alternatives in life to persons whose major contribution to society lies in the past, has only indirect bearing on the intergenerational continuity of poverty. For this reason, an income maintenance program specifically for the aging period has not been considered in this paper.

CONCLUSION

Analysis of the family life cycle has indicated two stages when some type of governmental income maintenance program would be effective in raising the quality of family life. In both the childbearing and adolescent stages, the family's vulnerability to losing control over its own and, by extension, the next generation's development is high. Shoring up the economic base by governmental support would give all families increased alternatives while providing the poor and near poor an escape from forced decisions. With the assurance of some measure of economic security, today's poor families would be able to look beyond the spirit-dulling problems of daily sustenance and begin setting higher standards of individual and family performance.

---

higher the education level of the homemaker, the lower the proportion of children with educational retardation and the greater the possibility of educational advancement." Burgess and Price, op. cit., p. 113.

[32] The authors' purpose in this paper is not to advocate any specific governmental income supplement program such as the negative income tax or family allowance. It is to identify the points in the family cycle when supplementation would be most effective in strengthening the family.

Strategies to make bureaucrats responsive

by Delbert A. Taebel

Since the early 1960s vast segments of American society have become more active politically. This has been a striking characteristic of the nation's politics in the past decade. No longer are groups and organizations content to let formal governmental bodies monopolize political decision-making. Minority groups, especially blacks, were the first to become involved in political action at the beginning of the sixties, and others—such as student organizations, churches, and neighborhood groups—later became active. Even local garden clubs now participate in politics and make loud demands for protection of the environment.

Yet, there is growing awareness that these efforts have been largely fruitless, that the political system remains unresponsive. The governmental bureaucracy has been among the most unresponsive components. Both scholars and practitioners have offered a plethora of recommendations and exhortations to remedy this deficiency. Approaches have been espoused that either focus on the bureaucracy itself or on client groups.

In general, the former approach is viewed as more propitious. Indeed, the advocacy role of the bureaucrat is now a highly fashionable concept in the scholarly community, especially in schools of public administration, social work, public health, and the like. Within the last several years, a body of literature has developed that prescribes ways in which the governmental bureaucrat can play a truly meaningful and relevant role in ameliorating serious problems of the poor and disfranchised. For example, instead of the traditional bureaucracy, White posits a "dialectical organization" that would devote itself, even at the risk of self-destruction, totally to the client.[1] This dialectical organization of course would operate by an ethical code quite contrary to that of the traditional bureaucracy.

The second approach focuses on organizing client groups to make the bureaucracy

[1] Orion F. White, Jr., "The Dialectical Organization—An Alternative to Bureaucracy," *Public Administration Review*, Vol. 29, No. 1 (January/February 1969), pp. 32–42.

Reprinted with permission of the National Association of Social Workers, from SOCIAL WORK, Vol. 17, No. 6, (November 1972), pp. 38-43.

responsive. It is argued that only by marshaling their forces can these groups confront the bureaucracy with political strength and thus force it to become more sensitive to their needs. Advocates of this approach usually concentrate on political strategies that will, they argue, bring the bureaucracy to heel. This paper explores the strategies of clients and assesses their utility in relation to "street-level" bureaucrats—those in governmental agencies whose impact on the client is dramatically evident every day.[2]

In general, client groups use at present one of two major strategic thrusts to generate a more responsive governmental bureaucracy. One strategy that many groups have adopted is to apply political pressure on the bureaucracy. The pressure takes many forms, including marches, confrontations, and sit-ins, plus such traditional tactics as appeals to elected officials. This strategy is based on the explicit assumption that the bureaucracy will respond to pressure and that the way to achieve this pressure is through organization and forced communication.

The second strategy advocated is decentralizing the bureaucracy down to the neighborhood level. This proposal is based on the assumption that decentralized agencies are more responsive to neighborhood needs. Bureaucrats who are "neighborhood folks," it is argued, are more perceptive to the mores and norms of the residents. The central thesis of this paper is that the assumptions underlying these strategies are invalid and that the strategies tend only to further exacerbate bureaucrat-client relations.

BUREAUCRATIC STRESS

It is important to understand the types of stresses that the street-level bureaucrat faces and the effect of these stresses on relations with the client. Lipsky identifies the following three sources of stress: [3]

1. *Inadequate resources.* It is almost axiomatic that public organizations providing direct services to the people lack the resources to carry out their functions adequately. (Ironically, those that seem to contribute least to the public welfare—e.g., the Department of Defense and state highway departments—seldom seem strapped for funds.) The effects of inadequate resources are most directly felt by street-level bureaucrats in those organizations directly serving the public—such as schoolteachers, social workers, and policemen. When the gap between the bureaucrat's capability and the client's demand becomes too great, the bureaucrat devises various defense mechanisms that result in unequal client treatment which penalizes minorities and the poor most severely.

"Shorthand" techniques for dealing with situations are one such defense mechanism. For example, the teacher faced with an overcrowded classroom may hastily stereotype pupils, categorizing them on the basis of academic ability. Indeed, a ready-made tool—the IQ test—is at the teacher's disposal, which obviates any sense of personal responsibility for the classification. Since the teacher lacks the time to give all pupils the individual attention needed, top students are likely to receive priority. Those at the bottom then get catch-as-catch-can treatment. Thus they are shortchanged in the educational process.

The teacher justifies the unequal treatment on the basis that those at the bottom cannot be educated anyway, and when they fail in their courses and drop out of school, the prophecy is fulfilled. If this stereotyping technique was applied equally to those in all strata of society, the problem would be serious enough. What is especially onerous is that poor and minority-group pupils are affected most drastically. Their unequal status in society is thus compounded by unequal treatment in the classroom.

2. *Physical and psychological threats.*

[2] Michael Lipsky, "Street-Level Bureaucracy and the Analysis of Urban Reform," *Urban Affairs Quarterly*, Vol. 6, No. 4 (June 1971), pp. 391–409.

[3] Ibid., pp. 393–395. Lipsky's conclusions are quite different from those reached in this article.

"The assumption . . . is that the application of pressure should cause the bureaucrat to treat the client more favorably [but] the strategy has the reverse effect."

Although policemen are the most common targets of physical threat, other street-level bureaucrats also are subject to it, as shown by the fact that teachers are urgently demanding stronger sanctions against pupils who physically abuse them.

Why is this type of stress significant for street-level bureaucrats? The bureaucrat-client interaction is in most cases involuntary, and the bureaucrat seeks to control the situation. The teacher, for example, argues that discipline and order are necessary antecedents to the learning process. Control over the situation is considered so important for the lower court judge that the setting is designed to promote it: the judge sits on a dais, forcing the client to look up at him. Bureaucratic control of welfare clients is evident in such techniques as requiring them to fill out long forms and to wait for service. As Kotler notes:

> There is nothing more terrifying to a bureaucrat than the prospect of losing control over the lives of his clients. To lose these small opportunities means the loss of the personal power that our paternalistic system gives bureaucrats as a fringe benefit and calls a moral obligation. Having no political liberty themselves, administrators cannot understand the claim of local liberty—let alone appreciate it.[4]

What is the effect of this stress on the bureaucrat-client relationship? It obviously generates a hostile response in the client. If this hostility becomes overt, the bureaucrat takes even stronger measures to insure control over the situation. The client's hostile reaction merely reinforces the bureaucrat's perception of threat, and

the bureaucrat's response further antagonizes the client.

3. *Role conflict.* Most people play various roles, even in the course of a day. It is only when these roles clash that problems arise. The street-level bureaucrat is especially subject to conflicting or ambiguous roles. Usually one's role is derived from several sources, including superiors, peer groups, reference groups, and the general public.

The social worker, a rather ambiguous bureaucrat anyway, may receive contradictory signals regarding the role he is expected to play. His superiors may require or expect certain attitudes and actions. The head of the agency may expect the worker to be loyal to the agency, efficient, and properly deferential to organizational authority. Peer groups may initiate demands. Colleagues may, for example, appeal for group cohesiveness, a realistic approach to the job, and restrictions in the work load. Reference groups, including professional organizations and client groups, may present role expectations. Professional groups may expect the social worker to pay homage to a code of professional ethics that he considers ambiguous and to articulate what he regards as the platitudes and myths of the profession.

The agency is the source of the most compelling rewards—such as promotion and prestige—and thus largely shapes the social worker's orientation. Unfortunately, client groups are not likely to have much impact on his role definition. As a consequence, client and bureaucrat usually approach their interaction process from different levels of expectations. Yet only when the social worker adopts a role that accords with the client's expectations is the interaction viable.

[4] Milton Kotler, *Neighborhood Government* (Indianapolis, Ind.: Bobbs-Merrill Co., 1969), p. 77.

DYSFUNCTIONAL STRATEGIES

The outcome of interaction between street-level bureaucrats and clients is naturally influenced by the stresses that bureaucrats face. How do these stresses relate to the two major strategies of citizen action groups—(1) asserting political pressures and (2) demands for decentralization down to the neighborhood?

The assumption underlying the first strategy is that the application of pressure should cause the bureaucrat to treat the client more favorably. Looking at the three stresses from this point of view, two factors indicate that the strategy has the reverse effect: it provokes less favorable treatment of the client and increases bureaucrat-client antagonism. First, much of this pressure seeks to have the bureaucrat take actions that would greatly over-extend his resources. Second, pressure threatens to undermine the bureaucrat's control of the situation. To capitulate would merely heighten his sense of fear. Also, the pressure implicitly demands an alteration or even a rejection of the bureaucrat's dominant role. In sum, the strategy of pressure politics as applied by many client groups only aggravates the stresses that undermine bureaucrat-client relationships in the first place.

The second strategy, decentralization down to the neighborhood, assumes that a local bureaucracy would be more responsive than one covering a large geographic area. Again, examination indicates that this strategy would compound the stresses on bureaucrats. First, since decentralization is generally a costly venture, the financial resources of bureaucracies would be stretched even more thinly. Second, decentralization—depending on its degree—would tend to isolate the bureaucrat and thus would heighten his apprehension of physical and psychological threats. Third, peer group support and its impact on role orientation would be curtailed, thus increasing role ambivalence. Finally, there is no evidence that bureaucrats recruited from the neighborhood would be more responsive to the client. Indeed, some evidence suggests that such bureaucrats tend to become "more royalist than the king." [5]

ALTERNATIVE STRATEGIES

If the strategies of political pressure and decentralization are dysfunctional, what are the alternatives? One might begin with the assumption that any strategy should be based on the following proposition: The more dependent the client is on the bureaucrat, the more unresponsive the bureaucracy will be. This might be considered a working hypothesis. Although it has not been empirically tested, it seems intuitively sound and offers a starting point for further research. Obviously, if the client must depend on the agency for service, the agency has little motivation to accommodate itself to client demands.

One should understand that governmental agencies and their client groups have a symbiotic relationship and that agencies depend on clients as well as clients on agencies. Even the police department depends on criminals—who are the main client group of law enforcement agencies—in the sense that the elimination of crime would mean the elimination of most policemen. This mutual bureaucrat-client relationship must be recognized. Nevertheless, the dependency relationship is one of degree. In terms of the client groups on which this article focuses, the client is at least more visibly dependent on the agency than the converse.

If this proposition regarding dependency is valid, then client strategies need to be devised that either reduce the client's dependency on the agency or increase the agency's dependency on the client. What kinds of strategies would accomplish these goals?

The following four strategies might instill a greater degree of responsiveness in agencies toward their clients:

[5] V. Subramaniam, "Representative Bureaucracy: A Reassessment," *American Political Science Review*, Vol. 61, No. 4 (December 1967). pp. 1010–1019.

"The agency is the source of the most compelling rewards—such as promotion and prestige—and thus largely shapes the social worker's orientation. Unfortunately client groups are not likely to have much impact on his role definition."

1. *Competitive structure.* First, competitive public service organizations should foster bureaucratic responsiveness. This strategy, of course, is sheer heresy to the doctrinaire bureaucrat who subscribes to "coordinated monopolization," which means the centralization of services and the elimination of duplicate programs. As Warren notes, this approach

> . . . tends to create a monopoly situation, to limit free competition, and to reduce the options to the client. . . . There is no reason . . . to believe that a monopoly situation induces nonprofit agencies to give the consumer a better break any more than it induces profit organizations to do so.[6]

A competitive structure would offer the client the option of shopping for an agency. The services performed and the number of client-customers could determine the funds allocated to agencies. This suggestion is especially applicable to the public school system, which has encountered serious proposals for instituting some kind of voucher system. Whether restructuring to make bureaucratic institutions competitive could be done across the board is doubtful, but if it could be done, it would offer a way out of the dependency syndrome.

2. *Positive input.* A second strategy of those seeking to alter the bureaucracy's responsiveness could be to make more diversified and more positive input into the system. For the political activist of the 1960s input meant one thing only: demands on the system. For the political scientist, however, input means both demands and supports.[7] The input of activists may have been largely unsuccessful because it has been negative. Bureaucratic agencies need the support of their clients. One cannot expect to have his demands heard unless he is willing to pay the cost—and the cost is some form of political support. The mere possibility might sound treasonable to a hard-core radical, but what would happen if representatives of a minority group showed up at a city council meeting to support pay raises for policemen? Or at a school board meeting to support a proposal for smaller classes? Client groups might offer many kinds of political support.

A review of the tactics of the groups that have been most successful vis-à-vis the political system reveals that the input of such interest groups has supported the system.[8] Indeed, these groups seldom have to make demands because agencies depend greatly on their support and have become more sensitive to their needs.

3. *Self-help programs.* A third strategy might be to develop self-help programs to offset the client's dependency on the bureaucrat. Obviously, ghetto development—including job training, housing, and the financing of business ventures—is expensive. If governmental agencies provide programs of this type, they may find that it is cheaper and more productive to

---

[6] Roland L. Warren, "The Model Cities Program," *Social Welfare Forum, 1971* (New York: Columbia University Press, 1971), p. 156. *See* also E. S. Savas, "Municipal Monopoly," *Harper's Magazine*, Vol. 243, No. 1459 (December 1971), pp. 55–60.

[7] *See,* for example, David Easton, "An Approach to the Analysis of Political Systems," *World Politics*, Vol. 9, No. 2 (April 1957), pp. 383–400.

[8] The classic work in the quite extensive literature on interest group activity is Vladimer O. Key, Jr., *Politics, Parties and Pressure Groups* (4th ed.; New York: Thomas Y. Crowell, 1958).

eliminate the middle-man, that is, the social service bureaucrat.

4. *Unconditional surrender.* If the bureaucracy does not respond to the foregoing strategies, it may be preferable to dissolve the bureaucrat-client relationship altogether. In a word, a bureaucratic agency that fails to respond needs to be junked, either by a general boycott or by overloading it.[9] As already noted, threats merely aggravate the conflict between bureaucrats and clients. Thus the only viable strategy in such a situation is to achieve unconditional surrender. Some might consider this a cut-off-your-nose-to-spite-your-face strategy, but it might be more appropriate to classify it as long-range versus short-range strategy. To perpetuate an unresponsive agency might yield minimal benefits at a high cost.

One objection to the unconditional-surrender strategy is that clients who suffer most—and therefore most need to use this kind of strategy—are least likely to have the staying power to accomplish such action. There must be an organization that supports the client who pits himself against the bureaucracy and can sustain him through the process, just as there is the labor union to support workers on the brink of and through a strike. There are many such client organizations, but they generally dissipate their resources and thus attenuate their efforts.

SUMMARY

The increasing activism in American politics has been directed toward altering the political system as a whole, but changing the street-level bureaucracy is the most critical concern for minority groups and the poor. The two strategies most often adopted—pressure politics and decentralization down to the neighborhood—exacerbate the stresses that street-level bureaucrats now face. These stresses undermine the bureaucrats' relations with their clients and provoke certain defense mechanisms that place minority groups and the poor at a disadvantage. Consequently, both strategies are highly dysfunctional in achieving the goals of minorities and welfare groups.

Four strategies for reducing the dependence of clients on bureaucracies are proposed: a competitive bureaucratic system, a more diversified and positive input by clients, self-help programs, and the "unconditional surrender" of unresponsive agencies.

Strategies for changing the political system must take into account the behavioral patterns of the organizations that comprise the system. To persist with the futile strategies devised in the 1960s will only immobilize the bureaucracy and penalize the client. Until strategies are devised that merge bureaucratic goals and client needs, the promise of America cannot be realized.

---

[9] For an analogous argument, *see* Richard A. Cloward and Francis Fox Piven, "The Weight of the Poor: A Strategy to End Poverty," *The Nation*, Vol. 202, No. 18 (May 2, 1966), pp. 510–517.

BY FRANCIS P. PURCELL AND HARRY SPECHT

The House on Sixth Street

■ *A case history of a tenement house illustrates factors necessary for the selection of intervention methods by the social worker. Residents of the tenement were encouraged and aided in their attempt to make their needs known to the public agencies. Out of these attempts, a community action group was initiated.* ■

THE EXTENT TO WHICH social work can affect the course of social problems has not received the full consideration it deserves.[1] For some time the social work profession has taken account of social problems only as they have become manifest in behavioral pathology. Yet it is becoming increasingly apparent that, even allowing for this limitation, it is often necessary for the same agency or worker to intervene by various methods at various points.

In this paper, the case history of a tenement house in New York City is used to illustrate some of the factors that should be considered in selecting intervention methods. Like all first attempts, the approach described can be found wanting in conceptual clarity and systematization. Yet the vital quality of the effort and its implications for social work practice seem clear.

The case of "The House on Sixth Street" is taken from the files of Mobilization For Youth (MFY), an action-research project that has been in operation since 1962 on New York's Lower East Side.[2] MFY's programs are financed by grants from several public and private sources. The central theoretical contention of MFY is that a major proportion of juvenile delinquency occurs when adolescents from low-income families do not have access to legitimate opportunities by which they can fulfill the aspirations for success they share with all American youth. The action programs of MFY are designed to offer these youths concrete opportunities to offset the debilitating effects of poverty. For example, the employment program helps youngsters ob-

FRANCIS P. PURCELL, MSW, *is now Professor of Social Work, Rutgers University, Graduate School of Social Work, New Brunswick, New Jersey. He was formerly Chief, Training and Personnel, Mobilization For Youth, New York, New York.* HARRY SPECHT, Ph.D., *now Assistant Executive Director, Research Projects, Contra Costa Council of Community Services, Walnut Creek, California, was formerly Assistant Chief, Community Development, Mobilization For Youth.*

[1] Social work practitioners sometimes use the term "social problem" to mean "environmental problem." The sense in which it is used here corresponds to the definition developed by the social sciences. That is, a social problem is a disturbance, deviation, or breakdown in social behavior that (1) involves a considerable number of people and (2) is of serious concern to many in the society. It is social in origin and effect, and is a social responsibility. It represents a discrepancy between social standards and social reality. Also, such socially perceived variations must be viewed as corrigible. See Robert K. Merton and Robert A. Nisbet, eds., *Contemporary Social Problems* (New York: Harcourt, Brace, and World, 1961), pp. 6, 701.

[2] A complete case record of the Sixth Street house will be included in a forthcoming publication of Mobilization For Youth.

Reprinted with permission of the National Association of Social Workers, from SOCIAL WORK, Vol. 10, No. 4 (October 1965), pp. 69-76.

tain jobs; other programs attempt to increase opportunities in public schools. In addition, there are group work and recreation programs. A wide variety of services to individuals and families is offered through Neighborhood Service Centers: a homemaking program, a program for released offenders, and a narcotics information center. Legal services, a housing services unit, a special referral unit, and a community development program are among other services that have been developed or made available. Thus,˝ MFY has an unusually wide range of resources for dealing with social problems.

THE PROBLEM

"The House on Sixth Street" became a case when Mrs. Smith came to an MFY Neighborhood Service Center to complain that there had been no gas, electricity, heat, or hot water in her apartment house for more than four weeks. She asked the agency for help. Mrs. Smith was 23 years old, Negro, and the mother of four children, three of whom had been born out of wedlock. At the time she was unmarried and receiving Aid to Families with Dependent Children. She came to the center in desperation because she was unable to run her household without utilities. Her financial resources were exhausted—but not her courage. The Neighborhood Service Center worker decided that in this case the building—the tenants, the landlord, and circumstances affecting their relationships—was of central concern.

A social worker then visited the Sixth Street building with Mrs. Smith and a community worker. Community workers are members of the community organization staff in a program that attempts to encourage residents to take independent social action. Like many members in other MFY programs, community workers are residents of the particular neighborhood. Most of them have little formal education, their special contribution being their ability to relate to and communicate with other residents. Because some of the tenants were Puerto Rican, a Spanish-speaking community worker was chosen to accompany the social worker. His easy manner and knowledge of the neighborhood enabled him and the worker to become involved quickly with the tenants.

Their first visits confirmed Mrs. Smith's charge that the house had been without utilities for more than four weeks. Several months before, the city Rent and Rehabilitation Administration had reduced the rent for each apartment to one dollar a month because the landlord was not providing services. However, this agency was slow to take further action. Eleven families were still living in the building, which had twenty-eight apartments. The landlord owed the electric company several thousand dollars. Therefore, the meters had been removed from the house. Because most of the tenants were welfare clients, the Department of Welfare had "reimbursed" the landlord directly for much of the unpaid electric bill and refused to pay any more money to the electric company. The Department of Welfare was slow in meeting the emergency needs of the tenants. Most of the children (forty-eight from the eleven families in the building) had not been to school for a month because they were ill or lacked proper clothing.

The mothers were tired and demoralized. Dirt and disorganization were increasing daily. The tenants were afraid to sleep at night because the building was infested with rats. There was danger of fire because the tenants had to use candles for light. The seventeen abandoned apartments had been invaded by homeless men and drug addicts. Petty thievery is common in such situations. However, the mothers did not want to seek protection from the police for fear that they would chase away all men who were not part of the families in the building (some of the unmarried mothers had men living with them—one of the few means of protection from physical danger available to these women—even though mothers on public assistance are threatened with loss of income if they are not legally married). The anxiety created by these conditions was intense and disabling.

The workers noted that the mothers were not only anxious but "fighting mad"; not only did they seek immediate relief from their physical dangers and discomforts but they were eager to express their fury at the landlord and the public agencies, which they felt had let them down.

The circumstances described are by no means uncommon, at least not in New York City. Twenty percent of all housing in the city is still unfit, despite all the public and private residential building completed since World War II. At least 277,500 dwellings in New York City need major repairs if they are to become safe and adequate shelters. This means that approximately 500,000 people in the city live in inferior dwelling units and as many as 825,000 people in buildings that are considered unsafe.[3] In 1962 the New York City Bureau of Sanitary Inspections reported that 530 children were bitten by rats in their homes and 198 children were poisoned (nine of them fatally) by nibbling at peeling lead paint, even though the use of lead paint has been illegal in the city for more than ten years. Given the difficulties involved in lodging formal complaints with city agencies, it is safe to assume that unreported incidents of rat bites and lead poisoning far exceed these figures.

The effect of such hardships on children is obvious. Of even greater significance is the sense of powerlessness generated when families go into these struggles barehanded. It is this sense of helplessness in the face of adversity that induces pathological anxiety, intergenerational alienation, and social retreatism. Actual physical impoverishment alone is not nearly so debilitating as poverty attended by a sense of unrelieved

[3] Facts About Low Income Housing (New York: Emergency Committee For More Low Income Housing, 1963).

impotence that becomes generalized and internalized. The poor then regard much social learning as irrelevant, since they do not believe it can effect any environmental change.[4]

INTERVENTION AND THE SOCIAL SYSTEMS

Selecting a point of intervention in dealing with this problem would have been simpler if the target of change were Mrs. Smith alone, or Mrs. Smith and her co-tenants, the clients in whose behalf intervention was planned. Too often, the client system presenting the problem becomes the major target for intervention, and the intervention method is limited to the one most suitable for that client system. However, Mrs. Smith and the other tenants had a multitude of problems emanating from many sources, any one of which would have warranted the attention of a social agency. The circumstantial fact that in individual contacts an agency that offers services to individuals and families should not be a major factor in determining the method of intervention. Identification of the client merely helps the agency to define goals; other variables are involved in the selection of method. As Burns and Glasser have suggested:

It may be helpful to consider the primary target of change as distinct from the persons who may be the primary clients. . . . The primary target of change then becomes the human or physical environment toward which professional efforts via direct intervention are aimed in order to facilitate change.[5]

The three major factors that determined

[4] Francis P. Purcell, "The Helping Professions and Problems of the Brief Contact," in Frank Riessman, Jerome Cohen, and Arthur Pearl, eds., Mental Health of the Poor (New York: Free Press of Glencoe, 1964), p. 432.

[5] Mary E. Burns and Paul H. Glasser, "Similarities and Differences in Casework and Group Work Practice," Social Service Review, Vol. 37, No. 4 (December 1963), p. 423.

MFY's approach to the problem were (1) knowledge of the various social systems within which the social problem was located (i.e., social systems assessment), (2) knowledge of the various methods (including non-social work methods) appropriate for intervention in these different social systems, and (3) the resources available to the agency.[6]

The difficulties of the families in the building were intricately connected with other elements of the social system related to the housing problem. For example, seven different public agencies were involved in maintenance of building services. Later other agencies were involved in relocating the tenants. There is no one agency in New York City that handles all housing problems. Therefore, tenants have little hope of getting help on their own. In order to redress a grievance relating to water supply (which was only one of the building's many problems) it is necessary to know precisely which city department to contact. The following is only a partial listing:

No water—Health Department
Not enough water—Department of Water Supply
No hot water—Buildings Department
Water leaks—Buildings Department
Large water leaks—Department of Water Supply
Water overflowing from apartment above—Police Department
Water sewage in the cellar—Sanitation Department

The task of determining which agencies are responsible for code enforcement in various areas is not simple, and in addition one must know that the benefits and services available for tenants and for the community vary with the course of action chosen. For example, if the building were taken over by the Rent and Rehabilitation Administra-

tion under the receivership law, it would be several weeks before services would be re-established, and the tenants would have to remain in the building during its rehabilitation. There would be, however, some compensations: tenants could remain in the neighborhood—indeed, in the same building—and their children would not have to change schools. If, on the other hand, the house were condemned by the Buildings Department, the tenants would have to move, but they would be moved quickly and would receive top relocation priorities and maximum relocation benefits. But once the tenants had been relocated—at city expense—the building could be renovated by the landlord as middle-income housing. In the Sixth Street house, it was suspected that this was the motivation behind the landlord's actions. If the building were condemned and renovated, there would be twenty-eight fewer low-income housing units in the neighborhood.

This is the fate of scores of tenements on the Lower East Side because much new middle-income housing is being built there. Basic services are withheld and tenants are forced to move so that buildings may be renovated for middle-income tenants. Still other buildings are allowed to deteriorate with the expectation that they will be bought by urban renewal agencies.

It is obvious, even limiting analysis to the social systems of one tenement, that the problem is enormous. Although the tenants were the clients in this case, Mrs. Smith, the tenant group, and other community groups were all served at one point or another. It is even conceivable that the landlord might have been selected as the most appropriate recipient of service. Rehabilitation of many slum tenements is at present nearly impossible. Many landlords regard such property purely as an investment. With profit the prime motive, needs of low-income tenants are often overlooked. Under present conditions it is financially impossible for many landlords to correct all the violations in their buildings even

---

[6] Harry Specht and Frank Riessman, "Some Notes on a Model for an Integrated Social Work Approach to Social Problems" (New York: Mobilization For Youth, June 1963). (Mimeographed.)

if they wanted to. If the social worker chose to intervene at this level of the problem, he might apply to the Municipal Loan Fund, make arrangements with unions for the use of non-union labor in limited rehabilitation projects, or provide expert consultants on reconstruction. These tasks would require social workers to have knowledge similar to that of city planners. If the problems of landlords were not selected as a major point of intervention, they would still have to be considered at some time since they are an integral part of the social context within which this problem exists.

A correct definition of interacting social systems or of the social worker's choice of methods and points of intervention is not the prime concern here. What is to be emphasized is what this case so clearly demonstrates: that although the needs of the client system enable the agency to define its goals, the points and methods of intervention cannot be selected properly without an awareness and substantial knowledge of the social systems within which the problem is rooted.

DEALING WITH THE PROBLEM

The social worker remained with the building throughout a four-month period. In order to deal effectively with the problem, he had to make use of all the social work methods as well as the special talents of a community worker, lawyer, city planner, and various civil rights organizations. The social worker and the community worker functioned as generalists with both individuals and families calling on caseworkers as needed for specialized services or at especially trying times, such as during the first week and when the families were relocated. Because of the division of labor in the agency, much of the social work with individuals was done with the help of a caseworker. Group work, administration, and community organization were handled by the social worker, who had been trained in community organization. In many in-

stances he also dealt with the mothers as individuals, as they encountered one stressful situation after another. Agency caseworkers also provided immediate and concrete assistance to individual families, such as small financial grants, medical care, homemaking services, baby-sitting services, and transportation. This reduced the intensity of pressures on these families. Caseworkers were especially helpful in dealing with some of the knotty and highly technical problems connected with public agencies.

With a caseworker and a lawyer experienced in handling tenement cases, the social worker began to help the families organize their demands for the services and utilities to which they were legally entitled but which the public agencies had consistently failed to provide for them.

The ability of the mothers to take concerted group action was evident from the beginning, and Mrs. Smith proved to be a natural and competent leader. With support, encouragement, and assistance from the staff, the mothers became articulate and effective in negotiating with the various agencies involved. In turn, the interest and concern of the agencies increased markedly when the mothers began to visit them, make frequent telephone calls, and send letters and telegrams to them and to politicians demanding action.

With the lawyer and a city planner (an agency consultant), the mothers and staff members explored various possible solutions to the housing problem. For example, the Department of Welfare had offered to move the families to shelters or hotels. Neither alternative was acceptable to the mothers. Shelters were ruled out because they would not consider splitting up their families, and they rejected hotels because they had discovered from previous experience that many of the "hotels" selected were flop-houses or were inhabited by prostitutes.

The following is taken from the social worker's record during the first week:

Met with the remaining tenants, several

Negro men from the block, and [the city planner]. . . . Three of the mothers said that they would sooner sleep out on the street than go to the Welfare shelter. If nothing else, they felt that this would be a way of protesting their plight . . . One of the mothers said that they couldn't very well do this with most of the children having colds. Mrs. Brown thought that they might do better to ask Reverend Jones if they could move into the cellar of his church temporarily. . . . The other mothers got quite excited about this idea because they thought that the church basement would make excellent living quarters.

After a discussion as to whether the mothers would benefit from embarrassing the public agencies by dramatically exposing their inadequacies, the mothers decided to move into the nearby church. They asked the worker to attempt to have their building condemned. At another meeting, attended by tenants from neighboring buildings and representatives of other local groups, it was concluded that what had happened to the Sixth Street building was a result of discrimination against the tenants as Puerto Ricans and Negroes. The group—which had now become an organization—sent the following telegram to city, state, and federal officials:

> We are voters and Puerto Rican and Negro mothers asking for equal rights, for decent housing and enough room. Building has broken windows, no gas or electricity for four weeks, no heat or hot water, holes in floors, loose wiring. Twelve of forty-eight children in building sick. Welfare doctors refuse to walk up dark stairs. Are we human or what? Should innocent children suffer for landlords' brutality and city and state neglect? We are tired of being told to wait with children ill and unable to attend school. Negro and Puerto Rican tenants are forced out while buildings next door are renovated at high rents. We are not being treated as human beings.

For the most part, the lawyer and city planner stayed in the background, acting only as consultants. But as the tenants and worker became more involved with the courts and as other organizations entered the fight, the lawyer and city planner played a more active and direct role.

RESULTANT SIDE-EFFECTS

During this process, tenants in other buildings on the block became more alert to similar problems in their buildings. With the help of the community development staff and the housing consultant, local groups and organizations such as tenants' councils and the local chapter of the Congress of Racial Equality were enlisted to support and work with the mothers.

Some of the city agencies behaved as though MFY had engineered the entire scheme to embarrass them—steadfastly disregarding the fact that the building had been unlivable for many months. Needless to say, the public agencies are overloaded and have inadequate resources. As has been documented, many such bureaucracies develop an amazing insensitivity to the needs of their clients.[7] In this case, the MFY social worker believed that the tenants—and other people in their plight—should make their needs known to the agencies and to the public at large. He knew that when these expressions of need are backed by power—either in numbers or in political knowledge—they are far more likely to have some effect.

Other movements in the city at this time gave encouragement and direction to the people in the community. The March on Washington and the Harlem rent strike are two such actions.

By the time the families had been relocated, several things had been accomplished. Some of the public agencies had

---

[7] See, for example, Reinhard Bendix, "Bureaucracy and the Problem of Power," in Robert K. Merton, Alisa Gray, Barbara Hockey, and Horan C. Sebrin, eds., Reader in Bureaucracy (Glencoe, Ill.: Free Press, 1952), pp. 114–134.

been sufficiently moved by the actions of the families and the local organizations to provide better services for them. When the families refused to relocate in a shelter and moved into a neighborhood church instead, one of the television networks picked up their story. Officials in the housing agencies came to investigate and several local politicians lent the tenants their support. Most important, several weeks after the tenants moved into the church, a bill was passed by the city council designed to prevent some of the abuses that the landlord had practiced with impunity. The councilman who sponsored the new law referred to the house on Sixth Street to support his argument.

Nevertheless, the problems that remain far outweigh the accomplishments. A disappointing epilogue to the story is that in court, two months later, the tenants' case against the landlord was dismissed by the judge on a legal technicality. The judge ruled that because the electric company had removed the meters from the building it was impossible for the landlord to provide services.

Some of the tenants were relocated out of the neighborhood and some in housing almost as poor as that they had left. The organization that began to develop in the neighborhood has continued to grow, but it is a painstaking job. The fact that the poor have the strength to continue to struggle for better living conditions is something to wonder at and admire.

IMPLICATIONS FOR PRACTICE

Social work helping methods as currently classified are so inextricably interwoven in practice that it no longer seems valid to think of a generic practice as consisting of the application of casework, group work, or community organization skills as the nature of the problem demands. Nor does it seem feasible to adapt group methods for traditional casework problems or to use group work skills in community organiza-

tion or community organization method in casework. Such suggestions—when they appear in the literature—either reflect confusion or, what is worse, suggest that no clearcut method exists apart from the auspices that support it.

In this case it is a manifestation of a social problem—housing—that was the major point around which social services were organized. The social worker's major intellectual task was to select the points at which the agency could intervene in the problem and the appropriate methods to use. It seems abundantly clear that in order to select appropriate points of intervention the social worker need not only understand individual patterns of response, but the nature of the social conditions that are the context in which behavior occurs. As this case makes evident, the social system that might be called the "poverty system" is enduring and persistent. Its parts intermesh with precision and disturbing complementarity. Intentionally or not, a function is thereby maintained that produces severe social and economic deprivation. Certain groups profit enormously from the maintenance of this system, but larger groups suffer. Social welfare—and, in particular, its central profession, social work—must examine the part it plays in either maintaining or undermining this socially pernicious poverty system. It is important that the social work profession no longer regard social conditions as immutable and a social reality to be accommodated as service is provided to deprived persons with an ever increasing refinement of technique. Means should be developed whereby agencies can affect social problems more directly, especially through institutional (organizational) change.

The idea advanced by MFY is that the social worker should fulfill his professional function and agency responsibility by seeking a solution to social problems through institutional change rather than by focusing on individual problems in social functioning. This is not to say that individual expressions of a given social problem should be left unattended. On the contrary, this approach is predicated on the belief that individual problems in social functioning are to varying degrees both cause and effect. It rejects the notion that individuals are afflicted with social pathologies, holding, rather, that the same social environment that generates conformity makes payment by the deviance that emerges. As Nisbet points out ". . . socially prized arrangements and values in society can produce socially condemned results." [8] This should direct social work's attention to institutional arrangements and their consequences. This approach does not lose sight of the individual or group, since the social system is composed of various statuses, roles, and classes. It takes cognizance of the systemic relationship of the various parts of the social system, including the client. It recognizes that efforts to deal with one social problem frequently generate others with debilitating results.

Thus it is that such institutional arrangements as public assistance, state prisons, and state mental hospitals, or slum schools are regarded by many as social problems in their own right. The social problems of poverty, criminality, mental illness, and failure to learn that were to be solved or relieved remain, and the proposed solutions pose almost equally egregious problems.

This paper has presented a new approach to social work practice. The knowledge, values, attitudes, and skills were derived from a generalist approach to social work. Agencies that direct their energies to social problems by effecting institutional change will need professional workers whose skills cut across the broad spectrum of social work knowledge.

---

[8] Merton and Nisbet, *op. cit.*, p. 7.

BY HYMAN J. WEINER

Toward Techniques for Social Change

IT IS DIFFICULT, if not impossible, to read a social work publication or attend a conference where reference is not made to the need to "put the 'social' back into social work." The authors or speakers plead with the social worker to interest himself in social conditions affecting the client. Yet in spite of these many exhortations, relatively little concrete social action is evident. Why is this?

One must respond to the question on many levels. Herbert Bisno emphasizes the social work profession's quest for status and the consequent fear of "rocking the boat." [1] Lloyd Ohlin highlights the rapid rate of organizational change in the field as well as the conformity process built into social work practice.[2] The purpose of this paper is to identify still another dimension—the social worker's view of agency as a major obstacle in assuming social change functions—and to suggest an alternate view.

The basic assumption is that the social worker is being simultaneously bombarded with the need for his activity in the social change process and hampered by lack of opportunity to translate this conviction into concrete action. Subjective interest in altering a profession's direction is not enough; one must have the avenues and opportunities as well. Currently, a social worker may become active in his professional association or in his community as a citizen, but little possibility exists for him to integrate a social change role with his daily job. The contemporary call for social action is creating a new strain in our recent graduates, who leave school anxious to help individuals and also to "change the world"—only to find themselves doing so one client at a time. Cynicism flourishes with this disparity between aspiration and opportunity. This paper will attempt to show that by altering the "traditional" view of the agency, a number of paths should be revealed along which the social change role can become more of a reality.

To date a rather static approach to teaching of social agency characterizes both educational and field arenas. The implicit assumption is that the social agency is the "house that houses" the client-worker relationship. It serves to define the direction of the relationship as well as the social services given, but is more or less reduced to a background phenomenon. Emphasis on the need to "identify with agency" marks this point of view. Thus the tendency is to limit the social worker's understanding of the metamorphosis of agencies—how they change, and how social work is *more than* casework or group work method.

Another consideration is the fact that the interests of the social work profession and of any given agency may be identical, may not wholly coincide, or may actually conflict. Robert Vinter states the position well.

The profession has an existence that is both independent of and more inclu-

HYMAN J. WEINER, M.S.W., *is research instructor in rehabilitation medicine at the Albert Einstein College of Medicine and at Yeshiva School of Social Work, New York City.*

[1] Herbert Bisno, "How Social Will Social Work Be?" *Social Work*, Vol. 1, No. 2 (April 1956).

[2] Lloyd Ohlin, "Conformity in American Society Today," *Social Work*, Vol. 3, No. 2 (April 1958).

sive than agencies and services. Professionals are presumably dedicated to selfless service and the enhancement of their special competencies. They receive a more or less clear mandate from the public to use their skills in a given area of service and are ultimately accountable to the public for this mandate. Agencies are essentially instrumental means, rationally organized in the pursuit of specific goals. Although agencies and professionals function interdependently, they are different entities and have different interests.[3]

The inability to separate the interests of the profession from those of the agency leads to many complications in our field. Unfortunately, a number of schools of social work still tend to function as "vocational schools" for agencies rather than as free-wheeling, educational-professional institutions.

There are two important trends in agency development which make it all the more essential that we review our previous assumptions. First, agencies are increasingly assuming a multifunctional character. Second, they are increasing in size, degree of professionalization, and tendency toward bureaucracy. We will here attempt to focus theoretical material dealing with agency structure and social change on the following two questions:

1. How can we best appraise a social agency with a view toward social change possibilities? (What are the realistic targets within both the agency and the community it serves?)

2. What is the optimum role a social work department and social worker can play in the agency as a social change agent? (What considerations does each different target require? What are the leverage points?)

A public crisis in a large municipal hospital is presented as a case study in order to throw light on these questions. A crisis situation is used because it illuminates the anatomy of an agency as it struggles to restore its equilibrium.[4] Sykes believes that organization can be conceived as a series of crises held within limits—that routine may be simply an ideal around which actual behavior fluctuates.[5] We will examine here a situation in which a small incident in the life of a hospital touched off a crisis. In many ways it was an event in the normal life of the hospital coming at a time when public criticism was organized to exploit it. The etiology of the event, as well as the hospital's response to it, will be reviewed.

FOOD RIOT: A CASE STUDY

On a weekday afternoon in November, a leading newspaper carried the following headline and story:

FOOD RIOT AT CITY HOSPITAL

Fifteen patients in the new University Memorial Hospital rioted over the weekend because of bad food conditions. They said, "We are hungry and we just couldn't take it any longer." Near bedlam reigned for 10 minutes about 5:00 P.M. Sunday in the third-floor rehabilitation dining room, patients revealed. "They served us some kind of dark soup and eggs so old they were practically green. We just couldn't stand it." About fifteen dumped their trays. Food, dishes, and liquids flew all over the place. No one was hurt but an aide's uniform got splashed. Hospital Commissioner Williams, informed of the incident and complaints, said he would have "an immediate and complete investigation and report" of conditions there. On the surface the sleek $20,-000,000 institution for aged and ill who

[3] Robert Vinter, "Group Work: Perspectives and Prospects," in *Social Work with Groups 1959* (New York: National Association of Social Workers, 1959), pp. 128–129.

[4] In this discussion a hospital is viewed as one kind of agency. Others include prisons, treatment homes, and family counseling or group service agencies.

[5] Gresham Sykes, *The Society of Captives* (Princeton, N. J.: Princeton University Press, 1959), p. 109.

need help is a model of cleanliness and comfort. Its floors and walls fairly gleam. The most modern-style couches grace the lounges.

It was the younger ones who rebelled. "The older patients don't complain," they said. "They know they will never have any other place to go and they just accept it. But we are here to be rehabilitated, but everyone passes the buck. The doctors say, 'What can we do about it?' The hospital people say, 'Oh, that's good food, what is the matter with you?'" One claimed that the care was nearly as bad as the food, explaining, "My feet haven't been washed since July, because I can't do it myself . . . the P.N.'s [practical nurses] sit around and crochet. . . ."

The newspaper continued this story line as a special feature for the next five days. Special investigators and newspapermen descended upon the normally quiet hospital scene.

For a month prior to this incident, patients had been expressing discontent with the food. The young adults were the most vociferous objectors. At least twenty-four hours before the tray-throwing, the group worker and chief nurse were jokingly told by a few patients, "Something sure is gonna take place around here." At supper next day, at a prearranged signal, three patients threw their food-laden trays off the table (the news account exaggerates the number). At that precise moment another patient wheeled herself to the public telephone and called the newspaper.

The following day a group of doctors and medical administrators from the Department of Hospitals visited University Hospital. They quizzed the superintendent, her staff, and selected groups of patients. The dietary division felt the brunt of the main critical blows. They tried to shift the blame to the nursing division, whose responsibility it is to serve the food. A series of staff meetings were called on the rehabilitation service and the following recommendations were approved:

1. Physicians and therapists in the rehabilitation department will eat lunch on the wards with the patients on a rotating basis.

2. A ward administrative committee will be organized, under the leadership of the director of clinical service, to be concerned with ward living problems.

3. Consideration will be given the special needs of the young adult population on the ward.

4. There will be the establishment of a new administrative nursing position, to be responsible directly to the director of rehabilitation as well as to the director of nursing.

Simultaneously, representatives of University Hospital, the Department of Hospitals, and the medical school associated with the hospital agreed to: (1) carefully review the situation in the dietary division and consider ways of improving it (within three months the chief dietitian resigned and was replaced by a young and dynamic person); (2) meet regularly with the (then infant) patients' council and open lines of communication between patients and administration.

Two weeks following the food incident the director of rehabilitation invited reporters from the interested newspaper to visit the hospital. They were given a tour, met with patients and staff, and next day printed a story describing how the hospital was sincerely moving in a constructive direction to improve the situation.

REDISTRIBUTION OF POWER

Certain stresses and strains in the hospital set the stage for this crisis, and certain conflicts touched it off. A temporary breakdown of accommodation between patients and staff occurred. Description and location of the underlying as well as of the immediate stresses and strains are in order. A basic assumption of this paper is that the crisis marked a momentary redistribution of power both within and outside the hospital. It was especially during the week following the incident that the hospital structure and the interest groups directly involved [6] or simply interested in the hospital's functioning became visible as they maneuvered with each other.

University Hospital can be conceived as a point in social space where a number of interest groups converge (medical school, Department of Hospitals, and so forth). Each of these groups, in the process of pursuing its own interests, moves in and out of coalitions with others. Interest groups within the hospital interlock with groups in the larger medical beaucracy or in the community at large. Power is distributed unequally among these groups. *It is in redistributing this power that significant change takes place.* In order to redistribute this power, understanding of the relations of the interest groups to each other, both within and outside the hospital, is a necessary prerequisite.

The use of the concept *power* requires clarification. This idea is generally associated with authority and force, and carries negative connotations. It is widely understood to be "that which makes people do what they may not choose to do voluntarily." [7] This partial view obscures a deeper comprehension of the relation of power to the process of social change. Under the above formulation we think of it in static terms—"those who have it and those who don't." This is a definition of power at the extreme end of a continuum that ranges from influence to force.

Power is differentially distributed in any social system, *i.e.,* organization or institution. Each social system can be conceived to be in a state of tension, a sort of "tug-of-war" between the different holders of power. It is helpful to view power as energy, which flows in many directions and can be created as well as mobilized. As with energy, one cannot subject power itself to examination, but one can study its effects on the social system and even locate its source and basis of generation.

The view presented here is that power is generated by interest groups through the ability of the group to control or influence the necessary resources that enable the social system to survive.[8] Each interest group may have its own "version of order" or "policy" that it wishes to impose upon the total system. Each may control some aspect of the resources, but the groups that wield major control are those that seriously influence policy. Versions of policy can be modified, even greatly altered, when other interest groups enter into coalition and begin to mobilize their latent power. The crisis described above set in motion some of these groups, which mobilized enough power to introduce certain changes in the organization. Let us first examine the network of interest groups in some way implicated in the functioning of University Hospital (see diagram on next page).

FEATURES THAT PRODUCE STRAINS

The diagram reveals at least three significant structural features serving to produce basic strains in the system: (1) nonconcentration of power, (2) departmental autonomy, and (3) informal power structure.

---

[6] Lloyd Ohlin states that "the term 'interest' is used to denote a line of current or future activity in which a person or group has invested action, resources and expectations." *See* "Interest Group Conflict and Correctional Objectives" in *Theoretical Studies of the Prison* (New York: Social Science Research Council, 1960), p. 111. The writer expresses his appreciation to Lloyd Ohlin for the fundamental ideas pertaining to interest group theory used in this paper.

[7] Elaine and John Cummings, "The Locus of Power in a Large Mental Hospital," *Psychiatry,* Vol. 19, No. 4 (November 1956), p. 362.

[8] For an interesting discussion in this vein *see* Robert Lynd, "Power in American Society as Resource and Problem," in Arthur Kornhauser, ed., *Problems of Power in American Democracy* (Detroit, Mich.: Wayne State University Press, 1956), pp. 36–38. Emphasis on the redistribution of power does not imply that the total amount of power in the social system remains fixed. The range of interest groups involved affects the amount of power generated, as well as its redistribution.

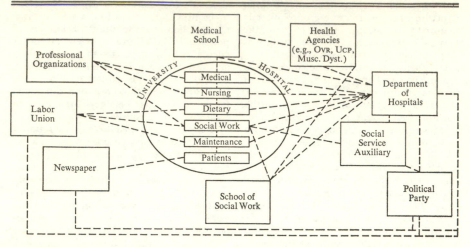

Nonconcentration of power. As stated above, power is unequally distributed through this hospital social system, and there exists no monopoly in any single group. The Department of Hospitals actually derives its power from responding to a multitude of interest groups, some of which are in sharp disagreement with each other. This is a common feature in the *public* large-scale organization in which policy is more visible to public scrutiny and particularly sensitive to open criticism. The nonconcentration of power encourages policy formation at a *least-common-denominator level,* which may not please but at least will not antagonize too many interest groups in this loose coalition. Basic patient need coverage—medical care, food, living facilities—becomes the level of service aimed for. A custodial rather than a therapeutic philosophy emerges and flourishes in this situation. (A therapeutic philosophy of care raises controversial questions of budget, nature of the case load, and eventually the need to institute far-reaching changes. This would require a clear mandate to the hospital administration, fully supported by enough power in the Department of Hospitals willing to risk alienation of certain interest groups.) Organizational maintenance at the least-common-denominator level of care becomes the hospital goal, and power is diffused through the total social system.

Departmental autonomy. The diagram shows that each department in the hospital—medical, nursing, and so on—has its counterpart in the Department of Hospitals. University Hospital tends to function as a combination of autonomous divisions co-ordinated by a superintendent. Thus a situation of dual authority exists. The administrative authority of the hospital superintendent tends to be undercut in this situation. The boundary of this bureaucracy is actually not University Hospital but the Department of Hospitals. Professional and departmental allegiances flourish, rather than a common focus on problems of patients in the hospital. In part, this explains why the chief dietitian became the central object of attack in the crisis rather than the hospital superintendent. Accountability travels in a horizontal rather than a vertical direction.

258

Informal power structure. As a result of the above two features (nonconcentration of power and departmental autonomy), the need arises for informal accommodations in a vertical direction between departments. A continual process of *trading in power* occurs, and an informal power structure evolves. This informal system may or may not be in harmony with the ascribed power dictated through the formal bureaucratic structure. At University Hospital this situation can be illustrated as follows from the most to the least power. The numbers signify ranking of ascribed and actual power, and do not have any numerical significance.

Groups [9]	Ascribed Power	Actual Power
Medical	6	4
Nursing	5	6
Social work	4	3
Dietary	3	5
Maintenance	2	3
Patients	1	1

As can be seen, medical authority has been abrogated. The medical school, responsible for medical care at University Hospital, is primarily interested in teaching and research. Its view of a physician's responsibilities does not include administrative control over medical and social care, and by default yields to the nursing division for supervision of these functions. More power accrues to the dietary division than is called for in the formal structure, as a result of the sensitivity of the social system to public criticism of poor food. The need for supplies and repairs in an economically impoverished institution permits the steward, carpenter, and store clerk to wield equal power with social workers. Staff expectations of each other's behavior

---

[9] The Rehabilitation Service at University Hospital functions administratively as a department and encompasses many medical and therapeutic professions. Actually it is the major power in the hospital, but this power is delegated by the medical school rather than as a department in the hospital hierarchy.

are shaped under the impact of a social structure which permits the accumulation of power to be based on access to needed resources rather than professional skill.

PRECIPITATING CIRCUMSTANCES

The above three features result in basic strains on the organization which set the stage for the crisis. In addition to the poor food situation, we shall consider two immediate circumstances that resulted in the food incident. They are (1) succession (replacement of one medical superintendent by another six months prior to crisis), and (2) administrative "buck-passing."

Succession. Six months earlier a well-liked, somewhat authoritarian but patient-centered superintendent had resigned and was replaced by a patient-centered but passive administrator. In the absence of aggressive and affirmative administration at University Hospital, the three basic strains began to assert themselves. These strains exist normally only as tendencies, which may be affected and even neutralized by unusually competent administration, in which informal ties develop and staff of all departments voluntarily accepts administrative leadership. The transition from assertive to passive leadership created a situation where petty nursing tyrants on some wards reasserted their power, and the physicians in turn became preoccupied with teaching and research. Within the bounds of bureaucratic role designations, paternalism became noticeable in each department.

Administrative buck-passing. One of the patients in the newspaper story complained, "Everyone passes the buck." The patients do not know *who has the power*. Only certain lines of authority are evident to them—*i.e.*, the physician okays discharge and weekend passes, but they are unclear about who takes responsibility for ward living problems. The patients run directly into a departmental autonomy situation in which the nurse passes responsibility to the doctor, the doctor to the administrator, and around it goes. Occasionally, group meetings are organized for patients to voice their dissatisfaction and offer recommendations, but administrative follow-through is lacking. In addition to the departmental autonomy described above, another dual authority problem remains.[10] Power is ascribed to each department in the hospital hierarchy, but any physician who so chooses may exercise authority outside this hierarchical scheme. At University Hospital this is done only in regard to individual patients and not in relation to the ward as a whole. The philosophy of treatment does not attach much significance to the ward as a living unit. It is viewed as a backdrop phenomenon in which the patient resides between therapy periods. As a result, the physician avoids taking any responsibility for ward living, and power in turn reverts to the nurse. In this buck-passing routine even the nurse is unable to follow through effectively, for she is involved in a complex network of accountability systems. The dietitian and the maintenance man, in given situations, may be in a better position to guarantee follow-up in their respective areas than the nurse, for they control needed resources.

These basic strains and immediate circumstances in the University Hospital social system generated the "incident," but the readiness of a public audience is necessary if the incident is to become a crisis. The Department of Hospitals had been under periodic attack by the city newspaper that decided to feature the food situation. This newspaper had been critical of the city administration during the previous year. It supported the mayor, but most reluctantly. When a middle-aged patient, formerly a professional (thus considered reliable), called them, they

jumped at the opportunity to attack the city administration. The Department of Hospitals publicly replied that it would investigate and immediately examined the University Hospital administration as well as its dietary department and counterpart in the Department of Hospitals. The health agencies that were in part subsidizing programs of the medical school began to urge that the situation at University Hospital be immediately improved. The medical school, in turn, began to hammer at the Department of Hospitals. Once public pressure began to mount, the labor union which had recently organized six hundred of the eighteen hundred employees revealed that employees as well as patients were the scapegoats. There was an absence of any organized coalition at the outset, but within three days two loose coalitions could be identified. The Department of Hospitals and the medical school constituted one, while the newspaper, two health agencies in the city, the labor union, and the school of social work comprised the other. These two coalitions reflected different policies. The first favored a custodial approach, the second a shift to more active treatment.

IMPLICATIONS FOR SOCIAL WORK

This case study is not submitted as a social work, or social change, success story. The purpose is rather to suggest a framework within which to view the social institution defined broadly as "agency." An agency is seen as a network of interlocking interest groups. The interests of the agency and of the social work profession are not necessarily identical. Policy formation is regarded as the resultant of power distributed unequally throughout each agency's network of interest groups.

Lydia Rapoport in a recent issue of *Social Service Review* makes the following statement: "Social workers, therefore, have to maintain a dual identification and loyalty, both to the agency and to the profes-

---

[10] *See* Harvey Smith, "Two Lines of Authority: The Hospital's Dilemma" in E. Gartly Jaco, ed., *Patients, Physicians and Illness* (Glencoe, Ill.: The Free Press, 1958).

sional body, with *the primary tie being to the agency* [emphasis supplied]." [11] This assertion that the social worker's primary identification belongs to the agency serves as a serious obstacle, limiting social change possibilities within both the agency and the larger community it serves. It does so by viewing agency policy as having monolithic unity. It does not take into consideration different versions of policy held by various interest groups. This holds true in social work agencies as well as in settings where social work is one among a number of disciplines. We do not suggest that a social work department is capable independently of seriously changing large bureaucratic settings or communities, but rather that significant inroads can be made through the mobilization of interest groups and subsequent generation of power.

In this case study, the social work department did not seek to set in motion the interest groups related to it or sympathetic to its position during the crisis period. There was a reservoir of at least five such groups, including (1) a school of social work, (2) the professional social work organization, (3) the social service auxiliary, (4) the labor union representing social workers, and (5) the social service department in the Department of Hospitals. A coalition among some of these groups might have enabled the social work department to increase its power as a social change force. Throughout the crisis period the social work department refused to "placate" the patients. The social workers were unable to accomplish as much as they would have liked—that is, they were able to counteract the view that individual "trouble-makers" among the patients constituted the core problem and to help establish medical authority in ward living, but little more. A more ambitious social change target could have been considered within a coalition approach: that of altering the custodial approach to treatment in favor of a more therapeutic one. The psychologists, therapists, and certain sections of the medical staff may well have been ready to enter such a coalition.

LEVERAGE POINTS

It is not enough to identify the existence of power relations if we wish to alter them. One must provide handles or leverage points which can help us to effect their rearrangement. C. Wright Mills' *The Power Elite* [12] dramatically describes our national network of power and interest groups but leaves one with the unanswered question, "What can we do about it?" It is interesting to note that *The Dynamics of Planned Change* is being snapped up in our profession, for, though less dramatic, it does provide a way of assessing a situation with suggestions for active intervention.[13]

In reconceptualizing our view of agency it is equally important to reconsider certain internal features characteristic of social work functioning. These include (1) extension of the diagnostic process, (2) alterations in the clinical role model, and (3) new division of labor within a social work department.

Diagnostic process. The diagnostic process should be extended to include problems transcending individual clients, either within the agency or in the community. This implies that the term "client" or "unit of service" may not be identical with an individual. A social change target would become the object of systematic social work intervention. The crisis situation was submitted as a diagnostic statement involving the total hospital as the actual client or unit of service. The call for extension of the diagnostic process refers to the application of a systematic problem-solving procedure. Unfortunately, there is a decided absence of social science theory in the area

---

[11] Lydia Rapoport, "In Defense of Social Work," *Social Service Review*, Vol. 34, No. 1 (March 1960), p. 71.

[12] New York: Oxford University Press, 1956.

[13] Ronald Lippitt, Jeanne Watson, and Bruce Westley, *The Dynamics of Planned Change* (New York: Harcourt, Brace & Company, 1958).

of social change. As was true in social work, earlier social scientists defined their core role in connection with the social problems of the day. Currently most social science theory avoids controversial questions, and when it does address itself to the change process it is with an interest in maintaining equilibrium. It is particularly in this area that the combined efforts of social work and social science can probably make their most significant contribution. In any given period of professional endeavor, a social work department could enumerate a number of social change targets, each calling for a different plan of intervention. The diagnostic procedure would seek to identify specific "treatment" approaches.

Clinical role model. Currently social work departments shape their clinical model around method competence. Thus medical social work is defined as casework in a medical setting, or the group worker in a residential treatment setting makes his claim to social work identity via the application of group skills. But social work is more than competence in any single method. Sound assessment of a social problem cannot be made effectively if the social worker is wedded to a given method diagnostically. He then tends to define each problem in terms of his capacity to deal with it. It is interesting to note how often caseworkers define agency and community problems in terms of the personality of the administrator or community leader.[14] The group worker characteristically reduces these problems to group interaction or the need for democratic processes. The call is not for treatment competence on individual, group, and community levels, but for the ability to *appraise* a given problem within this threefold perspective—though this would suggest, certainly, that more social workers should become adept in group and community processes in a "treatment" role.

In emphasizing the need for social action the cry "We are too oriented to technique and methodology!" is often heard, implying that social change content thus is abandoned. This is a misleading assertion, for one cannot separate technique from content. It is not that we have been too technique-oriented, but rather that the content has been the individual client, with emphasis on intrapsychic phenomena. Actually we are not technical enough in the social change arena, and unless we develop methodology in this content area there will be little action. The new clinical model should include the social change component. This development cannot come about as long as social work defines its core contributions as casework, group work, or community organization method.

Division of labor. In most situations the supervisor or administrator is able to play a more active role in social change matters than the staff social worker. The practitioner's contribution is generally reduced to one of communicating the problem to his supervisor, who in turn sends it up the hierarchy. A new division of labor is in order if the social change component is to be added to the social work role model. Current developments in the area of supervision have created a fertile field for this shift of functions. A more independent worker is required to fulfill social action expectations. *A total departmental view of social change is required.* Staff meetings may be used to appraise social problems, followed by a division of labor necessary for particular problems. The nature of the social change target may require assignments not consistent with a division of labor based upon method, or supervisory responsibility.

---

14 Even when a social worker happens to be in the role of administrator, he is not a free agent. He is functioning in the role of mediator among interest groups, and as representative of the board or of the dominant groups, not *necessarily* his group of origin: the social work profession.

CONCLUSION

Separation of the interests of the agency from those of the profession is suggested in this paper as one conceptual scheme that may offer new social change opportunities to social workers. A case study was used in order to elevate social change considerations to the same diagnostic and intervention significance as is necessary to help individual clients. The time for social change theory to address itself to practice principles is now. It is doubtful whether exhortations produce anything more than guilt, and subsequent anxiety. If social change technique is to be an integral part of social work skill, it is primarily the social workers who will have to do it. Our field and the social problems it deals with are currently attracting the interest of social scientists, but we cannot look to social science research teams to provide us with immediate answers. These researchers are caught in the same interest group arrangement as the social workers.[15] It is a rare social agency that encourages a research team to engage in studying controversial questions. Only when our profession is represented by a sound and powerful profession organization, and supported by policies of schools of social work less responsive to agency dictates, will social workers be able to implement a social change role. The less conservative political climate, recent demands for complete racial integration, and interest in extending health and welfare services have set the stage for new social change possibilities. It is up to the social work profession to take advantage of this positive objective situation and translate words into action. This paper has attempted to identify some of the roadblocks interfering with such a translation.

---

[15] Arthur Kornhauser, "Power Relationships and the Role of the Social Scientist," in Kornhauser, ed., *Problems of Power in American Democracy, op. cit.* This is a particularly good discussion of the problem. The author inquires (p. 191) "What parts of society want what types of knowledge, to be used by whom, toward what ends? The point of the question is sometimes put to us in the sharper and more cynical form: 'Whose social scientist are you?'"

BY GEORGE A. BRAGER AND VALERIE JORRIN

Bargaining: A Method in Community Change

■ Community change efforts entail the use of bargaining. This paper explores three factors that determine the nature and outcome of a bargaining process: (1) the power resources of the bargainers, (2) the formulation of issues, and (3) skill in the use of strategy. The paper also reviews the respective roles of the social worker and the community group in the bargaining transaction. ■

THE EFFORTS OF social workers to encourage environmental change and their advocacy on behalf of the disenfranchised poor require knowledge of bargaining and skill in using it. Bargaining is a process that takes place in all forms of human interaction, and it is practiced by all social workers in all settings. This paper deals specifically with bargaining as it relates to change-oriented community organization with an impoverished clientele, but much of its content is generic to other types of social work practice.

Bargaining, as the authors use the term, refers to a process between two parties, the intent of which is to reach an accommodation regarding a disputed issue. Bargaining may be serious or spurious.[1] In this paper, the authors are concerned only with bargaining in good faith, which implies that each party would rather concede something to the other than fail to reach agreement at

all. The resultant bargain is often unstable. Since bargaining requires compromise, neither party may be satisfied and the peace will be an uneasy one.[2]

Bargaining may be explicit or implicit. Explicit bargaining means negotiations, i.e., the parties engage in direct trading and in offering demands, arguments, and concessions. Implicit bargaining entails "positioning." It may occur without direct communication between the parties, as, for example, when a group makes a public attack on an adversary in order to obtain a future concession. A group's development of a

[1] Spurious bargaining occurs when the objective is to prevent actual bargaining from taking place. As is often the case in competitive or conflictual interaction, form may be used to obscure function. Bargaining may be promoted by both sides to obfuscate their unwillingness to accommodate or trade, as much as to obtain agreement. For officials, it may constitute a delaying tactic. For neighborhood groups, it may be a means of exposing venality or intractability of officialdom.

[2] One Community Action Program, for example, negotiated a teacher–home visiting program with the public schools in exchange for a guidance counseling package in which only the schools were interested. The CAP then devoted its efforts to shaping the guidance program in directions of interest to it, while the schools busily subverted the home visiting effort. See George A. Brager, "Effecting Organizational Change Through a Demonstration Project: The Case of the Schools," in Brager and Francis P. Purcell, eds., *Community Action Against Poverty* (New Haven, Conn.: College and University Press, 1967), pp. 116–117.

GEORGE A. BRAGER, Ph.D., *is Professor of Social Work, Columbia University School of Social Work, New York, New York.* VALERIE JORRIN, MSW, *is Director of Special Community Programs, New York City Housing and Development Administration, New York, New York. This paper was prepared as part of the Community Organization Curriculum Development Project conducted by the Columbia University School of Social Work with the support of the Office of Juvenile Delinquency and Youth Crime, U.S. Department of Health, Education, and Welfare, Washington, D.C.*

Reprinted with permission of the National Association of Social Workers, from SOCIAL WORK, Vol. 14, No. 4 (October 1969), pp. 73-83.

"line" for purposes of maneuvering constitutes implicit bargaining.

The shape and outcome of a bargaining process are determined by a number of factors, three of which will be discussed in this paper: (1) the power resources of the bargainers, (2) the formulation of issues, and (3) skill in the use of strategy. The authors will conclude by commenting on the respective roles of the social worker and the inexperienced community group.

POWER RESOURCES OF THE BARGAINERS

Differences in perspective between institutional officials and community groups are inevitable. Whatever their social goals, officials heed the requirements of administrative efficiency and organizational maintenance. Community groups, on the other hand, are more apt to be concerned about the consequences of institutional policy for people. The superior power of the officials in this contest is evident. They are, in large part, in control of the decisions at issue, while the community groups are clamoring at the gates. The officials have the advantage of greater knowledge; they can share information differentially or shield their operations from public scrutiny.[3] They are better organized and command vastly superior resources. Yet for bargaining to occur at all, there must be some parity or some appearance of parity between the parties.

Therefore, community groups often resort to dramatic action before bargaining can begin. This prenegotiation phase serves to establish them as a seriously contending party by demonstrating their ability to invoke sanctions. Bargaining that eventuates from public confrontation between community groups and officials carries the implicit or explicit threat of further contest should an impasse develop. Community groups

[3] The importance of knowing the system as a source of power is exemplified by the refusal of welfare officials to allow welfare client groups access to the regulations of their department, although they do make such information available to social agencies.

are therefore often involved in a bargaining process that follows a pattern of alternating public confrontation and private discussion.

The ability of neighborhood groups to sustain public demonstrations depends in large measure on the nature of the issue and the structure of the group. Public confrontation, as program activity, may promote membership involvement and provide the social glue necessary for further encounters. But it also may exhaust the group or produce internal conflict. However, it is a major source of community influence. Threats of embarrassing the officials or of causing disruption are levers that, when pressed, may encourage institutional responsiveness.

Identifying these points of influence is a prime task of bargaining. Negotiators must constantly examine their own reactions and responses in light of what they have to offer that their adversaries want or what they can inflict that the latter wish to avoid. To miscalculate by underestimating one's potency is to risk settling for less than one may otherwise earn. To miscalculate by overestimating can lead to defeat and group disarray.

LEVERAGE POINTS

The potential damage it can do to an institution's public image is an important leverage point for a group whose case has strong public appeal. Another is the response the group can elicit from its adversary's superordinates or other persons or groups whose opinions are important to organizational leaders. In dealing with a local district school system, for example, a community group may be able to exploit the officials' concern regarding the reaction of the board of education (since open conflict subjects the local officials to board criticism about their handling of the conflict, even when they agree on the issue in contention). Or the community group may find leverage in the educators' apprehensions about the response of the city's elected officials.

A threat of appeal need never be made explicit. Its potency as a leverage point is most likely to rest in the officials' awareness that the community group understands their vulnerability and is prepared to act on this understanding, if necessary. A sentence in passing may be enough to accomplish this end.

Another leverage point may be found in the laws or regulations that guide the operations of public organizations. If these are violated in practice, the organization may be especially vulnerable. When laws are evaded rather than directly violated, action to compel their widespread application causes dislocation or administrative inconvenience, which is another point of leverage. It has been noted, for example, that welfare officers try to avoid fair hearing procedures. A fair hearing costs them more in time, money, and manpower than it costs contending welfare rights groups and, in addition, may be regarded as evidence of their inhumane application of welfare provisions.[4]

A leverage point often overlooked in bargaining is the self-image of a group of officials. If they are professionals, internalized professional norms may require that they see themselves as client focused. However much their actual practice may violate a client orientation, there is likely to be some tension between this self-standard and their willingness to pursue restrictive organizational policy. Appeals to their personal or professional sense of justice may therefore be effective. A reasonable approach, which reaches out to the positive features in officials and assumes their good faith, may encourage their acquiescence. It offers them the good feeling of making voluntary concessions as a result of their own righteousness or the merit of a case. Reasonableness may be effective when officials and groups share social goals. An appeal to the merits of the case by community bargainers can sometimes maximize the divisiveness among their adversaries as well and strengthen the hand of their supporters within the institution.

Strength at the bargaining table rests with the party who is better able to afford protracted negotiation, bear the unpleasantness, and muster the required energy. This ability, in turn, is influenced by the relative desire for or resistance to the change, as well as the respective cohesiveness of the parties. The greater a contender's relative capacity to fight, the greater his power at the bargaining table. Thus negotiators try to convey an inflated impression of their willingness to do battle.

Tests of endurance pose a serious trial for neighborhood groups. Their fluidity is in sharp contrast to the solidity of a bureaucratic organization. Many such groups come together for a single purpose, impelled by a strong sense of immediacy; they generally have not developed the informal norms necessary to mediate internal disputes. In the face of bureaucratic resistance and delay, their resolve may wear thin.

Intensely committed and cohesive groups are likely to be further galvanized by official resistance, however, because the intransigence of officials provokes increased hostility. In this sense, to be headstrong and militant in the face of overwhelming odds is a source of power. The very weakness of people who have nothing to lose may constitute a significant source of strength.[5] The less one risks, the greater one's resolve for continued battle is likely to be.

FORMULATING DEMANDS

Formulating demands for a bargaining encounter is a central aspect of bargaining strategy. It has been suggested that skill in bargaining may be the ability "to set the

---

[4] Ted Seaver, "The Care and Feeding of Southern Welfare Departments," (Washington, D.C.: Poverty/Rights Action Center, 1966), p. 1. (Mimeographed.)

[5] Industrial relations specialists make this point as well, noting that the weakest employers are inevitably the strongest labor bargainers. *See* Robert H. Hoxie, *Trade Unionism in the United States* (New York: D. Appleton & Co., 1920), p. 255.

stage in such a way as to give prominence to some particular outcome that would be favorable." [6] In this view, the outcome of bargaining may be determined by the way in which the situation is defined rather than by the merits of the case or the pressures applied during bargaining.

How extensive or extreme should demands be? The ritual form of labor-management bargaining is suggestive in this regard. The union offers an extensive and grandiose series of demands that neither it nor management takes seriously. The company, in turn, makes a niggardly counter-offer that is also not serious. So common a ritual must have functional uses; the following are three such uses.

Making extreme demands appears to lessen the disadvantage inherent in being the initiator. The party that originates a proposal reveals information about its eagerness for settlement and in so doing risks divulging too much too soon. The practice of making unrealistic demands offsets this disadvantage, since such demands can hardly be taken as a proposal at all. Management, which then becomes the de facto initiator, responds in kind.

Starting at polar points also allows the parties to test points of "give" and "firmness" in each other's positions. As in foreign diplomatic negotiations as well as labor-management disputes, what is *not* said may be as important as what *is* said. While considerations of strategy may require that each partner at first opposes all offers put forth by the other, each will voice greater objection to some provisions than to others. In effect, testing is taking place.

Furthermore, *demands define the limits of trading*. Extreme demands, then, "up the ante," so that the ultimate compromise may be more advantageous than the proposer anticipated, while it appears to be a victory to the other party.

These points about the functions of extensive and extreme demands can also be applied to negotiations between community groups and officials as well as to labor-management bargaining. However, the differences in structure between a community group and the parties in formal collective bargaining (e.g., the often ad hoc and non-institutional character of community bargaining, the inexperience of the participants, and the public nature of the transaction) require that community bargainers take other factors into account. To erect a smoke screen of extensive nonessential demands may obscure the group's own understanding of its purpose and consequently risk a loss of focus on essentials. Unless there are special circumstances, probably no more than one or two basic demands should be presented. These might be embellished with related and subsidiary items for trading purposes, but, in that case, priorities should be clearly (if secretly) delineated by the neighborhood group or its negotiating team.

Since community bargaining is not so legitimate a practice as collective bargaining, extreme demands often unnecessarily harden official resistance to any bargaining at all. This is an important consideration for community groups that, because of their weak power resources, cannot otherwise compel responsiveness. A more critical consideration, however, may be the effect of extremist demands on the public case of community groups. Those who embark on potentially public controversies must weigh the persuasiveness of their arguments, self-consciously and with minimal self-deception. Whether important others can be brought to the bargaining table as silent partners determines the success of some transactions. Particularly for groups with limited resources, a public case and public support may be the major access to influencing officials.

AUDIENCES

A demand will seem extreme or not, depending on its audience. Experiments in

---

[6] Thomas C. Shelling, *The Strategy of Conflict* (Cambridge, Mass.: Harvard University Press, 1963), p. 68.

social psychology indicate that one-sided communications—those which omit arguments in support of an opposing viewpoint—are most effective with audiences predisposed to agreement. Two-sided communications are more convincing to those with less favorable initial attitudes. The educational level of the audience is an additional factor. Two-sided arguments, which are less extreme by definition, are more effective with better educated audiences, regardless of their initial attitudes; one-sided arguments are overwhelmingly more effective for those with less education who are more predisposed to agree.[7]

Much, then, depends on the audience to which an appeal is directed. If the organizer and the community group wish to strengthen the resolve of their low-income constituency or expand support within the low-income community, extreme demands are likely to be effective because of the probable receptivity of low-income persons to self-interest arguments, as well as their limited educational attainment. If, however, the appeal is to a broader middle-class public, which is more educated and less convinced about the injustices of impoverishment, a moderate two-sided argument will probably have greater short-term impact.[8]

The foregoing relates to the persuasiveness of extreme demands. There are, however, other considerations that may become important. Extreme demands may convey a sense of strength to one's adversary. They may be used to arouse fear and threaten disruption.

CONTENT OF DEMANDS

What about the content of demands? Should low-income community action groups limit themselves to identification of problems, or should their demands include program remedies as well? Is it sufficient, for example, for them to dramatize the existence of decayed slum housing and its consequences for poor people, or should the group also propose solutions? If they should do both, how specific and how comprehensive should the solutions be? Proposals might logically run the gamut from altering the tax structure to adding more building inspectors.

Arguments can be advanced on both sides of the question. Community groups that limit themselves to identifying problems are less likely to be deflected from a focus on change-oriented action. Program development activities tend to absorb time, energy, and attention that might otherwise be devoted to building support or intensifying pressure. Furthermore, when a group suggests remedies, it is forced into a defensive posture, a considerably weaker situation from which to argue than a concentrated attack on things as they are. That program development by community groups works at least in part to their detriment is suggested by the frequency with which community officials counsel such activity in the name of group responsibility. But the real responsibility for solving housing problems rests with housing officials and others rather than with community groups, as the officials themselves would quickly point out under other circumstances.

On the other hand, a group that engages in detailed planning demonstrates its commitment and seriousness of purpose. It says, in effect, that it intends to remain "in the ball game," that its attention will not easily be diverted. If its plans indicate

---

[7] Edward E. Jones and Harold B. Gerard, *Foundations of Social Psychology* (New York: John Wiley & Sons, 1967), pp. 448–449.

[8] Sometimes extreme demands are effective even with a middle-class public, however. This is so when the intent is long-range change, rather than an immediate settlement. An idea is extreme or moderate in relation to competing notions and the general ideological climate. Over an extended period, therefore, extreme demands may appear to be less radical as they become more familiar. Their presence in the marketplace of ideas may also serve the important function of making other, relatively radical notions seem mild in comparison. For example, in the movement of blacks for social justice, the ideas of Martin Luther King, sweeping and absolute in and of themselves, seemed moderate to the white middle class in comparison to the positions of some other black leaders.

knowledge of the housing, welfare, or educational systems, they serve notice that the community group cannot easily be put off or deceived. Furthermore, if the long-range intent of the group is to play a continuing role in decision-making, program planning moves it in that direction. The knowledge acquired in planning is necessary for consistent involvement in decision-making.

The interest and capacity of the community group to a great extent determine whether its demands should emphasize only identification of problems or should also include program solutions. For example, a mothers' group was concerned about the quality of their children's education in a slum school. The group, composed of a core of ten Puerto Pican women with perhaps fifty others who could be called on to participate in specific events, did not have the experience or sophistication to map a course through the shoals of educational program and policy. Nor was this an area of its concern. It knew at first hand, however, the lack of respect with which its members and their children were treated and limited its demands to this problem.[9] Had the organizer encouraged the members to devote attention to wider ranging educational issues at that point in the group's life, the result might have been the dissolution of the group or its transformation from an action to a study focus.

Timing is a further consideration. Demands may be escalated in both intensity and significance as groups gain experience and success. The campaign for minimum clothing standards by welfare rights groups is a case in point. Such a demand is effective because it goes to a basic need, is tangible and visible, and holds out the possibility of immediate relief to those who participate in the bargaining transaction. As the leaders and members of stable welfare clients' groups gain experience and are successful with more limited demands, it may be expected that their demands will increase in scope and complexity.

OTHER BARGAINING STRATEGIES

Bargaining is an art, say Bakke and Kerr, "composed of almost equal parts of bluffing and bulldozing."[10] A union statement describes it more delicately as a blend of "diplomacy, reason, and power."[11] But however euphemistic the definition, it is plain that some bargaining strategies strain the limits of the accepted values and norms of professional social work.[12]

Awareness and sensitive handling of the dialectics of the bargaining session constitute a major aspect of bargaining skill. One's best move is dependent on the adversary's move, as his in turn is dependent upon one's own. Consideration of strategic action cannot be divorced from consideration of the countermoves it will evoke. One must also anticipate what options for further action will be available to the group following a countermove, so that the countermove may be encouraged or avoided by one's own activity. In essence, one must analyze the opponent's goals and predict his moves, while at the same time revealing as little as possible of one's own goals and moves.

Schelling notes that such analysis is

. . . the art of looking at the problem from the other person's point of view, identifying his opportunities and his interests, an art that has traditionally been practiced by diplomats, lawyers, and chess players.[13]

[9] "I know it's not popular to say this," a school principal told the group, "but you're culturally deprived. You hardly understand what I'm saying, so how can you expect your children to understand the teachers?" Case record, Mobilization For Youth, New York, New York, February 1964.

[10] E. Wight Bakke and Clark Kerr, *Unions, Management and the Public* (New York: Harcourt, Brace & Co., 1948), p. 353.

[11] *Handbook of Trade Union Methods* (New York: International Ladies' Garment Workers' Union, 1937), p. 62.

[12] The authors make reference to the value issue to show that they are not unmindful of it. However, it will not be dealt with in this paper. For a discussion of the value issues involved in advocating the interests of the poor, *see* George A. Brager, "Advocacy and Political Behavior," *Social Work*, Vol. 13, No. 2 (April 1968), pp. 5–15.

[13] T. C. Schelling, "Strategic Analysis and Social

Community bargainers might now be added to this list. The art of looking at a problem from another's point of view requires learning as much about that person as possible—his judgments and prejudices, his role and its requirements, and the other persons and groups to whom he is responsive.

A search for goal convergence between the parties is part of all bargaining processes. Organizers and groups need to argue their demands, not only in regard to the merits of the case, but also in the context of their adversary's interests. Awareness of the other's goals and the political factors that determine his responses aids in identifying points of commonness. Demands then may be revised and alternative formulas developed, to make the community group's purposes more palatable in actuality or appearance.

THREATS

A major condition of bargaining strategy is the effective regulation of threat. Too often, the intensity and mode of expression of a threat owe more to the style of the community group and its organizer than to the specifics of the situation. Conversely, the threat may be overcautious, bound by the constraints of a sponsoring agency. Threats that are disproportionate to an issue or its strategic requirements are unlikely to be believed. Furthermore, they allow little room for escalation as the bargaining process continues. When an adversary is predisposed to concession, too strong a threat may harden resistance.

Threats are often more effective than carrying them out would be. This point is illustrated by the experience of a group of slum tenants who wished to force their landlord to make repairs. Without informing the landlord, the group scheduled a picket line demonstration at his suburban home. Wiser persons advised the group that the actual demonstration should be postponed, so that news of its imminence might be "leaked" to the landlord. The threat succeeded in bringing the landlord to the bargaining table and ultimately in persuading him to perform the repairs. The anticipation of embarrassment before his neighbors was the influencing factor, whereas the demonstration, by accomplishing the embarrassment, would have provided little incentive for settlement. If the threat had not worked, the group would have had to hold the demonstration in order to protect its credibility. But the single action would probably have been ineffective. An ongoing series of actions that raised the level of embarrassment would then have been required.

Threats, to be effective, must be credible. An insufficient but necessary condition for maximizing a threat's credibility is the intention of carrying it out. Groups that cannot do so risk permanent loss of status as contenders. However ferocious their growl, they may henceforth be viewed as paper tigers. A demonstrated readiness to act or implement a threat, such as involvement in the planning required for its implementation, will make it somewhat more convincing.

Credibility is increased when the threat seems to have been conveyed unintentionally. Communications that are overheard are more persuasive than those obviously intended for the listener.[14] There are a number of ways of being "overheard." A popular technique involves the use of a disinterested third party who reports supposedly confidential material. In the bargaining between community groups and organizational officials, the group may have allies within or related to the organization who can serve as conveyers of the threat.

A significant aspect of the credibility of a threat is the cost of fulfilling it. If to act on a threat would require greater re-

Problems," *Social Problems,* Vol. 12, No. 4 (Spring 1965), p. 370.

[14] For experimental evidence, *see* E. Walster and Leon Festinger, "The Effectiveness of Overheard Persuasive Communications," *Journal of Abnormal and Social Psychology,* Vol. 65 (1962), pp. 395–402.

sources than the community group seems to have or if to do so could cause the group great pain or damage, the threat is not likely to be believed. In these and other instances, the following are two ways in which plausibility may be increased.

Irrevocable commitments. Schelling refers to the ability to "bind oneself," i.e., to make so firm a commitment that retraction would be virtually impossible.[15] The irrevocable commitment may relate either to a threatened action in the event of official intransigence or to the terms under negotiation. A dramatic example was the position taken by a group of railroad workers striking for better wages, who chained themselves to the tracks in order to halt railroad operations. That they threw away the keys so they could not escape even if they wished to was the critical action.[16] This is a more literal example of binding oneself than is ordinarily available, of course, but there is a range of actions that can make the commitment of a group to a fixed position difficult to retract and, therefore, more persuasive to its adversary. It is for this reason, among others, that leaders stir the passions of their constituency and thereby limit their own opportunity for flexibility. When reputation is clearly important to a person or group, public commitment to take a threatened action puts one's reputation on the line and thus makes the threat more credible.

Irrationality. Threats of action that would cause pain or damage to the threateners are more likely to be believed when the threatener is perceived to be irrational. Schelling calls this "the political uses of madness," and notes:

[A] self-destructive attitude toward injury—"I'll cut a vein in my arm if you don't let me" . . .—can be a genuine strategic advantage; so can a cultivated

inability to hear or comprehend, or a reputation for frequent lapses of self-control that make punitive threats ineffectual as deterrents.[17]

One need not carry this as far as irrationality to note that similar advantages accrue to the bargainer who is moved by an excess of anger, is erratic, regards compromise as defeat, or has little to lose. Irrationality is by no means necessarily unproductive in community bargaining.

REASONABLENESS VERSUS OBSTINACY

There are, of course, advantages and disadvantages in both reasonableness and obstinacy, in hard and soft "sells." This is why negotiating teams sometimes embody both approaches in different team members. Seaver, describing the process of bargaining with southern welfare departments, refers to two roles—the "Mau Mau" and the "Moderate."

The job of the Mau Mau is to raise the maximum amount of hell in the most militant and annoying way possible. . . . The Moderate then comes on the scene, dripping with sweet reason and terms like "the breakdown of communications" and "what can we do constructively". . . . The Moderate takes the attitude that the Welfare Department is trying to help, and that he is there to help them help.[18]

This example represents an attempt to press a number of leverage points simultaneously.

A polite but firm stance by a negotiating team is another way of balancing the advantages and disadvantages of reasonableness and obstinacy. The indirect or implicit threat may serve this purpose as well. To imply rather than state allows one to communicate without taking responsibility for the communication. It constitutes a bluff that cannot be called since, on the face of it, the bluff was never made. It lets one deny the intent of the communication, if strategy so requires. From this point of view, it has been suggested that bargaining

---

[15] Schelling, *op. cit.*, pp. 22–28.
[16] Alan McSurely, *How to Negotiate* (Louisville, Ky.: Southern Conference Educational Fund, 1967), p. 2.

[17] Schelling, *op. cit.*, p. 17.
[18] Seaver, *op. cit.*, pp. 2–3.

is "an exercise in graceful retreat—retreating without seeming to retreat." [19] The implicit threat also permits the one who is threatened to save face. He may, if he wishes, appear to concede on the merits of the case, rather than as a consequence of pressure.

To help one's opponent find a face-saver is important in bargaining. Here, as elsewhere in the transaction, one must relate one's own interests to an adversary's. Whether in relation to the threats he has made or the terms he has insisted were his final offer, an adversary's face-saving is important. If he has bound himself to a commitment from which he wishes to withdraw, his ability to justify withdrawal may determine his willingness to concede at all. When his opponent can help him rationalize the change, settlement becomes possible.

Ambiguity also permits face-saving. An agreement may have the net effect of meeting a demand but yet be cast in such a way as to appear otherwise. Both parties are then satisfied, one because the demand was met, the other because it seemed not to be. Trust in each other's understanding and promises is a condition of ambiguous settlements, however. In effect, both parties must be clear about what their lack of clarity means for the ultimate payoff.

The intercession of a third party is also a face-saving mechanism. Prestigious third parties and formal mediators serve many functions in bargaining, one of which is to permit one of the contenders to concede without seeming to succumb to the other. Thus the president of Columbia University acceded to the "request" of New York City's mayor to halt construction of a gymnasium to which sitting-in students objected. [20]

THE WORKER AND THE GROUP

Strategy is one of the organizer's many concerns in his bargaining work with in-

experienced community groups. Demands, arguments, threats, concessions, and moves toward reconciliation must be shaped not only to maximize the vulnerability of the adversary, convince important audiences, or even promote a substantive victory, but must also take into account the community group itself—its needs and interests, experience, capacity, style, and internal and external relationships.

Should the worker use the strategies of bargaining set forth in this paper directly, as the group's leader or negotiator, or should he be a behind-the-scenes adviser and teacher? Space does not permit an exploration of this question. Fortunately, there is much in the literature regarding the organizer's role that is applicable to the bargaining agent of a community group. [21] However, some broad comments may be made.

An organizer's stance at a specific time requires the fine calibration of a series of sometimes conflicting considerations. For example, negotiations between a group and officials provide an opportunity for the organizer to demonstrate his allegiance to the group and its cause. A hard line by the organizer serves to dispel the suspicions of some low-income clients about his professional motivation and commitment. The organizer's firm stance is also likely to make officials seem less awesome to group members and serve as a model of courage for apprehensive participants who are unused to challenging authority figures. An unyielding position by the organizer exacts a political price, however, for it may give the impression that it is the professional, not the group, who is exercised about the issue. [22] The appropriateness of the stance

---

[19] Bakke and Kerr, op. cit., p. 353.
[20] New York Times, April 25, 1968.

[21] For one particularly relevant example, see Charles F. Grosser, "Staff Role in Neighborhood Organization," in John B. Turner, ed., Neighborhood Organization for Social Action (New York: National Association of Social Workers, 1968), pp. 133–145.
[22] It is suspected, however, that the accusation will be made in any case, regardless of the reality of the situation.

depends on which of these and other con siderations is most important in the specific instance.

The important point is that there is a wide range of professionally acceptable behaviors. In helping a group pursue its objectives, the organizer may find it necessary to take a primary role, actively contributing his expertise to the group's efforts. The contention that the worker's activity divests group members of a share in the process and thus deprives them of the emotional rewards of a self-help achievement may in part be justified, but it has probably been overemphasized.[23] Even in his role as a teacher, the organizer may properly be a doer. People learn, after all, from observation and identification with a role model as well as by doing themselves.

One need not define the question in either/or terms, of course. However much the demands of a situation call for the worker's activity, the professional must see himself principally as a catalyst, consultant, or trainer in the bargaining transaction. For strategic and other reasons, the group should carry as much of the work as possible in the sessions with officials.

PREPARATION

This requires, whenever circumstances allow, investment in adequate preparatory time. Demands, lines of argument and defense, and potential concessions need to be rehearsed. Focus is essential so that the group will not be deflected from its purposes. Who will pursue what lines of arguments and assume which roles must be decided. Whether the group will be militant or moderate, or who among them will be either one or the other, will be determined by the personalities of individual

members, the differing interests that members represent, and their respective knowledge of the substantive issues, as well as by strategic factors regarding the group's impact on the opposition.

Inexperienced groups need help to anticipate the responses of officials and to fortify themselves against spurious counterarguments. They need to analyze with whom they are dealing, to assess who is most vulnerable, and who might be a sympathizer. Depending on the circumstances, they may need to realize that compromise is essential in bargaining and that not all their demands will be met.

Negotiations involving an inexperienced community group must often be undertaken by the whole group. In addition to the educational value of observing the process as it unfolds, there may be a strategic advantage to appearing with large numbers. Appearance at the session may also relieve the suspicion that members often have of their leaders, the fear that leaders will too easily capitulate or be co-opted. In continuous bargaining, this testing may be followed by the creation of a smaller negotiating committee that has the group's confidence.

Of critical importance to effective bargaining is the relationship of the negotiating committee to its constituency or of individual negotiators to each other. Officials are no less aware than grass-roots organizers that there is strength in dividing one's opponent and they may be expected to act accordingly. New and ad hoc groups are especially subject to factionalism as a consequence of the fluidity of the group structure. A cardinal principle for the negotiators, then, is that differences must be aired privately and cooled publicly. To maintain unity and integrity, members and negotiators must be in constant contact, developments must be reported as they occur, and broad guidelines must be agreed on and revised as necessary. Frequent caucuses during lengthy negotiations serve the same purpose for the negotiators.

---

[23] This concern may be more relevant to an individual or group treatment situation than to task-oriented group action. The achievement of purpose, with or without extensive help by the worker, is likely to make the group feel an enhanced ability to affect community decision-making processes.

CONCLUSION

The effective involvement of the poor in community decision-making ultimately requires the institutionalization of bargaining mechanisms, just as collective bargaining arrangements have come to be the normal practice in labor-management relations. In a complex and highly bureaucratized society, solutions to institutional problems may need to be somewhat bureaucratized. New and consumer-oriented bureaucratic mechanisms, organized to challenge and counteract other formal organizations, are one means by which individuals may be protected from official inequity. Institutionalized bargaining can be regarded as a step toward control by service recipients. But whether or not community bargaining is ultimately institutionalized, social work with the poor requires expertise in applying its strategies and techniques.

BY DAVID WINEMAN AND ADRIENNE JAMES

The Advocacy Challenge to Schools of Social Work

■ Schools of social work teach their students theory, technology, and ideals that often are rendered useless by the abusive and dehumanizing practices toward clients students may witness in field work agencies, especially in captor-captive settings. The authors argue that the school of social work must "put its action where its mouth is" and fight the battle for human rights by using the power of the school to protect students who advocate in behalf of clients—and in so doing to engage in the teaching and practice of advocacy. ■

THERE ARE PRISONS with and without walls. A prison is here defined as a social arrangement in which a captor-captive relationship exists. Public assistance, probation, and parole agencies are prisons without walls. All forms of incarceration—jails and mental hospitals—are virtual prisons. And the American public school system chronically oscillates between potential and actual prisonhood.

Captor-captive states are inherently inimical to the human condition because they jeopardize the humanity of both captor and captive. Yet they appear to be inevitable in most complex societies. The degree of civilization of a society is demonstrated by how it treats its various classifications of captives, by the extent to which it displays a consciousness of its destructiveness, and by its readiness to undertake countermeasures against dehumanization.[1]

The social work profession is currently experiencing its main moral outrage and drive toward advocacy with respect to one of these client captivity statuses: the public assistance recipient. The other client statuses or states of captivity through which one may be equally attacked and buried in a subhygienic world have for the most part

[1] Treatment is the inverse of dehumanization. It is significant in this respect that a body of law is beginning to develop in which the right of the mentally ill to treatment is upheld. Cardinal to the court decisions that have begun to lay the foundation for this evolving juridical principle is the concept that when government (society) deprives a person of his right to liberty, that person is entitled through constitutional protections to prompt treatment so that his chance to regain the freedom of community life is maximized. See, for example, the three landmark decisions written by Chief Judge David Bazelon for the U.S. Circuit Court of Appeals (D.C.) dealing with the criminally insane, the sexual psychopath, and the senile aged in *Rouse* vs. *Cameron*, 373 F2 451, *Millard* vs. *Cameron*, 373 F2 468, and *Lake* vs. *Cameron*, 364 F2 657. The *Rouse* decision is especially noteworthy since it clearly reflects the court's opinion that in some cases an order of conditional or unconditional release may be the appropriate remedy in the absence of treatment. In an especially striking decision, one claimant has been granted damages of $300,000 from the state for negligence of state doctors in providing psychiatric and ordinary medical care in a state hospital. The opinion notes: "We believe we understand the immense difficulties faced by the State in financing, staffing, and administering as vast a complex as Mattawan State Hospital, as well as the other state hospitals. However, society denominates these institutions as hospitals and they should be so conducted. If they are to be no more than pens into which we are to sweep that which is offensive to 'normal society' then let us be honest and denominate them as such. . . ." *Whitree* vs. *State*, 290 NYS 2d 486, in *The Mental Health Court Digest*, Vol. 12, No. 3 (September 1968), pp. 3–4.

DAVID WINEMAN, MSW, *is Professor and Chairman of the Human Behavior Sequence, School of Social Work, Wayne State University, Detroit, Michigan.* **ADRIENNE JAMES, MSW,** *is Executive Director of Operation Friendship and a part-time instructor at Wayne State University.*

Reprinted with permission of the National Association of Social Workers, from SOCIAL WORK, Vol. 14, No. 2 (April 1969), pp. 23–32.

failed to excite recent writers on client advocacy. The statuses of schoolchild, mental hospital patient, probationer, parolee, and detention home, training school, or prison inmate have been virtually ignored.[2]

There is a kind of "bandwagon vision" operating that makes the poor and the black visible mainly in the status of public assistance client but not in these other statuses.[3] The stark horror of these more shadowy statuses of captivity should be spotlighted. There is a need to broaden the advocacy will of social work to attack the breakdown of democratic decency in whichever client statuses it occurs.

In the complex struggle for change that is visualized in building an advocacy norm into the profession, the school of social work is in an embarrassingly undefined position. A large number of social work students are spread among courts, public welfare, correctional agencies and institutions, mental hospitals, and schools. On campus, schools float out theory, technology, and ideals that represent the knowledge-value mix of the social work profession.[4] Theory may be weak, and sometimes techniques melt in front of the worker's eyes. A more eclectic program with a unified theory of social and human behavior is needed. But even if all these problems were solved immediately, it would not make much difference, because any model of theory, technology, and ideals, regardless of what it is or might become, will be useless the minute the student tries to apply it in the face of the contamination of the field work settings.[5]

A critical index of the integrity of the school of social work will increasingly be found in its willingness to engage in a

[2] Perhaps the clearest exhortation for broad client advocacy comes from Scott Briar, who uses the poor in his examples but also stresses that the principles of advocacy are "no less applicable to other groups in the society." A survey of *Social Work, Social Casework, Social Service Review, Journal of Education for Social Work, Social Work Education Reporter,* and *New Perspectives: The Berkeley Journal of Social Welfare* since 1965 reveals that captor-captive settings other than public assistance are seldom dealt with as specific advocacy targets. Exceptions to this are Specht, who uses a probation example; Brager, who cites school systems and housing authorities as possible targets for advocacy interventions; and Miller, whose focus on the involuntary status of certain clients includes the settings described in this paper. *See* Scott Briar, "The Social Worker's Responsibility for the Civil Rights of Clients," *New Perspectives: The Berkeley Journal of Social Welfare,* Vol. 1, No. 1 (Spring 1967), pp. 89–92; Harry Specht, "Casework Practice and Social Policy Formulation," *Social Work,* Vol. 13, No. 1 (January 1968), pp. 42–52; George A. Brager, "Advocacy and Political Behavior," *Social Work,* Vol. 13, No. 2 (April 1968), pp. 5–15, and Henry Miller, "Value Dilemmas in Social Casework," *Social Work,* Vol. 13, No. 1 (January 1968), pp. 27–33.

[3] Hollingshead and Redlich, for example, show that among neurotic patients, "Custodial care [as a type of treatment] is limited largely to Class V [lowest]" and "There is clearly a strong inverse relationship between class status and whether a psychotic patient is in the state hospitals." August B. Hollingshead and Fredrick C. Redlich, *Social Class and Mental Illness* (New York: John Wiley & Sons, 1958), pp. 267, 282.

[4] The words theory and technology refer to the theory and technology base of psychoanalytic ego psychology. The settings in question, it is being argued, are incompatible with the therapeutic ideology drawn from this model. The inference (if it were to be made) that there would be a higher compatibility with drastically different approaches —e.g., the sociobehavioral—is distinctly dubious. Examination of the sociobehavioral approach, or any rationally based extrapolation of a variety of current change models, will reveal that none of them could coexist with the capricious and arbitrary handling of human functioning endemic in these settings.

[5] Obviously, the focus on dehumanization and comments on the inutility of knowledge in captor-captive settings does not imply that there is no body of knowledge that, if followed, will permit the development of humane and useful settings. In the children's field, for instance, the works of Fritz Redl and Bruno Bettelheim alone present a detailed theoretical exposition of such humanely based and therapeutically focused residential care. John Brown's efforts in Canada, so vividly portrayed in the movie *Warrendale,* are provocative in this regard. Gisela Konopka has also written productively for this field, and a further contribution is A. E. Trieschman, L. K. Brendtro, and J. K. Whittaker, *The Other 23 Hours* (New York: Aldine Press, in press).

re-examination of the relationship between its teaching and the action imperatives of its field work agencies. In facing this challenge, the school finds its place in the crisis of higher education today: the confrontation between knowledge and social injustice.

FORMS OF DEHUMANIZATION

The following kinds of things, which frequently occur in captor-captive settings, are destructive to the total functioning of the person and preclude any rational application of the theory, technology, and ideals of the social work profession.[6] With respect to all of the following, social work students (and others) either are direct witnesses or are so close that de jure-tight cases could be made from their testimony.[7] There are other types of dehumanization, but those cited are meant to be representative of the most severe forms.

1. *Physical brutalization.* This occurs in the form of beatings, food deprivation, enforced immobility (e.g., standing for hours without being allowed to move), sensory deprivation (e.g., the use of quiet rooms for hours with little light or other signs of reality), spontaneous use of group sadism "to teach a kid a lesson," to mention but a few.

When they occur in state agencies, these may violate the constitutional right to freedom from cruel and unusual punishment.

2. *Psychic humiliation.* This includes a variety of tactics for stripping a person of all semblance of human dignity. Examples are shaming, exploiting weaknesses, needling and teasing, refusing to permit a person to tell his side of a conflict, arbitrary use of authority, surveillance activities in public assistance and corrections, and the use of invidious terms like "animal," "bastard," and "nigger" directed by persons in authority to patients, inmates, clients, and public school students.

3. *Sexual traumatization.* This occurs in settings where more powerful and institutionally sophisticated residents force the homosexual equivalent of rape on the weaker and less sophisticated.

4. *Condoned use of feared indigenous leaders for behavioral management.* A usually tacit but sometimes open deal is made between those in authority and such leaders, who are then permitted wider leeway than normal, given certain privileges, and the like, in exchange for the exercise of brutal control measures on weaker group members.[8]

5. *Chronic exposure to programless boredom.* Certain settings simply provide nothing for people to do. They sit and deteriorate mentally or engage in physical conflicts with each other in outbursts of tension and/or "symptom blowups" because of a systematic drainage of activity structures.

6. *"Unclean" grouping.* This includes enforced living together of clinically incompatible mixtures of human beings who cannot avoid symptom and trait clashes that worsen their problems. Too wide a range of sophistication, toughness, psychosis, delinquency, developmental levels, socioeconomic classes, and cultural styles is clearly contraindicated by any profes-

[6] Many of the areas mentioned—especially those identified as civil liberties or constitutional issues—have been investigated by the Metropolitan Detroit Branch of the American Civil Liberties Union of Michigan, primarily through its Committee on Civil Liberties of Children and Youth. Mimeographed material on these issues is available from the committee, 234 State Street, Detroit, Mich. 48226.

[7] In those areas in which the possibility of a constitutional or other legal violation may occur, co-operation of the legal profession is essential and represents a resource that social workers have encouragingly utilized in public assistance but not with other captor-captive client statuses. *See,* for example, Charles F. Grosser and Edward V. Sparer, "Legal Services for the Poor: Social Work and Social Justice," *Social Work,* Vol. 11, No. 1 (January 1966), pp. 81–87; and Betty Mandell, "The Crime of Poverty," *Social Work,* Vol. 11, No. 1 (January 1966), pp. 11–15.

[8] This phenomenon is described vividly in Howard W. Polsky, *Cottage Six* (New York: Russell Sage Foundation, 1962).

sionally based theory but may occur under certain conditions of policy stupidity, downright decadence, shortage of institutional space and personnel, and/or neglect.

7. *Symptom-squeezing forms of punishment.* Punishment of disturbed children and adults is contraindicated because of their ego impairment. In many residential settings for disturbed people, however, there is wholesale violation of this principle. Moreover, in the eagerness of the authorities to get some kind of pleasure/pain hold on the person, a special attack on his functioning is mounted by selection of certain punishment experiences that squeeze already existing symptom-loaded areas.

Thus, for example, restriction of home visiting privileges is apt to do just that. These are people who have broken down in the family system in a society in which the family unit is viewed as the basic protective and status-giving experience. Yet this pathology-infected area becomes the very one used to control the person's behavior in the institution. This is not to imply that home visiting should be uncontrolled—the criteria that control it should give priority to individual needs, not the behavioral control requirements of the institution. Another example of symptom-squeezing is the use of dark isolation rooms, regardless of whether the person has a severe phobia about being alone and in the dark.[9] Restriction of food with severely regressed people and the use of suspension from school with poor learners are cases in point—so are physical punishment of youths already fixed on a delinquent identity stressing toughness and any punishment at all of an individual whose ego functioning is heavily masochistically oriented.

8. *Enforced work routines in the guise of vocational training.* While it is possible that an educationally well-designed work training program may be integrated with housekeeping and maintenance chores, this is rare in most public institutions. Usually it is designed more to take the place of programming, which is ignored, or to save on administrative costs. When there is no central theory that relates it to the patient's or inmate's problem, it is simply not defensible and arguably constitutes a violation of the right to be free from involuntary servitude.

9. *Violations of privacy.* These range all the way from having to live in extremely overcrowded quarters in institutions to unauthorized searches of person and property. The latter occur in institutions and schools, in the operation of welfare and probation and parole agencies, and in the form of unauthorized home visits in which the client, probationer, or parolee must admit the worker or suffer some penalty. These assaults on pesonal dignity may represent violations of constitutionally guaranteed rights.

What is new about this list? Nothing. There is a tradition—a culture of abuse— in these captor-captive settings that is protected by a complex web of human weakness and deceit, including the most treacherous form, self-deceit.[10]

CONVENTIONAL FACULTY REACTIONS

Students go into these settings every year— like so many ants marching out of the hill —all with their shiny new theory and methods gear in their little knapsacks, ready to "help." (None of them was ever born that naïve, but that is the pretend game they and their faculty play.) They are systematically taught to abandon reality.

---

[9] Isolation need not be antitherapeutic. *See,* for example, William C. Morse and David Wineman, "The Therapeutic Use of Social Isolation in a Camp for Ego-Disturbed Boys," *Journal of Social Issues,* Vol. 13, No. 1 (January 1957), pp. 32–39.

[10] The captor-captive phenomenon described in this paper is presented in a highly conceptualized form by Goffman in his focus on the dehumanization of prisons and mental hospitals. Erving Goffman, *Asylums* (Garden City, N.Y.: Doubleday & Co., 1961). In the writings of Szasz the same theme is certainly implicit, but his main thrust is to reveal and indict what he considers the subversion of the psychiatric profession as the means by which the state creates a condition of captivity of the mentally ill. *See* especially Thomas S. Szasz, *Law, Liberty and Psychiatry* (New York: Macmillan Co., 1963).

From out of the wasteland of the field work settings students come back with angry perplexity: "Do you know what the attendants are doing at ———?" "I saw a principal knock a kid across the office!" "This counselor cut this kid down, wouldn't listen to him. How can I get anywhere if I can't protect the kid from that?" "Did you ever see the Hole at ———?" [11] "This boy at ——— is terrified of the older guys' sexual attacks. Nobody will talk about it there." "Dr. X threatens the patients with shock if they act up." "This student has been suspended for six weeks with no plan." "The kids at the youth home have to stand for hours 'on the line.'" [12]

When students express these concerns, the faculty more or less falls back on avoidance responses, which can only be characterized as a system of defense against change:

1. *Avoidance through instant clichés* is represented by the following examples: (a) That is work among the heathen—"You have to *work* with these people, to help them because 'they know not what they do.' We have the tools and they need to learn from us." (b) The child still knows you are his friend—"You can still help the kid even if you can't stop some of these things from happening. It's important to him that you're there and *understand*." (c) Search for the silver lining—"Are you sure it's that bad? Isn't there anything the client gets that's useful?" (d) Study it—"Do a process record of one of those and let's have a look at it, *or* "Why don't you make that your term paper topic?" (e) The staff is human, too—"The girl does have to know that staff have feelings (although I don't think the attendant should have hit her). Maybe you can work on that with her." (f) The administrator is getting ulcers from it, too—"I'm sure the administrator would do something if he could. I've known him for a long time. But he's got the legislature to deal with. He suffers, I'm sure. He's got a pretty good record. . . ."

2. *Avoidance through the emotional control demand system of the professional model.* How many students have been challenged with: "Are you sure you're not over-identifying with your client? You're pretty angry, you know." There is something wrong with the fear of affect in the casework and group work model. The importance of feeling is stressed, but students are taught never to show it to the client. Students are taught that their subjective lives are dangerous to the client's interests. It is necessary to be clear about this: It is true that worker needs and client needs should not be confused. But the way in which this has been incorporated in teaching and supervision has resulted in enculturating generations of caseworkers and group workers with fear of feelings for the client, not only those they may show *to* him but those they may show to their supervisor *about* him. That "sin" of overidentification with the client is avidly sought and rated low on evaluations. But identification with the agency, with the profession, is *good* and gets high ratings. (Has anyone ever heard of a student or worker about whom it was noted in an evaluation that he overidentified with the agency or the profession? That is a sin beyond imagination!)

There is something seriously amiss in the eager embrace of identification with the agency as the hallmark for the emerging professional identity, while warning of the

[11] The "hole" refers to isolation facilities in detention homes, state training schools, and prisons. It is typically a dimly lit, locked cubicle about $9 \times 9 \times 12$, sometimes with a small window either dirt-encrusted or deliberately glazed to screen out light, a slot in the door through which food is passed, a grade toilet and washbowl, and a concrete slab practically at floor height on which a mattress without linen and a blanket may be provided. There is no clock on the wall and the person being isolated typically is not permitted to have any activity materials, including reading matter.

[12] "On the line" refers to the punishment practice by which a person is required to stand in one spot without moving for a stipulated length of time, e.g., thirty minutes to an hour. If he moves, time is added.

precariousness of such identification with the client. The objection to this does not mean that self-discipline in relating to clients should not be taught or that theory, technique, and ideals should be abandoned. But agencies and professions are tools, instrumentalities toward an end: helping the client. To inject agency identification into the professional ego by dint of reward/punishment techniques inherent in evaluation and admission to elite membership among the "anointed" is really a betrayal of the fundamental values of the profession.

3. *Obsession with big-system change magic* is the newest avoidance tool that has come along as part of the enthusiasm about social movements and institutional reform. This should be supported, but not at the cost of the total expenditure of social work advocacy will and energy. The phenomenologically real system for caseworkers and group workers is what they experience in their dealings with the human beings they are committed to serve. The system is ubiquitous, but it comes in different sizes, shapes, and organizational patterns. Social work should continue to experiment with different-size targets for mediating and changing the system in its constraints on human functioning and human happiness. These should, however, be maneuverable targets, lest the advocate become like everyone else who has been shown the big-system world and its fierce determinism, powerless before the god of macro-organization.

TEACHING BY DOING

What should schools of social work do, then, when the "ants" come marching back with their embarrassing questions? *Schools must back their students in unflinching criticism and attempts at changing the settings they are in when those settings hurt the people they (and the schools) serve.*

Imagine the student—caseworker, groupworker, or community organization practitioner—who is witness to an act of client dehumanization. If he wants to enter the lists of advocacy in behalf of a client, only one condition is both necessary and sufficient for initiating such action: that his school will regard his action with enthusiasm and support.[13] This can occur if the traditional partnership between school and agency and their complementarity on the teaching continuum, which gives them power over the student, is somehow restructured so that the student's normal fear of reprisal is liquidated sufficiently for him to take the moral and tactical actions implied in the advocacy concept.

Of these two partners in the student's educational destiny, it may be validly asserted that the school is the more powerful. In the final analysis, when the agency complains about a student, it is still the school that determines his ongoing status as student. This power differential, while both complex and not absolute, is still extremely critical in the over-all strategy and tactics of evolving a training model that "builds in" student advocacy. For it is the superior power of the school that opens the door to deliberate and planned protection of the student advocate, and this protection will itself involve the school in direct confrontation with agency systems.

This asserted power differential in favor of the school has always existed and been used. Thus, the school has not always bowed to agency perceptions of student incompetence. Schools have refused to accept such judgments and subsequently arranged another placement or negotiated retention in the original agency. That there may have been far fewer instances of such an outcome than acceptance of the agency's recommendation does not vitiate the argument with respect to the school's possession of the "final vote" on the student.

[13] It seems unnecessary to point out that NASW should also support its member (and nonmember) advocates, and the authors note that Briar's paper, *op. cit.*, which was accepted in October 1966 as a working paper of the NASW Commission on Social Casework, has been approved by the Cabinet of the Division of Practice and Knowledge and referred to the Ad Hoc Committee on Advocacy.

LIMITATIONS ON SCHOOL POWER

Yet, for reasons that are quite clear, schools have been chary in using this power. First, the schools have not felt free to reject the agency's judgment about a student; they fear they will lose the agency's goodwill and participatory zeal in student training, which may extend to loss of placements. Second, they face a certain embarrassment and loss of status in graduating students whom agencies regard as inferior candidates. These strings on the use of school power are illustrative of the complexity and relativity of its freedom to differ with co-operating agencies.

However, it must also be remembered that these limitations have been most urgently operative outside the issue of advocacy. The typical case of the student whom the agency considered untrainable involved his presumed lack of potential as a clinical change agent and focused on what were considered defects that dulled or obviated such potential.[14]

If, however, a student should present evidence to the school that a given agency behaves toward the client in ways that violate the requirements of the professional action model, this certainly would constitute a totally new paradigm of agency-student-school conflict. There is a vast difference between a student who is a passive target of a field instructor's criticism of his suitability for social work and a student who is an active critic of an agency's social work morality—especially in the context of a school's sympathy and support of such sensitivity.

In the face of such novelty the two strains on the school enumerated could be inverted:

1. *Loss of placements.* Should the school keep such placements in the name of good education without at least trying to change them?

2. *Loss of status.* Should the school feel embarrassed about graduating students who point to such defects?

Yet, some may say, schools will still lose placements and still be maligned for graduating "crackpots." And do students know enough to criticize the agency? Is that not a contradiction in terms (a student who faults his teacher)?

It should be kept in mind that what is being dealt with is not a complex knowledge problem. It does not take intensive training, or perhaps any training at all, to recognize gross dehumanization. The student's sense of decency may be enough. Further, students vary widely in degree of social work knowledge, standing in the formal training process (i.e., newly arrived to almost graduated), previous practical experience, pre-social work education, individual intellectual endowment, and value dispositions. While some advocacy issues are more borderline than others and some do require technical training, many do not. Primarily, the considerations here are basic human values that must be guaranteed before treatment can be launched.[15] Many students,

---

[14] In referring to clinical social work training and the criteria employed by agency field instructors in making judgments about student potential, the authors are not in any way attributing to this a negative or anti-advocacy taint. The whole judgment-making process about who will or will not be a good clinical worker is drawn from a totally different set of data, with different motives and for different reasons than those that would apply if a student took an advocacy position and then was attacked by a field agency and labeled undesirable.

[15] Of course, the student may react to a treatment method with which he disagrees or that he misunderstands as dehumanization. So may a fully fledged professional. Professional colleagues may have sharp differences about the "right" approach such that one terms the other's therapeutic plan as ruinous to a client's interests. Such conflicts cannot reasonably be approached through an advocacy procedure. Dehumanization is simply something that in commonsense terms is qualitatively distinct from conflict arising out of competing theoretical orientations. There is usually no theory base in the situation in which dehumanization occurs except perhaps the belief that people can be forced to change by pain and humiliation. Lay rather than professional thinking dominates, often accompanied by open ridicule of the more sophisti-

especially in today's academic environment, are keenly aware of these issues and have been for a long time. In fact, their instructors' apparent apathy, uncertainty, and evasiveness have caused many students to wonder about the integrity of the profession.

As to loss of placements and status, one does not know without testing the model under discussion how things will turn out. Obviously one can visualize (or hypothesize) other than negative outcomes.

Certainly ability to maintain placements is a serious and critical issue.[16] Still, given an aggressive stance on the part of the school, an agency (or an administrative department of the state that controls certain placements) cannot with impunity just terminate placements. Schools have options they can use under such conditions. There are legal, political, and public relations moves that could restrain such agency or bureaucracy responses. Obviously, this is important.

Schools *should* fear losing placements, not because they will not have places to send students and thus will thwart their own enterprise, but because the client will be the loser. So schools that support student advocacy may have to resort to complex strategies and tactics in order to keep placements for the sake of the client. In so doing they will at the same time be fighting the very issue of dehumanization.

In this way the double function of schools becomes clear vis-à-vis teaching and advocacy: (1) they support the trainee in protest against defection from the values of the profession in which they are training him and (2) they fight the issue of dehumanization and in this respect realize a completely separate function in becoming themselves active agents of system change. So, paradoxically enough, the school that supports its student advocates as a matter of policy and action tries to keep "inferior" placements, but in the act of keeping them calls attention to them and engages in change attempts.

The question might be asked that if students with school backing begin to launch protests against such practices, will agencies not come to regard them as spies and schools as spy-breeding organizations, a kind of CIA? This pejorative argument can be quickly voided when schools make known to agencies in advance their explicit policy of backing students in stands against client dehumanization. Espionage does not proceed by public announcement. The act of announcing to the professional community that schools are concerned with client dehumanization and that they will support and participate with their students in doing something about it effectively vitiates the spy argument. At the same time, such an act is a form of preconfrontation by the school itself of client mistreatment by agencies.

IMPLEMENTATION MODEL

So far a principle has been argued. In what form should it be implemented? Imagine that a school has put itself on record as

---

cated or professional rationale. Creature needs of the dehumanizers tend to be served, not the needs of the client. Frequently, disregard for and contempt of the client are openly present. Further, there is an entirely separate and important conceptual issue relating to the compatibility between the treatment and advocacy functions of the social work role. The authors believe that many clinicians tend to be hung up on this but that there are guidelines for positive balancing of these two functions that could be described in a more theoretical and technically relevant analysis of this issue. This is needed for both teaching and practice of clinical social work, especially in the client-service ecologies discussed in this paper.

[16] A question that will occur to some is whether the student's job future is jeopardized by his "advocacy history." If he becomes somehow labeled as a "troublemaker," even in an advocacy-protected school, does he not possibly face some difficulty in being hired? This eventuality cannot be discounted. The strongest credential for a job in social work, however, is the MSW degree, and the disproportion between social work manpower and jobs is certainly in the student's favor. Furthermore, a record of advocacy may be considered a plus in some agencies.

being in support of student advocacy against client dehumanization and has so notified students and agencies.[17] Beginning experimentation appears to have three essential ingredients: informality, simplicity, and protection of the client's right to self-determination.

"Implementation form" refers to just that and not to content, i.e., how and with what theory, strategy, and tactics a given advocacy action would be carried out. Simplicity, informality, and protection of client self-determination are conceived of as basic ingredients for setting a climate for advocacy experimentation by schools. Content would be supplied by analysis of given incidents of dehumanization and selection of strategy and tactics from a number of options described in the pertinent literature. While none of these deals directly with school-based, student-supported advocacy, they could be reviewed for their adaptability to this.[18]

[17] The faculty of Wayne State University School of Social Work unanimously adopted and distributed to students, field instructors, and agency directors on April 8, 1968, an official position statement supporting client advocacy as a viable option for its students and on June 17, 1968, adopted an implementation model that had been proposed by a committee of faculty, students, and agency representatives. "Advocacy of Action Against Client Dehumanization" and "Memorandum," and "Advocacy Implementation Model" (Detroit, Mich.: School of Social Work, Wayne State University, April 8, 1968, and June 17, 1968, respectively). (Mimeographed.)

[18] In addition to articles previously cited, see, for example, George A. Brager, "Institutional Change: Parameters of the Possible," Social Work, Vol. 12, No. 1 (January 1967), pp. 59–69; Wilbur J. Cohen, "What Every Social Worker Should Know About Political Action," Social Work, Vol. 11, No. 3 (July 1966), pp. 3–11; Charles F. Grosser, "Community Development Programs Serving the Urban Poor," Social Work, Vol. 10, No. 3 (July 1965), pp. 15–21; Irving Piliavin, "Restructuring the Provision of Social Services," Social Work, Vol. 13, No. 1 (January 1968), pp. 34–41; Martin Rein and Frank Riessman, "A Strategy for Antipoverty Community Action Programs," Social Work, Vol. 11, No. 2 (April 1966), pp. 3–12; Paul Terrell, "The Social Worker as Radical: Roles of Advocacy," New Perspectives: The Berkeley Journal of Social Welfare,

Informality. In an advocacy-committed school, the freest and most spontaneous use of faculty resources is visualized as the desideratum for the student witnessing client dehumanization and wondering what he can do. Setting up a procedure that requires him to meet with a standing committee, with the executive office of the school, or to submit to any screening device must be avoided simply because it becomes too cumbersome in the climate of a felt need for active intervention. Collegial rapport and esprit between student and faculty are indispensable.

Thus, when a student becomes aware of and/or observes policies and practices that dehumanize clients and when he has decided to advocate in behalf of such clients, he should be encouraged to go directly to a faculty member or members of his choice. This structure would enable the student to view the faculty as a resource pool and would free him to select among them in terms of their expertise and interest in specific areas. Thus, the student should not be required to select his own adviser or field instructor as consultant, although he may do so if he chooses. This student-faculty cadre is then free, without other faculty review and consent, to develop an action plan based on analysis of the circumstances.

Simplicity. The fewer the number of steps and tasks required, the more feasible the procedural model becomes. Yet terse, succinct documentation cannot be dispensed with. The student should be required to describe in writing the policy or practice that dehumanizes the client. Records of each case should be kept and periodic reports to the total faculty should be planned (for purposes of information only).

Protecting client self-determination. No advocacy action should be undertaken without client consultation and consent whenever such action will result in identification

Vol. 1, No. 1 (Spring 1967), pp. 83–88; and Daniel Thursz, "Social Action As a Professional Responsibility," Social Work, Vol. 11, No. 3 (July 1966), pp. 12–21.

of the client either by name or implication. With some clients this will prove a stumbling block either because of the predicament they are in or because (as would be the case with some mentally ill clients and some children) they simply are unable to conceptualize the problem.

The predicament they are in might be illustrated by the following example: Suppose the student has for a client a child who is in a youth home and has been brutalized. The student wishes to carry out a protest action, but the child is fearful that he will be mistreated more if this happens. Such a step will then have to be forgone, although there may be some permissible leeway for trying to work it through with him, especially if meaningful protection that he can comprehend can be thrown around him. On the other hand, when the advocacy action is directed at a policy per se or a procedure that is applied to a group, client consent may not be at stake.

TOWARD A NEW PROFESSIONAL IDENTITY

The thesis of school-based client advocacy is not limited to a heroic adventure of students and their teachers. Involved is not only a redirection of the energy and power of the school to change agencies but equally to change the professional identity of the social work practitioner it graduates. The reaction patterns described earlier of the typical faculty to students' anguished questions about the indecencies of captor-captive settings point to one set of factors explaining why so few professionals have gained distinction in the battle for agency reform. Their ingenuous strivings in this direction as students have been extinguished by the avoidance behavior of their teachers.

But the student who emerges from an advocacy-centered school will have had the antithetical experience to the above: he will have seen his school "put its action where its mouth is." He will have been witness to real struggles and will have experienced some of these together with his teachers. Instead of having been exhorted by inactive teachers to carry the activist torch in his professional future, he will have been a participant with his teachers in carrying that torch as a student. Not the least of such torch-bearing, while moral in its nature or source, will have been shared technical thinking about advocacy and examination of both failure and success by student and faculty.

Such an academic environment and its constituent experiences provide the germ plasm for a new breed whose preprofessional moral distaste for human injustice will have been honed and hardened to the level of professionally informed instinct. Such professionals will find it unavoidably natural to stand and fight for client rights as a first priority, instead of fleeing to the "suburbs of the professional environment" —the agencies with better standards—postcommitment refugees who could not wait to get out.[19] Or, lacking the energy required for such mobility, to remain self-committed captives, bitter, cynical, and passively helpless in agencies that dehumanize.

Thus, if social work's dream of the client-advocating professional is a real dream, the profession, along with the schools, ought to welcome the challenge of the shift to advocacy of social work faculties and to back this one tiny but tough step toward bringing that dream closer to reality.

---

[19] "One of the favorite ploys of social work supervisors and educators is to advise students that when conditions become intolerable in agencies and they can no longer support their administrator, they should resign and go elsewhere. *This is too easy*, for it leaves those whom social workers are supposed to help to the tender mercies of the inhumanity they themselves cannot stomach. A better answer might be not only to refuse to quit but also refuse to engage in unethical acts." Russell E. Smith, "In Defense of Public Welfare," *Social Work*, Vol. 11, No. 4 (October 1966), p. 97.

BY GEORGE A. BRAGER

Advocacy and Political Behavior

■ This paper explores some of the methodological implications of the role of the social worker as advocate, especially in the case when advocacy requires political behavior. Although manipulation is proscribed in social work, professional purity may be most costly to the victims of social problems. Political behavior is, in any case, inevitable and guidelines must be developed for its use. Four are suggested here: (1) who benefits and who loses by the political behavior, (2) who is subject to or the target of the political activity, (3) which values are inherent in the substantive end or principle that occasions the political behavior, and (4) what is the nature of the act itself? Circumstances that impinge on the effectiveness of political behavior are suggested. ■

SOCIAL WORK'S QUEST for new techniques is a response to the social climate. The dynamism of the times has resulted in dissatisfaction with such concepts as worker neutrality or adherence to enabling as a major tenet of method.[1] Agencies that assist the poor to participate in community activities cannot, with equanimity, proclaim their neutrality when controversial issues are engaged. The contradiction of a community agency able and willing to help residents challenge community conditions,

GEORGE A. BRAGER, MSW, is Associate Professor, Columbia University School of Social Work, New York, New York, and a member of the Editorial Board of this journal. This paper was prepared as part of the Community Organization Curriculum Development Project conducted by the Columbia University School of Social Work with the support of the Office of Juvenile Delinquency and Youth Crime, U.S. Department of Health, Education, and Welfare. It was presented at the NASW Eastern Regional Institute, October 1967, Philadelphia, Pennsylvania, and will appear as part of a forthcoming monograph on the changing demand for social services to be published by NASW.

but unable or unwilling to put itself "on the line" as well is not lost on its constituency.[2] In the face of passion, neutrality

[1] Rothman defines the enabling role as "providing an accepting and facilitating social climate and procedural means through which individuals are encouraged to think their problems through and make valid decisions from their own internal resources. . . . The parallel to Rogerian nondirective psychotherapy with individuals is obvious." Jack Rothman, "An Analysis of Goals and Roles in Community Organization Practice," Social Work, Vol. 9, No. 2 (April 1964), pp. 26 and 27.

[2] Examples from work with individuals are available as well. Although enabling and nondirectiveness are not synonymous, they have a natural affinity, and in practice are associated with one another. In such cases, a client might be expected to respond as follows: "Miss K., the social worker, gave us a letter to take to Welfare. If she had gone with us instead, it would have been different. . . . She's very nice, Miss K., but I don't know what she's going to do for me. She looks at me, smiles, and says, 'Hm-um, hm-um!' Well, life just isn't that calm for us." George Brager and Sherman Barr, "Perceptions and Reality: The Poor Man's View of Social Agencies," in Brager and Francis Purcell, Community Action Against Poverty (New Haven: College and University Press, 1967), p. 79.

Reprinted with permission of the National Association of Social Workers, from SOCIAL WORK, Vol. 13, No. 2 (April 1968), pp. 5-15.

seems like timidity and enabling seems unresponsive.

Methodological questioning has also been furthered by the infusion of social science knowledge into the field of social work. Of particular significance in this regard is the increased understanding of the contextual aspects of events. Attitudes develop, behavior is shaped, interactions take place, and incidents occur in response to current structural arrangements, not merely as reflections of the psychological patterns of individual actors or their past environmental conditions.

These currents impel, in their turn, a consideration of the role of the social worker as advocate.[3] Although the concept is both important and in current use, its methodological implications have not yet been seriously considered. The worker as advocate identifies with the plight of the disadvantaged. He sees as his primary responsibility the tough-minded and partisan representation of their interests, and this supersedes his fealty to others. This role inevitably requires that the practitioner function as a political tactician. It is this aspect of advocacy with which this paper deals.

REDISTRIBUTION OF POWER

The context in which change is espoused, clients are helped to achieve it, or are taught how to work effectively for desired social ends must be taken into account. When this is done, one turns inevitably to the making of the community's agenda. Who defines the problems that need remedy? Or their causation and solutions? As has been noted elsewhere:

> The groups that are feeling the impact of "bad" social conditions frequently lack the strength or voice to be heard. Such

groups as the victims of poverty, neglected children, unemployed youth, migrants, the uneducated, the victims of discrimination, and the aging cannot compete easily in the market of ideas and vested interests.[4]

These groups are also the least likely to be involved in community decision-making processes or, when involved, to be influential participants. One of the advocate's objectives may be conceptualized as the redistribution of community power so that programs and policies that benefit the disadvantaged may receive more vigorous and receptive attention. This does not mean, of course, that low-income persons or groups have a lien on either virtue or wisdom. It means, rather, that in a pluralistic and democratic society disproportionate differentials in influence must be adjusted.

The social worker, himself hardly a powerful figure in our society, is not in a commanding position. His authority is weak and the resources at his disposal that would influence the community decision-making process are sharply circumscribed. Fear of abusing his professional power through its untrammeled application is, in this context, unrelated to reality—although to believe otherwise may be irresistibly appealing to his professional self-image. For the social worker in his role as a model to eschew political behavior or to counsel his clients or constituents to avoid it, even indirectly, is to diminish still further the ability of the disadvantaged and their professional advocates to influence community change. Professional purity is likely to be most costly to the victims of social problems.

VIOLATING PRINCIPLES

The social agency—the worker's own and his colleagues'—must also be seen as part

---

[3] The concept of advocacy as a professional strategy was introduced into the social work literature by Charles Grosser in "Community Development Programs Serving the Urban Poor," *Social Work*, Vol. 10, No. 3 (July 1965), pp. 15–21.

[4] Nathan E. Cohen, "A Social Work Approach," in Cohen, ed., *Social Work and Social Problems* (New York: National Association of Social Workers, 1964), p. 374.

of the worker's field of forces. Social work is a profession practiced largely from an agency base, and yet it is only recently that organizational requisites have begun to receive attention.[5] The agency provides the workers with both opportunities and constraints, but what counsel is there for maximizing the former and minimizing the latter?

Social workers have perhaps been unduly simplistic; they have advised their fellow workers that they have a responsibility to influence changes in policies with which they disagree but have not specified the professionally acceptable and effective means of doing so. They have suggested that if agency policy violates principle and cannot be influenced to change, the professional may—sometimes should—leave. But this leaves the clients in the lurch and the violated principle intact. Furthermore, to counsel such a course ignores the manifold influences on the worker, one of which is his need for a job.

The fact is that all organizations violate principles at one time or another. Agencies can be ranged on a continuum as to their amenability to influence and their violation of practice norms, yet this has not really been considered. Is the same advice offered to the welfare department employee, the social worker in the public schools, the neighborhood center group worker, and the psychiatric caseworker in the family agency? And, if so, are workers not being implicitly encouraged to seek employment in the small voluntary agency, in which professional norms tend to be observed and professional influence is greatest?

[5] See, for example, George Brager, "Institutional Change: Perimeters of the Possible," Social Work, Vol. 12, No. 1 (January 1967), pp. 59–69; Martin Rein and Robert Morris, "Goals, Structures and Strategies for Community Change," Social Work Practice, 1962 (New York: Columbia University Press, 1962), pp. 127–145; Mayer N. Zald, "Organizations As Polities: An Analysis of Community Organization Agencies," Social Work, Vol. 11, No. 4 (October 1966), pp. 56–65.

If social workers believe that agencies are dedicated to client interests, they face little conflict between their organizational and professional responsibilities. If they believe that agencies are sufficiently interested in their clients' welfare to respond to a reasoned appeal for policy change, they successfully avoid the issue. But what if they are convinced that the maintenance and enhancement needs of organizations take precedence over clients' needs, even in the best of agencies? Or that conflict between the needs of the organization and the needs of its constituents is inevitable? This is likely to be the advocate's perception, since his single-minded focus on the client will make him most sensitive to unmet needs and to policies that act to the detriment of clients.

To whom, then, is the worker's primary responsibility: the agency or the client? If the former, the issue is simply met. If the latter—as in the case of the advocate— the agency may well become a target for change. The worker who has thus opted in favor of his clients' interests is likely to feel he owes it to them to be as effective as possible. Considering the structure of influence in the social agency, his own potency as a member of the staff group— not to mention his clients' or constituencies' power—is likely to be limited. To be effective, he may have to use political strategies. To avoid them on the grounds of professional purity may once again be most costly to the victims of social problems.

INGROUP DEFENSES

And all of this is likely to apply equally or more in the advocate's dealing with colleagues and their agencies. All professions develop self-protective mechanisms, shielding their members from outside criticism or intrusion. Thus the doctor, for example, does not reveal what he has observed in the operating room, and thereby protects his colleagues from lay scrutiny. Similarly, a study of the public schools reports the perception of teachers that one of the principal's major functions is to protect them from faultfinding by parents.[6] The norms are understandable. Commonness of experience and shared interests lead inevitably to ingroup defenses. It may also be that the norms make it possible for the system to function smoothly, by keeping each actor aware of the support he may expect from the others.

To sanctify norms as professional ethics is another matter, and to deny their self-serving nature would be untoward in a field that emphasizes self-knowledge and understanding. The worker who is strongly client-identified will be aware of this, especially since much of his work entails helping clients to negotiate with workers in massive service systems. In dealing with his colleagues he may or may not appear to observe the norms, but he will surely violate them in fact.

Organizations also are circumspect in their relationships with one another; one social agency is responsive to the interests of another. Social work literature is replete with references to the advantages of co-ordination among agencies, with little attention given to the disadvantages. This is not meant to challenge interagency co-ordination, but to note that the concept of co-ordination may be used by agencies to protect their "turf." Devising geographic boundaries as a basis for service does, after all, insure that agencies will not compete for clientele.

It is curious that a nation devoted to free enterprise and competition does not hold these values for its service agencies. Yet the principle is the same. If clients could choose from among a number of welfare agencies, it is likely that the service at all these agencies would be better than it is.

Co-ordination may be more beneficial to the serving agencies than to the served.[7]

Norms that regulate interorganizational relationships also pose issues for the advocate social worker; his focus on clients' needs may threaten to impair his agency's relationship with other important organizations. He must then walk the tightrope between conflicting demands. If client identification is uppermost to him, he will present the case to his agency in a way most likely to garner support for a client-oriented course of action. This may require that he minimize the risk to his agency while underscoring the importance of his client's interests. He may even argue the case with more passion than he feels, if he believes that his emotional tone will positively affect his gaining administrative support. He will, in short, engage in political behavior.

POLITICAL BEHAVIOR

What is meant by political behavior? It must be clear so far in this paper that it does *not* mean a relation to government or skill in governing. The term does, however, encompass many other meanings. The dictionaries include the following as synonyms for "politic": artful, shrewd, crafty, expedient, and prudent. In order to sharpen the inquiry into the advocate's technology, one aspect of "artfulness" will be emphasized—the conscious rearranging of reality to induce a desired attitudinal or behavioral outcome.

Reality may be arranged with the knowledge of those affected, as when social workers artificially create interracial groups and explain their interest in changing interracial attitudes, or it may be rearranged without their knowledge, as when the groups are created without giving an interpretation. There is also the gray area, in which reality is not arranged but infor-

[6] Howard S. Becker, "The Teacher in the Authority System of the Public School," in Amitai Etzioni, ed., *Complex Organizations: A Sociological Reader* (New York: Holt, Rinehart & Winston, 1961), pp. 243–251.

[7] This idea was suggested to the author by Professor Irving Miller of the Columbia University School of Social Work, New York, New York.

mation is withheld, as when a worker does not share a perception with a client because he believes the client is not "ready" for it or when a student is led by his supervisor's questions to an answer the supervisor knew all the time.[8]

Generally, the values of social workers allow reality rearrangements when the fact is shared with those affected although even here questions of values can be raised. It is when the arrangements are secret or ill defined that negative prescriptions are invoked and the action is called "manipulative." It is the argument of this paper that in the context in which social workers function, advocacy requires political behavior, and political behavior includes manipulation.

MANIPULATION

In recent years, Richard Christie and other social psychologists have conducted intensive studies of manipulation. A scale has been developed by culling from Machiavelli's writings those statements that appear to have relevance to the ways in which people view one another or to their means of controlling or influencing the behavior of others. The scale, intended to measure the respondent's acceptance of manipulation or the use of guile in interpersonal relations, appears to have predictive validity; academicians who were identified by their colleagues as "smooth operators" scored higher than others.[9] In laboratory experiments involving a series of three-person games, those who scored high on

the scale were consistently and dramatically the victors.[10]

Unfortunately, there have been no samples of social workers in these experiments. Although a related professional group—the social psychologists—score consistently high as a group, the studies done of the medical profession are most interesting. Physicians' scores vary depending on their medical specialization. They are as follows in descending order: psychiatry, pediatrics, internal medicine, obstetrics, and surgery.[11] This finding is reported, not to indicate that psychiatrists are less moral or principled than their fellow physicians or the rest of us, but to point up Christie's interpretation that the degree of interpersonal manipulation required by a person's formal role (or job) is the most salient factor in explaining his response to the scale. Persons oriented to social roles that involve influencing others, he notes, are more in agreement with Machiavelli than are persons who are oriented primarily to the manipulation of things or pure ideas.[12] The point, of course, is not that artfulness is necessarily desirable, but that it is an inevitable concomitant of certain roles and tasks.

PROCESS ORIENTATION

This finding may profitably be applied to social work. There are three general professional approaches, each fashioned by its objectives: the process orientation, the clinical, and the social reform. Although the terminology is loose because all approaches in social work are concerned with process, the process orientation is distinct from the others in that process is valued for its own sake. The professional facil-

---

[8] These examples are not offered with the intent of being judgmental but because it is believed that the technique of leading a student to a predetermined answer by questioning, although a common pedagogical device, is basically dishonest. It is better for the supervisor to express an opinion and to follow it by questions in a climate that encourages students to challenge the supervisor's ideas.

[9] Richard Christie, "The Prevalence of Machiavellian Orientations," paper presented at the annual meeting of the American Psychological Association, Los Angeles, September 1964. (Mimeographed.)

[10] Florence Geis, "Machiavellianism and the Manipulation of One's Fellow Man," paper presented at the annual meeting of the American Psychological Association, Los Angeles, September 1964. (Mimeographed.)

[11] Christie, op. cit., pp. 12–13.

[12] Ibid., p. 14.

itates and guides the interaction among persons or mediates between persons and institutional officials without his own preconceived notions about desired outcomes. Goals are set by the participants and the professional's task is to insure that issues are effectively confronted.

Assuming that professional practice without goals is possible, the process-oriented worker is likely to be less manipulative than others.[13] Ideally, he is neutral; with no stake in the outcome, he feels little pressure to influence the attitudes or behavior of others and, therefore, less need for artfulness as it has been defined previously. But although he is freer of value conflict than his colleagues, he is probably also less effective in dealing with behavioral change or significant issues.

Process orientation ignores context. It assumes, for example, that communication itself may solve problems, without sufficient regard for the circumstances in which the communication takes place or the differentials in influence among the communicators. The worker who initiates a process between tenants and public housing officials without, in practice, accounting for the differences in power between the parties is hardly likely to affect public housing arrangements. He may even run the risk of being defined as a "cop out" by the tenants and a "do-gooder" by the officials.

CLINICAL ORIENTATION

A second approach to social work may be referred to broadly as a clinical or treatment orientation. The professional seeks improved functioning of his clients —changes in their personality, attitudes, or behavior. Although the client seeks

the help and the changes are ultimately his own, the professional assumes responsibility for diagnosing the problem and "prescribing" the treatment. The social worker does, of course, have ends in mind and a stake in the outcome. For these reasons, and because he attempts, as does the psychiatrist, to influence others, he is likely to engage in manipulative activity. If Christie is correct, the formal role of the clinician makes this inevitable.

The field's negative prescriptions may thus be problematic, since they encourage or require the denial of guileful behavior and this makes its proper examination impossible. Its inevitability cannot be explored without emotional overtones, nor can consideration be made of whether there are circumstances in which artfulness is professionally justified or appropriate, what those circumstances are, in regard to whom, and within what limits.

SOCIAL REFORM

The objective of the third approach is reform. It seeks to make an impact on social problems by influencing change in organizations and institutions. Although advocacy *may* be found in any professional interaction in which a client's interest is opposed by some other person or institution, it *must* be a part of the worker's armamentarium when environmental change is the objective. The necessity for political-manipulative behavior by the advocate has already been argued; it need only be added that the reformer is more likely to embrace this activity than are his professional colleagues with different orientations. There are at least two reasons for this in addition to those referred to earlier.

Collectivities that press for change will try to make the most effective case for their position rather than the most complete or reasoned one. They will scale their demands for change to strategic considerations, asking for more than is achievable or less than they need, depending on what

---

[13] The author does not, in fact, make the assumption that professional practice without goals is possible. Quite the contrary; he believes that goal-less practice is not possible, and that its proponents have a difficult time making a case for it. They say, for example, that workers have "purposes" but not goals. But this is outside the scope of the current discussion.

is deemed tactical. They will be concerned as much with their appearance of strength or influence as with the reality, since the two are related. They will, in short, engage in politics. The advocate-reformer is likely to be at least as interested in the specific change pursued by these groups as they are and may even be more so. He will therefore join them in the manipulative activity.

Furthermore, the advocate-reformer is less likely than other social workers to be concerned with a role of authority or the imposition of his beliefs. Imposition and manipulation do, of course, entail different behaviors and are to some extent opposed to one another.

A worker who is overbearing may impose his point of view, but this is not being manipulative. On the other hand, successful manipulation necessarily involves imposition. The client's choice is bent to the worker's desire if the worker distorts information or if environmental conditions are arranged to induce the outcome to which the worker aspires. In any case, the power relations between clients and social workers are likely to be quite different, depending on the context of their relationship. Clients are dependent on the professional when they are engaged in an intense treatment relationship.

On the other hand, the worker who needs constituent support for a social action effort is the seeker in the relationship and, consequently, wields less authority. In petitioning for community change, he is again the suppliant and his influence is often considerably less than that of the officialdom with which he deals. Lesser authority and power—in combination with client identification and social change commitment—are likely to foster in the social worker a belief in both the necessity and the justification of employing political strategies. There is, therefore, less need to deny the professional relevance of these methods.

If manipulation is inevitable for the professional who attempts to influence others or is justified by particular objectives or a specific context, one must address the issues thus posed. For it could hardly be proposed that there be a moratorium on morality or suggested that "anything goes." Rather, it is necessary for professional guidelines to be imposed on the use of political methods. One set of rules is needed having to do with values; another, with effectiveness or expediency (although at times the two do merge).

WHO BENEFITS, WHO LOSES?

To make value judgments one must assess situations on an individual basis, taking a number of factors into account. Although it is not possible to establish rigid rules, broad standards may nevertheless be developed, relating to (1) who benefits and who loses, (2) the subject of the political activity, (3) the principle involved or the end pursued, and (4) the nature of the political act.

Professional ideals require that the end of political behavior must not be the interest of the professional himself. Although, unconsciously or otherwise, this rule may be breached in the reality, such behavior should not be encouraged or condoned, especially when it might conflict with the client's needs. The justification for violation of any cherished value must be its inherent conflict with some other value of equal or greater import. It follows, then, that manipulation should generally be eschewed except when it is clearly in the best interests of the disadvantaged client. The magnitude of the need, the powerlessness of the client, and the rules of the game as played by his adversaries dictate the conclusion that manipulation is sometimes justified. This is at the other end of the continuum from using it to further the professional's self-interest. Falling midway between the two are the interests of one's agency and other clients or constituents.

Certain cautions must be introduced before artfulness may be counseled comfortably, even in the "best interests" of the client. One has to do with risk. For example, a strategy might be pursued that is in the long-term interest of the client but that risks losses to him in the short run. (Some advocates' fervor for change makes this a ready possibility.) Thus, an advocate of the rent strike as a tactic for housing improvement may try to convince tenants to withhold their rent no matter what the cost. On the other hand, if he understands the risks to the tenants, he will avoid both imposition and manipulation; instead he will try to make clear to them what their choices are and the dangers that might be involved, however much this approach might inhibit the success of the effort.

Social workers working in a labor union setting recently found themselves in a situation like this. Union officials favored creating an incident that would force an eviction so that the attendant uproar would attract attention to the problem. In this instance the social workers' advocacy led them to insist that no eviction be promoted without the understanding and concurrence of the tenants and the union's assurance of support.

The worker's wish to serve the best interests of his client is a necessary but not a sufficient condition to justify manipulation. Good intentions have been used, sincerely and otherwise, to excuse base actions. To arrange events or shape information in order to control another's action may be inevitable, but it should not be professionally approved unless other factors are also considered, such as the importance of the issue involved and the object of the manipulation.

OBJECTS OF POLITICAL BEHAVIOR

Considering the possible objects of an advocate's political behavior raises a complex question, especially in community organization, in which there is confusion as to who the client is. To say that the community is the organizer's client is to deal in an abstraction that has scant meaning. "Community" is too broad a term to have a discernible empiric referrent. One may more profitably conceptualize the organizer's (and other advocates') relations to three systems: client, action, and target.

Client system. The term "client" usually refers to one who engages the services of a professional and, in this sense, social workers do not ordinarily have clients. In social work usage the term connotes those whose interests are served. This has been taken to mean persons in interaction with a professional. In community organization, however, until quite recently direct contact has been with the providers, rather than the recipients, of service and this remains a significant component of community organization practice. Defining the client system to mean those who benefit or are intended to benefit from the worker's activity alters one's professional perspective. Prescriptions are different when the beneficiaries of a committee's process and, therefore, the primary concern for the professional, are not the participants. His activity may be appropriately evaluated by how well he represents the absent client rather than by how well he serves the member in attendance.

Action system. The action system may be viewed as composed of those who are engaged in the planned action, e.g., the committee mentioned previously. Other examples would be the worker, client, and perhaps the worker's agency in cases of individual advocacy when intercession is necessary with another service system. Client and action systems overlap when the beneficiaries and those who are actually involved in the planned action are the same, as when groups of the poor organize to affect service systems in which they are recipients.

Target systems. Target systems are those groups, programs, or institutions that are strategic to the change attempt and that need to be modified if the objective of the process is to be attained. A school system, welfare department, or housing authority might constitute a target for change. In such instances interaction between the professional and the target system might or might not take place.

This prescription would permit worker politicking in descending scale from target systems to action and then client systems. Four considerations guide this viewpoint: (1) the similarity of objectives between the advocate and others, (2) the quality of their interaction, (3) their relative influence, and (4) the rules by which the game is played.

When there are both similarity of objectives and interaction that permits shared understanding, as is the case with professionals in their dealings with most clients and many action systems, manipulative behavior violates a trust. On the other hand, as disparity of influence widens between the parties, guile becomes more understandable and more justifiable. In this view, a dependent client's manipulation of a worker is more understandable than is a professional's manipulation of the client. And if the structure of an action group is such that it inhibits or forecloses decision-making by client groups, political activity may be the only appropriate professional response.

Furthermore, as advocacy is accepted as an appropriate strategy, social workers become increasingly involved in arenas broader than social services. To play by one's own rules without cognizance of others' rules may be to suffer irreparable disadvantage (although again, perhaps, only to the clients).

One sharp illustration would be when a government official lies in his dealings with social workers. For example, when Mobilization For Youth, the Lower East Side's (New York City) delinquency prevention and antipoverty project, was under attack for "agitating the community," it was discovered that New York City's deputy mayor was feeding false information to the press. When confronted by agency officials with his press quotations, the deputy mayor categorically denied, contrary to all evidence, that he had made the statements. It could hardly be expected, for value reasons at any rate, that agency officials would feel bound to be utterly truthful in their dealings with him.

A third important standard in evaluating the appropriateness of political strategies relates to the values inherent in the substantive end or principle at issue. Risks to life and limb, basic needs, and social justice are areas that justify political intervention. Manipulation by or on behalf of the victims of discrimination in a case of clear social injustice would thus be appropriate, e.g., in response to the jailing of civil rights workers. Similarly, one could condone a lie to entice a potential suicide off a ledge, although one would be highly critical of such behavior in other instances.

IMAGE MANAGEMENT

Moreover, there is the nature of the act itself. One important aspect of political skill is image management. It takes many forms and is engaged in by almost everyone.[14] It is a feature of organizations as well as of people. Banfield, for example, in a study of civic associations in Chicago, describes a technique:

A common, indeed almost invariable, feature of the process by which an issue is prepared for settlement is a ceremonial appeal to the authority of "objective facts." . . . although the issue must . . . always be settled on grounds that are political in the broad sense, and although crucial judgments that are involved . . . cannot possibly be made in a purely . . . technical way, nevertheless the almost unvarying practice is to make it appear that the decision rests upon "objective" and even "factual" grounds. . . . This extraordinary devotion to "facts" is often

[14] For a cogent and diverting exposition of this viewpoint, *see* Erving Goffman, *The Presentation of Self in Everyday Life* (New York: Doubleday & Co., 1959).

associated with an extraordinary determination to conceal what is really at issue. . . .[15]

Images may be fabricated in a number of ways. One may withhold information or exaggerate, distort, or lie. The supervisor who counsels a graduate student worker not to indicate his student status to a client is guilty of the first; undue expressions of psychological support to clients on scanty bases are examples of the second. These may be professional errors, but they do not violate professional sensibilities. The point is that manipulative actions are of different orders of morality. In the present view, the appropriateness of a guileful act must be evaluated by the act itself in combination with the other standards that have been suggested. It is the balancing of these factors in the particular instance that determines the morality.

Moral relativism is an uncomfortable thing. Fortunately, professional choices are limited by factors of effectiveness or expediency as well as by one's value framework. Although the latter has been a major focus of this paper, it is not so distinct from pragmatic concerns as may have been implied.

There are those who maintain that manipulation is self-defeating in the long run. They do not explain, however, the prevalance of this self-defeating behavior. And they would undoubtedly find it difficult to account for the results of the experiments cited earlier or for such findings that show that male students, controlled for ability, score higher on the Machiavelli scale and get better grades in the universities.[16]

Political behavior requires the same sensitivity to oneself and others as is required in all human interaction. It may even require more. Manipulation is neither self-defeating nor effective. The potential costs of political strategies must always be assessed against their potential gains, so that one's morality is supported by expedience. Social workers may use up their currency as, for example, when a person develops a reputation for guile. With his motives suspect, his hidden agendas revealed to view, and his word in doubt, he can hardly be an effective advocate. Since people resent being treated as means to an end rather than as ends in themselves, those who appear to use them instrumentally are likely to be ineffective.

Different individuals and groups are differentially tolerant of being the target of political activity and will evaluate the experience differently. The value prescriptions mentioned earlier are also relevant in this regard. People are likely to be more charitable toward guile exercised in behalf of disadvantaged clients concerning a significant issue than toward guile exercised in a professional's self-interest or concerning a matter of small moment. Most significantly, perhaps, the nature of the relationship or situation creates an expectation that either minimizes or maximizes the consequences of political behavior. Three such may be cited.

Adversary situations. In adversary situations there is considerable margin for political behavior; both parties ordinarily expect it, and discovery would cause little further disruption. Thus, target systems, for example, become ready candidates. The welfare worker whom the advocate is flattering, cajoling, disputing, intimidating, or threatening in behalf of his client questions the advocate's information, quietly makes assessments of his strength, and would not be shocked by the suggestion that he was lacking in candor.

Differences of interest. Situations short of conflict, in which there are differences of interest clear to both parties, allow a smaller margin of safety. The prospective

[15] Edward C. Banfield, *Political Influence* (New York: Free Press of Glencoe, 1961), p. 183.
[16] Jerome E. Singer, "The Use of Manipulative Strategies: Machiavellianism and Attractiveness," *Sociometry*, Vol. 27, No. 2 (June 1964), pp. 128–150. Ability was measured by the admissions test battery.

employer hardly expects complete openness from the job applicant. The professor is likely to expect to be, in some measure, "conned" by the student. The conning becomes problematic only when it is stupidly or grossly done, is the student's predominant way of relating, or takes place after a significant relationship has developed.

Ongoing relationships. In an ongoing relationship or process the dangers of manipulation are significant. For here trust is expected between the parties and discovery may be seriously damaging to the attainment of immediately desired objectives and, more important, to the long-range relationship. In part, a determination of strategy depends on an evaluation of the importance of the present instance as compared with future need. One might not distort the truth to the potential suicide teetering on the ledge if one were his worker, anticipated a continued treatment relationship with him, and could conceive of any alternative method of deterring him. Manipulation in an ongoing relationship, which contravenes the rules understood by both parties, is not only of dubious morality but fraught with risk.

CONCLUSION

There is, of course, risk in any case. Professionals function at the fulcrum of a field of interacting interests—agency board and executive, supervisor, those who are supervised, clients, community groups, government officials, and the like. Treading the path through the varying expectations, values, and demands of these disparate groups requires risk-taking and a high order of political skill. It is the author's argument that the advocate—the professional who identifies with the victims of social problems and who pursues modification in social conditions—will need to have the professional dedication to take the risk and to be political.

THE MODEL AGENCY APPROACH TO GRADUATE SOCIAL WORK EDUCATION

Morley D. Glicken

The ability of social work education to perceive problems
confronting the profession and the society has been severely
limited by an orthodoxy with which social work educators
approach the task of preparing practitioners for future work.
There seems no limit to the amount of information concerning
the ineffectiveness of social work practice, yet rather than
facing the obvious implication that practitioners are ill
prepared for providing effective social work intervetion,
schools of social work essentially continue to instruct from
the same model. While the curriculum might be changed somewhat,
the essential bias of instructors and the necessity of a
university based school of social work to be academic in an
apparently visibly way to others in the academy make for a
situation which not only disserves the profession but also
disserves the society. Academy based social work education
often gears itself to a model of training which may be
inconsistent with the needs of social work education. There
is considerable evidence that social work practitioners, to
be effective, not only need a broad base of didatic information,
but also should have personal characteristics consistent
with successful work with client groups. Rather than producing either a rich didatic base of information or providing
opportunities to improve facilitative effectiveness in relationships, schools of social work appear to do a minimal job
of either. Let's examine the approach schools of social
work take in providing graduate training.

To begin with, the selection process often provides
little opportunity to adequately measure whether or not
students have adequate people skills. While in some schools
an interview is used, in most schools there is no contact
with the student other than his grades, perhaps a GRE report,
references which tell us little in a believable way about the
applicant, and a personal statement which tells us more about
his ability to write and to perceive the social reality of
what the school wants him to say than it tells us about his
people interest, his value system, and his understanding of
social work. Schools of social work take far too many
applicants for the present market and are consequently, much
too large to provide a quality educational experience.

Once in graduate school, the student is confronted
with field experiences based in agencies which often provide
a model of practice not at all consistent either with social
work ethics or with what is considered to be positive and
effective practice. Our relationship with these low level
agencies in effect gives the community the message that social

Paper presented at the Council on Social Work Education Regional Meeting on the Structure of Social
Work Education in Los Angeles, California, April 1974.

work education operates in a competitive vacuum and that
standards are set at the very lowest level of practice.
David Wineman characterizes these agencies as people
hating. Even in those settings considered more adequate,
the student tends to learn little about service to clients
in light of modern, effective technique. Instead he
learns how to dictate properly, how to write psychosocial
histories, to process record, and how most significantly,
to understand the reality of social work practice - which
is to do and say nothing which might upset agency structure.
    And what of the reality of the classroom? Well, in
the classroom students are often given material which, to
say the least, is not current and often has dubious
relevance. Dogma tends to replace information. Often little
is done to coordinate information given between field and
classroom so that the student has every right to feel
disjointed. Much in the graduate experience is repetitive
of the undergraduate experience and students often report
that what happened in the undergraduate experience tended
to be far more stimulating. Rather than individualizing,
students are thrown together in one pot providing essentially
the same experience with little concern for past work and
educational endeavors. Instead of involving the student
in what is current, students are often asked to learn what
seems to have little relevance either to effectiveness or
current practice because of instructor bias or laziness.
Consequently, very little which is innovative comes out
of the academy as it relates to practice. When students
rebel we label it adolescent anger when in reality the
student is in considerable despair over the low quality of
the experience. Rather than face up to the fact that social
work education is in a tremendous amount of difficulty
and is beginning to lose support in the community, the
educational institutions fail to concern themselves with
answers to significant problems confronting the community.
At best they provide a minimum amount of criticism of
current practice, or tell students in more candid moments,
that while the experience in the school is a painful one,
have faith, that practice will be better. Well, in fact,
practice is not better. Often times practice is a continuation of the negative experience felt in the school. And
the existential apathy which allows students to cope with
two years of trivia often extends itself into practice.
There are no ends to the horror stories that one can tell
about poor educational experiences in schools of social
work. They are notorious, they are prevalent, they need
not be documented statistically. We have all had our
experiences with them and we all know full well that they
are present. What is agonizing is the fact that while

we are in the midst of feeling the crunch from students, we are at the same time unwilling to really confront ourselves with how drastically inappropriate the social work educational experience has become.

These are admittedly serious problems which many of us are increasingly aware of. However, I'm beginning to believe that elimination of the concerns outlined lie less in our awareness of the problem and more in our determination to maintain university based social work education. Which is to say that I no longer believe that a university based training approach is capable of training effective workers. Consequently, with an eye toward what we have at present and its ineffectiveness, I'm suggesting that graduate education concentrate its forces on preparing workers for practice. One might call my orientation to education a model agency approach. The model agency, by definition, is a service providing institution which trains workers in the context of helping people. The advantages of the model agency are as follows: Rather than operating from a university setting which often times isolates instructors and limits contact with people and their problems, the model agency would center itself in the community. Physically separated from the university setting, but still an administrative part of it, that is a part of it in terms of funding and employee security, the model agency would contract with existing agencies to provide client services covering numerous areas of social work concern including direct practice to clients, development of new social agencies, research, community action, etc. In the context of providing varied innovative services, the student could conceivably be part of an exciting, dynamic social service operation where learning takes place as students and teachers work together to provide sophisticated, broadly general services in the geographic area served by the school. In the model agency, didactic information would be included in small seminars as students and instructors process what may have happened in a specific practice experience. Rather than learning theory about areas of practice not often touched in field experience, the student would find himself part of the administrative functioning of the school; he would take part in actual research which could have an effect on the community; he would be involved in developing new social services for the geographic area served by the school; he would be involved in developing social policy; he would have contact with the political structure of the geographic area served; he would provide direct, innovative services to clients; he would be involved in community action.

Rather than separating the classroom from the field, the academic experience would be held in conjunction with the field experience. The student's learning could be programmed so that he would move from the simple to the complex with academic input properly timed to fit his field experience. As such, he might more readily feel at one with the two experiences than may be the case at present. The goal of training would be to educate for sophisticated generalist practice which views the graduate experience as practice oriented but much more broadly applicable to complex social work tasks than may be the function of the student prepared at present for practice as a generalist.

The model agency would hopefully set standards for other agencies in the geographic area served. In a sense, it would be the best or the most innovative agency in that area, and in a sense it would also be somewhat competitive. In rural areas, such as my state of Arizona which has one school of social work in a four state geographic area, it becomes increasingly important that one service center provide a quality service which other agencies might consider representative of quality practice, and which might be referred to as an example of successful social work.

If the model agency is to physically separate itself from the academy, I agree with Richan and Mendelsohn that it should locate itself in that part of the community which includes our primary service population, the economically disadvantaged. There is such a vast difference between theoretically viewing poverty and living in it, that model agency practice might more readily involve instructors in the reality of practice, something not often done in the academy. Out of that involvement might come the new practice skills we should be developing.

In terms of the selection process, students would be screened thoroughly to select only those few applicants with greatest potential for successful practice. One possible approach is to require applicants to be physically present in the agency for a sufficient period of time to be placed in stress situations with clients, faculty, and other students to adequately evaluate their potential for the profession in a way which might more closely approximate their performance in graduate school.

The model agency might further consider new approaches to information giving which would increase the amount of information available to the students. One idea which is presently being developed in Canada is the notion of a central data collection agency which can provide any member agency almost instantaneous data through the use of computers and cable connections. In this system, one central agency collects and microfilms journals, magazines, sections of books, etc. When a member agency requests a specific set of material, the central agency, through the use of its computers sends that agency the information requested which is then placed on video tape for use whenever the instructor wants it. The benefit of this approach is to greatly reduce the need for libraries and other systems which reduce the efficiency of the learning experience. Additionally, there is room for the notion of programmed information. It is conceivable that programmed information packages might replace present, more traditional training approaches such as the lecture. Further programmed learning might substantially broaden the areas covered in the graduate experience.

One of the prime supportive strengths of the model agency is that experiencial learning increases facilitative skills at no specific reduction in the amount of information learned. One might anticipate, for example, greater involvement in research if the student is actively involved in projects commissioned by the community which could possibly affect social policy. Additionally, direct involvement in administering the school or providing new delivery systems involves the student at a level where theory more realistically fits practice and might significantly broaden the practice abilities of the student. In any event, there is ample evidence that experiencial learning produces significantly higher levels of those facilitative characteristics necessary for successful work with people. Truax and Carkhoff have demonstrated for example, that experiencial training programs can produce in lay, untrained workers similar levels of facilitative skills as highly regarded professionals in 100 hours of training, a significant reduction over present training programs.

The model agency approach to summarize, is an attempt to prepare the worker for sophisticated generalist practice. The sophisticated generalist is seen as a worker capable of dealing effectively with problems which may be mishandled by the less adequately trained baccalaureate degree worker and just as readily mishandled by the graduate trained specialist. The model agency is seen as a possible way to reconcile the growing rift between the needs of the community and the isolated condition of schools of social work. At its very worst, it couldn't be much less in touch than present orientations to training workers. At its best, perhaps it might be an alternative direction in social work education, one which could help us recoup lost ground in preparing effective social work practitioners capable of meeting the varied and complex needs of the community.

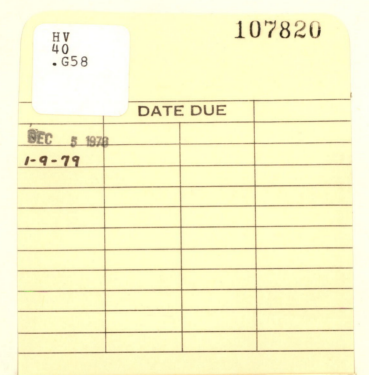